C & DATA STRUCTURES BY PRACTICE

C & DATA STRUCTURES BY PRACTICE

Ramesh Vasappanavara
BE (ECE), M. Tech. (CSE, IIT KGP) (PhD)

Anand Vasappanavara
B. Tech(IIT Madras), (ME)(IISc)

Gautam Vasappanavara
B. Tech (IT), (ME)(BITS, Pilani)

PUBLISHING FOR ONE WORLD

NEW AGE INTERNATIONAL (P) LIMITED, PUBLISHERS
(formerly Wiley Eastern Limited)

New Delhi • Bangalore • Chennai • Cochin • Guwahati • Hyderabad
Jalandhar • Kolkata • Lucknow • Mumbai • Ranchi

Visit us at www.newagepublishers.com

Published by New Age International (P) Ltd., Publishers
First Edition: 2007

ISBN : 81-224-2021-4

Rs. 250.00

C-06-12-1199

Printed in India at Nisha Enterprises, Delhi.
Typeset at in-house

PUBLISHING FOR ONE WORLD

NEW AGE INTERNATIONAL (P) LIMITED, PUBLISHERS
(formerly Wiley Eastern Limited)
4835/24, Ansari Road, Daryaganj, New Delhi - 110002
Visit us at **www.newagepublishers.com**

In Loving Memory of

V Prahlad

V Indira Prahlad

V Thunder

FOREWORD

In the early days of computers, many programming languages had come into vogue but programming in C language had very quickly taken the leading position soon after its introduction in early Seventies. Enormous capabilities and usefulness of C language are reflected in the fact that it is reigning supreme as the most important programming language for more than 30 years and is taught invariably in all engineering institutions across the globe.

The large number of students who want to learn the C programming language need good text books for their self study to supplement their classroom learning. Hence, it is no wonder that many authors attempted to present the learning material in their respective individual styles. Sensing the need for a "practice oriented" textbook, Prof. Ramesh Vasappanavara and his two well-qualified sons, Anand and Gautam, have joined together to produce the new book "C and Data Structures - By Practice".

Prof. Ramesh and his co-authors have adopted a distinctively different style of presenting the material, similar to the adage that swimming can be learnt only by jumping into the swimming pool and not by getting theoretical lessons in a classroom. It avoids unnecessary repetition of what is taught in the classroom but serves as a true supplement to traditional classroom teaching by laying emphasis on practical examples.

Prof. Ramesh must have chosen this unique style based not only on his almost decade long experience in teaching the subject as Professor of Computer Science and Engineering at Gayatri Vidya Parishad College of Engineering but also on his vast practical experience in heading a team of competent computer specialists during his earlier career in R&D and Industry. His close contacts with almost all the leading software companies in the country as Professor of CSE and as an enormously successful Professor-in-charge of placement at GVP College of Engineering have given him an insider's knowledge of what the industry expects out of a potential employee once he/she comes out of the college. He has used this knowledge to the fullest extent in writing this book.

I congratulate Prof. Ramesh Vasappanavara and his coauthors on the painstaking efforts they have taken to put their ideas together in the form of the present book. I am sure not only the students and teachers of the subject in various Universities but also the practicing professionals will find the book extremely useful and that it would help them to attain greater and greater proficiency as they go along in their careers.

Dr. P. Srinivasa Rao

Formerly Professor of Structural Engineering
Dean, Industrial Consultancy &
Dean, Academic Affairs
IIT Madras, Chennai.

PREFACE

This textbook is written for those who would like to learn C & Data Structures by themselves and become experts on their own steam. The focus is on teaching you the methods and the theory in an easy and understandable manner, that makes you confident. The approach taken in this text is to teach by practice and examples. We have taught the C and Data Structures for several years to graduate and post-graduate students and our experience shows that considerable effort is needed both on the part of instructors and students to cover the entire requisite material. This is mainly due to negligible or no previous knowledge of programming skills available with the student. Hence our C coverage has been extensive and almost on talking terms with you, explaining the details, the art of programming and so on.

In the first chapter itself, we have introduced most of the concepts of C like loops, arrays and structures and even a small program on files. Our idea is that you should become conversant with bare minimum skills to program, so that you can handle laboratory and other works. However, you may proceed to Chapter 2 directly, should you so wish.

In succeeding chapters, we have introduced basics of programming, control loops and functions. Arrays and pointers are dealt with extensively, keeping in view their importance. Concepts like memory management and storage type and pre-processor directives have been explained with the help of programming examples.

Chapters on structures and files have been designed to introduce you to all the concepts involved through examples. Examples are so chosen that each example, while reinforcing your learning, will introduce a new concept. This way we feel the practice and concepts stay with you.

We have defined the data structure and its need and linked the concepts to other linear data structures. Each problem is explained with the help of a diagram, an algorithm, and a function code. The programming style chosen is consistent so as to make the student adept at writing such programs. Non-linear data structures like trees and graphs have been presented in an easy to understand manner. Each iteration and an event has been explained with an illustration.

This text lays importance on understanding the algorithm and program. The chapter on Searching and Sorting will answer all your queries on efficiency of sorting, programming techniques etc.

All the chapters have been provided with running examples. At the end of each chapter we have provided:

- Objective questions
- Review questions
- Solved examples
- Assignment questions.

Note that the questions in *italics* have been set by University. In addition, we have included eight question papers by JNTU completely solved, three in the text and five in resource CD. All the programs have been tested under Linux, VC++, and Turbo C environments.

We highly appreciate and express our thanks to Mr MPJ Santosh Kumar and Mr M Srinivasa Rao and V Poojita of Computer Science department who have helped in preparation of the manuscript and testing of programs. The staff of Computer Science and Engineering department deserve special thanks. We would like to express our thanks to scores of our students, both past and present, who have rendered invaluable assistance by checking out the programs. We are highly indebted to teachers, both past and present, for their valuable suggestions and their painstaking effort to make this subject easier for students.

We appreciate and thank Dr B Kanta Rao, Senior Professor, Dr M N Seetaramanath, Professor, Dept of CSE, AUCOE and Dr NB Venkateswarlu, Head of Dept. IT, GVPCOE for their encouragement and suggestions.

We are thankful to Prof P Srinivasa Rao, Director IGIAT, Visakhapatnam and formerly Professor of Structural Engineering and Dean, IIT Madras, Chennai, Prof P Somaraju, Secretary, Gayatri Vidya Parishad and Prof NSVVSJ Gandhi, Principal, Gayatri Vidya Parishad College of Engineering for their encouragement and wholehearted support.

While every effort has been made to make this publication error free, the authors would very much feel obliged for feedback.

We thank the editors and the staff at New Age Publishers, who have brought out this high quality textbook.

Finally, we express our thanks to V Usha Ramesh and V Thunder for their wholehearted support for this project.

Ramesh Vasappanavara
Anand Vasappanavara
Gautam Vasappanavara

CONTENTS

6. Pointers 125

7. Structures & Unions 151

8. Files 179

LIST OF EXAMPLES & SOLVED PROBLEMS

There are numerous examples throughout the textbook to enhance understanding and improve the art and science of writing programs.

Chapter 1

Chapter 2

Chapter 3

Chapter 4

Chapter 5

Chapter 6

Chapter 7

Chapter 8

Chapter 9

Chapter 10

Chapter 11

Chapter 12

Chapter 13

Chapter 14

CHAPTER 1

AROUND THE WORLD OF C

1.1 WELCOME TO C LANGUAGE

We want to make you reasonably comfortable with C language. Get ready for an exciting tour. The problem we would consider to introduce C language is that , we have a Foot Ball spherical in shape. We would like to compute surface area of the ball, given it's radius, given by formula 4 * PI * r * r The C code for the above problem is given below:

//Example 1.1 area.c Program to calculate surface area of a ball

```
# include <stdio.h> // library file for standard I/O Ex. printf & scanf
# define PI 3.141519 // PI is a symbol for constant

/* Declare function prototype that will compute surface area
given radius of float (real number) data type and returns area
again of float data type*/

float FindArea(float radius);

void main( )
{
  // You will need float (real numbers) data types for holding radius and area
  float radius, area;
 /* Obtain radius from the user. User can enter 0 to stop the
 process of  computation of surface area.*/
  printf(" Enter radius of the ball. To stop enter 0 for the radius \n");
  printf("\n Radius = ? ");
  scanf("%f", &radius); // What user enters for the radius is entered by computer at
                    //address of radius denoted by & operator
```

```
/* We would like to compute surface areas of the various ball.
        So user enters various radii. User can stop by entering 0
        for the radius. We will use while statement.*/

  while (radius != 0) //i.e. till user does not enter 0
     {
       if ( radius < 0)
           area = 0;  // if radius is negative area =0
       else
            area = FindArea(radius); // calling out function. We have supplied radius
                                              // We store the result returned by FindArea() at area

       // print out put
       printf("Area =  %f\n", area); // %f is used to print float data type area
      /* what is in quotes appears as it is in the output. \n means leave a line after print
      We are inside while statement. We have just completed printing of area.
      What should we do next? Ask the user for next problem i.e. next radius. Ask it.*/
       printf("Enter radius of the ball. To stop enter 0 for the radius \n");
       printf("\n Radius = ? ");
       scanf("%f", &radius);
     }// end of while
  }// end of main

// function definition. Here we will tell what FindArea function does

float FindArea (float radius)
{   float answer; // we will store the area
   answer = 4* PI * radius * radius;
   return answer;
} // end of function definition
                                   /* OR

We could simply write in one line above definitions as

float FindArea ( float radius ) { return  4 *PI*radius*radius;} */
/*
OUTPUT:
 Enter radius of the ball. To stop enter 0 for the radius
 Radius = ? 2.0
```

```
Area  =  50.240002
Enter radius of the ball. To stop enter 0 for the radius
Radius = ? 1.0
Area  =  12.560000
Enter radius of the ball. To stop enter 0 for the radius
Radius = ? 3.0
Area  =  113.040001
Enter radius of the ball. To stop enter 0 for the radius
Radius = ? 0
*/
```

Note : // or /* .... */ are comments. They are there to improve the understanding of the program. They are not compiled.

include < > statements are preprocessor directives. They tell the C compiler to include the standard definitions that are included in header files supplied by the standard C Library.

Function Prototype like float ***FindArea(float radius);*** tells the compiler that function definition is after main( ) but its usage will be in the main( ). It is like advance information to the compiler to accept usage prior to definition.

Global Declarations and Definitions. All statements included before main() function. All include sections, define statements, function prototype declarations, and structure definitions are global declarations. Hence they are available to all functions also.

Structure of a C Program. Include section, function prototype declarations, structures and other global declarations and definitions if any, main function, and function definitions.

Simple IO Statements printf() and scanf() statements. The general syntax of these IO statements are printf("control format", data); and scanf("control format", address of data items);

CREATION COMPILATION AND RUNNING YOUR PROGRAM

Use any text editor like notepad, vi editor etc and enter your code and save it as ball1.c.

Compile it using #gcc ball.c   Output using # a.out for Linux based system

Run —— Compile —— Execute for Turbo C

Compile and Run your program. Now we are ready for dabbling our foot ball using arrays!

Programming and executing in Linux environment:

1. Switch on the computer.
2. Select the Red hat Linux environment.
3. Right click on the desk top. Select 'New Terminal'.
4. After getting the $ symbol, type ***'vi filename.c'*** and press Enter.
5. ***Press Esc+I*** to enter into Insert mode and then type your program there.

The other modes are Append and Command modes.

6. After completion of entering program, press ***(Esc + Shift*** + :).

This is to save your program in the editor.

7. Then the cursor moves to the end of the page.
   Type 'wq' and press Enter.
   (wq=write and quit)
8. On $ prompt type, cc ***filename.c*** and press Enter.
9. If there are any errors, go back to your program and correct them. Save and Compile the program again after corrections.
10. If there are no errors, run the program by typing
    ./a.out and press Enter.
11. To come out of the terminal, at the dollar prompt, ***type 'exit'*** and press Enter.

■■■ 1.2 ARRAYS IMPLEMENTATION

In the C program in section 1.1, we have taken in the radius and immediately declared the result and continued the process till user entered 0 to exit. Instead, it would be nice, if we had taken all the radii of several foot balls together and stored in memory location, compute corresponding surface areas of these foot balls and stored them as well and declared the results. Array comes to our rescue here. We will define array named radius with maximum of 10 elements of type float as;

```
float radius[10];
```

	2.0	3.0	4.0	5.0	6.0	7.0	8.0	9.0	12.0	12.0
radius	**0**	**1**	**2**	**3**	**4**	**5**	**6**	**7**	**8**	**9**

In C language, it is customary to number the cells of the array starting with 0. Accordingly radius[0] holds a value 2.0 and radius[9] holds value of 12.0. With this knowledge, let us attempt array implementation of Foot Balls.

Example 1.2 ***array1.c***

```
//Arrays implementation to determine surface area of Foot balls

# include <stdio.h>    // library file on standard i/o
# define PI 3.14159    // PI is a symbol for constant
// declare function prototypes
float FindArea(float radius);
void main()
{   int n, i =0; //  i we will use as array index, n for keeping count
    float radius[50]; // Array of radius, numbering max of 50
    float area[50];  // Array of area, numbering max of 50
    printf(" To stop enter 0 for the radius \n");
    printf("\n Radius = ? ");
    scanf( "%f", &radius[i]); // we are storing at address of radius[i]
   while (radius[i] != 0)
     {  if (radius[i] < 0)
              area[i] = 0;
         else
              area [i]= FindArea(radius [i]);// store the result in array area
         // get the next set of data. we have to increment i prior to getting new radius
         // else old data will be over written and hence lost
         ++i;
         printf("To stop enter 0 for the radius \n");
         printf("\n Radius = ? ");
         scanf("%f", &radius[i]);
     }// end of while
     n = — i; // This is because you have increased the count
              // for i for radius = 0 case also. We will use n in for loop.
    // display array elements
    printf ("\n Surface area of balls\n");
   // You have n balls (i.e 0 to n-1 as per C convention). Therefore print  i <=n
   for (i=0; i<= n; i++)
         printf("radius = %f   area = %f \n", radius[i], area[i]);
}// end of main
// function definition
float FindArea(float radius) {return (4*PI * radius * radius);}
/*
 To stop enter 0 for the radius
 Radius = ? 2.0
```

```
To stop enter 0 for the radius
Radius = ? 3.0

To stop enter 0 for the radius
Radius = ? 4.0
To stop enter 0 for the radius
Radius = ? 0.0
Surface area of balls
radius = 2.000000  area = 50.265442
radius = 3.000000  area = 113.097237
radius = 4.000000  area = 201.061768
```

■■■ 1.3 USE OF STRUCTURE TO IMPLEMENT FOOT BALLS PROBLEM

While arrays store same type of data in contiguous locations, structure can be used to store different types of data, bundled together as an instance of structure. For example you can store details of Sports Ball, like color, radius, and surface area etc in a structure. We can define structure in C language

```
  struct SportsBall
  {
   char color[20];
   float radius;
   float area;
  };
typedef struct SportsBall stsb;
stsb ball[10]; //max of 10 Foot balls
```

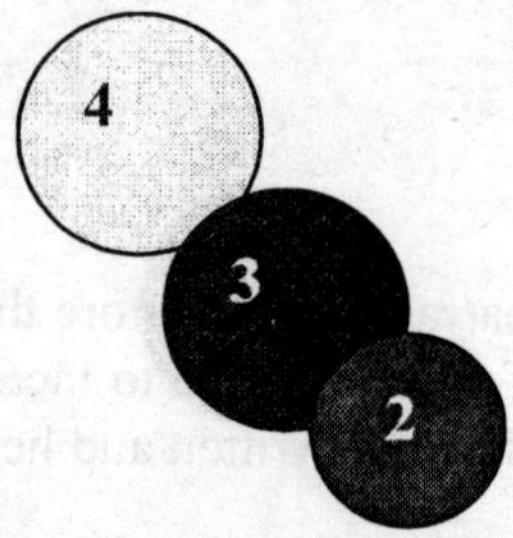

Structure Sports Ball holds Red, Blue, and Yellow balls. Radii are 2, 3, and 4

We have used typedef statement so that we can use stsb in lieu of lengthy struct SportsBall.User can enter color of the ball, radius of the ball. Program computes the surface area of the ball and stores it in the structure as ball[i]. Later you can refer to items inside the structure using

ball[i].color, ball[i].radius, ball[i].area

```
//Example 1.3  areadiff.c
//Use structures to find surface area of different colored balls
# include <stdio.h>     // library file on standard i/o
# define PI 3.14159    // PI is a symbol for constant
// declare function prototypes
float FindArea(float radius);
// declare a structure
```

```
struct FootBall
  {
   char color[20];
   float radius;
   float area;
};
typedef struct FootBall stsb;
stsb ball[10]; //maximum of 10 Foot balls
void main( )
{
  int n, i=0;  // i we will use as structure index, n for keeping count

  printf("To stop enter STOP for the color field \n");
  printf("\n Enter color of the ball :");
  scanf("%s", ball[i].color);
 /* if any one of sub expression is true enter the loop. For example if first letter is not
   S enter while loop. Similarly enter if 2, 3, 4 letters are not T, O, P*/
 while (  ball[i].color[0] != 'S'|| ball[i].color[1] != 'T' || ball[i].color[2] != 'O'|| ball[i].color[3] != 'P')
  {
        printf("\n Radius = ? ");
        scanf("%f", &ball[i].radius);
        if (ball[i].radius < 0)
              ball[i].area = 0;
        else
              ball[i].area = FindArea(ball[i].radius);
        ++ i;
        printf("To stop enter STOP for the color field \n"); // get next set of data
        printf("\n Enter color of the ball :");
        scanf("%s", ball[i].color);
  }// end of while
  n = — i; // this is because you have increased the count for i for color =STOP case also.
 // display structure elements

printf("\n Surface area of Foot balls\n");
 for(i=0;i<= n; i++)
        printf("color   %s radius = %f area = %f \n",ball[i].color, ball[i].radius,
               ball[i].area);
}// end of main
// function definition
float FindArea (float radius)
{float answer;
 answer = 4*PI * radius * radius;
 return answer;
 } // end of function definition
/*output
```

```
To stop enter STOP for the color field
 Enter color of the ball :RED
 Radius = ? 2.0
To stop enter STOP for the color field
 Enter color of the ball :BLUE
 Radius = ? 3.0
To stop enter STOP for the color field
 Enter color of the ball :STOP
 Surface area of Foot balls
color   RED radius = 2.000000 area = 50.265442
color   BLUE radius = 3.000000 area = 113.097237*//*
```

■■■ 1.4 EXPLOIT C FILES TO STORE DATA ABOUT FOOT BALLS

In daily life, you would have used files. For example, your certificates and marks lists are probably stored in a file. C language also provides files to store your data. File contain papers, here we will call them records. Each record in the file holds details of RED ball viz color, radius, surface area. We will now write a program to read the data and store the records in a structure and later record the details in a file called SportsBalls. Our program also opens the file, reads the details and displays on the screen.

Example 1.4 fptr.c Program to demonstrate the use of file to store details of different Foot balls.

```
/*We will make use structure to store the details like, color, sport, and radius, and area
 write to file data stored in structure & finally read details from file and display . write to file using
pointer fptr in fprintf statement*/
//Program to store details of different Sports Balls using files
# include <stdio.h>    // library file on standard i/o
# include <stdlib.h>   // to use standard C file definitions
# define PI 3.14159    // PI is a symbol for constant
// declare function prototypes
float FindArea(float radius);
// declare a structure
struct SportsBall
  { char color[20]; // array
    char sport[20]; //array
    float radius;
    float area;
  };
typedef struct SportsBall stsb;
stsb ball[10];  //maximum of 10 sports balls
void main( )
{ int i=0;
  char stg[20]; // This is an array. we will use it to store what we read from file.
  FILE *fptr; // fptr points to object FILE. You can access definitions contained therein.
  fptr=fopen("SportsBalls","w"); // open SportsBalls for writing data
```

```
 if (fptr==NULL)
   {     printf("File could not be opened\n");
         exit(1);
   }
  printf(" To stop enter END for the color field \n");
  printf("\n Enter color of the ball :");
  scanf("%s", ball[i].color);

  while (ball[i].color[0] != 'E'|| ball[i].color[1] != 'N'
        || ball[i].color[2] != 'D')
   {  fprintf(fptr," %s", ball[i].color);
     // get details of sport, radius, and compute area
      printf("\n Sport = ? ");
     scanf("%s", ball[i].sport);
     fprintf(fptr,"%s", ball[i].sport);
     printf("\n RADIUS = ? ");
     scanf("%f", &ball[i].radius);
     fprintf(fptr,"%f", ball[i].radius);
     ball[i].area=FindArea(ball[i].radius);
     fprintf(fptr,":%f", ball[i].area);
     i++;
      //get the next set of data
    printf(" To stop enter END for the color field \n");  // get next set of data
    printf("\n Enter color of the ball :");
    scanf("%s", ball[i].color);
   }// end of while
  //close file SportsBalls
  fclose(fptr);
  // now open the file in read mode
  fptr=fopen("SportsBalls","r"); // open sportsballs for reading data
if (fptr==NULL)
   {     printf("File could not be opened\n");
            exit(1); // exit to operating system
   }
printf(" Details of FootBalls fetched from file are...\n");
 printf("color : sport : radius : area \n");
 // do while end of file not reached
  while(!feof(fptr))
   { //fscanf reads entire line as an array. store it in array stg
     fscanf(fptr,"%s", stg); //
     //print stg using printf command
     printf("%s\n", stg);
   }
```

```
fclose(fptr);
}// end of main

// function definition
float FindArea (float radius) {return (4*PI * radius * radius);}
/*OUTPUT:
To stop enter END for the color field
 Enter color of the ball: RED
 Sport = ? CRICKET
 RADIUS = ? 2.0

 To stop enter END for the color field
 Enter color of the ball: BLUE
 Sport = ? TENNIS
 RADIUS = ? 2.5
To stop enter END for the color field
 Enter color of the ball: END

 Details of SportsBalls fetched from file are...
color : sport : radius : area
RED: CRICKET: 2.000000:50.265442
BLUE: TENNIS: 2.500000:78.539749*/
```

We have finished telling you what we wanted to tell you before we commence in depth. It is like you will learn at home with mother most of the things they formally teach you at lower KG in school. Look back, you will notice, you have already learnt about functions, passing arguments, arrays, structures, and files. Make sure you enter the code yourself by hand and execute them if you have access to computer or write the code on paper if you do not have one. Both methods of learning are equally effective. In the next chapter we will learn about problem solving techniques like flow charts and algorithms.

OBJECTIVE QUESTIONS

1. Standard library file —————— is included to use printf & scanf functions
2. For using clrscr() function, the standard library file to be included

   a) stdio.h b) conio.h d) math.h d) stdstream.h
3. To go to new line the escape sequence required is

   a) '\a' b) '\new' c) '\t' d) '\n'
4. For using getch() function, the standard library file to be included

   a) stdio.h b) math.h c) conio.h d) stdstream.h

5. Conversion specifier for integer in scanf statement are

a) %d b) %f c) %c d) %s

6. Conversion specifier for float in scanf statement are

a) %d b) %f c) %c d) %s

7. Conversion specifier for string in scanf statement are

a) %d b) %f c) %c d) %s

8 Function prototype statement will have a semicolon True/False

9 Function definition statement will have a semicolon True/False

10 Global Declarations and Definitions are available to all functions True/False

11 Structure declaration and definition and are placed above void main(). Which one of the following statements are NOT true.

a) its required by all functions
b) Its global declaration
c) Space available
d) They are global declaration and available to all

12 Type defining a structure would allow shorter names in lieu of key word struct and structure name True/False.

13 #define symbol value. Value can be changed in side function True/False

14 Include sections are called pre processor directive True/False

15 FILE object contains standard definition for accessing file functions True/False

REVIEW QUESTIONS

1 What are global declarations?

2 What does <stdio.h> contain?

3 Why function prototypes are declared before main( ) function.

4 Declare an array of integers X to hold 25 values. Draw pictorially and put a value of 25 in X[10].

5 Declare a structure called BankCustomer. Show the fields name, acctno, balance. Type define structure as customer and creates an array of customers called cust to hold 25 customers of type BankCustomer.

SOLVED PROBLEMS

1. Write and test a function that takes two arguments radius and height and returns surface area of the cylinder.

```
//surarea.c
// We will pass two arguments radius and height
# include <stdio.h>    // library file on standard i/o
# define PI 3.14159   // PI is a symbol for constant
// declare function prototypes
float FindArea(float radius, float height );

void main()
{ float radius, height;
  float area;
  printf(" To stop enter 0 for the radius \n");
  printf("\n Radius = ");
  scanf("%f", &radius);
  printf("\n Height = ? ");
  scanf("%f", &height);
  while ( radius != 0)
   { if (radius < 0)
        area = 0;
     else
         area = FindArea(radius, height);
     // print out put
       printf("Area of cylinder = %f\n", area);
       printf(" To stop enter 0 for the radius \n");
       printf("\n Radius = ");
       scanf("%f", &radius);
       printf("\n Height = ");
       scanf("%f", &height);
   }
 }// end of main
// function definition
float FindArea(float radius, float height) {return (2*PI * radius * height);}
/*Output:
To stop enter 0 for the radius
Radius = 4
Height = ? 4
Area of cylinder = 100.530884
To stop enter 0 for the radius
Radius = 3
Height = 6
```

Area of cylinder = 113.097237
To stop enter 0 for the radius
Radius = 0
Height = 0

2 Write and test a function that takes two arguments a and b and prints multiplication table.

```
// function definition
void Multiply(int a, int b)
{ // a implies a times table and b implies up to b
  // Ex a=5, b=20 means up to 5x20
  int i;
  for (i=1;i<=b;i++)
   {
      printf("\n %dX%d= %d\n", a, i, a*i);
   }
}//end of function main
```

```
/*Output:
Enter values for <a,b>5 5
5X1= 5
5X2= 10
5X3= 15
5X4= 20
5X5= 25
```

3. Write a program to compute larger of two float numbers. Function FindMax to turn larger of two float type arguments.

```
//findmax.c
# include <stdio.h>    // library file on standard i/o
// declare function prototypes
int FindMax(int a, int b);
void main()
{
   int a, b, ans;
   printf("\n Enter values for <a,b>");
  scanf("%d%d", &a, &b);
   ans = FindMax(a,b); // pass parameters
   printf("\n maximum of two given numbers %d and %d = %d\n", a, b, ans);
}
// function definition
int FindMax(int a, int b)
 {int ans;
  ans = (a>b)?a:b;
  return ans;
 }
```

```
/*Output:
Enter values for <a,b>23 45
maximum of two given numbers 23 and 45 = 45*/
```

4 **Write and test a program that uses three float type arrays : num[10], square[10]Squareroot[10]. Get the num from the user and write functions to compute square and squareroot and store in respective arrays. You can use n^0.5 for square root.**

```
//squar.c
#include <stdio.h>    // library file on standard i/o
#include<math.h>
// declare function prototypes
float FindSquare(float num);
double Squareroot(float num);

void main()
{  int n, i =0;  // i we will use as array index, n for keeping count
   float num[10]; // Array of numbers, numbering max of 10
   float square[10];  // Array of square, numbering max of 10
   double squareroot[10];  // Array of squareroot, numbering max of 10

  printf(" To stop enter 0 for the number \n");
  printf("\n Number = ");
  scanf("%f", &num[i]);
  while (num[i] != 0)
   {  if ( num[i]< 0)
        { square[i] = 0;
          squareroot[i]=0;
        }
     else
        { square[i] = FindSquare(num[i]);// store the result in square area
          squareroot[i] = Squareroot(num[i]); // store the result in squareroot
        }
     // get the next set of data. we have to increment i prior to getting new radius
     // else old data will be over written and hence lost
     ++i;
      printf(" To stop enter 0 for the number \n");
  printf("\n Number = ");
     scanf("%f", &num[i]);
   }// end of while
   n = — i;  // This is because you have increased the count
             // for i for radius = 0 case also. We will use n in for loop.
  // display array elements
  printf ("\n Square and square root of a given number\n");
```

```
// You have n balls (i.e. 0 to n-1 as per C convention). Therefore print  i <=n
for (i=0; i<= n; i++)
  printf("number = %f : square = %f : squareroot = %lf \n", num[i], square[i], squareroot[i]);
}// end of main

// function definition
float FindSquare(float num)
{ return num*num;
}
double Squareroot(float num)
{ return pow(num, 0.5);
}
/*Output:
To stop enter 0 for the number
Number = 4
To stop enter 0 for the number
Number = 5
To stop enter 0 for the number
Number = 6
To stop enter 0 for the number
Number = 0

Square and square root of a given number
number = 4.000000 : square = 16.000000 : squareroot = 2.000000
number = 5.000000 : square = 25.000000 : squareroot = 2.236068
number = 6.000000 : square = 36.000000 : squareroot = 2.449490*/
```

5 **Define a structure called Student. Field in the structure is name[20], int age, char class[20], float marks1, float marks2, and float total. Write and test the program to get the data, compute total through a function call and print all the details for 5 student records.**

```
//studstruct.c
#include<stdio.h>
#include<stdlib.h>
struct student
{       char name[20];
 int age;
 float marks1;
 float marks2;
 float total;
};
typedef struct student stud;
stud st[5]; //create 5 instances of students
```

```
void printdata();
void compavg();
void main()
{       int i;
        for(i=0;i<5;i++)
        {   printf("\nenter name :");
       scanf("%s", st[i].name);

            printf("\nenter age :");
             scanf("%d", &st[i].age);
            printf("enter marks1 and marks2 :");
             scanf("%f%f", &st[i].marks1, &st[i].marks2);
   }
   compavg();
   printdata();
}
void compavg()
{       int i;
      for(i=0;i<5;i++)
          st[i].total=(st[i].marks1+st[i].marks2);
}
void printdata()
{ int i;
  printf("\n printing details of students.......\n");
  for(i=0;i<5;i++)
  {  printf("name: %s\nage:=%d\n", st[i].name, st[i].age);
   printf("marks1=%f\tmarks2=%f\total=%f\n\n", st[i].marks1, st[i].marks2,
  st[i].total);
  }
}//end of main

/*Output:
enter name:ravi
enter age:23
enter marks1 and marks2:40 40

enter name:kalyan
enter age:22
enter marks1 and marks2:30 40

enter name:arvind
enter age:24
enter marks1 and marks2:60 40
```

```
enter name:anil
enter age:24
enter marks1 and marks2:40 50

enter name:rohit
enter age:21
enter marks1 and marks2:40 50

printing details of students.......
name:kalyan
age:=22
marks1=30.000000      marks2=40.000000      total=70.000000


name:ravi
age:=23
marks1=40.000000      marks2=40.000000      total=80.000000

name:rohit
age:=21
marks1=40.000000      marks2=50.000000      total=90.000000

name:arvind
age:=24
marks1=60.000000      marks2=40.000000      total=100.000000

name:anil
age:=24
marks1=40.000000      marks2=50.000000      total=90.000000
```

ASSIGNMENT PROBLEMS

1. *Write the various steps involved in executing a c program and illustrate it with the help of flowchart*
2. *What are different types of integer's constants? What are long integer constants? How do these constants differ from ordinary integer constants? How can they be written and identified?*
3. **Write a function program to convert Fahrenheit to centigrade using the formula Celsius=5*(farenheit-32)/9.**
4. **Write a c module to compute simple and compound Interest using the formula SI =P*N*R/100 and CI= P*(1+R/100)^N**
5. **Write a program to prepare name, address, and telephone number of five of your friends. Use structure called friend.**

6. Write a program to store number, age and weight in three separate arrays for 10 students. At the end of data entry print what has been entered.
7. Using the formula A=Squareroot(s*(s-a)*(s-b)*(s-c)) compute area of the triangle. S=(a+b+c)/2, and a, b, and c are sides of the triangle

Solutions to Objective Questions

1. stdio.h	2. b	3. d	4. c	5. a	6. b
7. d	8. True	9. false	10. True	11. c	12. True
13. False	14. True	15. True			

CHAPTER 2

PROGRAMMING BASICS

2.1 INTRODUCTION

We have a problem on hand of finding maximum of three numbers using a computer and C language. For this problem to be executed by a computer, you will need C compiler and a C program to get us the result. C compiler is a tool, where as C program is to be developed by you after understanding the process involved in obtaining the results. What are the tools available for making the program understand the problem better and thus develop an optimal C Code. The following techniques / tools help you in better understanding the problem at hand.

Algorithm : ***It is a step by step logical procedure to be adopted for achieving the solution.***

Flow Chart : ***Graphical and diagrammatic presentation, using standard flow chart symbols, of logical steps in a procedure to be adopted for obtaining the solution for a give problem.***

Let us solve the problem of finding maximum of three numbers using above techniques.

2. 1.1 Flow Charts

The symbols used to describe logical steps in a procedure are given at Fig. 2.1

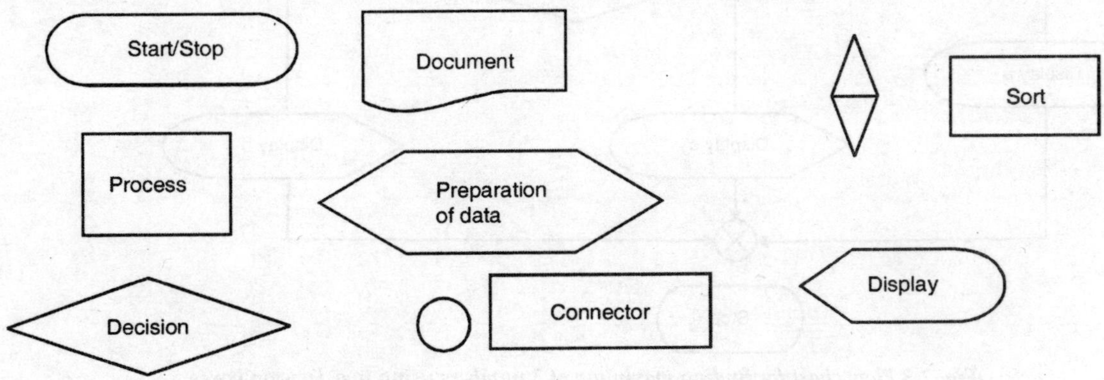

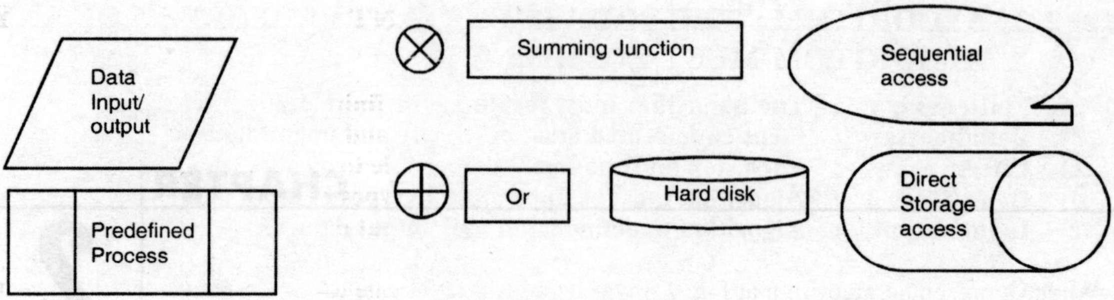

Fig. 2.1 Flow chart symbols

Look at the flow chart we have presented at Fig. 2.2 carefully. It does solve our problem. But does it solve efficiently? For example, there are 3 decision boxes in the flow chart. Can we redesign the flow chart with only 2 decision boxes so that our C code is efficient ? Here is the improved version of flow chart placed at Fig. 2.3a that uses only two decision boxes.

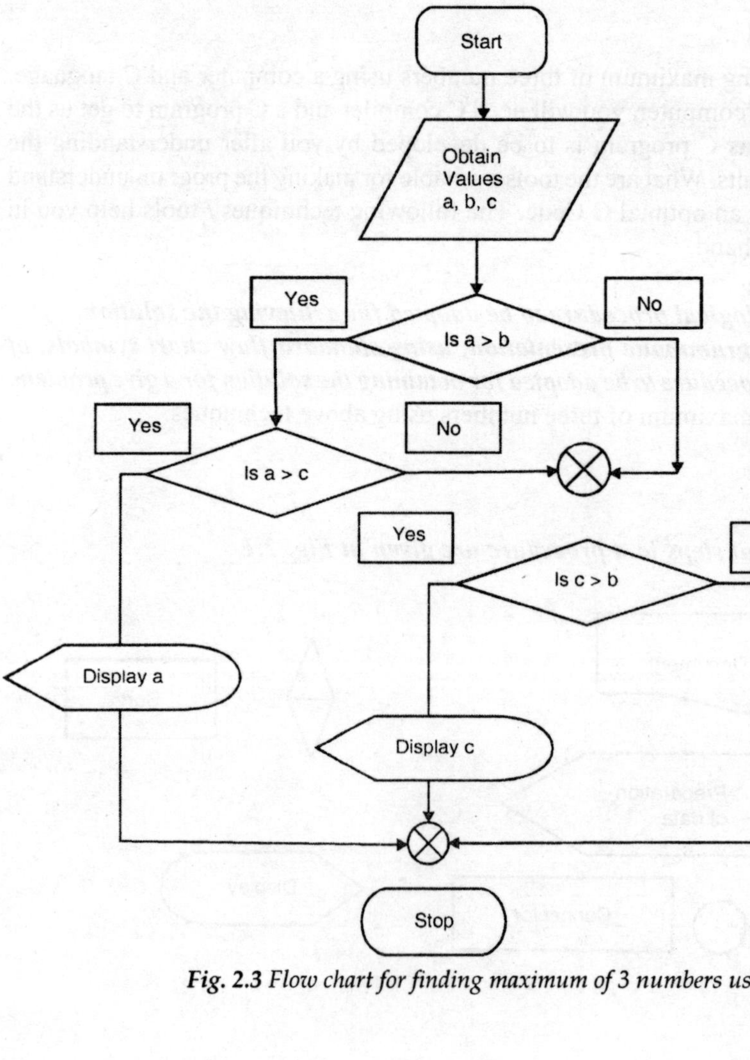

Algorithm

Step1 **:** ***Obtain values a,b,c***
Step2 **:** ***Max = a***
Step3 **:** ***Check if Max < b***
let max = b.
Step4 **:** ***Check if max< c. If yes***
let max = c
Step 5 **:** ***display max***
Step 6 **:** ***End***

Fig. 2.2

Fig. 2.3 Flow chart for finding maximum of 3 numbers using two decision boxes

2.2 ALGORITHM : THE FOUR IMPORTANT PROPERTIES OF ANY ALGORITHM MUST POSSESS ARE

a)	**Finiteness**	**:**	**The algorithm must terminate in finite number of steps.**
b)	**Definiteness**	**:**	**Steps enumerated must be precise and unambiguous.**
c)	**Effectiveness**	**:**	**Each step must be easily convertible to a code.**
d)	**Generality**	**:**	**Algorithm must be applicable all types of input data**
e)	**Input/output**	**:**	**Algorithm to define input and output data.**

We have presented algorithm at Fig. 2.3b, to demonstrate the one to one correspondence between the algorithm and flow chart. Further note that a well developed algorithm and flow chart greatly simplifies writing of the C code and further testing. From the basics you have learnt from chapter 1, we can convert above algorithm and flow chart in to a C code.

Example 2.1 : *max.c* C code for finding maximum of 3 numbers

```
//Program to find Maximum of 3 values
#include<stdio.h>
/* declaration of Function prototype. Function FindMax receives
three arguments of type integers, find out maximum of the three
numbers and returns this maximum value to main function*/
int FindMax(int a, int b, int c);
void main()
 {  int a,b,c;
   int max; // maximum of three numbers
   // get input data a, b, c from the user
   printf("enter values of a, b, c \n");
   scanf("%d%d%d", &a, &b, &c);
   // call the function. Use max to store the value returned by function
   max = FindMax(a,b,c);
   //display the result
   printf("\nMaximum Value of %d, %d, %d is %d", a, b, c, max);
   getch();
}//end of main
// Function definition
int FindMax(int a, int b, int c)
 { int max;
   max = a;
   if (max < b)
     max= b;
   if (max < c)
     max = c;
   return max;
 } // end of function FindMax
/*
OUTPUT:
enter values of a, b, c
2 5 8
Maximum Value of 2, 5, and 8 is 8
*/
```

2.3 PROGRAM DEVELOPMENT STEPS

a) Understand the problem at hand.

b) Identify what are the inputs and outputs required. It will help you to conceptualize the problem as shown below

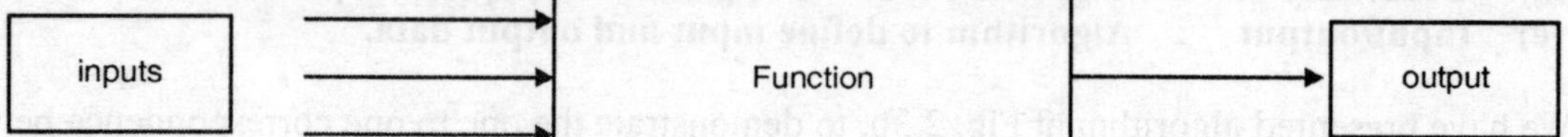

Fig. 2.4 Conceptualization of a problem

c) Use flow chart or algorithmic approach to define functionality.

d) Test the functionality by using test data.

e) Writing of C code.

   i) Write the main program and call the function to achieve desired results. For example in 2.1, we have called a function FindMax.

   ii) Write C code for function declared in the main program.

f) Debug and remove errors

i) Syntax errors. These errors are easy to remove. Compiler pin points syntactical errors.

   ii) Logical Errors. Compiler can not catch these errors. Only extensive testing can resolve these errors.

   iii) Run time errors. The examples are linking errors or errors that can occur at run time of the program like

   - division by zero.
   - array out of bounds.
   - exceeding of allocated limits.
   - errors due to data type.

g) Testing and Validation. Design the test data, called test cases that would test the correct functioning of the algorithm under

   i) normal conditions.

   ii) Best case considerations

   iii) worst case considerations.

Test cases chosen must be exhaustive to test boundary conditions of the algorithms.

h) Documentation to keep track of development and changes incorporated in the programs so that program maintenance becomes easier later.

■■■ 2.4 ABOUT A, B AND C

Dennis Ritchie of Bell Telephone Laboratories, now known as AT&T Bell labs, originally developed C language. C is a successor of two other languages known as A and B at the same laboratories. Later, in the year 1978, Brain Kennigan and Dennis Ritchie jointly published, description of C language. This language has become very popular owing to its rich features and found itself to be popular among students and Industry. American National Standards Institute(ANSI) has standardized the c language.

C is very versatile as it combines the features of high level languages and also low level language like assembler and hence often called as middle level language. Unique feature of C language is that it allows user to control hardware directly, in addition to providing conventional features of a high level language like good user interfaces and high computational and commercial processing ability.

C language abets structured programming, in that modules can be developed independently and can be compiled separately and can be linked to perform the desired tasks. Modularity and good program organization make C programs readable and easily maintainable.

■■■ 2.5 STRUCTURE OF C LANGUAGE

C Language program will have :

a) Include section wherein all the header files provided by the supplier of the compiler or written by the user are declared. For example, we have defined stdio.h to include standard input and ouput routines.

b) Preprocessor directives like #define etc. for example, we have defined #define PI 3.14159 in programs in chapter 1.

c) Function Prototypes. These are advance information to compiler that program uses these functions, but definitions can be found after main program. A function prototype will have

ReturnType Function name (Argument List);

↙ ↙ ↙

int FindMax (int a, int b, int c);

Function Definition is given after main program as

```
int    FindMax ( int a, int b, int c)
{
 // Function Code here
}
```

d) Structure and Union Declarations. Refer to program using structures we have dealt in Chapter 1. Recall the structure called sportsball

```
// declare a structure
struct SportsBall
{ char color[20];
  float radius;
  float area; };
typedef struct SportsBall stsb;
stsb ball[10]; //maximum of 10 Foot balls
```

The structure defined before main section are globally available to all functions.

e) Main function. This is the main function and contains declarations and definitions of variables. We generally obtain the data from the user in main function. Main function in turn calls a function and supplies the inputs to the function through arguments. Main also displays the solution to the user. In effect, we can call the main as interface with the user i.e. obtain the inputs, call a function and process the input and finally display the result.

d) Note that C language is a case sensitive and each statement is separated by a semi colon. Except group statement that precedes opening brace { . For example observe that void main ( ) and function definition statement int FindMax (int a, int b, int c), did not have semi colons.

2.6 C LANGUAGE BASICS

Declaration of Variables: In C language all variables must be declared before they are used. A variable can consist alphabet and digits. Either upper and lower case or mixtures of both cases are allowed. A variable can **not** start with a digit. It can start with an _. The allowable characters in C language are alphabets A to Z, a to z, numbers 0 – 9 and following special characters.

!	*	^	#	%	/	+	%	(	)
-	"	|	=	{	}	[	]	'	<
>	:	;	,	~	? &	_	.	BLANK	

Identifiers : Identifiers are names given to variable, function names, a structure names etc.
The valid variables are : basic_pay, hra, FindArea( ), d2000k, _std
The invalid variables and the reasons are :

2found	can not start with a digit
basic-pay	illegal character -.
Your Age	blank space

Keywords : Reserved and have special meaning in C language. A few of the important and commonly used keywords are:

auto	break	case	char	const	continue	double	default
do	else	extern	enum	float	for	goto	if
int	long	register	return	short	signed	sizeof	static
struct	switch	typedef	union	unsigned	void	volatile	while

Tokens : A token is an atomic word that is recognized by the compiler and that which will not be broken further. It can be a single character or a group of characters that can be recognized by a C compiler. Ex case, default, main, and goto etc.

■■■ 2.7 DATA TYPES

What is a data type ? simply put it defines range of permitted values and operations that can be performed on the data type. Data Types, also called intrinsic data types supported by C language is given at Fig. 2.5. The ranges allowed for a 32 bit IBM PC and memory requirements are highlighted at Table 2.1.

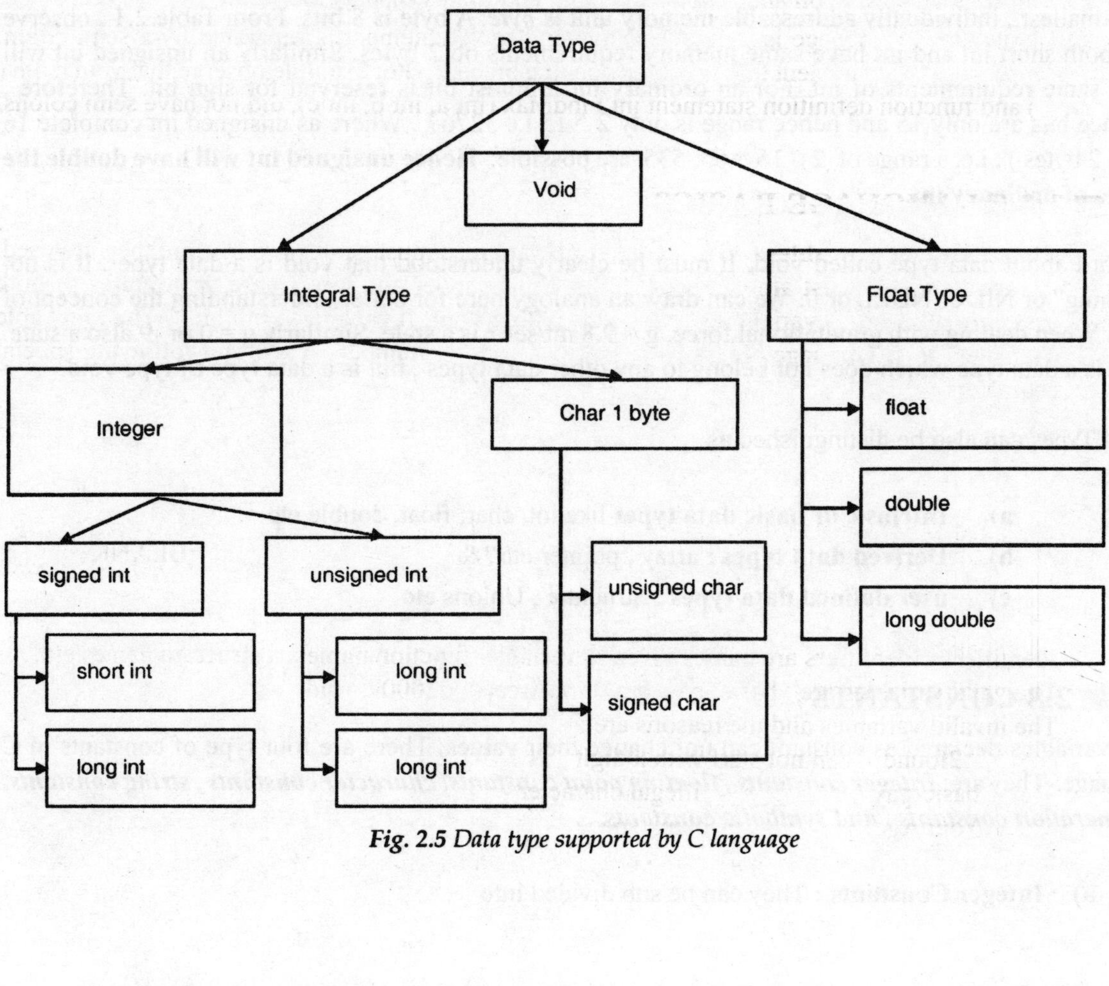

Fig. 2.5 Data type supported by C language

Table 2.1: Ranges allowed for various data types for a PC

Data type	Size(bytes)	Range allowed	Remarks
signed char	1	–128 - 0 - 127	–A , –d etc
Unsigned char	1	0-127	A , B , a , b etc
short signed int	2	–32768 to 0 to 32767	–129 , +31560 etc
short unsigned int	2	0 - 65,535	34560 , 789 etc
long signed int	4	–2,147, 483, 648 to 2, 147, 483, 647	
long unsigned int	4	0 to 4 , 294, 967, 295	
Float	8	– 3.4e 38 to +3.4 e 38	
Double	8	– 1.7 e 308 to +1.7e 308	double precisionmeans more bits for significant and exponent.
long double	10	–1.7 e 4932 to + 1.7 e 4932	

The smallest , individually addressable memory unit is ***byte.*** A byte is 8 bits. From Table 2.1 , observe that both short int and int have same memory requirements ob 2 bytes. Similarly an unsigned int will have same requirements of int. For an ordinary int leftmost bit is reserved for sign bit. Therefore , balance bits are only 15 and hence range is only 2 ^ 15 i.e 32767 . Where as unsigned int complete 16 bits (2 bytes) , i.e. a range of 2 ^ 16 = 65, 535 are possible. **Hence unsigned int will have double the range of ordinary int.**

A word about data type called void. It must be clearly understood that void is a data type . It is not "nothing" or NIL or NULL or 0. We can draw an analogy here for better understanding the concept of void. When dealing with gravitational force, g = 9.8 mt/sec ^{2} is a state. Similarly g = 0 or -9 also a state. Void is a data type which does not belong to any other data types , but is a data type of type void.

Data Types can also be distinguished as

a) **Intrinsic or basic data types** like int, char, float, double etc

b) **Derived data types :** array , pointer etc

c) **user defined data types** : Structure , Unions etc

2.8 CONSTANTS

The variables declared as constant can not change their values. There are four type of constants in C language. They are: ***Integer constants , floating point constants, character constants , string constants, enumeration constants , and symbolic constants.***

a) **Integer Constants :** They can be sub divided into

Decimal integer constants : 0 10 -745 999

Unsigned integer constant an be specified by appending letter U at the end . Ex : 55556U or 55556u

Long integer constant can be specified by appending the letter l s at the end . For example 789654234L or 7896s

Octal integer constants :only digits between 0 to 7 are allowed. All Octal numbers must start with 0 digit to identify as octal number
Allowed octal constants : 0777, 001 , 0117 , 07565L (octal long)
Illegal octal constants are : 089 - 8 is illegal , 777 - does not start with 0
: -0675.76 - . is illegal

Hexa decimal constants : A hexa decimal number must start with 0x or 0X followed by digits 0 to 9 or alphabets a to f, both upper case or lower case allowed. Allowed hexa decimal constants are : 0xffff , 0xa11f , 0×1, 0x65000UL
Illegal hexa decimal constants are : 0x14.55 , illegal character "."

b) **Floating point constants.** They are base – 10 number that can be represented either in exponent form or decimal point representation.Valid floating point constants are : 0.01 , 789.89765, 5E-5 , 1.768E+9 Invalid floating point declarations are:
6 invalid . must contain exponent or float point.
5E+12.5 Invalid as exponent can not be float.
6,789.00 Invalid character","

c) **Character constants.** Character constants can be declared based on the character set followed in a computer. ANSI have standardized these values as shown below. Appendix A gives ASCII character set.

A	65	a	097	NULL	000
B	66	b	098	LF(line feed)	010
Z	90	z	122	CR(carriage return)	013

A character constant contains a single character enclosed within a pair of single quote marks. Examples of character constants are:

'5' 'X' ';' ' '

Note that the character constant '5' is not the same as the number 5. the last constant is a blank space. Character constants have integer values known as ASCII values. For example, the statement

```
printf("%d",'a');
```

would print number 97, the ASCII value of letter a. Since each character constant represent an integer value it is also possible to perform arithmetic operations on character constants.

Special Characters that can not be printed normally, double quote(") ,apostrophe(') , question mark(?) and backslash(\) etc can be represented by using ***escape sequences. An escape sequence always starts with \ followed by special character stated above.***

d) String Constants . String constant can contain any number of characters in sequence , but enclosed in double quotation marks.

"new delhi" , "14 Nov 1954" , an empty string is "".

Please note that NULL character \0 indicates NULL character and is used by C language to indicate the end of a string.

Table 2.2 Escape sequences and its special effects

Special Character	Escape sequence	ASCII value
Bell	\a	007
Back space	\b	008
Horizontal tab	\t	009
Vertical tab	\v	011
New line	\n	010
Carriage return	\r	013
Quotation mark	\"	034
apostrophe	\'	039
Backslash	\\	092
Null	\0	000

e) Enumeration Constants

Enumeration is a user defined data type and its members are constants. It can be used effectively to associate integer values to variables. The syntax and example are shown below

Syntax storage class enum variable { var1, var2, var3 ....};

Examples are : enum bool { FALSE,TRUE};
enum colors { RED,BLUE,GREEN};
enum waitque { P0 , P1,P2=5,P6};

Then integer values assigned with above enum declarations are

FALSE =0 TRUE =1
RED =0, BLUE =1, GREE=2
PO=0,P1=1,P2=5,P6=6 and so on

We can create instances of enum variable and assign data as shown below.

color color1,color2;
color1=2; // means color1 will be GREEN

In C language , enumeration is a list of constant integer values. This enumeration type of declaration is useful , when we want to assign constant integer values to names , for example 0 and 1 to a variable. Consider the example shown below

```
enum bool { no, yes} ;  no has a value 0 and yes has a value = 1
enum month {jan, feb, mar, apr};
enum color   { red , yellow=3 , green }; // red = 0 , yellow =3 and green =4
```

f) **Symbolic Constants.** A symbolic name substitutes a sequence of characters or numerical value that follows it.

```
# define PI 3.14159
# define MAX  50
# define NAME thunder
```

Note that there is no semi colon at the end of statement

2.8.1 Declaration and Assignment Values to Variables. Declaration means mapping the association between the variables and data types. Following are valid declarations

```
int  x , y , z;
float  radius =  2.56 . //This is declaration and also assignment of value to the
                          variable. We can also call this activity as definition.
float radius[25] ;      // declaration of array of data type float with size 25
double root1 = 0.3123e-10; // we have used exponent form. 0.3123*10^10
short x , y=0 , z;      // you can declare variables as short or short int
short int x , y=0 ,z;  // Similarly long int can be declared as long int or long
```

char **text[]** = "New Delhi"; // The string contains 9 characters . It will be stored in an array as shown below. Note that we have left blank for size of the array.

You could also declare specifying the size , but size to be correctly specified , taking care of null character as char text[9] = "New Delhi"

name of the array	**: text :**	**N**	**e**	**w**		**D**	**e**	**l**	**h**	**i**	**\0**
Subscript value	:	0	1	2	3	4	5	6	7	8	9

text[0] contains character N

text[9] contains null character(\0)

■■■ 2.9 EXPRESSIONS

An expression can comprise any one of the following

a) A single character or a number.

b) A single constant or a variable.

c) A combination of variables or constants , inter connected by operators.

d) A logical condition that is true (value 1) and false (value 0).

Examples of expressions are:

```
root1=(-b+sqrt(d))/(2*a);   x=y;   ++i;   x = = y; x=oyez;
```

Example 2.2 *roots.c* A program to compute roots of a quadratic equation. In this example observe, declaration , assignment , expressions , math function

```
/*This program finds the roots of a quadratic equation
Formula to compute the roots are  (-b+sqrt(b*b-4*a*c))/(2*a)
and (-b-sqrt(b*b-4*a*c))/(2*a)
*/
#include<stdio.h>
#include<conio.h>
#include<math.h> // for square root function
// function prototype
void FindRoot(float a , float b , float c);
void main()
{       // declare three variables as double precision numbers
        int a,b,c;
        // obtain the coefficients
        printf("\nenter coefficiants of x^2 , x , and constant:");
        scanf("%f %f %f",&a,&b,&c);
        // Call FindRoot function. We are sending a , b , c values as arguments
        FindRoot(a,b,c);
        getch();
}// end of main
// function definition
void FindRoot(float a,float b,float c)
 {      double d,root1,root2;
        d = ((b*b)-(4*a*c));
        if(d>=0)
        {       printf("\n roots are real\n");
                root1=(-b+sqrt(d))/(2*a);
                root2=(-b-sqrt(d))/(2*a);
                printf("\n root1=%f",root1);
                printf("\n root2=%f",root2);
        }
        else
        {       printf("\n roots are imaginary\n");
                printf("\nroot1=%e+i%e",-b/(2*a),sqrt(-d)/(2*a));
                printf("\nroot2=%e-i%e",-b/(2*a),sqrt(-d)/(2*a));
        }
}// end of function call
/*
OUTPUT:
enter coefficiants of x^2 , x , and constant: 1 -3 2
roots are real
root1=2.000000
root2=1.000000
*/
```

■■■ 2.10 ARITHMETIC OPERATORS

The basic (also known as intrinsic) operators are

\+ **addition** – **subtraction** * **multiplication**

/ **division** % **modulus (remainder after division).**

It may be noted that C language does not support exponentiation. Although we will use ^ symbol to denote exponentiation in expression , we have to use a library function call pow to calculate the exponentiation.

Type conversion : If the variable involved in an operation are of different type , then type conversion is carried out before the operation.

If the operation is between a float and double , the float will be converted to double and the result will result in double

If the operation is between a float or double or long double and a char or int , then char or int will be converted to float or double or long double and the result will result in float or double or long double.

If the operation is between a int and long int, the int will be converted to long int and the result will result in long int.

If the operands are not float or long int , they will be converted to int.

Type Cast : Suppose , we want to declare the result in particular data type , we can type cast as shown below.

```
int a , b;
float x;
x=(float)a/b; //  a/b is integer division and the result is converted to float .
```

Unary operators : In unary operator , operator precedes a single operand. Unary operators are : - , ++ , —. sizeof . Examples are :

- 4.0 , -5*(A+B)
++ i , i++ , —i , i—

++ , — operators are called increment and decrement operators. If they precedes the operand , then first the variable is incremented , then operation is performed. If they follow the operand , then the operation is performed first , and the variable is incremented.

```
int  count = 1;
printf("%d" , count);   // out put will be 1
printf("%d" , ++count);
/* count will be incremented by one and then operation of
print is performed . Output will be 2. Now , if you use*/
printf("%d" , count++);
/* count will be printed first. Output is 2. Then count will
be incremented by 1 to 3.*/
printf("%d" , count);   // out put will be 3.
```

sizeof **operator will be useful for determining the size allocated for a data type by the computer.**

```
char city[]="New Delhi";
 printf("Size of integer: %d", sizeof(int));
  printf("Size of float: %d" , sizeof(float));
  printf("Number of characters in String constant  city :%d" , sizeof (city) );
```

Output of above statements would be

```
Size of integer :  2
Size of float    :  4
Number of characters in String constant  city:9
```

■■■ 2.11 RELATIONAL AND LOGICAL OPERATORS

The relational operators are : **>** **>=** **<** **and** **<=.** These four relational operators have same precedence. However , they have lower priority than arithmetic operators.
The two more operators , known as equality operators = = and ! = have priority just below relational operators.

Logical Operators : These are && and ||. Evaluation of expressions connected by logical operators are done from left to right and evaluation stops when either truth or false hood is established. In the statement shown below

```
while ( (iflag==0) && ( text[i]!='E') )
```

first iflag == 0 is evaluated , if it is true , then only second expression text[i]=!E is evaluated. In other words , evaluation stops as soon as truth or false is established.

Conditional Expressions : Question Mark operator.

Suppose , you want to allot 10 additional bonus marks to students , who put in 100 percent attendance , and all others additional 2 marks. This would result in statements like

```
If ( attendance > 100)
  marks += 10; // this is a compound statement . It means Marks=Marks +10
Else
  marks +=2;
```

C language gives you facility of conditional operator, using which above 4 lines can be coded as a single line

```
marks = (attendance > 100) ? marks + 10 : marks + 2;
```

The syntax is :   z = exp1 ? expr 2 : exp3. Exp1 is evaluated first. If it is true z is equated to the result of exp2 . Else z is equated to exp3.

Bit Wise Operators :

Bit wise operators available in C Language are

& **Bit wise AND.** Used for masking operation. For example if you want to mask first four bits of a number 'n' , then we will mask n with a number whose last four bits are 1s. i.e. 0001111. In Octal representation it is 017(Remember an octal number starts with 0 and a hexa number starts with 0x)

n= 1 0 0 1 0 1 0 1 =149(decimal)

& 0 0 0 0 1 1 1 1 = 017(octal)

result n = 0 0 0 0 0 1 0 1

Note that last four bits are 0101 and are unaffected i.e. they are just reproduce in the result , whereas , the left four bits are all 0s. i.e. they are *masked.*

| **Bitwise OR**. This operator is used when you want to set a bit. For example , we want to set 0th and 2nd bit to 1 for n=144 , then we will use | operator with n and as shown below

n= 1 0 0 1 0 0 0 0 =144(decimal)

| = 0 0 0 0 0 1 0 1 = 005(octal)

result n = 1 0 0 1 0 1 0 1 =149(decimal)

^ **Bit wise Exclusive OR.** Exclusive OR also known as odd function , produces output 1 , when both bits are not same (odd) and produces a 0 when both bits are same.

n = 1 0 0 1 0 1 0 1 =149(decimal)

^ = 0 0 0 0 0 1 0 1 = 005(octal)

result n = 1 0 0 1 0 0 0 0 =149(decimal)

<< **Left Shift.** Shifting left by one position , bits of a binary number is equal to multiplying the number with 2.

n = 1 0 0 1 0 0 0 0 =144(decimal)

n<< 1 1 0 0 1 0 0 0 0 0 = 288(decimal)

n<< 2 1 0 0 1 0 0 0 0 0 0 = 576

>> **Right Shift.** Shifting right by one position , bits of a binary number is equal to division of the given number with 2.

n = 1 0 0 1 0 0 0 0 =144(decimal)

n>> 0 1 0 0 1 0 0 0 = 72(decimal)

n>>2 0 0 1 0 0 1 0 0 = 36(decimal)

~ **Tilde operator . one's complement Operator.** This is a unary operator , used to find one's complement of a given number .

n = 1 0 0 1 0 1 0 1 =149(decimal)

~n = 0 1 1 0 1 0 1 0 = bit wise complement

Example 2.3 bitwise.c

```
//A program to demonstrate the working of bitwise operators.

#include<stdio.h>
int main()
{
  int n = 149;
  int res;
  res = n & 0017;
  printf("The resultant of Bit wise AND operator is : %d \n", res);
  res = n | 0017;
  printf("The resultant of Bit wise OR operator is : %d \n", res);
  res = n && 0017; // this is logical AND . Truth or false will be output
  printf("The resultant of Logical AND operator is : %d \n", res );
  res = n || 0017; // this is logical OR . Truth or false will be output
  printf("The resultant of Logical OR operator is : %d \n", res);
  res = n ^ 0017;
  printf("The resultant of Exclusive operator is : %d \n", res);
  res = n <<2;
  printf("The resultant of shift left ( by 2 bits) operator is : %d \n", res);
  res = n >>2;
  printf("The resultant of shift right ( by 2 bits) operator is : %d \n", res);
  res = ~n;
  printf("The resultant of NOT operator is : %d \n", res);
  return 0;
}

The resultant of Bit wise AND operator is : 5
The resultant of Bit wise OR operator is : 159
The resultant of Logical AND operator is : 1
The resultant of Logical OR operator is : 1
The resultant of Exclusive operator is : 154
The resultant of shift left ( by 2 bits) operator is : 576
The resultant of shift right( by 2 bits) operator is : 36
The resultant of NOT operator is : -150*/
```

2.12 PRECEDENCE AND ASSOCIATION OF OPERATORS

The precedence and association of the operators are shown at Table 2.3. The operators at the top have priority more than those that appear later in the table , i.e. operators priority is highest at the top of the table and lowest at the bottom of the table. Operators on the same line have same priority.

- , / and % have all same priority
- Unary operators like + , - , and * have more priority than binary operators

■■■ 2.13 INPUT AND OUTPUT STATEMENTS

2.13.1 Scanf Function : The statement format is

scanf(format , arg1 ,arg2 .....)

format specifiers and the data types they handle is shown below:

%c	Character
%d	Decimal integer
%h	Short integer
%i	Decimal , octal(prefix by 0) , Hexadecimal(prefix by 0x)
%o	Octal integer
%u	Unsigned decimal integer
%x	Hexadecimal
%f	Float
%e	Float , double precision
%g	Float
%s	String followed by null character (\0 will be added automatically)
[...]	String that includes white space characters like tabs , blank etc

Table 2.3 Precedence and association rules for the operators.

<table>
<tr><th>Operator</th><th>Association</th></tr>
<tr><td>Function call ( ) , [] ,-> .</td><td>Left to right</td></tr>
<tr><td>! ~ ++ —+ - ,^, sizeof</td><td>Right to left</td></tr>
<tr><td>* / %</td><td>Left to right</td></tr>
<tr><td>+ -</td><td>Left to right</td></tr>
<tr><td><< >></td><td>Left to right</td></tr>
<tr><td>< <= > >=</td><td>Left to right</td></tr>
<tr><td>= = !=</td><td>Left to right</td></tr>
<tr><td>&</td><td>Left to right</td></tr>
<tr><td>^</td><td>Left to right</td></tr>
<tr><td>|</td><td>Left to right</td></tr>
<tr><td>&&</td><td>Left to right</td></tr>
<tr><td>||</td><td>Left to right</td></tr>
<tr><td>?:</td><td>Right to left</td></tr>
<tr><td>= += -= *= /= %= ^= != <<= >>=</td><td>Right to left</td></tr>
<tr><td>,</td><td>Left to right</td></tr>
</table>

2.13.2 Printf Statement: The format for printf statement is : printf(format, arg1,arg2..)

%c	Character
%d	Decimal integer
%h	Short integer
%i	Decimal , octal(prefix by 0) , Hexadecimal(prefix by 0x)
%o	Octal integer
%u	Unsigned decimal integer
%x	Hexadecimal
%f	Float
%e	Float , double precision
%g	Float
%s	String followed by null character (\0 will be added automatically)

You have already experimented with integers and float , and double variables. In this section , we will understand usage of other format specifiers. For example consider following statements.

Example 2.4 ***inout.c*** **.**

```
/*inout.c . A program to demonstrate usage of input and out put statements of
C Language using scanf and printf functions*/
#include<stdio.h>
void main()
{       int i;
        int n=149; // arbitary integer . we will use it to display in octa & hexa
        short int j;
        long int k;
        float a,b,c;
        double root1,root2;
        char d;
        char city[20];

        printf("\nEnter value  < int>:");
        scanf("%d",&i); // enters into slot of i
        printf("\nValue of <int >signed decimal integert> %d" ,i);

        printf("\nEnter <long int>  value:");
        scanf("%ld",&k); // enters into slot of i
        printf("\nValue of <long intl> %ld \n",k);

        printf("\nEnter decimal value:");
        scanf("%i",&i); // enters int slot of i
        printf("\nValue of <decimal> %i \n",i);
        printf("\nEnter octal(0-prefix) value:");
```

```
        scanf("%o",&i); // enters into slot of i
        printf("\nValue of <decimal> %d \n",i); //item displayed without leading 0.
        printf("\nEnter hexa (0x-prefix) value:");
        scanf("%x",&i); // enters into slot of i
        printf("\nValue of <decimal> %d \n",i); //item displayed without leading 0x.

        // print n in octal and hexa decimal number representations.
        // You can use these formatting command to convert decimal to binary.
        // item displayed without leading 0x.
        printf("\n Value of <n=149> in hexa %x ",n);
        // item displayed without leading 0.
        printf("\nValue of <n=149> in octal  %o ",n);
        /* for input and output statements for real variables , we can use
        float and double precision. In float we can use decimal or exponent
        notation. Note that we can use following statement to control output
        format %8f width of float is 8 %8.2f total width is 8 out of which
        two charaters after decimal %.2f two charaters after decimal*/

        printf("\nenter float values<a,b,c>:");
        scanf("%f%f%f",&a,&b,&c); // float variable in decimal format
        printf("\nvalues of <a,b,c in decimal float format> %f:%f:%f " , a,b,c);
        printf("\nusage of <8.2f>:");
        printf("%8.2f%8.2f%8.2f\n",a,b,c);

        printf("\nusage of <double precision float number >:");
        printf("\nenter double precision float values<root1,root2>:");
        scanf("%e%e",&root1,&root2); // root1& 2 are read as exponent format
        printf("\nvalues of root1& 2 in double  form : %e%e",root1,root2);
        /* another form for outputting float variable is 'g' type of
        conversion.Here display is either in f format or e format. Trailing
        zeros are suppressed*/
        printf("\n%g%g\n",root1,root2);
} // end of inout.c
/*OUTPUT:
Enter value  < int>:1
Value of <int (signed decimal integert> 1
Enter <long int>  value:1234567
Value of <long intl> 1234567
Enter decimal value:12
Value of <decimal> 12
Enter octal(0-prefix) value:012
Value of <decimal> 10
Enter hexa (0x-prefix) value:0xf
Value of <decimal> 15
```

Value of <n=149> in hexa 95
Value of <n=149> in octal 225
enter float values<a,b,c>:3.5 4.5 6.5
values of <a,b,c in decimal float format> 3.500000:4.500000:6.500000
usage of <8.2f>: 3.50 4.50 6.50
usage of <double precision float number >:
enter double precision float values<root1,root2>:1.00005 0.000565
values of root1& 2 in double form : -9.255960e+061-9.255960e+061
-9.25596e+061-9.25596e+061

2.13.3 Single Character Input & Output Statements

Commands getchar() and putchar() can be used to input single character at a time from keyboard. Consider the following program , where in we will read characters into an array and output the array in upper case.

Example 2.5 ***getchar.c***

```
//C program for demonstrate usage of getchar and putchar
#include<stdio.h>
void main()
{
        char city[80]; // declare an array of 80 characters length
        char c; // we will use it to store the character input
        int i=0,j=0; // i & j we will use them as counters

        // read in line .'\n' is a end of line recognized when 'enter' is pressed
      while ( (c=getchar())!='\n')
          city[i++]=c; // store it in city[i] and then post increment i.
        // store the value in j. This is because we will use i as counter once again.
        j=i;
        i=0;
        while ( i<j) // output the character in uppercase
                putchar(toupper(city[i++])); // post increment i
} // end of main.
/*
OUTPUT:
hai srinivas <pressed enter>
HAI SRINIVAS
*/
```

Observe that in using while loops we have used brace brackets only for clarity. These while loops have only one line in the body , hence could have been written with out brace brackets as

```
        while ( c!='\n')
              city[i++]=c;
```

2.13.4 Commands Gets and Puts.

These commands are used to input and output strings

```
#include<stdio.h>
void main()
{
        char city[80]; // declare an array of 80 characters length
        printf("\nEnter any line: \n");
        gets(city);    // read a line till 'enter'(new line character is pressed ).
        puts(city);         // output a line
}

/*
OUTPUT:
Enter any line :
This is taken by gets function.
This is taken by gets function.
*/
```

OBJECTIVE QUESTIONS

1. Is the given program valid? Valid/invalid

```
main()
{    int n=10;
     printf(
     " value of n is %d ",
     n);
}
```

2. The real constants can be written in ——————and ——————form.

3. What is the output of the following program? ——————and——————

```
main()
{    char ch=65;
     printf(" %d  %c ", ch,ch);
}
```

4. What is the output of the following program? ——————

```
main()
{printf(" %d ", -4 % -3);
}
```

5. Given a>c>b , a=d What is the value of the following expression?

a>b?(a>c?(c>d?4:5):3):(b>c?6:8)

a) 20 b) 5 c) 10 d) 15

6. The statement int i=j=k=l=m=10; is valid/Invalid

7. what is the output of the following program?

```
int i=10;
while(i = = 0)
{
    printf("%d\n ",i);
    i—;
}
```

output ——————————————————

8 What is the output of following code

```
int i=0;
printf("%d%d%d",i++,i++,i++);
```

output : —————————

9 What is the output of following code output: ——————————

```
main()
{  int d,i=3;
   d=i++ + ++i;
   printf("%d \t %d",i,d);
}
```

10 Given a= 00110010 (50) . Write C statements to determine whether bit 1 in the above pattern is ON/OFF.(least significant bit is bit 0)

a) a & 0x03 b) a|0x03 c) a & 0x02 d) a | 0x02

11 ASCII value for A , Z are

a) 66 ,91 b) 65,90 c) 97 , 122 d) 96 121

12 ASCII value for a , z are

a) 66 ,91 b) 65,90 c) 97 , 122 d) 96 121

13 To find a raised to power of b , the function we would use is

a) a^b b) a**c c) pow(b,a) d) pow(a,b)

14 What is ascii value for 0 and 9

a) 30 39 b) 31, 40 c) 31,39 d) 56, 64

15 To read a character and echo the character on to screen , with out the need to press enter key, appropriate function is

a) getch() b) getche() c) getchar() d) gets()

16. A variable can start with a number True/False

17. Int and short occupy ——————————bytes of memory

18 Declaration of variable can be done anywhere in the program True/False

19 Range of character data type is ________________

20 Range of signed integer data type is ________________

REVIEW QUESTIONS

1. What are different data type of c
2. Distinguish a variable and constant with examples.
3. What is a token.
4. Explain program development steps.
5. What are logical errors and run time errors.
6. What are the key words? Explain with example.
7. What are Integer and float type constants?
8. What are character constants.
9. How string constants are declared and stored. Explain with examples.
10. What are enumeration constants.
11. Explain escape sequences for new line , tab .
12. Explain type conversion operator used in printf statements
13. Explain typecasting with examples.
14. What are relational and logical operators. Discuss their priorities.
15. What is the difference between & , && operators.
16. What is the difference between = , = = operators.
17. Explain ? operator.
18. Show the working of bitwise AND operator with example. What is masking operation.
19. Show the working of bitwise OR and Exclusive OR operators with example.
20. Distinguish unary and binary operators.

SOLVED PROBLEMS

1 Write a program to find out the maximum of 2 given numbers using conditional operators*/

```
// max.c #include <stdio.h>
#include<conio.h>
//function prototype declarations
int MAX(int a,int b);
main()
{
        int p,q,r;
        clrscr();
        printf("enter values for p,q\n");
        scanf("%d%d",&p,&q); //input from the user
        r=MAX(p,q); //function call
        printf("maximum no. is: %d\n",r);
        getch();
} //end of main
int MAX(int a,int b)//function definition
{
        return(a<b?b:a); //return the max value to main
}//end of function MAX

/*
OUTPUT:
enter values for p,q:
2 5
maximum no. is: 5
*/
```

2 Write a program that reads the 3 sides of a triangle and prints and checks whether its rightangled or not

```
// check.c
#include<stdio.h>
#include<conio.h>
//function prototype declarations
void RIGHTANGLED(int p,int q,int r);
void main()
{
        int a,b,c;
        clrscr();
        printf("enter the sides a,b,c\n");
```

```
        scanf("%d%d%d",&a,&b,&c);              /*input sides from the user*/
        RIGHTANGLED(a,b,c);   /*function call*/
        getch();
} /*end of main*/
void RIGHTANGLED(int p,int q,int r)        /*function definition*/
{       p*=p;
        q*=q;
        r*=r;
        /*checking the condition of right angled triangle*/
          if( ( (p+q)==r) || ( (q+r)==p) || ( (p+r)==q) )
                  printf("rightangled\n");
          else
                  printf("not rightangled\n");
}       /*end of function RIGHTANGLED*/
/*
OUTPUT:
enter the sides a,b,c
3 4 5
rightangled
*/
```

3. Write a C program to print the following figure:

```
        *
        * *
        * * *
        * * * *
```

```
// star.c
#include<stdio.h>
#include<conio.h>
void figure5(int m); //function definition
void main()
{       int n;
        clrscr();
        printf("enter number of lines\n");        /*how many lines*/
        scanf("%d",&n);
        figure5(n);          /*function call*/
        getch();
}                 /*end of main*/
void figure5(int m)          /*function definition*/
{       int i=0,j=0;
        for(i=0;i<=m;i++)     /*outer loop begins*/
        {
                for(j=0;j<i;j++)        /*inner loop begins*/
                {       printf("*");
```

```
        }       /*end of inner loop*/
        printf("\n");     /*print in next line*/
    }                 /*end of outer loop*/
}                 /*end of function figure5*/
/*
OUTPUT:
enter number of lines:4
    *
    * *
    * * *
    * * * *
*/
```

4 Write a program to find out whether a given year is leap or not

```
// leap.c
#include<stdio.h>
#include<conio.h>
void LEAP(int n); //function definition
void main()
{
    int x;
    clrscr();
    printf("enter the year\n");
    scanf("%d",&x);        /*input year from the user*/
    LEAP(x);           /*function call*/
    getch();
}/*end of main*/
void LEAP(int n)           /*function definition*/
{
    if((n%400==0)||((n%4==0)&&(n%100!=0)))
    printf("leap year\n");
    else
    printf("not leap year\n");
} /*end of function LEAP*/
/*OUTPUT:
enter the year:
2000
leap year*/
```

5 While a program that reads a string and prints yes if all the chars are vowels else prints no*/

```
// vowel.c
#include<stdio.h>
#include<conio.h>
#include<string.h>
```

```
#include<ctype.h>  // to facilitate using of tolower() and toupper functions
void main()
{
        int i,nv;
        char x[20];
        clrscr();
        printf("enter any string\n");
        scanf("%s",x);                  /*input from the user*/
        nv=0;                   /*nv=number of vowels,initially 0*/
        i=0;            /*i is the number of chars,initially 0*/
        while(x[i]!='\0')               /*when the char of string is not null*/
        {       switch(toupper(x[i]))
                {       case 'A':
                        case 'E':
                        case 'I':
                        case 'O':
                        case 'U': nv++;break;
                }
                i++;
        }
        if(i==nv)               /*when value of  nv equals to i*/
           printf("yes\n");
        else
           printf("no\n");
        getch();
} /*end of main*/
/*OUTPUT:
enter any string
education
no  */
```

6 Write a program to find out whether the given number is even or odd

```
//.even.c
#include<stdio.h>
#include<conio.h>
void EVENODD(int x); //function definition
void main()
{
        int n;
        clrscr();
        printf("enter a number\n");
        scanf("%d",&n);                 /*input from the user*/
        EVENODD(n);                     /*function call*/
        getch();
}                               /*end of main*/
```

```
void EVENODD(int x)            /*function definition*/
{
        if(x%2==0)
        printf("even\n");
        else
        printf("odd\n");
}                       /*end of function evenodd*/
/*OUTPUT:
enter a number
123
odd
OUTPUT:
enter a number
222
even
*/
```

7. Write a program to print the following figure:

```
          1
        2 3 4
      5 6 7 8 9
    0 1 2 3 4 5 6
  7 8 9 0 1 2 3 4 5
```

```
//format.c
#include<stdio.h>
void figure3(int n);           /*function definition*/
void main()
{       int x;
        printf("enter x value");
        scanf("%d",&x);         /*how many lines*/
        figure3(x);           /*function call*/
        getch();
}
void figure3(int n)            /*function definition*/
{       int i,j,l,k=1;
        l=n-1;
        for(i=1;i<=n;i++,l--)       /*outer loop begins*/
        {       for(j=0;j<l;j++)
                    printf(" ");
                for(j=0;j<(2*i-1);j++)
                    printf("%d",k++%10);
                printf("\n");       /*print in next line*/
        }                   /*end of outer loop*/
}                       /*end of function figure3*/
```

```
/*
OUTPUT:
enter x value7
    1
   234
  56789
 0123456
789012345
67890123456
7890123456789*/
```

8. Write a program to find the GCF of 2 integers

```
//.gcf.c
#include<stdio.h>
#include<conio.h>
int GCF(int a,int b);              /*function definition*/
void main()
{
        int p,q,r;
        clrscr();
        printf("enter the values of 2 integers\n");
        scanf("%d%d",&p,&q);           /*input from the user*/
        r=GCF(p,q);                  /*function call*/
        printf("the GCF of %d and %d is %d\n",p,q,r);
        getch();
}                          /*end of main*/
int GCF(int a,int b)               /*function definition*/
{
        int x;
        x=(a<b)?a:b;
        while(x)                /*loop begins*/
        {
                if((a%x==0)&&(b%x==0))
                        return(x);    /*returning the value of x to main*/
                x—;
        }                  /*end of loop*/
}               /*end of function GCF*/
/*
OUTPUT:
enter the values of 2 integers
2 5
the GCF of 2 and 5 is 1*/
```

9. Write a program to find whether a given num is prime or not

```
// prime.c
/*Program to find whether a given num is prime or not*/
#include<stdio.h>
void isprime(int x);                /*function definition*/
void main()
{       int n,p;
        printf("enter a number");
        scanf("%d",&n);             /*input from the user*/
        isprime(n);                 /*function call*/
}                       /*end of main*/
void isprime(int x)             /*function definition*/
{       int i,j=0;
        for(i=1;i<=x;i++)           /*loop begins*/
        {       if(x%i==0)
                j++;

        }                       /*end of loop*/
        (j==2)?printf("yes.prime\n"):printf("not a prime\n");

}                       /*end of function isprime*/
/*
OUTPUT:
enter a number13
yes.prime*/
```

10. Write a program to find the number of digits in a number*/

```
// number.c
#include<stdio.h>
#include<conio.h>
void NUM(int x);                /*function definition*/
void main()
{       int n;
        printf("enter the number\n");
        scanf("%d",&n);             /*input a number from the user*/
        NUM(n);                     /*function call*/
        getch();
}                       /*end of main*/
```

```
void NUM(int x)                   /*function definition*/
{       int i=0;
        while(x>0)                /*when xis greater than 0*/
        {       x=(x/10);
                i++;              /*increment i*/
        }
        printf("no. of digits=%d\n",i);
}                         /*end of function NUM*/
/*
OUTPUT:
enter the number
1234
no. of digits=4
*/
```

ASSIGNMENT PROBLEMS

1. Write a c program to count number of lines , number of words , no of open braces , number of close braces in an input file.
2. Write a c program to compute vlue of e from the series

$$1 + \frac{1}{1!} + \frac{1}{2!} + \frac{1}{3!} + \ldots\ldots$$

3. Write a c program to compute value of e^x from the series

$$1 + \frac{x}{1!} + \frac{x^2}{2!} + \frac{x^3}{3!} + \ldots\ldots$$

4. Write a program to convert a given integer into
   a) Hexa decimal number
   b) Octal number
5. Write a program to shift given integer to 2 positions to left.
6. Write program to test if the given integer has 1 in 4 bit position. If its 0 set it to 1.
7. Write a C program to mask given integer of the low 4 bits.
8. Using priorities of the operators evaluate z= 4 * 5/6 + 10 / 5 + 8 – 1 + 7/8.
9. Write a program to take in 6 subjects marks of a student in to an array called marks. Calculate the average and store it on the same array. Declare the division

i division if avg >=60

ii division if avg >=50 and < 60

10 Write a program to print the ASCII table for range 30 to 122 .

Solutions to Objective Questions

1) Valid n=10	2) fractional and exponential		3) 65 , A	4) 1
5) b	6) Invalid	7) infinite loop	8) 0 0 0	9) 5 , 8
10) c	11) b	12) c	13) d	14) a
15) b	16) false	17) one	18) false	
19) -128to 127	20) -32768 to 32767			

CHAPTER 3

CONTROL STATEMENTS

Computer program is a sequence of steps. Control statements tell the order in which these sequential steps are to be executed. For example , we have already used while and for statements. We will formalize and consolidate our understanding of these concepts.

Statement & Blocks : C language consists of statements and blocks. Statements are expression in c language , terminated with ; . Following are examples of statements:

```
Sum+=100;  // increment sum by 100 i.e sum=sum +100
root1 =  -b/a ;
```

{ and } are used to denote start and end of block of statements in C language. Observe that there is no semicolon after close brace. Block is also called a compound statement as it contains several of the statements. All the variable declared in a block are local to the block. For example , the variables declared in a function block , with in brace brackets , are local to that function and are not available out side the function.

■■■ 3.1 CONDITIONAL AND BRANCHING STATEMENTS

3.1.1 If Statement

The syntax is simple and straight forward

```
if (expression)
  statement;
```

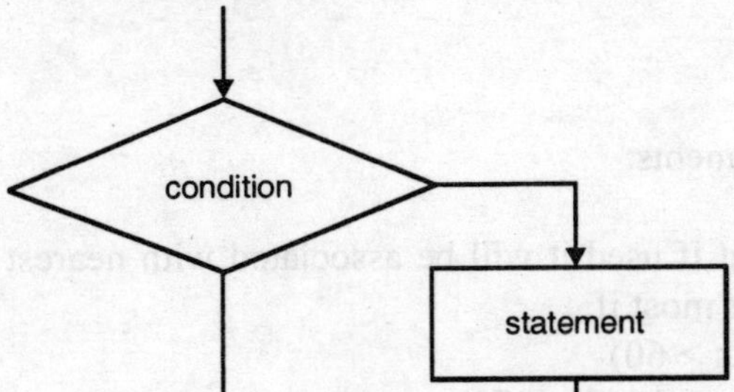

Fig 3.1 control flow in if statement

Example 3.0 : ***checkhigh.c***. //A program to find higher of two temperatures

```
#include<stdio.h>
#include<conio.h> // console input /output for getch() and clrscr()
void main()
{
        float temp1,temp2 ;
        float max; // to store higher of the two temperatures
        printf("Enter <temperature1 and Temperature2>\n");
        scanf("%f %f",&temp1,&temp2);
           max=temp1;
        if (max<temp2) // temp1<temp2 , hence equate max with temp2
           max=temp2;
           printf("\n Higher of the two given temperatures %f and %f = %f \n" ,
                       temp1,temp2, max);
        getch(); // to observe the result on console
}// end of main
/*
OUTPUT:
Enter <temperature1 and Temperature2>
1.2 3.4
Higher of the two given temperatures 1.200000 and 3.400000 = 3.400000
*/
```

Note that we have included ***conio.h*** for console in and out library. This would facilitate us to use console functions like clear screen (clrscr()) and getch() for get character operation. Use of getchar() would make computer wait for input through console. It will only proceed further only when it receives the input. This feature we can use to observe the result on console. Linux based compilers like gnu C does not support conio.h.

3.1.2 If – Else Statement: The syntax is

```
if (expression)
{
        statements;
}
else
{
        statements;
}
```

Else statement is optional. But if used it will be associated with nearest if statement.In the example shown else is attached to inner most if.

```
if ( totalMarks > 60)
        if ( total Marks > 70)
          printf("passed with distinction\n");
    else
          printf("passed with first class\n");
```

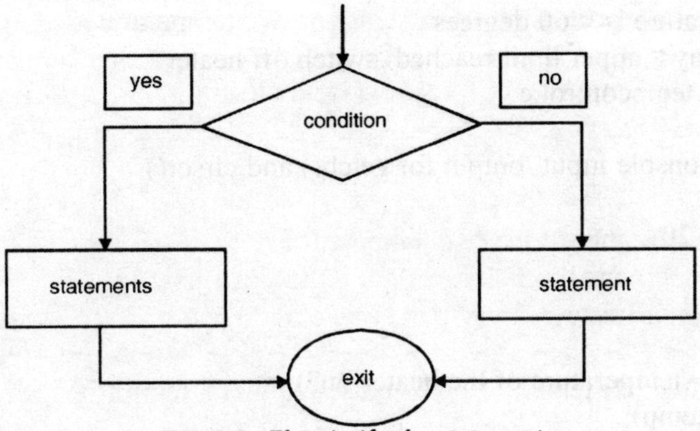

Fig. 3.2 : Flow in if –else statement

Use of brace brackets dictate the association rule for else statement. Else in the following code is linked up with first if statement

```
if ( totalMarks > 60)
  {  if ( total Marks > 70)
         printf("passed with distinction\n");
  }
 else
       printf("passed with first class\n");
```

■■■ 3.2 IF - ELSE-IF STATEMENT

In real life , we need to evaluate , several conditions in sequence, called multi way decision making and *else if* statements are very useful for this purpose. The syntax and example are shown below

```
if ( expression)          : if ( totalMarks >= 70)
   statement                       printf("passed with distinction\n");
else if ( expression)        else if ( totalMarks >= 60)
   statement                       printf("passed in first class\n");
else if (expression)            else if( totalMarks >= 50)
   statement                       printf("passed with second class\n");
else                            else
   statement                       printf("unsuccessful \n");
```

Example 3.1 tempcontrol.c . In this problem , we would consider the algorithm shown below

Read the temperature
If temperature < 20 °
    Display " Temperature is lukewarm. Switch on heater".
Else if temperature < 40 °
    Display " switch heater to simmer mode"

```
        else if  temperature is < 60 degrees
                  Display " upper limit reached .switch off heater"
 // Listing for program tempcontrol.c
#include<stdio.h>
#include<conio.h> // console input /output for getch() and clrscr()
#define MAX 60
#define LUKEWARM 20
#define WARM 40
void main()
{       float  temp ;
        printf( "Enter <temperature of the heater>\n");
        scanf("%f",&temp);
        if (temp < LUKEWARM)
            printf("\n Temperature is lukewarm. Switch on heater\n");
        else if (temp < WARM)
            printf("\nWater is warm. Switch heater to simmer mode\n");
        else
            printf("\nWater is hot. Switch off the heater \n");
} // end of main
/*
OUTPUT:
Enter <temperature of the heater>22
Water is warm. Switch heater to simmer mode*/
```

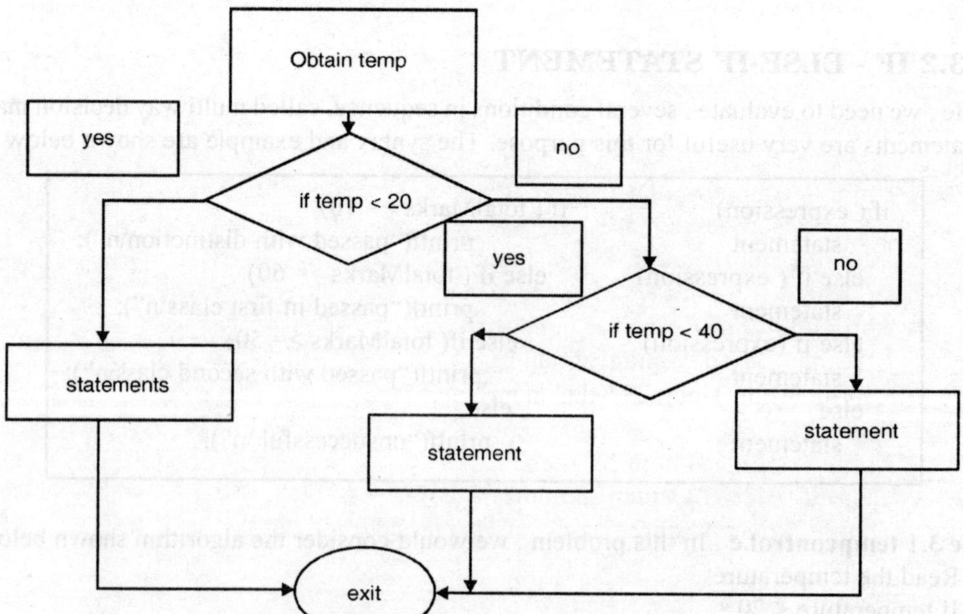

Fig. 3.3 Flow chart for If Else IF Statement

3.3 SWITCH AND CASE STATEMENTS

Switch statement evaluates an expression and depending on the numerical value of the evaluation control is branched to corresponding block of statements. The syntax and example problem are shown below.

```
switch ( expression)
        case constantexpression1 : statements1
        case constantexpression2 ; staements2
        default statements
```

Example 3.2 *switch.c* to show the usage of switch and case

```
//program to demonstrate the switch statement
#include<stdio.h>
void main()
{
  int choice;
  int num1,num2;
  printf("1.Addition\n");
  printf("2.Substraction\n");
  printf("3.Multiplication\n");
  printf("4.Division\n");
  printf("5.Quit\n");
  do
       { printf("\nEnter your choice: ");
        scanf("%d",&choice);
        switch(choice)
        {
        case 1:printf("\nEnter <num 1& num2>: ");
                scanf("%d%d",&num1,&num2);
                printf("num1+num2=%d\n",num1+num2);
                break;
        case 2:printf("\nEnter <num 1& num2>: ");
                scanf("%d%d",&num1,&num2);
                printf("num1-num2=%d\n",num1-num2);
                break;
        case 3:printf("\nEnter <num 1& num2>: ");
                scanf("%d%d",&num1,&num2);
                printf("num1*num2=%d\n",num1*num2);
                break;
        case 4:printf("\nEnter <num 1& num2>: ");
                scanf("%d%d",&num1,&num2);
                printf("num1/num2=%d\n",num1/num2);
                break;
```

```
        case 5:printf("exiting from program\n");
               exit(0);
        default: printf("Invalid choice<enetr no between 1 and 5 only>\n");
        } // end of switch
    }while(choice!=5);
}//end of main
/*
OUTPUT:
1.Addition
2.Substraction
3.Multiplication
4.Division
5.Quit

Enter your choice: 3
Enter <num 1& num2>: 3 5
num1 * num2 = 15
Enter your choice: 5
*/
```

Note that switch statement directs flow to the block of statements depending on the integer constant choice. Further it is necessary to separate blocks in a switch statement through ***break*** statement. Break statement simply put breaks the nearest brace bracket block , in this case it is switch block brace brackets. Also note that , the while loop continues till you enter choice of 5. It exits the program through exit(0) statement

■■■ 3.4 CONTROL LOOPS

3.4.1 While Loop

While loop is written by a programmer , if he is not sure if the while block will be executed. A condition is checked first. If it is true , the while block is executed. The syntax of while statement is

```
While (expression)  //body of while contains a single line
        Statement;  // no brace brackets required
While(expression)
{       statement1;
        statement2;
}
while(1)                    // expression is always true
{ block of statements;  // the loop is called for ever while loop
}
```

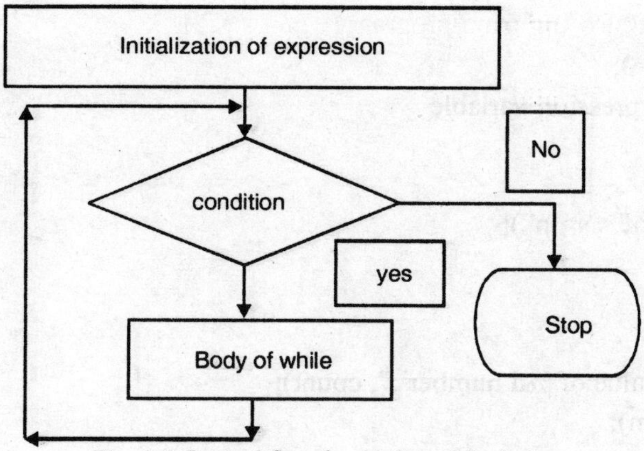

Fig. 3.4 Control flow for while and for loops

Example 3.3 CheckLimit.c. In this program , we will use while loop to turn off the heater if upper cut off temperature has reached. The algorithm is

Read the temperature
While temperature < upper cut off
    Switch on the heater
Switch off the heater

```
// Listing for program checklimit.c
#include<stdio.h>
#include<conio.h> // console input /output for getch() and clrscr()
#define MAX 60
void main()
{       float temp ;
        printf("Enter <temperature of the heater>\n");
        scanf("%f",&temp);
        while (temp<MAX)
                printf("\n Temperature is lukewarm. Switch on heater\n");
        printf("\nWater is hot. Switch off the heater \n");
} // end of main
/*
OUTPUT:
Enter <temperature of the heater>
Water is hot. Switch off the heater
*/
```

Example 3.4 *sumwhile.c* **//Program to find sum of n numbers and their average using while loop.**

```
#include<stdio.h>
#include<conio.h> // console input /output for getch() and clrscr()
void main()
```

```
{   int n;
   int num ,sum = 0, avg=0;
   //initialize the while expression variable
   int count =1;
   // input N
   printf("\n Enter value of <N>\n");
   scanf("%d",&n);
   // control loop
   while (count <= n )
   {     printf("\n Enter value of %d number :", count);
         scanf("%d",&num);
         sum+=num;
         count++;
   }
   avg=sum/n;
   printf("\n Sum of %d numbers = %d ",n,sum);
   printf("\n Average of  %d numbers = %d",n,avg);
   getch();
} // end of main
/*
OUTPUT:
Enter value of <N>3
Enter value of 1 number : 1
Enter value of 2 number : 2
Enter value of 3 number : 3
Sum of 3 numbers = 6
Average of 3 numbers = 2
*/
```

3.4.2 Do-While Loop

The syntax is

```
Do
  {
     block of statements
  } while (expression);
```

The block is executed first and the condition is checked . If true , the loop is executed , till the condition becomes true. We will use do – while loop , when we know that the loop needs to be executed at least one time . Whereas , while loop is used when we are not aware if loop needs to be executed or not. Control flow is shown in Fig. 3.5.

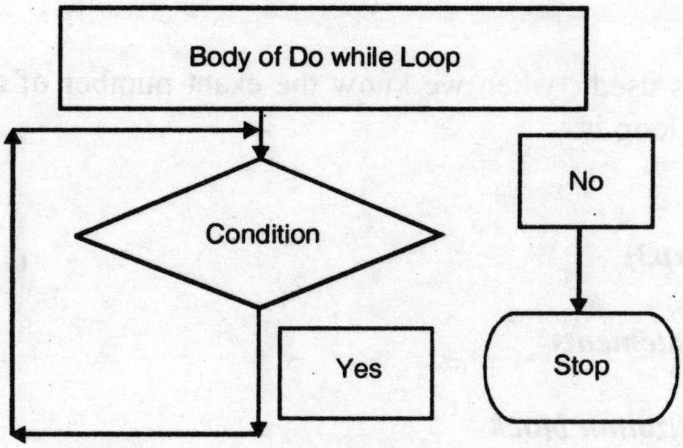

Fig. 3.5 Control flow for do-while loop

Example 3.5 ***sumdowhile.c*** /*Program to find sum of n numbers and their average using do-while loop.*/

```
#include<stdio.h>
#include<conio.h> // console input /output for getch() and clrscr()
void main()
{
   int n;
   int num ,sum = 0, avg=0;
   //initialize the while expression variable
   int count =1;
   // input N
   printf("\n Enter value of <N>\n");
   scanf("%d",&n);
   // control loop
   do
   {
          printf("\n Enter value of %d number :", count);
          scanf("%d",&num);
          sum+=num;
          count++;
   }while (count <= n );
   avg=sum/n;
   printf("\n Sum of %d numbers = %d",n,sum);
   printf("\n Average of  %d numbers = %d",n,avg);
   getch();
} // end of main
/*
OUTPUT:
Enter value of <N>3
Enter value of 1 number : 1
Enter value of 2 number : 2
Enter value of 3 number : 3
Sum of 3 numbers = 6
Average of 3 numbers = 2
*/
```

3.4.3 For Loop

for loop , as control loop is used , when we know the exact number of times the loop needs to be executed. The syntax of for loop is

```
for ( exp1 ; exp2 ; exp3)
  {
        block of statements
  }
where exp1 is initialization block
      exp2 is condition test block
      exp3 is alter initial value assigned to exp1
```

Forever for loop is shown below.

```
for ( ; ; )
{
   statement;
}
```

for loops can be nested. That means we can write for loop with in a for loop. In nested for loop , the inner loop is executed for each value of outer loop. For exmple , inner loop is executed for i=0 and value of j is varied from 0 final condition. Outer loop is executed for values of i varying from 0 to n-1.

The syntax is

```
for ( i=0;i<n;i++)
 {
   for ( j=0;j<n;j++)
     {
       statement
     }
 }
```

Example 3.6 *sumfor.c* . //A program to compute sum and average of given numbers using for loop.

```
#include<stdio.h>
#include<conio.h> // console input /output for getch() and clrscr()
void main()
{
   int n;
   int num ,sum = 0, avg=0;
   //initialize the while expression variable
   int count;
   // input n
   printf("\n Enter value of <n>\n");
```

```
    scanf("%d",&n);
    // for control loop
    for(count=1; count<=n ; count++)
    {
          printf("\n Enter value of %d number :", count);
          scanf("%d",&num);
          sum+=num;
    }
    avg=sum/n;
    printf("\n Sum of %d numbers = %d",n,sum);
    printf("\n Average of  %d numbers = %d",n,avg);
    getch();
} // end of main
/*
OUTPUT:
Enter value of <N>
3
Enter value of 1 number : 1
Enter value of 2 number : 2
Enter value of 3 number : 3
Sum of 3 numbers = 6
Average of 3 numbers = 2
*/
```

Control flow is shown in Fig.. 3.4. Note that the Fig. 3.4 also shows the control flow for *while* loop also. We have also shown through the examples 3.5 and 3.6 that code also is same in both cases.

Example 3.7 ***nest.c*** . //A program to demonstrate nested for loop

```
#include<stdio.h>
#include<conio.h> // console input /output for getch() and clrscr()
void main()
 {     int  i , j ; // counters for outer and inner for loop
   for (i=15; i<20; i++)    // outer loop
   {
        printf("\n Multiplication table for %d X %d", i,j);
        for (j=1; j<20 ; j++)   // inner loop
        {
                  printf( "\n %d X %d = %d ",  i , j , i*j);
        } // end of inner for loop
        } // end of outer for loop
 } // end of main
/*
 OUTPUT:
Multiplication table for 15 X 1 = 15
                               2 = 30
                               3...*/
```

3.4.4 When to Use for or While or Do-while

for loop is best suited , when programmers have exact knowledge of initialization and final conditions to be met.

```
for ( exp1 ; exp2 ; exp3)
    {
            block of statements
    }
```

where exp1 is initialization block
exp2 is condition test block
exp3 is alter initial value assigned to exp1

The above for loop is equivalent to following while loop. ***While*** loop, is used when programmer does not know if the while block will be executed at all or not. In other words , in a situation , where we have to check a condition and then only execute block , we will use while loop.

```
exp1;
while(exp2)
  { statement;
   exp2;
  }
```

Do – while loop , on the other hand is used when we know that block is to be executed at least once. In other words , we have to execute the block and then check for a condition.

■■■ 3.5 BREAK AND CONTINUE

3.5.1 Break. Break statement is used to exit from the switch control or control loop. We can use break statement to exit from for , while and do while, and switch control statements. You have already seen use of break statement in Switch statement. Observe how break is used to come out of if statement below

break.c //Program that demonstrates Break statement.

```
#include<stdio.h>
void main()
{
    int count=0;
    int sum,num;
    int avg;
    for ( ;;)    // for ever for loop
    {          if(count == 5)
               { printf("\n reached upper limit of 5: breaking the for loop");
                 break;
               }
               else
               {
```

```
            printf("\n Enter value of %d number :", count);
            scanf("%d",&num);
            sum+=num;
            count++;
        }
    } // end of for
} // end of main
/*
```

OUTPUT:

```
Enter value of 0 number : 1
Enter value of 1 number : 2
Enter value of 2 number : 3
Enter value of 3 number : 4
Enter value of 4 number : 5
reached upper limit of 20: breaking the for loop*/
```

3.5.2 Continue Statement

Continue is used when we want to stop further processing of loop statements and start at the beginning of the control loop. In the example shown below , we would like to add 10 points to all odd number between 0 to 10 and skip adding to even numbers

continue.c

```
#include<stdio.h>
  void main()
      {   int count=0;
          int sum;
           int avg;
          for ( ;;)   // for ever for loop
           { if( (count %2)== 0)  // the number is even. % operator gives remainder
               { printf("\n even number: breaking the for loop:%d " count);
               continue;                          //control goes to here
               }
             else
               { count+=10; // means count = count + 10
               printf("\n odd number : added 10%d",count);
               }
           } // end of for
      } // end of main
/*
```

OUTPUT:

```
even number: breaking the for loop:0
*/
```

3.6 GOTO STATEMENTS

Goto statement is rarely used due to fears that it would lead to unstructured programs. Goto statements can be conditional and unconditional .The syntax is

```
goto label      // unconditional branch
```

goto.c

```
#include<stdio.h>
void main()
{
        int num ,sum=0,count=0;
        start:
                printf("\n Enter value of <number> number :");
                scanf("%d",&num);
                sum+=num;
                count++;
                printf("\n number: %d",num);
                if ( count > 3)
                        goto stop1;
                else
                        goto start;
        stop1:
                printf("\n exiting the main program");
} // end of main
/*
OUTPUT:
Enter value of <number> number : 1
number: 1
Enter value of <number> number : 2
number: 2
Enter value of <number> number : 3
number: 3
Enter value of <number> number : 4
number: 4
Enter value of <number> number : 5
number: 5
Enter value of <number> number : 6
number: 6
exiting the main program
*/
```

We do not recommend using of goto at all. It is always better to get used to while , do while and for loops for achieving the same result, but using structured programming style.

3.7 Exit function. You can force a program to stop what ever it is doing and return the control to operating system by using ***exit()*** function. For this function you have to include stdlib.h in the include section.

```
exit(0);  // return after successful completion to operating system(os)
exit(1);  // return to os on being unsuccessful
```

OBJECTIVE QUESTIONS

1. Break statement takes the control to
   a) goes out of the innermost loop that contains the break statement
   b) to the beginning of the program
   c) to the end of the program.
   d) goes out from all the nested loop.
2. Continue statement takes the control to
   a) to the bottom of the loop.
   b) to the beginning of the loop.
   c) to the next statement.
   d) to the end of the program
3. exit() function returns control to Operating system TRUE/FALSE
4. Which of the following are true statements
   a) goto can be used in for loop to come out of the loop
   b) continue takes you to beginning of the loop
   c) continue can be used in switch statement
   d) break can be used in switch statement
   a) Only statement (I) is correct b) Only statement (II) is correct
   c) Both statements b & c are' correct d) only d is correct
5. The following expression

   pay= (bp>=1000) ? bp : 1500;

   is equivalent to

a) if (bp==1000)
pay = bp;
else
pay = 1500;

b) if (bp<1000)
pay = bp;
else
pay = 1500

c) if (bp>=1000)
pay = bp;
else
pay = 1500;

d) if (bp>1000)
pay = bp;
else
pay = 1500

6. Following code converts c to

```
char c ='A'
        c=c+'a'-65
```

a) to upper case b) to lower case c) to a number d) to character c

7. To check the equality of two variables a and b , in C language

a) if (a=b) b) if (a equalto(b)) c) if (a==b) d)if((a,b)=0)

8 Do while statement executes body at least once prior to checking the conditions. True/False

9 What will be the out put

```
int i =0;
int k=1
do
{
        printf("%d" , ++i);
} while ( i<=k)
```

a) 1 b)2 c) 3 d) 4

10 What is the output of the following code:

```
int x=10;
  while(1)
  {
        if(m<1)
        break;
  m=m-8;
  }
  printf("%d",m);
```

a) 0 b) 1 c) 2 d) 10

REVIEW QUESTIONS

1. Distinguish the switch and if else statements.
2. When do you use for statement and while statements. State the situation when for statement is better than while statement.
3. Explain the differences of do while and while statements.
4. Why goto statement is not preferred?
5. Explain the continue and break statement with examples

SOLVED PROBLEMS

1. *sum.c* //Write a C program to find out the sum of the digits of a number

```
#include<stdio.h>
#include<conio.h>
// function prototype declarations
void sumdigits(int n);              /*function definition*/
void main()
{
        int x,s;
        clrscr();
        printf("enter a number\n");
        scanf("%d",&x);             /*input number from the user*/
        sumdigits(x);               /*function call*/
        getch();
}                   /*end of main*/
void sumdigits(int n)               /*function definition*/
{
        int r,sum=0;
        while(n)            /*when n is not 0*/
        {
                r=n%10;
                sum=sum+r;
                n=n/10;

        }
        printf("%d\n",sum);
}                   /*end of function sumdigits*/
/*
OUTPUT:
enter a number
123
6
*/
```

2. lupper.c Write a C program for converting a line of lower case text to upper case*/

```
/*Program for converting a line of lower case text to upper case*/
#include<stdio.h>
#include<conio.h>
#define EOL '\n'
//function prototype
void LU(char text[80]);
```

```
void main()
{
        char letter[80];
        clrscr();
        LU(letter);         /*function call*/
        getch();
}               /*end of main*/
void LU(char text[80])
{
        int tag,count=0;
        printf("enter the text\n");
        while((text[count]=getchar())!=EOL)  /*enter a line full of text*/
        ++count;
        tag=count;
        count=0;
        printf("the text in upper case is\n");
        while(count<tag)  /*loop begins*/
        {
                putchar(toupper(text[count])); /*converting to uppercase and printing*/
                ++count;
        }               /*end of loop*/

}                       /*end of function LU*/
/*
OUTPUT:
enter the text
hello
the text in upper case is
HELLO
*/
```

3. *reverse.c* Write a C program to find the reverse of a given number*/

```
/*Program to find the reverse of a given number*/
#include<stdio.h>
#include<conio.h>
void REVERSE(int n);            /*function definition*/
void main()
{
        int x;
        clrscr();
        printf("enter a number\n");
        scanf("%d",&x);         /*input from the user*/
        REVERSE(x);           /*function call*/
```

```
        getch();
}                /*end of main*/
void REVERSE(int n)              /*function definition*/
{
        int r=0,s=0;
        while(n>0)       /*when n is greater than 0*/
        {
                r=n%10;
                s=s*10+r;
                n=n/10;
        }
        printf("the reverse of the given number is:%d\n",s);
}        /*end of function REVERSE*/
/*
OUTPUT:
enter a number
1234
the reverse of the given number is: 4321
*/
```

4. *format1.c* /* Write a program to print the following figure:

```
            1
          1 2 1
        1 2 3 2 1
      1 2 3 4 3 2 1
    1 2 3 4 5 4 3 2 1
 */
#include<stdio.h>
#include<conio.h>
void figure2(int x);             /*function definition*/
void main()
{
        int n;
        clrscr();
        printf("enter n value\n");           /*how many lines*/
        scanf("%d",&n);
        figure2(n);                    /*function call*/
        getch();
}                    /*end of main*/
void figure2(int x)            /*function definition*/
{
        int i,j,l;
        l=x-1;
        for(i=1;i<=x;i++,l—)          /*outer loop  begins*/
        {
```

```
            for(j=0;j<l;j++)
            printf(" ");
            for(j=1;j<=i;j++)
            printf("%d",j);
            for(j=i-1;j;j—)
            printf("%d",j);
            printf("\n");          /*print in next line*/
      }                 /*end of outer loop*/
}               /*end of function figure2*/
/*
OUTPUT:
enter n value
5
        1
      1 2 1
    1 2 3 2 1
  1 2 3 4 3 2 1
1 2 3 4 5 4 3 2 1
*/
```

5. Write a C program to find the factorial of a given number

```
//fact.c
#include<stdio.h>
int fact(int n);            /*function definition*/
void main()
{       int x,ans;
        printf("enter a number");
        scanf("%d",&x);           /*input from the user*/
        ans=fact(x);    /*function call*/
        printf("\n factorial of a given Number : %d = %d \n", x,ans);
}
int fact(int a)     /*function definition*/
{       int fact=1;
        if ( a==0 || a==1)
         return 1;
      else
        {
          while ( a > 1)
            {  fact=fact*a;     //1*5*4*3*2*1
             a—;
            }
         }
}
/*output
enter a number5
 factorial of a given Number : 5 = 120*/
```

6. Write a c program to generate Fibonacci series with out using recursion

```
/*Program to generate the Fibonacci series*/
//fibsrs.c
#include<stdio.h>
void fib(int x);/*function definition*/
void main()
{       int n;
        printf("enter <no of terms n>");
        scanf("%d",&n);          /*input from the user*/
        fib(n);              /*function call*/
}               /*end of main*/
void fib(int x)          /*function definition*/
{       int a=0,b=1,i=0,c;
        printf("%d  %d",a,b);
        i+=2;                // increment i by 2 because a & b
        while(i<x)           /*loop begins,runs till i<x*/
        {       c=a+b;
                printf("  %d",c);
                a=b;
                b=c;
                i++;
        }/*end of while loop*/
}   /*end of function fib*/
/*
enter n:7
0 1 1 2 3 5 8
*/
```

7. Write a program to convert a given string from lowercase to uppercase.

```
// strupp.c
#include<stdio.h>
#include<conio.h>
#include<ctype.h>
void lowup(char cha[20]); /*function definition*/
void main()
{       char ch[20];
        clrscr();
        printf("enter a string\n");
        scanf("%s",&ch);          /*input string from the user*/
        lowup(ch);            /*function call*/
        getch();
}                 /*end of main*/
void lowup(char cha[20])          /*function definition*/
{       int i;
        char c;
```

```
        for(i=0;cha[i]!='\0';i++)       /*loop begins*/
        {       if(islower(cha[i])) /*if the char is in lowercase*/
                c=toupper(cha[i]); /*convert to uppercase*/
                else
                c=cha[i];
                printf("%c",c);      /*display the char*/
        }                         /*end of loop*/
}                              /*end of function lowup*/
/*
OUTPUT:
enter a string:
string
STRING*/
```

8. Write a program to calculate the value of the series
x+(x*x*x)/3!+(x*x*x*x*x)/5!+....7th digit accuracy*/

```
// series1.c
#include<stdio.h>
#include<conio.h>
void series1(int m,int y);/*function definition*/
void main()
{       int n,x;
        clrscr();
        printf("enter n and x values\n");
        scanf("%d%d",&n,&x);     /*input from the user*/
        series1(n,x);            /*function call*/
        getch();
}               /*end of main*/
void series1(int m,int y)          /*function definition*/
{       int i,j,p;
        double s,t;
        s=y;
        t=y;
        for(i=3;i<=m;i=i+2)        /*loop begins*/
        {
                p=1;
                for(j=i;j>0;j—)
                p=p*j;
                t=(t*y*y)/p;
                s=s+t;
        }       /*loop ends*/
        printf("sum=%12.7lf",s); /*printing upto 7th digit accuracy*/
}           /*end of function series1*/
/*
```

OUTPUT:

```
enter n and x values
 5 2
 sum = 3.3777778 */
```

9. Write a program to calculate the value of the series
1+(x^2)/2!+(x^4)/4!+...upto 10 terms

```
// series2.c
#include<stdio.h>
#include<conio.h>
void series2(int m,int y);          /*function definition*/
void main()
{
        int n,x;
        clrscr();
        printf("enter n and x values\n");
        scanf("%d%d",&n,&x);       /*input from the user*/
        series2(n,x);         /*function call*/
        getch();
}               /*end of main*/
void series2(int m,int y)          /*function definition*/
{       int i,j,p;
        double s=1,t;
        for(i=2;i<=m;i=i+2)        /*loop begins*/
        {       t = (t * y * y )/ ((i)* (i–i));
                s=s+t;
        }               /*loop ends*/
        printf("sum=%lf",s);
}           /*end of function series2*/
/*
OUTPUT:
enter n and x value:
5 2
sum=3.166667*/
```

10. Write a program to produce the pyramid

```
      1
    1 1 1
  1 1 1 1 1
```

```
//pyramid.c
```

```
#include<stdio.h>
//function prototype declarations
void figure1(int x);
void main()
{       int n;
        printf("enter n value\n");
        scanf("%d",&n);             /*input from the user asking how many lines*/
        figure1(n);                 /*function call*/
        getch();
}                                   /*end of main*/
void figure1(int x)                 /*function definition*/
 {      int i,j;
        for(i=1;i<=x;i++)       /*loop 1 begins*/
        {       for(j=0;j<x-i;j++)  /*loop 2 begins*/
                printf(" ");
                for(j=0;j<(2*i-1);j++) /*loop 3 begins*/
                printf("1");
                printf("\n");           /*print in next line*/
        } /*end of loop 1*/
}/*end of function figure1*/
/*OUTPUT:
enter n value: 3
          1
        1 1 1
      1 1 1 1 1*/
/*Program to print the following figure:
        1
      1 2 1
    1 2 3 2 1
  1 2 3 4 3 2 1
1 2 3 4 5 4 3 2 1*/
```

11. Write a program to produce the figure shown below

```
//numpid.c
#include<stdio.h>
void figure2(int x);//function prototype
void main()
{       int n;
        printf("enter n value\n");      /*how many lines*/
        scanf("%d",&n);
        figure2(n);                 /*function call*/
        getch();
}                       /*end of main*/
```

```
void figure2(int x)              /*function definition*/
{       int i,j,l;
        l=x-1;
        for(i=1;i<=x;i++,l--)          /*outer loop  begins*/
        {         for(j=0;j<l;j++)
                  printf(" ");
                  for(j=1;j<=i;j++)
                  printf("%d",j);
                  for(j=i-1;j;j--)
                  printf("%d",j);
                  printf("\n");          /*print in next line*/
        }                   /*end of outer loop*/
}                     /*end of function figure2*/
/*
OUTPUT:
enter n value:5
        1
       1 2 1
      1 2 3 2 1
     1 2 3 4 3 2 1
    1 2 3 4 5 4 3 2 1
*/
```

ASSIGNMENT PROBLEMS

1. **Candidates have to score 90 or above in the IQ test to be considered eligible for taking further tests. All the candidates who do not clear the IQ test are sent reject letters and others are sent call letters for further test. Represent the logic for automating this task.**

2. Write C code for following series

   a) $1+3+5+7+ \ldots\ldots\ldots\ldots+n$

   b) $1+x^2+x^4+x^6+\ldots\ldots\ldots\ldots$ n terms

   c) $(1-x)^n = 1 + nx + ((n(n+1)x^2)/ 1.2) ((n(n+1)(n+2)x^2)/ 1.2.3)$

3 write a program for computing

   a) $\cos(x) = 1 - (x^2/2!) + (x^4/4!) - (x^6/6!) + \ldots\ldots\ldots$

   b) $\sin(x) = x - (x^3/3!) + (x^5/5!) - (x^7/7!) + \ldots\ldots\ldots$

   b) $e^x = 1 + (x/1!) + (x^2/2!) + (x^3/3!)+ \ldots\ldots\ldots$

4. Write the following code using switch statement

```
if (color == 'r')
        printf("\n color is red\n");
else
        if ( color =='b' )
          printf("\n color is blue");
        else
          printf("\n colorless\n");
```

5. Write a program to compute electricity bill to be paid by a consumer as per following tariff

upto 100 units	2.30 /unit
up to 400 Units	2.70 / unit
>400 and <1000	4.50 / unit
> 1000 units	6.00 / unit

6. Write a program to compute Income Tax to be paid by a citizen as per following tax regime. Take the gross salary from the individual and compute the tax payable.

Upto 100000	NIL
> 100000 and < 1 60 000	10% of the amount exceeding 100000
> 160000 and < 250 000	20% of the amount exceeding 160000
> 250 000	30% of the amount exceeding 250000

add sur tax @ of 10% on the tax payable.

7. Write a program to display the ascii table.

8. Write a program to read a line from the keyboard and print the line using a suitable encryption. Simple encryption can be a substitution with next character A with B , a with b , and z with a and so on. De crypt and display the original message

Solutions to Objective Questions

1) a	2) b	3) true	4) c	5) c
6) b	7) c	8) true	9) b	10) c

CHAPTER 4

FUNCTIONS AND STORAGE CLASSES

■■■ 4.1 WHY USE FUNCTIONS ?

Its common knowledge that experts, who are dedicated to a particular job, will perform the job better and faster. We approach architect for making functional and aesthetic housing. Similarly we handover control to doctors to take care of our health. In C language, we hand over jobs to functions specially written for this purpose.

Idea is to decompose main problem into smaller modules and write functions to implement the modules. The main function in C Language is called : ***main().*** Interestingly, it is also a function, albeit, a main function. Main() function calls other functions. ***Calling function*** is one which calls a ***called function.*** The function prototype is declared before, void main (), in the global area, so that it is accessible by all other functions. The syntax is :

ReturnType Function name (Argument List) ; // note the semicolon

int FindMax (int a, int b, int c);

void main () calls the function FindMax() by supplying the arguments and receives the result through return type.

ans = FindMax (a, b, c) ; // a,b,c and ans are all integer data types

Function Definition is given after main program as

```
int   FindMax  ( int a, int b, int c)  // note the absence of semicolon
{
  // Function Code here
}
```

Example 4.1 swap.c. A program to demonstrate concepts of functions so far discussed and also bring out concept of pass by value.

```
#include<stdio.h>
#include<conio.h>
// function prototype declarations
void  Swap ( float x, float y); // to interchange values
void main() //Calling Function
 {
   float x= 100.00;  // x & y are local to main()
   float y = 1000.00;
   printf("\n Before calling Swap function <x and y >  %f   : %f ", x,y );
    // call the function and pass arguments x  & y
   Swap(x,y);  //Called Function
   printf("\n After return from Swap <x and y > %f   : %f ", x, y);
   getch();
 }//end of main
// function definition
void  Swap ( float x, float y)
  { float temp ; // temp is local to Swap  function
    temp = x; // store x in temp
    x=y;    // store y in x
    y=temp; // store temp in y
    printf("\n Inside Swap programme <x and y > %f   :  %f ", x, y);
  } // end of Swap

/*
OUTPUT
Before calling Swap function <x and y > 100.00  :  1000.00
Inside Swap programme <x and y >  1000.00  : 100.00
After return from Swap <x and y > 100.00  :  1000.00
*/
```

Observe the output. While the function Swap has done its job of interchanging the values of x and y, as shown by printf statement inside Swap, in the the main program, the values did not interchange. What does the mean ? Answer lies in the fact that variable values and operations you do on them are local to block i.e local to function Swap. It has no connection with variables x and y belonging to main() function.

Indeed, main() function passes arguments by copying these values in to stack area of the function Swap. Its like passing a Xeroxed document and retaining the original. Obviously, the changes you make on Xerox copy will not be reflected on the original.

We have shown function handling by C language in Fig. 4.1. While we will handle stack in detail in under data structures, understand that stack is Last in first out(LIFO) data structure. As an example consider, a student places(pushes) a book on the table first. He follows(pushes) it up with another book and an apple. Last item in is apple. So when the student tries to take out an item, the first one to come out (pop) is apple. This is LIFO structure. It has great many uses in computer science. For example, compilers use Stack data structure for evaluation of expressions written by programmers.

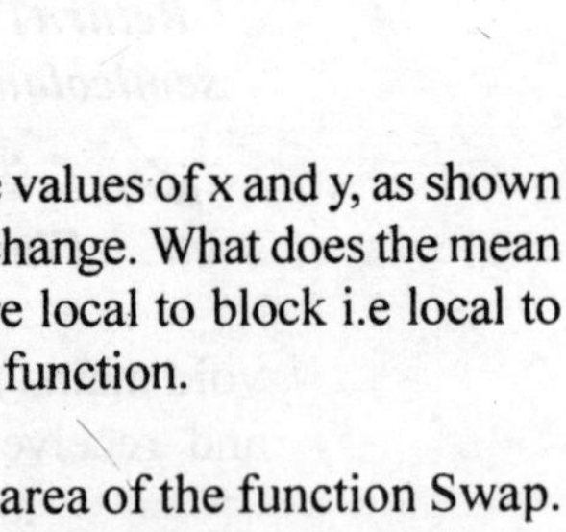

How are functions handled in C. We would like to give an example. Suppose a carpenter carrying out some job using the *chisel.* Now *chisel* has turned little blunt. What will the carpenter do? Simply, he marks and makes a note of his current work area or spot and proceeds to area where grinding stone and machines are situated. He sharpens his *chisel* and on completion, returns to his original spot and resumes his carpentry work. Surprisingly C also handles functions in the same manner

Store return address, copy arguments into function areas, branch to function,return to main and resume execution of main function

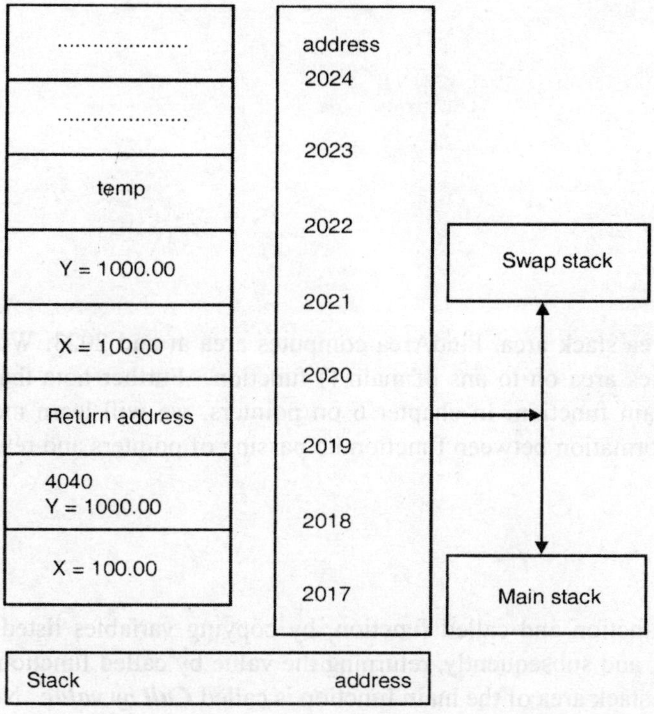

Main stores x and y at 2017 and 2018 addresses

When Swap is encountered, the address of next instruction, say 4040 from code area is pushed onto stack area i.e at 2019.

Arguments x & y of Swap function are pushed onto stack by main() function at address 2020 and 2021.

Swap allocates address 2022 to local variable temp.

Swap ,interchanges values of x and y at address 2020 & 2021. But note that x&y of main at 2017 &2018 are untouched. Printf ,in side Swap shows changed values.

When Swap encounters return or closing }, the control picks up return address and returns to main function. Here you will find x & y at address 2017 & 2018 unaltered

Fig. 4.1 Function handling in C language

■■■ 4.2 COMMUNICATION BETWEEN FUNCTIONS

We have seen how arguments are passed between calling and called function using stack structure. In the example 4.1, the function Swap did not return any value to main function. Now let us see, how a function returns a value

Example 4.2 comm.c A program to demonstrate returning of a value to main function

```
#include<stdio.h>
#include<conio.h>
// function prototype declarations
```

```
float FindArea ( float x, float y);
void main()
 {  float ans;
    float x =200, y =100;
    ans = FindArea(x,y);
    printf("\n area =%f", ans);
 }
 // function definition
 float FindArea(float x, float y)
 {
    float ans;
    ans=x*y;
    return ans;
}// end of FindArea
/*
Output:
 area =20000.000000*/
```

Note that x & y are copied on to FindArea stack area. FindArea computes area at add 2023. When ***return area*** is encounterd FindArea copies area on to ans of main () function. Further note that a function can return only one value to main function. In chapter 6 on pointers, we will learn more elegant methods of communication of information between function i.e passing of pointers and return of pointers from and to main functions.

■■■ 4.3 CALL BY VALUE

Mode of data transfer between calling function and called function, by copying variables listed as arguments into called function stack area, and subsequently, returning the value by called function to calling function by copying the result into stack area of the main function is called ***Call by value***. Note that as copying of the variables, both for forward transfer and return transactions are involved, it is efficient only if values to be transfered are small in number and basic data type. For group and user define data structures like structures and unions etc, call by value method is not used. Instead, we will employ call by reference method to move large data items.

■■■ 4.4 CALL BY REFERENCE

For large data items occupying large memory space like arrays, structures, and union, over heads like memory and access times etc become very high. Hence, we do not pass values as in call by value, instead, we pass the address to the function. Note that function once receives a data item by reference, it acts on data item and the changes made to the data item also reflects on the calling function. This is like passing address of original document and not a Xerox copy. Therefore, changes made on the original document applies owner of the document as well. Note that arrays are always forwarded by call by reference. Study the following example.

Example 4.3. arraycall.c. A program to demonstrate passing of array by reference. In this example we will pass the array of integers by reference to a function called intsort, which sorts the array in the ascending order.

```
#include<stdio.h>
#include<conio.h>
// function prototype declarations
void IntSort( int n, int a[]);  // recives number of items & array
void main()
{
        int i,n=10;// number of items
        int a[] ={ 67,87,56,23,100,19,789,117,6,1}; // array with 10 elements
        printf("\n Given input  array");
        for (i=0;i<n;i++)
        printf( "%d \t ", a[i]);
        // we are passing  array a. Note that array name is 'a'. Name is address.
        IntSort(n,a);
        printf("\n Sorted array \n");
        for (i=0;i<n;i++)
                printf( "%d\t", a[i]);
}//end of main
// function definition
void IntSort(int n, int a[])
{
        int  i,j, temp; // i for outer loop j for inner loop and temp for swapping
        for ( i=0; i< n-1; i++)  // last value need not be sorted
        {
        // find the smallest of remaining numbers and exchange it  with
                for ( j=i+1; j< n; j++)
                {
                        if (a[j] < a[i])
                        {       // swap
                                temp=a[i];
                                a[i]=a[j];
                                a[j]=temp;
                        }
                }
        }
}
/*
Output:
 Given  input array....
67    87    56    23    100    19    789    117    6    1
 Sorted array.....
```

```
1    6    19    23    56    67    87    100    117    789
*/
```

As array is a data structure comprising several data types, compiler passes it as reference. Note that we have called IntSort(n,a); a means name of the array. Name means the address of the array. In effect we have given the address of the array to IntSort function. The algorithm we have used for sorting integers is simple, though not very efficient.

In pass 1 , i=0, compare n-1 balance items with j as index, find out if a[j] < a[i], if yes exchange with a[i]. This ensures that at the end of pass 1, the smallest number bubbles to the top of the array.

In pass2, start the same procedure but with i = 1; Let 2 nd smallest number be swapped to 2nd position

Continue till all elements are exhausted. The algorithm requires a total of n-1 passes to completely sort the given list

We will learn more about call by reference through usage of pointers.

4.5 RECURSION

Recursion is an advanced feature supported by C Language. Recursion means a function calling it self. Consider the problem of finding a factorial of a number. In the example we can clearly see that Fact(5) is calling Fact(4) and so on.

```
Fact(5)  =  5 x 4 x 3 x 2 x 1
         =  5 x Fact(4)
         =  5 x 4 x Fact(3)
         =  5 x 4 x 3x Fact(2)
         =  5 x 4 x 3x 2 x  Fact(1)
         =  5 x 4 x 3x 2 x  1 x Fact(0)
         =  5 x 4 x 3x 2 x  1   ( Fact(0) =1)
```

Example 4.4 factrecur.c A program for finding factorial of a number using recursion feature.

```
#include<stdio.h>
// function prototype
int fact(int a);
void main()
{       int x,ans;
        printf("enter a number:\n");
        scanf("%d",&x);              /*input from the user*/
        ans=fact(x);                 /*function call*/
```

```
        printf("factorial=%d",ans);
        getch();
} /*end of main*/
int fact(int a)                /*function definition*/
{       int ans;
        if(a<=0)
          return(1);           // fact(0) = 1 by definition
        else
          ans =a*fact(a-1);  /*funtion call with recursion*/
        return(ans);          /*returns the value of fact to main*/
} /*end of function fact*/
/*
Output:
enter a number:7
factorial=5040
*/
```

We have also used non recurring technique in chapter 3. Then which one we should use recursion or control loop. Recursion is a powerful feature and if it is programmed correctly, would lead to elegant and less code. But otherwise we can also achieve the same result by using any of the control loops.

■■■ 4.6 STORAGE CLASSES IN C LANGUAGE

You are already familiar with intrinsic or basic data types like ***int, char, and float*** etc and allowable ranges and operations that can be performed on them. We have also studied that variables are declared and assigned memory locations. The manner in which memory is allocated and accessed depends on the type of ***storage class.*** Now we will study how these variables are allocated memory and accessed.

The variable are allocated required space either in ***memory or registers. Storage class*** determines

location	:	Where in memory or in CPU registers ?
initial values	:	What are the initial and default values? For example are they 0s or garbage values
scope	:	Which all functions can have access ?
life of variables	:	What is the life of variables ? Is it till the end of function, in which they are defined or is it till the end of main() function or is it that they are available even after end of main () function.

4.6.1 Memory Organization and Mapping of C Language

Memory can be broadly divided into data area or code area also called data segement and code segment. Based on the requirements of access times, scope, and life of variables, the memory is divided in to global, heap, code area, stack and static area as shown in Table 4.5

Table 4.5 Memory organization of C language

GLOBAL: Include section Function declarations Structures and global variables	**All declarations & definitions are accessible to all the functions.**
Heap Memory: Access to heap memory is only through pointers i.e through malloc() or calloc() unctions	Memory remaining after allocating space to global,code , and stack/static variables Code for all functions is stored here
CODE AREA: The C code, Functions etc are stored in this section	
STACK VARIABLES All variables you declare are stores on STACK STATIC VARIABLES	**Life of variable is till life of function in which it is declared. called local variables.** Life of static variable is till of main () .Accessible to all Fns

Global Variables: These are declarations such as include sections, define statements, function prototype declaration, and declarations of structures and unions etc, have scope that extends to all functions. It means, any variable declared in global section can be accessed by all functions. This section appears before main () function.

Code Area : All the functions and their code is stored here.

Stack Area : All the variable declared in a function are automatically allocated space in stack area of the memory. The scope of the variable is local. It means that a variable declared in a function, is accessible only within the function. Further the life of variables declared within the function is life of the function itself i.e within the brace brackets of the function. Hence these variables are called local variables or automatic or auto variable. Consider the example given in Table 4.6 for local or auto variables.

Static Variables : In several situations, you will need accessibility of variables declared in a function for all function, we will declare such variables as **static**. For example

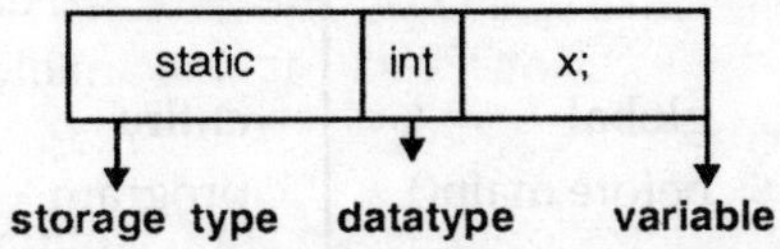

Table 4.6 Local or stack auto variables

void main()
{
float x =100, y=200,z;
float a[]= { 10.0,20.0,30.0};
………
z=FindArea(x,y);
printf("\n area =" , z);
} // end of main
	float FindArea(float x , float y)
	{ static int times=0;
	float ans;
	ans=x*y;
	return ans;
	}// end of FindArea

x , y , z ,and array a are local to main() They are stored on stack area x & y are passed as arguments to FindArea() FindArea copies the answer onto z Life of variables is life of void main()	ans is local to FindArea() return ans ; statement copies ans in to z belonging to main() Z is printed as output

Variable declared as static, are stored in contiguous memory locations. Only special feature of static area is that the variable in this static area are not erased, even if function terminates. For example, we have declared, times as static int, to keep track of number of times FindArea is called by main() function. We have also initialized times = 0; It is incremented when the first time function is called. Next time, when FindArea() is called it is incremented by one to 2.

Heap Memory or Free Space: After allocating mandatory spaces for all the above storage classes, the memory still free, is called heap memory or free space. This is dynamic memory available to programmer for requirements of memory at run time. But access to this space is available only through pointers. Malloc() and calloc() and free() are commands that are used for allocating and freeing space from heap memory. We will study these aspects in chapter 6 on pointers.

Now we are ready to discuss the storage types in the following section.

4.6.2 Types of Storage Classes

storage classes supported by C language is shown in Table 4.7

Table 4.7 Storage classes with their location, scope and life span

Storage class	Location	Scope	Life
a) Automatic or auto or stack storage	stack	local	within the block { }
b) Register storage	registers	local	within the block { }

c) Static storage	static	local	within the block { } value stays even after termination of function.
d) External	global before main()	entire program	When all functions need the value declare it as external.Tillmain ()

Note that while static global and external declarations have reach to all functions there is one vital difference. Static global declarations and definitions are available only throu a single main() function. Whereas, declarations and definitions using ***extern*** are available even to programs written separately with different file names but compiled and linked with main() program. Example will make the concepts clear.

Example 4. 5 stackstatic.c A program to demonstrate usage of static and stack(auto) variable..

```
#include<stdio.h>
#include<conio.h>
// function prototype declarations
float FindArea ( float x, float y);
void main()
{
  int i;
        float x =200, y =100, area=0,ans;
 // call function FindArea 10 times
 for (i=0;i<10;i++)
 {  ans = FindArea(x++,y++);
   printf("\n area =%5.2f", ans);
 }
 printf("\n Address of variable ans in the main function : %x", &ans);

   }// end of main
// function definition
float FindArea(float x, float y)
{  static int times=0; // static variable to keep track of number of times function is calles.
   float ans;
   ans=x*y;
   times++;
   printf("\n number of times we have called findArea function = %d",times);
   if (times ==10)
   printf("\n Address of variable ans in the FindArea function : %x", &ans);
   return ans;
}// end of FindArea
/*output

 number of times we have called findArea function = 1
 area =20000.00
 number of times we have called findArea function = 2
```

```
area =20301.00
number of times we have called findArea function = 3
area =20604.00
number of times we have called findArea function = 4
area =20909.00
number of times we have called findArea function = 5
area =21216.00
number of times we have called findArea function = 6
area =21525.00
number of times we have called findArea function = 7
area =21836.00
number of times we have called findArea function = 8
area =22149.00
number of times we have called findArea function = 9
area =22464.00
number of times we have called findArea function = 10
Address of variable ans in the FindArea function : 12ff04
area =22781.00
Address of variable ans in the main function : 12ff6c
*/
```

Example 4.6 reg.c. A program to demonstrate usage of register storage class usage.
Note that registers of CPU, resident on the processor chip, exact number depends on the hardware of the processor is considered as the primary memory and hence enjoy fastest access times. However, being limited memory, they have to be used sparingly. For example variable which are most frequently used by CPU can be declared as register variables thus saving access times. In the following example, we would use register memory to store counter of control loop, square and square root of a number.

```
//reg.c
#include<stdio.h>
void main()
{
    register counter,square,sqroot;
    for(counter=1;counter <=10; counter ++)
    {  square= counter* counter;
          printf("\nnumber : %d : square : %d ", counter, square );
    }
}
/*
Output:
number : 1 : square : 1
number : 2 : square : 4
number : 3 : square : 9
number : 4 : square : 16
```

```
number : 5 : square : 25
number : 6 : square : 36
number : 7 : square : 49
number : 8 : square : 64
number : 9 : square : 81
number : 10 : square : 100
*/
```

Example 4.7 extern.c A program to demonstrate usage of extern variable usage.

Variable declared out side void main() function comes under external storage class.

```
#include<stdio.h>
#include<conio.h>
// external function
void FindArea();
float x=10;
float y=10;
float area;
void main()
 {   extern float area;
     extern float x;
     extern float y;
     area=0;
     printf("\n area before calling FindArea %f",area);
     FindArea ();
     printf("\n area after return from FindArea %f",area);
     getch();
 }// end of main

// fn declaration
void FindArea()
 {
    extern float x;
    extern float y;
    extern float area;
    area = x*y;
    printf("\n area inside FindArea %f",area);
 }
/*
Output:
 area before calling FindArea 0.000000
 area inside FindArea 100.000000
 area after return from FindArea 100.000000
*/
```

Note that though, FindArea did not return the value of the area, the main program has shown the correct value of area. Thus, we can use external declaration for avoiding passing of variable to and from functions. We can also use extern declarations and definitions to link variables declared in two different files. We will attempt to demonstrate the concept through next example.

Example 4.8 externfile.c A program to demonstrate usage of external program stored in another file. Write C code for void FindArea() and save it as findarea.h in the current directory.

```
#include<stdio.h>
void FindArea()
 {
   extern float x;
   extern float y;
   extern float area;
   area = x*y;
   printf("\n area inside FindArea %f",area);
}
```

Write C code for void main () and include it along with other include statements as shown below

```
#include<stdio.h>
#include<conio.h>
#include"findarea.h" // findarea.h is stored in the current working directory
 // external function
void  FindArea();
float x=10;
float y=10;
float area;
void main()
 {  extern float area;
    extern float x;
    extern float y;
    area=0;
    printf("\n area before calling FindArea %f",area);
    FindArea ();
    printf("\n area after return from FindArea %f",area);
    getch();
 }// end of main
```

Note that you can use #include<findarea.h> if you copy the findarea.h into directory c:\tc\include

```
/*
Output:
 area before calling FindArea 0.000000
 area inside FindArea 100.000000
 area after return from FindArea 100.000000
*/
```

4.7 HEADER FILES

ANSI standards provided flowing standard header files.

stdio.h : facilitates input output statements.

ctype.h : contains functions that would facilitate manipulation of character data type. The functions supported are :

isalnum() : Checks whether a character is alphanumeric (A-Z, a-z, 0-9)

isalpha() : Checks whether a character is alphabetic

islower() is upper().Test if char is lower or upper respectively.

tolower() and toupper() : converts to lower and upper cases.

math.h : Contains library functions. Note that x can be float or double. C language does not support expression of type x ^a. We need to use pow(x,a).

sqrt(x) : determines square root of x

pow(,x,a) : computes x^a

exp(x) : computes e^x

sin(x) and cos(x): computes sin and cosine

log(x) : computes natural log

log10(x) : computes log to base 10

stdlib.h

abs(x) : computes absolute value of integer x

atof(s) : converts a string s to a double

atoi(s) : converts to integer

malloc() : allocates memory and returns a pointer to the location.

calloc() : same as malloc() but initializes the memory with 0s.

free(x) : frees heap memory space pointed by x

rand() : generates a random number.

4.8 C PREPROCESSOR

The preprocessor does some house keeping function before submitting the source code to the C compiler. The jobs it performs are:

a) inclusion of all include section files. For example it fetches and appends stdio.h from tc\include directory and includes in source file.

b) Macro expansion. Actually pre processor carries out substitution for declarations given in Macro statement. For example in the statement #define PI 3.14159, preprocessor searches for occurrence of symbol PI and replace it with 3.141519.

c) Conditional inclusion. To prevent, inclusion second and multiple number of times, we can employ conditional inclusion.

d) String Replacements

The standard directives available in C Language are:

#include	include text from the specified file
#define	define a macro
#undefine	indefine a macro
#if	test if a condition holds at compile time
#endif	end of if (conditional preprocessor)
#elif	if-else-if for multiple paths at compilation time
#line	provides line number

In chapter 1, we have already used #define PI 3.14159 macro and calculated areas. You have also used : #include<stdio.h> type of inclusion macros. In this section, we will use other type of macros.

4.8.1 Macro Expansion

Example 4.9 macro1.c

```
#include<stdio.h>
#define GETDATA  printf("\n Enter the value: ");
void main()
{
int x, y;
GETDATA;
scanf("%d",&x);
GETDATA;
scanf("%d",&y);
printf("\n values enetered are %d %d",x,y);
}
/*
Output:
Enter the value: 23
Enter the value: 34
Values enetered are 23 34
*/
```

Preprocessor directive like #define GETDATA printf("\n Enter the value: "); will simply substitutes all the occurrences of GETDATA with printf("\n Enter the value: ");

4.8.2 Macro Definition with Arguments. The general syntax of macro with arguments is
#define macro-name(arg1,arg2,arg3,..........argn). Examples are shown below

Example 4.10 macro2.c. A program to demonstrate the usage of preprocessor directives.

```
        #include<stdio.h>
#include<conio.h>
// substitution & macro definition macros
#define GETDATA  printf("\n Enter the value < number>");
#define WRITEDATA(ans)  printf("\n answer=%d",ans);
#define SUM(a,b) ((a)+(b))
#define PRODUCT(a,b)  ((a)*(b))
#define MIN(a,b)  ((a)>(b)?(a): (b))
void main()
{
        int x, y, ans;
        GETDATA;
        scanf("%d",&x);
        GETDATA;
        scanf("%d",&y);
        ans=PRODUCT(x,y);
        printf("\n product of numbers is ");
        WRITEDATA(ans);

        ans=SUM(x,y);
        printf("\n sum of numbers is " );
        WRITEDATA(ans);
        getch();
}
/*
Output:
    Enter the value < number>4
    Enter the value < number>5
    product of numbers is
    answer=20
    sum of numbers is
    answer=9
*/
```

4.8.3 File Inclusion

All include files are placed at directory c:\tc\include for turbo C compiler. Hence if you copy any heard file written by you into this directory, you can include this file as

```
#include <findarea.h>
```

If you have placed the file in the current directory, the you can include such a file with a preprocessor directive # include "findarea.h", as shown in example 4.7

4.8.4 Conditional Inclusion

Conditional Inclusion of some parts of source code is done using conditional inclusion macros. The syntax is

```
#if constant expression
        statement sequence
#endif

        or

#if constant expression
        statement sequence
#else
        statement sequence

#endif
```

Example 4.11elseifmacro.c A program to demonstrate the usage #if, #else, and #endif preprocessor directive.

```
#include<stdio.h>
#include<conio.h>
#define UPPER  5000
#define BONUS1 1000
#define BONUS2  500
#define bp 1000
void main()
{
        int netpay;
        printf("\n The basic pay is: %d",bp);
        #if bp<UPPER
        netpay=bp+BONUS1;
        #else
        netpay=bp+BONUS2;
        #endif
        printf("\n netpay = %d", netpay);
        getch();
} // end of main
/*
Output:
```

```
Enter the basic pay 1000
netpay = 2000
*/
```

4.8.5 Conditional Compilation #ifdef and #ifndef Statements.

In order to prevent inclusion of macros more than once and leading to multiple declarations, we can use macro #ifdef and #ifndef, to indicate if defined and if not defined. The general syntax is :

```
#ifdef macroname              #ifndef
   Statements          or     statements
#endif                        #endif
```

4.8.6 #undef

A macro must be undefined before it is redefined. Consider the macro definitions. In this module we will also use conditional inclusion like #ifdef

Example 4.12 undef.c

```
        #include<stdio.h>
#include<conio.h>
#define UPPER 100
#define LOWER 10
#define WRITEDATA printf("\n answer=%d",ans);

void main()
{
        int temp= 70,ans=10;
        if (temp<UPPER && temp>LOWER)
        WRITEDATA;

        #ifdef UPPER
        #undef UPPER
        #endif
        #ifdef LOWER
        #undef LOWER
        #endif
        // now we can set new limits for UPPER & LOWER
        #define UPPER 60
        #define LOWER 50
        if (temp<UPPER && temp > LOWER)
        WRITEDATA;
}// end of main
/*
```

Output:

Answer=10(printed from the 1st if statement, the second WRITEDATA is not executed as the 2nd if loop returns a false.)
*/

4.8.7 #error Macros

#error macro usage is shown below. When #error macro is encountered, the compiler displays the error message. Note that error message is not in double quotes

```
#ifdef UPPER
        #include<upper.h>
#elifdef            // this macr is similar to if-else-if
        #include<lower.h>
#else
        #error Incorrect inclusion of Header files
#endif
```

OBJECTIVE QUESTIONS

1. what is the value of y = floor(35.5)

   a) 35 b) 35.5 c) 36 d) 35.0

2. what is the value of y = ceil(35.5)

   a) 35 b) 35.5 c) 36 d) 35.0

3. sizeof() operator in C is a Library function true/false

4. getch() and getche() perform the same operation true/false

5. In #include<stdio.h> statement, stdio.h, under turbo C, is available at

   a) current directory b) tc\include c) tc\bin d) none

6. In #include "circle.h" statement, circle.h is available at

   a) current directory b) tc\include c) tc\bin d) none

7. What will be output for printf("%c", 65);

   a) 6 b) A c) 10 c) none

8. When two strings are equal strcmp(stg1,stg2) returns

   a) -1 b) 0 c) 1 d) true

9. How many times "Hi" will be printed.

```
{ int x=0;
  printf("Hi");
  findarea(x);
}
```

   a) 1 b) 2 c) infinite d) 0

10 Call by reference is default mode of transferring values to a function true/false

11 For recursive procedures we can use following storage allocations

a) static b) heap c) stack d) global

REVIEW QUESTIONS

1. Explain call by reference call by value ?
2. Explain the need to declare function prototype before main() function?
3. What are the storage classes?
4. Explain the difference between static and stack storage?
5. Distinguish global and external declarations.
6. What is the role of pre processors?
7. What are macros? Explain the #ifdef and #ifndef statements with exmples

SOLVED PROBLEMS

1 lcm.c Write a C program to find LCM of two integers

```
#include<stdio.h>
#include<conio.h>
// function prototype declaration
int LCM(int a,int b);
void main()
{       int p,q,r;
        clrscr();
        printf("enter any 2 numbers\n");        /*getting the input*/
        scanf("%d%d",&p,&q);
        r=LCM(p,q);                             /*function call*/
        printf("the lcm between %d and %d is %d\n",p,q,r);
        getch();
} /*end of main*/
int LCM(int a,int b)
{       int x;
        x=a<b ?b:a;                     /*use of conditional operators*/
        while(x<=(a*b))     /*loop begins*/
        {  if( (x%a==0) && (x%b==0) )
                return(x);/*returning the value of x to main*/
                x++;
        } /*end of loop*/
        return 0;
```

```
} /*end of function LCM*/
/*
OUTPUT:
enter any 2 numbers
4 10
the lcm between 4 and 10 is 20
*/
```

2 bincode.c Write a c program to find the binary code of a number

```
#include<stdio.h>
#include<conio.h>
// function prototype declaration
void Int2Bin(int n);
void main()
{
        int n;
        clrscr();
        printf("enter the number\n");     /*getting input from the user*/
        scanf("%d",&n);
        Int2Bin(n);                       /*function call*/
        getch();
} /*end of main*/
void Int2Bin(int n)                       /*function definition*/
{       if(n/2)
            Int2Bin(n/2);                 /*calling the function recursively*/
        printf("%d",n%2);
} /*end of function Int2Bin(int n)*/
/*
OUTPUT:
enter the number
4
100
*/
```

3 palen.c Write program to check whether the given number is palindrome or not*/

```
#include<stdio.h>
#include<conio.h>
//function prototype declarations
void PALINDROME(int x);
void main()
{       int x;
        clrscr();
        printf("enter a number\n");
        scanf("%d",&x);       /*input a number from the user*/
        PALINDROME(x);   /*function call*/
```

```
        getch();
    } /*end of main*/
    void PALINDROME(int n)    /*function definition*/
    {       int m,r,s=0;
            m=n;
            while(n!=0)             /*when the number is not 0*/
            {       r=n%10;
                    s=s*10+r;
                    n=n/10;
            }
            if(s==m)              /*if value of s equals m*/
                printf("palindrome\n");
            else
                printf("not palindrome\n");
    } /*end of function PALINDROME*/
    /*
    OUTPUT
    enter a number
    121
    palindrome
    */
```

4 exchg.c Write a C program to exchange the values of 2 variables. In this model, we do not use a variable temp

```
    algorithm   :   x=10    y=15
        x=x+y;      x=25
        y=x-y;      y=25-15 = 10
        x=x-y;      x=25-10 =15
        Therefore   x=15,   y=10
    */
    #include<stdio.h>
    #include<conio.h>
    //function prototype declarations
    void swap2(int a,int b);
    void main()
    {       int a,b;
            clrscr();
            printf("enter two numbers\n");
            scanf("%d%d",&a,&b);        /*input 2 numbers from the user*/
            swap2(a,b);             /*function call*/
            printf("%d\t %d\n",a,b);
            getch();
    } /*end of main*/
    void swap2(int x,int y)                 /*function definition*/
```

```
{       x=x+y;
        y=x-y;
        x=x-y;
        printf("incide Swap2 %d\t%d\n",x,y);
} /*end of function swap*/
/*
OUTPUT:
enter two numbers
22 43
incide Swap2 43 22
22 43
*/
```

5 armsg.c Write a C program to print yes if the given num is an armstrong number. In an Armstrong number sum of cube of individual digits will be the number it self. For example, consider a number 4 0 7.

Sum of cube of digits = $4^3 + 0^3 + 7^3 = 407$

```
#include<stdio.h>
#include<conio.h>
// function prototype declaraations
void armstrong(int n) ;
void main()
{ int x;
        clrscr();
        printf("enter a number\n");          /*input from the user*/
        scanf("%d",&x);
        armstrong(x);                        /*function call*/
        getch();
} /*end of main*/
void armstrong(int n)                        /*function definition*/
{       int p,r,s=0;
        p=n;                      /*storing the value of n in p*/
        while(n)                  /*checking for n,loop begins*/
        {       r=n%10;
                s=s+(r*r*r);
                n=n/10;
        }/*end of while loop*/
        if(p==s)          /*checking the value of s after the loop with p*/
                printf("yes. Given number is Armstrong number\n");
        else
                printf("no. Given number is NOT a Armstrong number \n");
}/*end of function armstrong*/
/*
```

```
OUTPUT:
enter a number
1234
no. Given number is NOT a Armstrong number
*/
```

6. **fibrecur.c Write a C function to generate Fibonacci series. In a Fibonacci series the series starts with 0 and 1 and next number will be a sum of previous two numbers. For example 3 rd number will be sum of 1 & 2 numbers i.e 0+1 = 2. The series for n=6 would be**

1 1 2 3 5 8 ..... and so on.

```
// now let us write a recursion version of Fibonacci number generator
// finds n the Fibonacci number. Algorithm used is for n<3,fibno = 1
// else fibno=fin(n-1)+fib(n-2).
// Programe stops if n=2 || n=1
/*Program to generate the fibonacci series*/
//fibrecur.c
#include<stdio.h>

int fib(int x);/*function definition*/
void main()
{
     int n,ans=0;

     printf("enter n:");
     scanf("%d",&n);                /*input from the user*/
     ans=fib(n);                    /*function call*/
     printf("\n Fibonacci number for a given <%d>: %d ", n,ans);
}                          /*end of main*/
int fib(int x)                  /*function definition*/
{    int ans;
     if (x<3) // i.e 1st and 2nd terms
       return 1;
     else
       ans = fib(x-1)+fib(x-2);
     return ans;
}
/*output
enter n:8
Fibonacci number for a given <8>: 21 */
```

ASSIGNMENT PROBLEMS

1. Write a program to compute sum of n natural numbers. Use recursion.
2. Write a function module to reverse the string.

3. Write c code for
    a) displaying error message using #error directive
    b) finding of maximum of two numbers.
4. Write a c code to sort the given array of integers.
5. Write a program to merge two sorted array in to a third array.
6. Write a function to compute the total of three subject marks. Another function to compute totals, average and declare the result. For example > 60 of average means first class else declare as second lass. Class comprises 50 students. Use functions and separate arrays for subjects, total, avg.

Solutions to Objective Questions

1) a	2) c	3) true	4) false	5) b
6) a	7) c	8) 0	9) c	10) false
11) c				

CHAPTER 5

ARRAYS & STRINGS

One dimensional & Two dimensional arrays, initialization, string variables-declaration, reading, writing, Basics of functions, Parameter passing, String handling function, user-defined functions, recursive functions, variables and storage classes, scope rules, block structure, header files, C preprocessor, example C programs.

In day to day life there are several occasions, where in we have to store, data of same type in contiguous locations, like marks obtained by a stûdent in six different subjects are shown in an array named ***marks in Fig. 5.1.*** Elements of the array are referenced by array name followed by subscript. we have shown an array named marks 3, six subject marks, scored by the student can be represented by marks[0]=80.0 and marks[5]=70.0 etc.

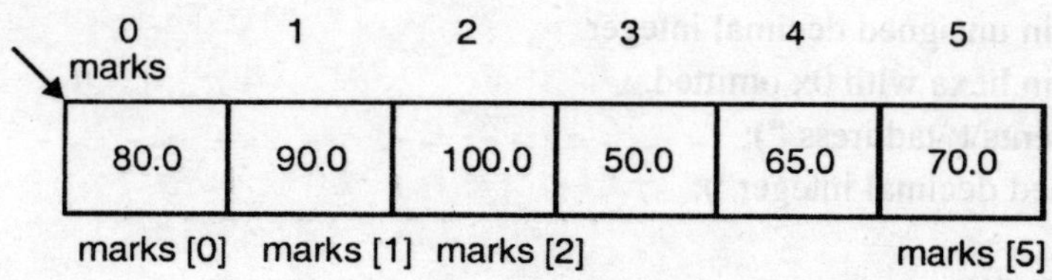

Fig. 5.1 Representation of an array

General syntax of array is *: storage class data type array [expression]*

Note that storage class is optional. Data type is data type of the array. Array is name and expression is a positive integer. Example of valid declarations of array are:

```
float marks[6] = { 60.0, 66.0, 70.0, 80.0, 90.0, 100};
float marks[] = { 60.0, 66.0, 70.0, 80.0, 90.0, 100.0};// no need to declare dimension
char stg[]={ 'g','o','o','d'};
```

5.1 HOW ARRAYS ARE STORED IN THE MEMORY

Consider an array named x, declared as int x[]= {80,90,100,50,65,70};

x ↘

80	90	100	50	65	70
x[0]	x[1]	x[2]	x[3]	x[4]	x[5]

memory **2000 2002 2004 2006 2008 2010 = 12 bytes**

Fig. 5.2 Representation arrays with memory locations shown

The addresses shown above are dummy addresses. Using of sizeof operator would tell us the memory requirement of data type int on your hardware. Assuming that it is 2 bytes, the memory of the array element are shown in Fig. 5.2.

Example 5.1 array.c write a program to display the array elements along with their address.
Sizeof operator provide size of data type in bytes.

```
#include<stdio.h>
//#include<conio.h>
void main()
 {  int i,n; //number of ements of array x
    int x[]={80,90,100,50,65,70};
    n= sizeof(x)/sizeof(int);
    printf("\n size of data type <int>%d ", sizeof(int));
    printf("\n Memory space allocated to x[6] : %d ", sizeof(x));
    printf("\n no of elements in array x = %d",n);
    // %u displays the address in unsigned decimal integer
    // %x displays the address in hexa with 0x omitted.
        printf("\n array elements\t:\taddress ");
    printf("\naddress in unsigned decimal integer");
        for (i=0;i<n; i++)
    printf("\n%d\t:\t%u", x[i],&x[i]);
     printf("\naddress in hexa with 0x omitted.\n");
        for (i=0;i<n; i++)
      printf("\n%d\t:\t%x", x[i],&x[i]);
        printf("\n");
 }
output
 size of data type <int>4
```

```
Memory space allocated to x[6] : 24
no of elements in array x = 6
array elements :      address
address in unsigned decimal integer
80    :    1245024
90    :    1245028
100   :    1245032
50    :    1245036
65    :    1245040
70    :    1245044
address in hexa with 0x omitted.
80    :    12ff60
90    :    12ff64
100   :    12ff68
50    :    12ff6c
65    :    12ff70
70    :    12ff74
Press any key to continue
```

■■■ 5.2 ARRAY INITIALIZATION

You have already seen declaration and initialization of the type:

```
float marks[6] = { 60.0, 66.0, 70.0, 80.0, 90.0, 100};
char stg[]={ 'g','o','o','d'};
```

We can use scanf to read into an array. In the following example, we will show use of scanf when we reverse the string.

Example 5.2 revstg.c a program to read the input string character by character from keyboard and reverse the string

```
#include<stdio.h>
#include<conio.h>
// function prototype declarations
 int length(char a[20]);
void main()
 {  int count=0,i;
    int len; // length of the string
    char c;
    char x[20]; // array of characters. string
    // get a character
   printf("\n Enter a word and press <enter>\n");
```

```
        c=getchar();
    while ( c!='\n')  // '\n' is end of line character  i.e. pressing enter key
      {
        x[count]=c;
        count++;
        c=getchar();
          }
    // we have reached end of line. Append '\0' to the string
    x[count]= '\0';
    len = count;
    // Now display the string you have just read
    printf("\n String inputted : %s ", x);
    printf("\n space allocated to single char : %d byte", sizeof(char));
    printf("\n Memory space allocated to string x[] : %d ", sizeof(x));
    printf("\n No of characters in the string x [] : %d ", length (x));
    // now reverse the string
    printf("\n string X reversed.\n");
    for ( i=len-1;i>=0;i—)
      printf("%c",x[i]);

}
  int length(char a[])              /*function definition*/
    {     int i=0;
            while(a[i]!='\0')       /*when the character is not null*/
              i++;
      return i;

  }/*end of function length*/
/*
 Enter a word and press <enter>
HELLO

 String inputted : HELLO
 space allocated to single char : 1 byte
 Memory space allocated to string x[] : 20
 No of characters in the string x [] : 5
 string X reversed.
OLLEH */
```

■■■ 5.3 MULTI DIMENSIONAL ARRAYS

Arrays can have more than one dimension. For example a matrix is two dimensional array, with number of rows and number of columns.

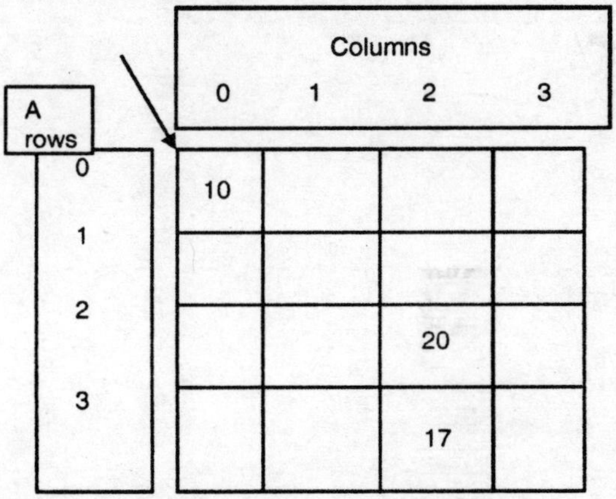

Fig. 5.3 Two dimensional array matrix A[4][4]

This is matrix A with dimensions 4 X 4. written as A[4][4]. First dimension is row and second dimension is columns.

As per C convention elements in row major representation is
A[0][0] A[0][1] A[0][2] A[0][3]
A[1][0] A[1[1] A[1][2] A[1][3]
A[2][0] A[2][1] A[2][2] A[2][3]
A[3][0] A[3][1] A[3][2] A[3][3]

Note A[0][0] = 10
A[2][2] = 20
A[3][2] = 17

Example 5.3 transpose.c. A program to find the transpose of a matrix

```
//transpose.c
#include<stdio.h>

// functional prototype declarations
void Transpose( int A[10][10], int n );// n is the order of square matrix
void ReadMatrix( int A[10][10], int n );
void PrintMatrix( int A[10][10], int n );
void main()
{
        int n,A[10][10];

        printf("Enter the order of square matrix <n>");
        scanf("%d",&n);
        ReadMatrix(A,n);
        printf("The elements of the Matrix are:\n");
        PrintMatrix(A,n);
        printf("The elements of the Transpose Matrix are:\n");
        Transpose(A,n);  /*function call. A is name of matrix. Name is address is */

} /*end of main*/

void Transpose(int A[10][10],int n)  /*function definition*/
{
        int i,j,t;
```

```
        for(i=0;i<n;i++) /*loop1. i=1 because you don't have to touch x[0][0]*/
        {
                for(j=0;j<i;j++) /*loop2*/
                {
                        t=A[i][j];
                        A[i][j]=A[j][i];        /*swapping*/
                        A[j][i]=t;
                }       /*end of loop2*/
        }

// output the matrix
        PrintMatrix(A,n);
}               /*end of furction transpose*/

void ReadMatrix( int A[10][10], int n)
{
        int i,j;
        printf("Enter the elements\n");
        for(i=0;i<n;i++)
          {
                for(j=0;j<n;j++)
                 scanf("%d",&A[i][j]); /*input elements*/
          }
}//end of ReadMatrix
void PrintMatrix( int A[10][10], int n)
{       int i,j;
        for(i=0;i<n;i++)
        {       for(j=0;j<n;j++)
                {       printf(" %d ",A[i][j]);
                }
                printf("\n");
        }
}//end of ReadMatrix
/*output
Enter the order of square matrix <n>2
Enter the elements
1 2 3 4
The elements of the Matrix are:
 1 2
 3 4
The elements of the Transpose Matrix are:
 1 3
 2 4 */
```

Example 5.4 matmul.c. A program to find the product of two matrices

```
//matmult.c
```

```
#include<stdio.h>
// functional prototype declarations
void MatrixMul( int A[10][10],int B[10][10],int C[10][10],int m,int n,int p );// m and n are the order of
square matrix
void ReadMatrix( int A[10][10],int m,int n );
void PrintMatrix( int A[10][10],int m,int n );
void main()
{
        int m,n,o,p,A[10][10],B[10][10],C[10][10];

        printf("Enter the order of 1st matrix\n");
        scanf("%d %d",&m,&n);
        printf("Enter the order of 2nd matrix\n");
        scanf("%d %d",&o,&p);
        if(n == o)
        {
                ReadMatrix(A,m,n);
                ReadMatrix(B,o,p);
                printf("\nThe elements of 1st Matrix are:\n");
                PrintMatrix(A,m,n);
                printf("\nThe elements of 2nd Matrix are:\n");
                PrintMatrix(B,o,p);
                MatrixMul(A,B,C,m,n,p);
                printf("\nThe elements of Resultant multiplication matrix are:\n");
                PrintMatrix(C,m,p);
        }

} /*end of main*/

void MatrixMul(int A[10][10],int B[10][10],int C[10][10],int m,int n,int p)  /*function definition*/
{
        int i,j,k;
        for(i=0;i<m;i++)
        for(j=0;j<p;j++)
                C[i][j]=0; //initializing the resultant matrix as 0

        for(i=0;i<m;i++)
        for(k=0;k<p;k++)
        for(j=0;j<n;j++)
                C[i][k] += A[i][j] * B[j][k]; //matrix multiplication
}//end of function MatrixMul

void ReadMatrix( int A[10][10],int m,int n )
{
```

```
    int i,j;
    printf("Enter the elements\n");
    for(i=0;i<m;i++)
    for(j=0;j<n;j++)
            scanf("%d",&A[i][j]); /*input elements*/
}//end of ReadMatrix

void PrintMatrix( int A[10][10],int m,int n )
{
    int i,j;
    for(i=0;i<m;i++)
    {
            for(j=0;j<n;j++)
            printf(" %d ",A[i][j]);
            printf("\n");
    }
}//end of PrintMatrix
/* output
Enter the order of 1st matrix
2 2
Enter the order of 2nd matrix
2 2
Enter the elements
1 2 3 4
Enter the elements
1 2 3 4
The elements of 1st Matrix are:
 1  2
 3  4
The elements of 2nd Matrix are:
 1  2
 3  4
The elements of Resultant multiplication matrix are:
 7  10
 15  22 */
```

5.4 CHARACTER ARRAY – STRING HANDLING IN C LANGUAGE

An array of characters is called string variable. A string variable will always be automatically terminated with '\0' (NULL) character. C compiler treats occurrence of NULL character to mean the end of string. In the following program, we would check for occurrence of '\0' to indicate the end of strings. Consider string declaration shown below and which type of declaration is best.

```
char city[6] ="Mumbai";  //incorrect as no space for adding '\0' (NULL) character.
char city[6] ="Mumbai";  // correct. '\0' (NULL) character is added automatically.
```

```
char city[] ="Mumbai"; // correct. '\0' (NULL) character is added automatically.
                        // This is preferred mode and we will be using this mode
                        // through out the textt
```

Example 5.7 concat.c A program to concatenate two strings

```
#include<stdio.h>
#include<conio.h>
void concat ( char x[],char y[]);
void main()
{
        char x[20],y[20];   // x 7 y are two strings
        clrscr();
        printf(":enter any 2 strings\n");
        scanf("%s%s",x,y);          /*input 2 strings from the user*/
        concat(x,y);            /*function call*/
        getch();
}/*end of main*/
void concat(char a[],char b[])          /*function definition*/
{       int i;
        for(i=0;a[i]!='\0';i++)   // check for '\0' occurence
                printf("%c",a[i]);
        for(i=0;b[i]!='\0';i++)
                printf("%c",b[i]);
} /*end of function concat*/
```

■■■ 5.5 STRING.H – LIBRARY FUNCTION

C compiler provides a library function called string.h. The functions supported by the header file string.h are:

strlen() : length of the char array
strcpy() : copies a string to another
strcat() : concatenates two strings
strcmp() : compares two strings
strlwr() : converts from upper case to lower case
struper() : converts from upper case to lower case
strrev() : reverses a string

To be able to use above library function we have to include <string.h> or <stdlib.h>. The best ways to learn programming is to write programs. Let us write our own code for achieving above. For all this function, you can write main program and forward the character array through a function call. For example ans=stglen(stg);, where char stg[20] ; is the character array declared. We provide a main program which you can use to test the functions.

Example 5.8. stg.c

```
//stg.c. main program to test the string handling functions
```

```
#include<stdio.h>
#include<conio.h>
#include<stdio.h>  // string functions line strlrn() etc
// Function prototype declarations
int stglen( char stg[20]);
int stgcopy( char stg2[20],char stg1[20]);

void main()
{ int len, flag ;  // flag = 0 to false, flag =1 means true

 char stg1[20],stg2[20], char stg3[20];

 printf("\n Enter<stg1>");
  gets(stg1);
  printf("\n Enter<stg2>");
  gets(stg2);
 len=stglen(stg1);
 printf(„\n length of the string thru our program : %d ",len);
  printf(„\n length of the string thru string.h : %d ", strlen(stg1));
 flag=stgcmp(stg1,stg2);
 if ( flag)   // i.e. if flag is true i.e. flag == 1
    printf("\n Both string stg1 and stg2 are identical);
 else
     printf("\n Both string stg1 and stg2 are not equal);
  getch();
} // end of main
```

5.8.1 String Length

```
int stglen( char stg[20])
  { int count=1;
    while ( stg[count] !='\0')  // '\0' is NULL character. Denotes end of string
        count ++;
    return count;
  }
```

We can also use the function provided by string.h : len=strlen(stg);

5.8.2 String Copy

stg1 is a source string and stg2 is a destination string. strcpy(stg2,stg1) of string.h would achieve the same result

```
void stgcopy( char stg2[20],char stg1[20])
  {    int count = 0;
```

```
        while( stg1[count] !='\0')
        { stg2[count]=stg1[count];
          count++;
        }
        stg2[count]= '\0'; // we have to insert NULL at the end
    }
```

5.8.3 String Compare

```
int stgcmp(char stg2[20],char stg1[20])
{   int count =0;
    while (  ( stg1[count] == stg2[count] ) && stg1[count]!='\0'
                                   && stg1[count]!='\0')
      count ++
   /* when you come out of loop, if both stg1 & stg2 are equal to '\0'
      then it can be said that both strings are identical.In such a case we will
      return 1.  Else, we will return a 0. */

    if    ( (stg1[count] =='\0')   && (stg2[count] =='\0') )
        return 1;
    else
        return  0;
}
```

5.8.4 Sub String Extraction from A String

In the main program, we need to pass as arguments the stg1 containing the string, stg2 to hold extracted string, substring start position, and length of sub string. For example consider the string:

I LOVE INDIA. We would like to extract INDIA. The
extractstg(stg1,stg2,8,5); INDIA at position 8 and 5 characters

```
void extractstg(char stg1[20], char stg2[20],int pos,int len)
{       int count =1;
        while(  count <= pos )
            count ++;
      count=1;
      while (count <= len )
          stg2[count]=stg1[count];
      stg2[count]='\0'; // insert NULL character
```

Example 5.8.5 chararraysort.c A program to sort strings.

```
#include<stdio.h>
```

```
#include<string.h>
#define gappu
//fn prototype declarations
void charraysort(char x[10][10],int n);
void main()
{       int count = 0,n=0;
        int i;
        char stg[10][10];
        // read in the string
       printf("\n Enter string<END to stop>: ");
        scanf("%s",stg[count]);
        while((strcmp(stg[count],"END")!=0))
          {   count++;
              printf("\n Enter string<END to stop>: ");
              scanf("%s",stg[count]);
          }
      charraysort(stg,count);
        printf("\n Sorted strings......");
      for( i=0;i<count;i++)
              puts(stg[i]);
} // end of main
// fun definition
void charraysort( char x[10][10],int n)
{       char temp[10];
         int i,j;
        for (i=0;i<n-1;i++)
        {
          for (j=i+1;j<n;j++)
            {
                    if(strcmp(x[i],x[j])>0)
                    {       // swap
                              strcpy(temp,x[j]);
                         strcpy(x[j],x[i]);
                              strcpy(x[i],temp);
                    }
              }
          }
}// end of charraysort()
output:
 Enter string<END to stop>: ramesh
 Enter string<END to stop>: usha
 Enter string<END to stop>: thunder
 Enter string<END to stop>: anand
 Enter string<END to stop>: gautam
```

Enter string<END to stop>: END
Sorted strings.......
anand
gautam
ramesh
thunder
usha

OBJECTIVE QUESTIONS

1. ____________method copies the value of an argument into the formal parameters of the subroutine.
2. ____________method copies the address of the actual parameters into the formal parameters.
3. Character array must be terminated with
   a) \0 b) \n c) \a d) \t
4. An array with out initial values contains
   a) all zeros b) all 1s c) garbage value d) none of the above
5. Array can be initialized at the time of declaration it self using
   a) square bracket b) braces c) (and) d) single quotes
6. The number in a square brackets of an array is called
   a) super script b) subscript d) dimension d) range
7. Subscript of an array A with m elements can be dimensioned as
   a) A[m] b) A[m-1] c) A[m+1] d) none
8. Array declared as array A[7] the elements are subscripted between
   a) 0....m b) 0....m+1 c) 1......m d) 0.....m-1
9. An array is always passed using pass by value to a function TRUE/FALSE
10. In a row major representation, the first subscript refers to row TRUE/FALSE
11. In an array, array elements are stored in contiguous locations TRUE/FALSE
12. An array is a collection of different data types TRUE/FALSE
13. If int A[6] is a one dimensional array of integers, which of the following refers to the value of fourth element in the array:
    a) A[4] b) A[2] c) A[3] d) none
14. Consider the following declaration of a two-dimensional array in C:

    char a[100][100];

    Assuming that the main memory is byte-addressable and that the array is stored starting from memory address 0," the address of a[40][50] is
    a) 4040 b) 4050 c) 5040 d) 5050

15. Suppose an array x contains the integer values [10,20,-10,25,0,-1]. The output of the following program segment is:

```
for(i=1;i<6;i++)
{
   if(x[i]<0)
      continue;
      if(x[i]==0)
        break;
      printf((“%d”,x[i]);
}
```

a) 10,20,-10,25,0,-1 b),-10,25,0,-1
c) 20,-10,25 d) 10,20,25

16) Spot the invalid array declarations

1) float c(20) 2) int x[]={1,5,8}; 3) int n(0..50) 4 char city[5]

a) 1,2 b) 1,3,4 c) 1,3 d) 1,2,4

REVIEW QUESTIONS

1 *Write in detail about one dimensional and multidimensional arrays. Also write about how initial values can be specified for each type of array?*

(a) *In what way array is different from ordinary variable?*

(b) *what conditions must be satisfied by the entire elements of any given array?*

(c) *What are subscripts? How are they written? What restrictions apply to the values that can be assigned to subscripts?*

(d) *What advantage is there in defining an array size in terms of a symbolic constant rather than a fixed integer quantity?*

2 *How are multidimensional arrays defined? Compare with the manner in which one- dimensional arrays are defined.*

SOLVED PROBLEMS

1 sum.c.Write a C program to find the sum of elements of an array with recursion

```
//sum.c
#include<stdio.h>
// function prototype declarations
int sumofelements(int a[] , int n);
void main()
{
```

```
        int a[10],n,i,ans;

        printf("enter the number of elements\n");
        scanf("%d",&n);          /*how many elements*/
        printf("enter the elements");
        for(i=0;i<n;i++)
           scanf("%d",&a[i]);      /*input elements from the user*/
        // forward array a to function by call by ref method
  ans=sumofelements(a,n);   /*function call*/
        printf("sum of all elements=%d",ans);

} /*end of main*/
sumofelements(int x[],int m)        /*function definition*/
{       if(m==1)          /*checking for value of m*/
           return(x[0]);
        else
           return(x[m-1]+sumofelements(x,m-1)); /*calling function recursively*/
}/*end of function sumofelements*/
/*
OUTPUT:
enter the number of elements
3
enter the elements 1 2 3
sum of all elements=6*/
```

2 extract.c.Write a C program that extracts a portion of the string starting from nth position upto mth position/

```
//extract.c
#include<stdio.h>
#include<conio.h>
#include<string.h> // allows use of library contained in string header
//function prototype declarations
void Extract( char x[],int m, int n ); // m=start position, n= ending position
void main()
{
        char x[40]; // x is a string of length 40
        int i,m,n;
        clrscr();
        printf("enter a string\n");
        scanf("%[^\n]",x); /*input from the user."%[^\n]" allows white spaces also*/
           printf("enter values of starting (n),and ending (m) positions,n>m\n");
        scanf("%d%d",&m,&n);     /*input from the user*/
```

```
        Extract(x,m,n);
        getch();
} /*end of main*/
void Extract(char a[], int m, int n)
{       int i;
        for(i=m;i<=n;i++)
         {
            printf("%c",a[i]);
         }
} /*end of function extract*/
/*
OUTPUT:
enter a string
education
enter values of starting (n),and ending (m) positions m,n> 2 4
uca
*/
```

3 stglen.c Write a program to find the length of a string/

```
//stglen.c
#include<stdio.h>
//function prototype declarations
int length(char x[]);
void main()
{  int ans;
   char x[20]; // dimension of string array x
        printf("enter a string:");
        scanf("%s",x);          /*input string from the user*/
        ans =length(x);              /*function call*/
   printf("length=%d\n",ans);
        getch();
}/*end of main*/
int length(char a[])        /*function definition*/
{       int i=0;
        while(a[i]!='\0')    /*when the character is not null*/
           i++;
        return i;
}/*end of function length*/
/*
enter a string:hello
length=5 */
```

4. matdet.c. Write a C program to find the determinant of a matrix

```
//Example 5.4 mat.c. A program to find the Det of a matrix
#include<stdio.h>
#include<conio.h>
#include<math.h>
// functional prototype declarations
int Det( int A[10][10],int n );// n is the order of square matrix
void ReadMatrix( int A[10][10],int n );
void PrintMatrix( int A[10][10],int n );
int det=0;
void main()
{
        int n,A[10][10];
        clrscr();
        printf("Enter the order of the matrix\n");
        scanf("%d",&n);
        ReadMatrix(A,n);
        printf("\nThe elements of the given Matrix are:\n");
        PrintMatrix(A,n);
        printf("The Det of the given matrix is : %d ",Det(A,n));
        getch();
} /*end of main*/

int Det(int A[10][10],int n )  /*function definition*/
{
        int k,l,p,q,i=0,j,temp[10][10],sign;
        if(n==2)
                return (A[0][0] * A[1][1] - A[0][1] * A[1][0]);
        else
        {
                for( j=0;j<n;j++)
                {
                        for(k=0,p=0;k<n && p<n-1;k++,p++)
                        for(l=0,q=0;l<n && q<n-1;l++,q++)
                        {
                                if(k==i) k++;
                                if(l==j) l++;
                                temp[p][q]=A[k][l];
                        }
                        printf("the sub matrix is:\n");
                        PrintMatrix(temp,n-1);
                        sign=pow(-1,i+j);
                        det += A[i][j] * sign * Det(temp,n-1);
                }
                return det;
```

```
    }
}//end of function Det
void ReadMatrix( int A[10][10],int n )
{
        int i,j;
        printf("Enter the elements\n");
        for(i=0;i<n;i++)
        for(j=0;j<n;j++)
                scanf("%d",&A[i][j]); /*input elements*/
}//end of ReadMatrix

void PrintMatrix( int A[10][10],int n )
{
        int i,j;
        for(i=0;i<n;i++)
        {
                for(j=0;j<n;j++)
                printf(" %d ",A[i][j]);
                printf("\n");
        }
}//end of PrintMatrix
/*
OUTPUT:
Enter the order of the matrix
3
The elements of the given Matrix are:
1 2 3 4 5 6 7 8 9
The elements of the given matrix are:
1 2 3
4 5 6
7 8 9
the sub matrix is:
5 6
8 9
the sub matrix is:
4 6
7 9
the sub matrix is:
4 5
7 8
The Det of the given matrix is : 0
*/
```

5 singular.c. Write a program to find the singular of a matrix. A matrix is called singular matrix if its determinant is zero

```
//Example 5.4 mat.c. A program to find the Det of a matrix
```

```
#include<stdio.h>
#include<math.h>
// functional prototype declarations
int Det( int A[10][10],int n );// n is the order of square matrix
void Determinent( int A[10][10], int B[10][10],int n);
void ReadMatrix( int A[10][10],int n );
void PrintMatrix( int A[10][10],int n );
int det=0;
void main()
{       int n,A[10][10],B[10][10];
        printf("Enter the order of the matrix\n");
        scanf("%d",&n);
        ReadMatrix(A,n);
        printf("\nThe elements of the given Matrix are:\n");
        PrintMatrix(A,n);
        Determinent(A,B,n);
        printf("\nThe Determinenet matrix is: \n");
        PrintMatrix(B,n);
        if(Det(B,n)==0)
                printf("The given matrix is Singular");
        else
                printf("The given matrix is not Singular");
        getch();
} /*end of main*/

void Determinent( int A[10][10], int B[10][10],int n)
{
        int k,l,p,q,i,j,temp[10][10],sign;
        for(i=0;i<n;i++)
        for(j=0;j<n;j++)
        {
                for(k=0,p=0;k<n && p<n-1;k++,p++)
                for(l=0,q=0;l<n && q<n-1;l++,q++)
                {
                        if(k==i) k++;
                        if(l==j) l++;
                        temp[p][q]=A[k][l];
                }
                sign=pow(-1,i+j);
                B[i][j] = A[i][j] * sign * Det(temp,n-1);
        }
}
int Det(int A[10][10],int n )  /*function definition*/
{
```

```
    int k,l,p,q,i=0,j,temp[10][10],sign;
    if(n==2)
        return (A[0][0] * A[1][1] - A[0][1] * A[1][0]);
    else
    {
        for( j=0;j<n;j++)
        {
            for(k=0,p=0;k<n && p<n-1;k++,p++)
            for(l=0,q=0;l<n && q<n-1;l++,q++)
            {
                if(k==i) k++;
                if(l==j) l++;
                temp[p][q]=A[k][l];
            }

            sign=pow(-1,i+j);
            det += A[i][j] * sign * Det(temp,n-1);
        }
        return det;
    }
}//end of function Det

void ReadMatrix( int A[10][10],int n )
{
    int i,j;
    printf("Enter the elements\n");
    for(i=0;i<n;i++)
    for(j=0;j<n;j++)
        scanf("%d",&A[i][j]);  /*input elements*/
}//end of ReadMatrix

void PrintMatrix( int A[10][10],int n )
{
    int i,j;
    for(i=0;i<n;i++)
    {
        for(j=0;j<n;j++)
        printf(" %d  ",A[i][j]);
        printf("\n");
    }
}//end of PrintMatrix
/*
OUTPUT:
```

Enter the order of the matrix
3
enter the elements
1 2 3 4 5 6 7 8 9
The elements of the given Matrix are:
1 2 3
4 5 6
7 8 9
The Determinenet matrix is:
-3 12 -9
24 -60 36
-21 48 -27
The given matrix is Singular
*/

ASSIGNMENT PROBLEMS

1. Write a program to count number of vowels in a given line of text.
2. write a complete C program to convert a lower case string to upper case. accept the input using scanf statement.
3. Write a program to print the given string in an alphabetical order.
4. Write function modules for finding
   a) string length
   b) string equality
   c) concatenation of two strings.
   d) Appending a string at the end of another string.
5 Write a file named mystring.h, comprising all above function modules. Include the header file in your driver program and test all the modules.
6. The annual examination is conducted for 50 students for three subjects.

   Write a program to the data and determine the following.
   (a) Total marks obtained by each student.
   (b) The highest marks in subject and the roll no of the student who Secured it.
   (c) the student who obtained the highest total marks.
7 Write a program to find the largest element in an array?

Solutions to Objective Questions

1) call by value	2) call by ref	3) a	4) c	
5) b	6) b	7) a	8) d	9) False
10) True	11) True	12) False	13) c	14) b
15) d	16) c			

CHAPTER 6

POINTERS

■■■ 6.1 WHAT, WHY AND HOW OF POINTERS

In C, we would like to use pointers because, they point to location in memory and not value and are very efficient to move multiple data items between main program and function as function arguments. In addition you can have pointers to a function. Pointer would facilitate reassignment of value just like you can point any one with your index finger.

How does Arjuna, the famous archer in Maha Bharata, use his arrows?

Firstly he removes an arrow from his storage.

Secondly he gives a name(mantra like Nag Astra).

Then he points it to ground while he thinks or gets address from his guide(Lord Krishna). He points it to ground so that the arrow does not take off accidentally and hit the passers by or unintended target.

Lastly, he aims at the address given and he lets it go!.
We will also do the same in case of pointers.

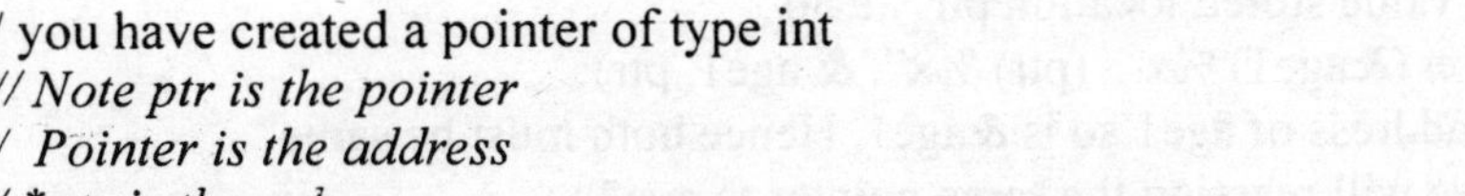

Fig. 6.1 A pointer example with terms

```
int *ptr; // you have created a pointer of type int
          // Note ptr is the pointer
          // Pointer is the address
          // *ptr is the value
Ptr = NULL:  // you have now pointed to NULL
```

■■■ 6.2 DECLARATION & USAGE

Let us say that at address 2513, we have stored a integer variable called age.
And at address 2613, we have integer variable age2.

```
int age =50;
int age2=18;
we want pointer ptr to point to age;
        age
```

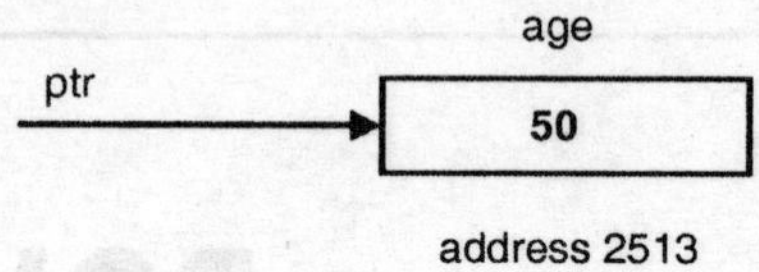

Fig. 6.2 Pointer in a memory

```
ptr = & age; // you have assigned ptr to age.
printf("my age %d : ", age); // displays 50
printf(("my age %d", *ptr); // displays 50
//*ptr which is value stored location i.e. 50
```

Once created you can reassign pointers

```
ptr = & age2;
printf(("your age %d", *ptr); // displays 18
//*ptr which is value stored location i.e. 18
```

Example:6.1

```
//ptr1.c
// program to introduce you to pointer concepts
#include<stdio.h>
#include<conio.h>
void main()
{ int age1 = 50;
  int age2 = 18;
  //create a pointer
  int * ptr;
  // assign it to age1
  ptr = & age1; // & is address of operator
  printf("\nmy age (age1) %d ", age1); // displays 50
  printf("\nmy age (*ptr) %d", *ptr); // displays 50
  //*ptr is value stored location ptr i.e 50
  printf("\n (&age1) %x   (ptr) %x", & age1, ptr);
  // ptr is address of age1 so is &age1. Hence both must be same
  // now we will reassign the same pointer to age2
  ptr = & age2;
  printf("\nyour age (*ptr) %d", *ptr); // displays 18
  //*ptr which is value stored location i.e. 18
  printf("\n(&age2) %x (ptr) %x", & age2, ptr);
// ptr is address of age2 so is &age2. Hence both must be same.
```

```
        printf("\n(&ptr) %x ", & ptr); // prints out address of variable ptr. We are not
                                       // interested in this address. It is just another address.
    }//end of main
/*OUTPUT:
my age (age1) 50
my age (*ptr) 50
 (&age1) 12ff7c    (ptr) 12ff7c
your age (*ptr) 18
(&age2) 12ff78  (ptr) 12ff78
(&ptr) 12ff74 */
```

A note about address scheme of Intel processors is appropriate:
When you ask for a display of address, the system would display a 32 bit address like ffff:fff4 in Hexa Decimal notation ; which means

1111 1111 1111 1111 : 1111 1111 1111 0100 in binary.

■■■ 6.3 CALL BY VALUE & CALL BY REFERENCE

(pointers) what are they? You can pass variables to a function by either of :

a) Call by Value. The value of arguments is copied on to formal arguments whenever a function is called. Thus there is a overhead of copying. As only copy reaches the function, the changes made in the local function are not reflected onto the original variable in the calling function. Further if the data to be copied is large, ex. structure, the method is inefficient. It is hence used only for small data.

b) Call by reference: Actual arguments are not copied but only addresses(pointers) are forwarded. The functions gets this addresses as arguments and works on the variables located at the addresses forwarded. Hence changes made to the variables are reflected on to variable from calling function. We are forwarding only addresses, there are no copying overheads as in Call by Value.

Example:6.2// program to highlight call by value and call by reference

```
//Example:3.2 ptr2.c
#include <stdio.h>
#include <stdlib.h>
// declaration of function prototypes
void Swap( int  a , int  b);  // call by value
void PtrSwap ( int *a, int * b); // Call by Ref. a & b are pointers by def.

void main()
{   int x = 5;
    int y=10;
    // call by value
```

```
        Swap( x,y);
        printf("\nafter call by value : x= %d  : y = %d ", x,y);
        // call by reference. Note that we have to send pointers i.e. addresses
        //of x & y. Hence we will pass &x , and & y.
        PtrSwap( &x, &y);
        printf("\nafter call by ref : x= %d  : y = %d ", x,y);
}//end of main
// Function definitions
void Swap ( int a, int b)
{  int temp ; // two local variables
   temp=a;
   a=b;
   b=temp;
   printf("\ninside Swap : a= %d  : b = %d ", a,b);
}
void PtrSwap ( int *a, int *b)
 { // a & b are pointers. Hence we need a pointer called temp
   int *temp ;
   *temp=*a;
    *a =*b;
   *b= *temp;
   printf("\ninside Swap : a= %d  : b = %d ", a,b);
 }
/*OUTPUT:
inside Swap : a= 10  : b = 5
after call by value : x= 5  : y = 10*/
```

In this module a few interesting results are there. Though inside Swap function values actually were interchanged they were not reflected in the main program as discussed. Whereas in the case of PtrSwap, wherein we have passed pointers, the result of PtrSwap were reflected to main programmers. This is in consonance with what we have learnt.

■■■ 6.4 DYNAMIC MEMORY AND MALLOC() AND CALLOC()

We can declare an array of 12 integers as int x[12]; This array declaration reserves 12 contiguous locations in memory. In case user does not use all 12 locations memory will be wasted. Array declaration is an example of static memory allocation. Instead we can also declare an array as

```
int  *x ; // x is a pointer variable
//allocate dynamic memory space using malloc()
x = (int *)malloc( 12 *sizeof(int));
```

malloc() function returns a pointer of *type int* by type casting it as (int*). This pointer points to a location in *heap memory*, that has 12 contiguous memory locations allocated by malloc(). Sizeof() is a C library function which tells the size of 'int' variable. To understand Dynamic memory and functioning of malloc(), we have to learn about C memory organization

GLOBAL: Include section **Function declarations** **Structures and global variables**	All declarations & definitions are accessible to all the functions.
Heap Memory: Access to heap memory is only through pointers i.e through malloc() or calloc() functions	Memory remaining after allocating space to global, code , and stack/static variables
CODE AREA: The C code, Functions etc are stored in this section	
STACK VARIABLES All variables you declare are stores on STACK	Life of variable is till life of function in which it is declared. called local variables.
STATIC VARIABLES	Life of static variable is till of main () .Accessible to all Fns

Fig. 6.3 Memory organization of C language

6.4.1 Function calloc() : Calloc requires two arguments instead of one argument for malloc(). For example consider

```
int *x;
x= (int*) calloc ( 10 * 4);
```

The above statement specifies that we would like to allocate 4 bytes to integer data type(space for 10 integers totaling 40 bytes) would be allocated. Most importantly calloc() after allocating memory, initializes the memory with zeros.

■■■ 6.5 POINTERS & ARRAYS: LET US UNDER STAND THE CONNECTION BETWEEN POINTER & ARRAYS

int x [10] = { 10, 20, 30, 40, 50, 60, 70, 80, 90, 100}

	x↘									
	10	20	30	40	50	60	70	80	90	100
pointer	x	x+1	x+3	x+4						x+9

Fig. 6.4 Array with addresses (pointer)

Note that 'x' is the name of the array. 'x' is also the address of the array and also the address of the first element of the array. Hence we can call 'x' as the pointer to the array too.

Suppose you want to print 4 th element i.e. 40, as per C convention you would write : printf("%d", x[3]);

Now as the element, we are interested in at position 4 (3 in case we are counting from 0) i.e. at address x+6.

We have learnt that if we want value from address we have to de-reference the address by using *.

Ex printf("%d", *(x+3));

Example: 6.3 samp7.c to pass an array to a function that receives an array by reference and sorts an integer array.

Let us write a program to pass an array to a function that receives an array by reference and sorts an integer array. We can define an array of 10 integers, using malloc() function as follows

```
//samp7.c
#include<stdio.h>
#include<conio.h>
// function prototype declarations
void IntSort( int n, int *a); // receives number of items & array
void main()
{    int i;
  int n=10;// number of items
  int a[10] ={67,87,56,23,100,19,789,117,6,1};
   printf("\n Given array ");
   for ( i=0;i<n;i++)
      {
         printf( "%d ", *(a+i));
      }
  // we are passing array a. Note that array name is 'a'. Name is address.
  IntSort(n,a);
  printf("\n Sorted array ");
                              for (i=0;i<n;i++)
      {
         printf( "%d ", *(a+i));
      }
 }//end of main
// function definition
void IntSort(int n, int *a)
  { int i,j, temp=0; //i for outer loop j for inner loop and temp for swapping
   for ( i=0; i< n-1; i++) // last value need not be sorted
     {
        // find the smallest of remaining numbers and exchange it with
        for ( j=i+1; j< n; j++)
           {
              if (*(a+j) < *(a+i))
                 { //swap
```

```
                temp=*(a+i);
                *(a+i)=*(a+j);
                *(a+j)=temp;
            }
        }
    }
}
```

```
/* output
 Given  array 67 87 56 23 100 19 789 117 6 1
 Sorted array 1 6 19 23 56 67 87 100 117 789
 */
```

■■■ 6.6 POINTERS & MULTI DIMENSIONAL ARRAYS

6.6.1 Two Dimensional Arrays & Pointers

Let us say that you have a two dimensional array 'a' with 12 rows and 20 columns. Then we can declare it as :

int a[12][20]

or

as a one dimensional array using pointers. For example

int *x[12]

pictorially following figure makes the concept clear. Therefore a[0] points to beginning of first row. a[11] points to beginning of 11 th row. Note that a[0]….a[11] are pointers to respective rows.

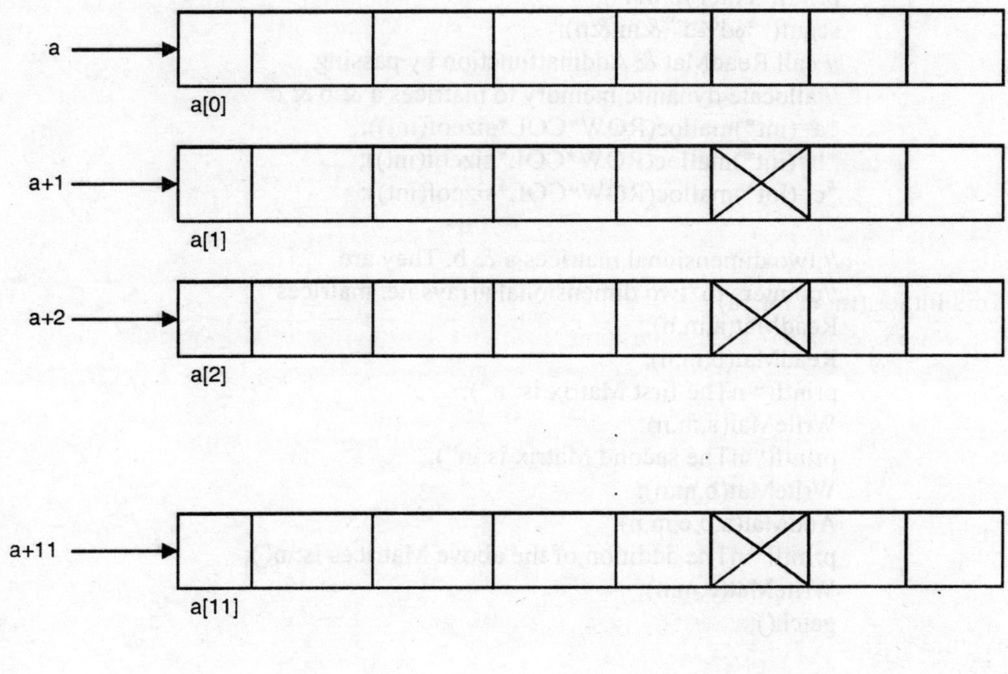

Now suppose you want to access 1 st row 5 element ; then
a[1] is the pointer to first row and 5 elements displacement is 5
We know we can write a[1] as *(a+1)
Therefore, address of desired element is a[1]+5 or *(a+1) +5
Value of element is : * (*(a+1) + 5).

Example 6.4 ptr4.c To add two matrices

To put into practice all the important concepts like two dimensional arrays and dynamic memory allocations, we will multiply two matrices A & B and put the result in matrix C

```
//ptr4.c A program to compute the matrix addition using dynamic memory allocation
#include<stdio.h>
#include<conio.h>
#include<stdlib.h>
#define COL 10
#define ROW 10
void AddMat(int *a[COL],int *b[COL],int *c[COL],int m,int n);
void ReadMat(int *a[COL],int m,int n);
void WriteMat(int *a[COL],int m,int n);
void main()
{
        int *a[COL],*b[COL],*c[COL];
        int m,n;

        //get ROWs and Columns
        printf("enter m,n\n");
        scanf("%d%d",&m,&n);
        // call ReadMat & Addmatfunction by passing
        // allocate dynamic memory to matrices a & b & c
        *a=(int*)malloc(ROW*COL*sizeof(int));
        *b=(int*)malloc(ROW*COL*sizeof(int));
        *c=(int*)malloc(ROW*COL*sizeof(int));

        // two dimensional matrices a & b. They are
        //pointers to two dimensional arrays i.e. matrices
        ReadMat(a,m,n);
        ReadMat(b,m,n);
        printf("\nThe first Matrix is:\n");
        WriteMat(a,m,n);
        printf("\nThe second Matrix is:\n");
        WriteMat(b,m,n);
        AddMat(a,b,c,m,n);
        printf("\nThe addition of the above Matrices is:\n");
        WriteMat(c,m,n);
        getch();
```

```
void ReadMat(int *a[COL],int m,int n)
{                    int i,j;
                     for(i=0;i<m;i++)
                     {
                          for(j=0;j<n;j++)
                          {
                                  printf("enter data for element (%d,%d) ",i,j);
                                  scanf("%d",&a[i][j]);
                          }
                     }
}
void AddMat(int *a[COL],int *b[COL],int *c[COL],int m,int n)
{                    int i,j;
                     for(i=0;i<m;i++)
                     {
                          for(j=0;j<n;j++)
                          { // two dimensional element access
                                  *(*(c+i)+j)=*(*(a+i)+j)+*(*(b+i)+j);
                          }
                     }
}
void WriteMat(int *c[COL],int m,int n)
{                    int i,j;
                     for(i=0;i<m;i++)
                     {
                          for(j=0;j<n;j++)
                          {
                                  printf("%d\t",*(*(c+i)+j));
                          }
                          printf("\n");
                     }
}
/*
OUTPUT:
enter m,n
2 3
enter data for element (0,0) 1
enter data for element (0,0) 3
enter data for element (0,0) 4
enter data for element (0,0) 6
enter data for element (0,0) 2
enter data for element (0,0) 4
enter data for element (0,0) 5
enter data for element (0,0) 2
```

```
The first Matrix is:
1          3
4          6
The second Matrix is:
2          4
5          2
The addition of the above Matrices is:
3          7
9          8*/
```

6.6.2 Three Dimensional Arrays & Pointers

To access an element a[3][4][5]

a) a is the pointer to first row. We need 3 row. Therefore it is a[3] or *(a+3)

b) Column displacement is 4. Therefore address is *(a=3)+4 and value is *(*(a+3)+4)

c) 3 dimensional displacement is 5. Therefore address is : *(*(a+3)+4)

Therefore value of element is: *(*(*(a+3)+4))

6.6.3 Array of Pointers. Pointers can be stored in arrays. You already know that pointer means address, hence array of pointers means collection of addresses. For example you can store a set of 5 pointers each pointing to a string variable like:

char * **ptr[5] = { "welcome", "to","self_learning","CDS", "Book" }**

ptr is a dimension 5 i.e. an array of 5 pointers. The following example will make the concept clear:

Example 6.5 Program to demonstrate use of array of pointers

```
//ptr5.c Program to demonstrate use of array of pointers
#include<stdio.h>
#include<conio.h>
void main()
{    int i;
    // array of pointers with 5 elements
    char *ptr[5]={"welcome","to","self_learning","CDS","Books"};
    char *x; // x is a pointer of type int
    x=ptr; // x now points to ptr, i.e. starting pointer in an array of pointers
    for ( i = 0 ; i< 5; i++)
        printf("\n %s", *(ptr+i));
    // following print statements will teach you more about array of pointers
    printf("\n %c", *ptr[3]); // you can expect value of starting element in CDS i.e. C
}
```

```
/*
OUTPUT:
welcome
to
self_learning
CDS
Books
C
*/
```

■■■ 6.7 POINTERS TO VOID

Remember 'void' is a data type. Usually we will declare pointer to point to a particular type of data. For example int * ptr or char * ptr etc. Suppose in your program you have multiple data types, the void can be employed. But typecasting is essential, when void pointer used.

Type casting a void pointer

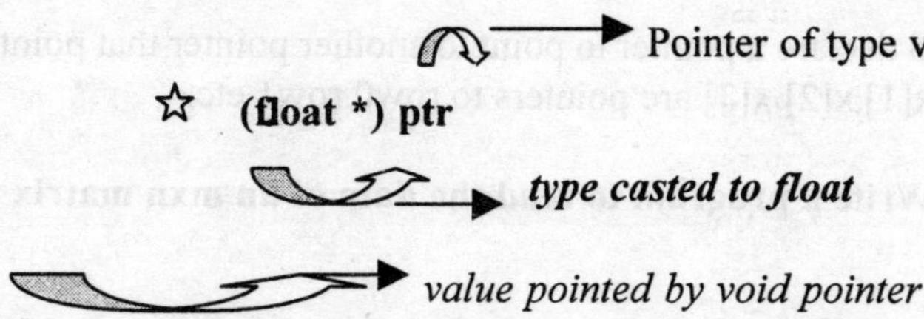

Example 6.6 voidpointer.c Program to demonstrate use of void pointers

```
#include<stdio.h>
#include<conio.h>
void main()
 {  int  x=100;
    float sal = 2000.00;
    void * ptr;// ptr is a pointer to data type void
    // assign void pointer to int
   ptr = &x;
  printf("%d", *(int*)ptr); // typecasting of ptr to int
  // assign void pointer to float
  ptr = &sal;
  printf("\n%f", * (float*)ptr); // typecasting of ptr to float
}//end of program

/*output
100
2000.000000 */
```

6.8 POINTER TO POINTERS

Let us say we have a two dimensional array as shown below

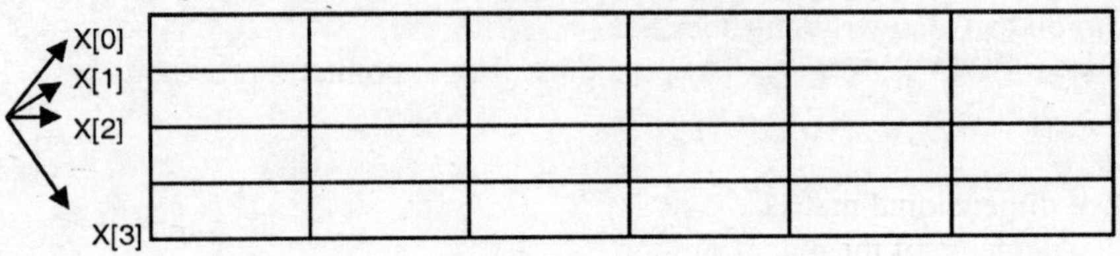

We could declare the above matrix as int x[4]][6]. Also we have learnt we could have declared as shown below and allocated space dynamically using malloc(). Note that x is a pointer to location that is starting address of a one dimensional array that stores entire two dimensional matrix.

```
int *x[][6];
x = (int *) malloc(rows*col*sizeof(int));
```

Alternatively, we could declare a pointer to point to another pointer that points to array. For example in the above figure x[0],x[1],x[2],x[3] are pointers to row0,row1 etc.

Example 6.7 ptr7.c Write a program to read the data of an mxn matrix using pointer to pointer

```
#include<stdio.h>
#include<stdlib.h>
void main()
{
        // Now define a pointer to pointer "x" to an mxn matrix
        int **x; // x is a pointer to a pointer
        int i,j,m,n;
        // allocate dynamic memory using malloc()
        //x[i] is a pointer to row i
        printf("\nEnter m and n: ");
        scanf("%d%d",&m,&n);
        for (i=0;i<m;i++)
        {
                x[i] = (int*) malloc( n*sizeof(int)); // n is size of each row
                // we could have written above also as:
                *(x+i) = (int*) malloc( n*sizeof(int)); // n is size of each row
        }
        // Read data into two dimensional matrix
        printf("\nEnter the elements of matrix...\n");
        for (i=0; i<m; i++)
        {
```

```
        for ( j=0; j<n; j++)
        {  printf("\nx[%d][%d] = ",i,j);
           scanf("%d",&x[i][j]);
           // you can also write the above as
           // scanf("%d",    *(*(x+i) + j)); // 2 dimensional pointer representation
        }
    }
    // Display two dimensional matrix
    printf("\nThe elements of the matrix are...\n");
    for (i=0; i<m; i++)
    {
        for ( j=0; j<n; j++)
        {  printf(" %d", x[i][j]);
           // you can also write the above as
           // printf("d",*(*(x+i) + j)); // 2 dimensional pointer representation
        }
        printf("\n"); // to print new row on a new line
    }
}// end of main

/*
OUTPUT:
Enter m and n: 2 3
Enter the elements of matrix...
x[0][0] = 1
x[0][1] = 2
x[0][2] = 3
x[1][0] = 4
x[1][1] = 5
x[1][2] = 6
The elements of the matrix are...
1 2 3
4 5 6
*/
```

OBJECTIVE QUESTIONS

1. The________pointer is used to specify a pointer whose base type is unknown and is a generic pointer.
2. ____________is the means by which a program can obtain memory during runtime.
3. Memory allocated by C's dynamic allocation functions is obtained from _______.
4. The malloc function returns a pointer of type ———————which means that we can assign it to any type of pointer.

5. Pointer arithmetic is restricted to _______ and_______type pointer.

6. The ____is a unary operator that returns the memory address of it's operand.

7. In Call by reference actual arguments are not copied but only addresses(pointers) are forwarded True/False.

8. The declaration of two dimensional arrays int a[12][20] and int *a[20] are one and the same. True/False

9. Only addition and subtraction operations are permitted on pointers (True /False)

10 Which among these is the indirection operator:

a) & b) + c) % d) *

11 Which of these is not a valid pointer operation?

a) p++; b) 5+(p*5); c) (p)++; d) (p+3);

12 What is the main advantage of allocating memory from dynamic memory for an array

a) The size of variable can be decided at run time
b) Easy to pass as arguments to a function.
c) Accessing array elements becomes easier
d) None of the above

13 Dynamic memory can be allocated with out use of pointers. True/False

14
```
void main( )
    {   int age1=50,age2=25, *ptr;
        ptr=&age1;
        &age2=ptr;
        printf("The value of y is %d",age2);
    }
```

a) The value of age2 is25 b) The value of age2 is 50
c) Run-time error may occur d) Compilation error

15 printf("%d", x[5]); is equal to

a) printf("%d", x[5]); b) printf("%d", x+5);
c) printf("%d", *x+5); d) printf("%d", *(x+5));

16. If int A[6] is a one dimensional array of integers, which of the following refers to the value of fourth element in the array:

a) * (A+4) b) * (A+3) c) A+4 d) A+3

REVIEW QUESTIONS

1. *What are pointers? List out reasons for using pointers.*

2. *state whether each of the following statements is true or false.*

Give reasons.

(a) An integer can be added to a pointer.

(b) A pointer can never be subtracted from another pointer.

(c) When an array is passed as argument to a function, a pointer is passed.

(d) Pointers cannot be used as formal parameters in headers to function Definitions.

3. *If m and n are declared as integers and p1 and p2 as pointers to Integers, then find out the errors, if any, in the following statements.*

   *(a) p1=&m; (b).p2=n; (c).m=p2-p1; (d).*p1=&n;*

4. *Explain the process of assessing a variable through its pointer. Give an example.*
5. *How to use pointers as arguments in a function? Explain through an example.*
6. *Explain the process of declaring and initializing pointers ? Give an example.*
7. *Distinguish pointer * operator (indirection operator) and address operator(&) with examples*
8. *Give examples of pointer arithmetic for +,-,++.*
9. *Explain dynamic memory operators malloc, calloc, and free.*
10. *Differentiate array of pointers and pointer to an array.*

SOLVED PROBLEMS

1. samp1.c Write a program using pointers to find maximum of an array // *(samp1.c)* program to find maximum in an array using pointers

```
#include<stdio.h>
#include<conio.h>
#include<stdlib.h>
// Function prototypes
int FindMax( int *a, int n);
void SortArray( int *a, int n);

void main()
{ int i, n, max; // n= no of values in an array
  int *x;  // x is a pointer to an array

  printf("how many elements in your array?<n>\n");
  scanf("%d",&n);

  // allocate dynamic memory space using malloc()
  x=(int*)malloc(n*sizeof(int));
  // read in the array
```

```
   for (i=0;i<n;i++)
     { printf("\n value for %d element=",i+1);
        scanf("%d",x+i); // scanf needs address. we have
     }                  // given address when we write x+i
   printf("\n The entered array is....\n");
   for (i=0;i<n;i++)
     printf("%d  ",*(x+i)); // same as writing x[i]
   // call Findmax function
   max=FindMax(x,n);//x is a pointer to array
   printf("\n maximum value of given array = %d ",max);
 }//end of main

// Fn definitions
int FindMax(int *x, int n)
{ int max,i;

  max=*x; // *x is the value of 1 element
  for(i=1;i<n;i++)
   { if (max<*(x+i))
       max=*(x+i);
   }
  return max;
 } // end of FindMax
/*
OUTPUT:
how many elements in your array?<n>5
 value for 1 element=2
 value for 2 element=6
 value for 3 element=4
 value for 3 element=2
 value for 3 element=4
The entered array is...
2 6 4 2 4
 maximum value of given array = 6
*/
```

2. samp2.c Write a c program to illustrate the use of indirection operator "*" to access the Value pointed by a pointer.

```
 //sort intarray using pointers
//sortarryptr.c
          #include<stdio.h>
          #include<conio.h>
```

```
// function prototype declarations
void IntSort( int n, int *a);  // receives number of items & array

void main()
                    {                    int i;
  int n=10;// number of items
  int a[10] ={ 67,87,56,23,100,19,789,117,6,1};
   printf("\n Given  array ");
                                         for ( i=0;i<n;i++)
      {
         printf( "%d ", *(a+i));
      }
  // we are passing  array a. Note that array name is 'a'. Name is address.
  IntSort(n,a);
  printf("\n Sorted array ");
                                         for (i=0;i<n;i++)
      {
         printf( "%d ", *(a+i));
      }
  }//end of main
  // function definition
void IntSort(int n, int *a)
  {  int  i,j, temp=0; // i for outer loop j for inner loop and temp for swapping
   for ( i=0; i< n-1; i++)  // last value need not be sorted
     {
        // find the smallest of remaining numbers and exchange it  with
        for ( j=i+1; j< n; j++)
           {
              if (*(a+j) < *(a+i))
                 {  // swap
                    temp=*(a+i);
                    *(a+i)=*(a+j);
                    *(a+j)=temp;
                 }
           }
     }
  }
```

```
/* output

Given  array 67 87 56 23 100 19 789 117 6 1
Sorted array 1 6 19 23 56 67 87 100 117 789
*/
```

3. samp3.c Write a c program using pointers to read in an array of integers and print it's elements in reverse orders.

```
// (samp3.c)Findreverse.c Program to find the reverse of elements of an array using pointers.
#include<stdio.h>
#include<conio.h>
#include<stdlib.h>
// Function prototypes
// a is one dimensional array of say 12 elements

void FindReverse( int *a,int *b, int n);
void main()
 { int i, n; // n= no of values in an array
   int *x;  // x is a pointer to an array
   int *y; // y is reversed array
   printf("how many elements in your array?<n>");
   scanf("%d",&n);

   // allocate dynamic memory space using malloc()
   x=(int*)malloc(n*sizeof(int));
   y=(int*)malloc(n*sizeof(int));
        // read in the array
   for (i=0;i<n;i++)
     { printf("\n value for %d element=",i+1);
      scanf("%d",x+i); // scanf need address. we have
     }          // given address when we write x+i

   // call FindReverse function
   FindReverse(x,y,n);//x& y are pointers to array
   printf("\n Given Array\n");
   for (i=0;i<n;i++)
     printf("%d ",*(x+i));

   printf("\n Reversed  Array\n");
   for (i=0;i<n;i++)
     printf("%d ",*(y+i));

 }//end of main
 // Fn definitions
 void FindReverse(int *x,int * y, int n)
 {  int i;
    for(i=0;i<n;i++)
      *(y+(n-1-i))=x[i];
 } // end of FindReverse
```

```
/*output
how many elements in your array?<n>5
 value for 1 element=10
 value for 2 element=20
 value for 3 element=30
 value for 4 element=40
 value for 5 element=50
 Given Array
10 20 30 40 50
 Reversed  Array
50 40 30 20 10 */
```

4. samp4.c Write a c program to find number of words, blank spaces, special characters, digits and vowels of a given text using pointers.

```
//samp4.c
#include<stdio.h>
#include<conio.h>
#include<string.h>
void main()//main function
{
int i,n,b=0,w=1,sp=0,d=0,v=0;
char *ch="Hello This is my Text (123)";
clrscr();//for clearing the screen
n=strlen(ch);
for(i=0;i<n;i++)
//counts words and blank spaces
if(*(ch+i)==' ')
{
        b++;
        w++;
}
//counts vowels
e                    l                    s                    e
if(*(ch+i)=='a'|*(ch+i)=='e'|*(ch+i)=='i'|*(ch+i)=='o'|*(ch+i)=='u'|*(ch+i)=='A'|*(ch+i)=='E'|*(ch+i)=='I'|*(ch+i)=='O'|*(ch+i)=='U')
        v++;
//counts digits
else if(*(ch+i)>=48 && *(ch+i)<=57)
        d++;
//counts special characters
else if(*(ch+i)=='!'||*(ch+i)=='.'||*(ch+i)=='('||*(ch+i)==')') sp++;
printf("\nThe given String is :  \n\n%s\n",ch);
printf("\nThe no. of Words is: %d",w);
printf("\nThe no. of Blank Spaces is: %d",b);
```

```
printf("\nThe no. of Digits is: %d",d);
printf("\nThe no. of Vowels is: %d",v);
printf("\nThe no. of Special Characters is: %d",sp);
getch();
}//end of main
/* OUTPUT:
The given String is :
Hello This is my Text (123)

The no. of Words is: 6
The no. of Blank Spaces is: 5
The no. of Digits is: 3
The no. of Vowels is: 5
The no. of Special Characters is: 2
*/
```

5. samp5.c. Write a c program to illustrate the use of pointers in arithmetic operations.

```
//(samp5.c)
#include<stdio.h>
void main()//main function
{
int *a,*b,*c;
clrscr();//function for clearing the screen
printf("\nEnter 2 numbers: ");
scanf("%d%d",a,b);
*c = *a + *b;
printf("\nThe Sum of the given no.s is: %d",*c);
*c = *a - *b;
printf("\nThe Difference of the given no.s is: %d",*c);
*c = *a * *b;
printf("\nThe Product of the given no.s is: %d",*c);
*c = *a / *b;
printf("\nThe Division of the given no.s is: %d",*c);
}//end of main
/*
OUTPUT:
Enter 2 numbers:
6 3

The Sum of the given no.s is: 9
The Difference of the given no.s is: 3
The Product of the given no.s is: 18
The Division of the given no.s is: 2
*/
```

6. samp6. Write a c program to compute the sum of all elements stored in an array using pointers.

```
// (samp6.c)Program to find the sum of elements of an array using pointers.
#include<stdio.h>
#include<conio.h>
#include<stdlib.h>
// Function prototypes
// a is one dimensional array of say 12 elements

int FindSum( int *a, int n);
void main()
 { int i, n, sum; // n= no of values in an array
   int *x; // x is a pointer to an array

   printf("how many elements in your array?<n>\n");
   scanf("%d",&n);

   // allocate dynamic memory space using malloc()
   x=(int*)malloc(n*sizeof(int));
   // read in the array
   for (i=0;i<n;i++)
     { printf("\n value for %d element=",i+1);
       scanf("%d",x+i); // scanf need address. we have
     }           // given address when we write x+i

   // call FindSum function
   sum=FindSum(x,n);//x is a pointer to array
   printf("\n sum of elements of given array = %d ",sum);
 }//end of main
// Fn definitions
int FindSum(int *x, int n)
{ int sum=0,i;

   for(i=0;i<n;i++)
      sum+=*(x+i);
  return sum;
 } // end of FindSum
/*
output
 how many elements in your array?<n>5
 value for 1 element=10
 value for 2 element=20
 value for 3 element=30
 value for 4 element=40
```

```
value for 5 element=50
sum of elements of given array = 150
*/
```

7. samp8.c Write a c function using pointers to exchange the values stored in the two locations in the memory.

```
//(samp8.c)
#include<stdio.h>
//function prototype
void Exchange(int *,int *);
void main()//main function
{
int *number1,*number2;
printf("\nEnter number1 :");
scanf("%d",number1);
printf("\nEnter number2 :");
scanf("%d",number2);
printf("\nNumbers entered are:\nnumber1=%d\nnumber2=%d", *number1, *number2);
Exchange(number1,number2);
printf("\nNumbers afterexchange:\nnumber1=%d\nnumber2=%d", *number1, *number2);
}//end of main
void Exchange(int *num1,int *num2)//function definition of Exchange
{
int temp;
temp=*num1;
*num1=*num2;
*num2=temp;
}//end of Exchange
/*
OUTPUT:
Enter number1 :4
Enter number2 :2
The numbers entered are:
number1=4
number2=2
The numbers after exchange:
number1=2
number2=4
*/
```

8. samp9.c Write a c program using pointers to determine the length of a character string.

```
//samp9.c
#include<stdio.h>
```

```
#include<string.h>
#include<stdlib.h>
// function prototype declarations
int Length(char *a);
void main()
{
        int count=0;
        int len; // length of the string

        char *x;// array of characters string
   x=(char*) malloc(10*sizeof(char));
        // get a character
        printf("\nEnter a string ");
        scanf("%s",x);
        len=Length(x);
        // Now display the string you have just read
        printf("\n String inputted : %s ", x);
        printf("\n length of  the string : %d", len);

}//end of main

int Length(char *a)
{  int len=0,count=0;
   while (a[count++]!='\0')
          len++;
   return len;
}

 /*OUTPUT:
Enter a string (to stop press enter)
education
String inputted : education
length of  the string *x : 9
```

9. addsum.Write a c program that uses a pointer as a function argument.

*/*In this program we will add three numbers in a function and returns sum as a pointer to the calling function*
AddSum.c**/*

```
#include<stdio.h>
#include<conio.h>
```

```
void AddSum( float * x,float *y, float * z,float *total);
void main()
 {
   float x=100,y=200,z=300;
   float total;
    AddSum( &x,&y,&z,&total);
   printf("\n Sum of three numbers x,y,and z :\n");
  printf("%5.2f\t%5.2f\t%5.2f = %5.2f\n", x,y,z,total);
}//end of program

void AddSum(float * x,float *y, float * z,float *total)

{ *total=(*x)+(*y)+(*z);
}

/*output
 Sum of three numbers x,y,and z :
100.00  200.00  300.00 = 600.00
Press any key to continue*/
```

10. samp11.c Write a C program to sort names in alphabetical order using a pointer.

```
//samp11.c
#include<stdio.h>
#include<string.h>
#include<stdlib.h>
//fn prototype declarations
void charraysort(char *x[],int n);
void main()
{          int count = 0,n=0;
           int i;
           char *stg[10];
           // read in the string
   stg[count]=(char*)malloc(10*sizeof(char));
           printf("\n Enter string<END> to stop>: ");
           scanf("%s",stg[count]);
           while((strcmp(stg[count],"END")!=0))
              {    count++;
                   stg[count]=(char*)malloc(10*sizeof(char));
                   printf("\n Enter string<END> to stop>: ");
                   scanf("%s",stg[count]);
                      }
   charraysort(stg,count);
```

```
        printf("\n Sorted strings\n");
       for( i=0;i<count;i++)
            puts(stg[i]);
} // end of main
// fun definition
void charraysort( char *x[10],int n)
{   char temp[10];
        int i,j;
        for (i=0;i<n-1;i++)
        {
          for (j=i+1;j<n;j++)
           {
                if(strcmp(*(x+i),*(x+j))>0)
                {        // swap
                         strcpy(temp,*(x+j));
        strcpy(*(x+j),*(x+i));
                         strcpy(*(x+i),temp);
                }
           }
        }
}// end of charraysort()

/*output
 Enter string<END> to stop>: ramesh
 Enter string<END> to stop>: gautam
 Enter string<END> to stop>: usha
 Enter string<END> to stop>: anand
 Enter string<END> to stop>: thunder
 Enter string<END> to stop>: END
 Sorted strings
anand
gautam
ramesh
thunder
usha
*/
```

ASSIGNMENT PROBLEMS

1 Write a program to find out sum of three numbers passed as pointers to a function. Function should return a pointer for the answer.
2. Write a c program to determine determinant of a matrix using pointers and dynamic memory allocations to matrix variables.
3. Write a c code to determine if the given matrix of order m x n is singular or not.
4 Write a c code to determine if the given matrix of order m is symmetric or not.
5. Write a c program using pointers to achieve basic calculator functions like +,-,*, and / operations..

Solutions to Objective Questions

1) void pointer	2) dynamic allocation	3) heap	4) void *
5) char,int	6) &	7) TRUE	8) TRUE
9) TRUE	10) d	11) b	12) a
13) FALSE	14) d	15) d	16) b

CHAPTER

7 STRUCTURES AND UNIONS

Arrays are useful for storing data of same type for example. int or char. But in real life you will face the need to store different data types in an array. Student record in a college contains information of several types of data. Consider the following example, where in a college maintains student details as records in a file;

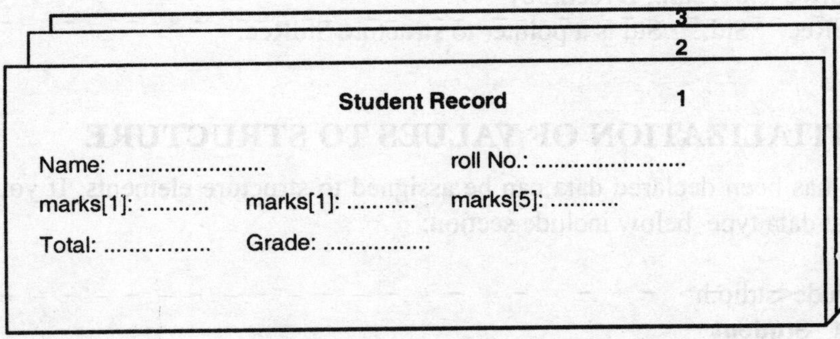

■■■ 7.1 LET US DECLARE & DEFINE A STRUCTURE IN C LANGUAGE FOR THE ABOVE RECORD IN A PHYSICAL FILE

```
struct   Student
{   char  name[20]; // array of name with  space for 20 characters
        int rollNo;
        float marks[5]; //marks as array for 5 subjects
        float total;
        char grade;
   };
typedef struct  Student  StdRec;  // StdRec typecasted to Student  structure
  StdRec  Std[5];  // array of structre of type StdRec.
```

An example of structure within a structure is given below

```
struct ToDate
{ int dd;
  int mm;
  int yy;
};
typedef struct ToDate date;
struct Student
 { char name[20]; // array of name with space for 20 characters
       int rollNo;
       float marks[5]; //marks as array for 5 subjects
       float total;
       char grade;
         date dt;   //structure with in a structure
 };
 typedef struct Student StdRec;
```

We can declare several variables of type StdRec structure.

```
Ex: StdRec std1, std2, BTech[50]
    StdRec *Std; // Std is a pointer to structure StdRec.
```

7.2 INITIALIZATION OF VALUES TO STRUCTURE

Once a structure has been declared data can be assigned to structure elements. If you have declared structure as global data type below include section:

```
#include<stdio.h>
struct Student
{ char name[20]; // array of name with space for 20 characters
     int rollNo;
     float marks[5]; //marks as array for 5 subjects
 };
 typedef stru Student stdrec;
 stdrec Std; //declare one record Std
```

Then in void main( ) you can assign values

```
Std = {'Govind',5050,78,95};
```

If you have declared structre with in main then you have to use static.

```
static Std= {'Govind',5050,78,95};
```

If you have declared an array of structure as stdrec Std[3]

```
Std[3]={
            {'Govind',5050,78,95},
```

```
                {'Anand',6060,94,88}'
            {'Gautam'7070,98,84}
            };
```

■■■ 7.3 FIRST PROBLEM USING STRUCTURE

Declare a structure of student as discussed above. Let your structure declare an array of marks for three subjects and total. Calculate and print student wise total for three students.

/* arrays with in a structure. You will see how to initialize data and calculate and print student wise totals*/

Example 7.1

```
//struct1.c
#include<stdio.h>
#include<stdlib.h>
// struct declaration
struct Employee
 {
 float credits[3]; // array of credits for 3 items
                         //basic,da,hra etc
 float total;
 };
 typedef struct Employee emprec;
 void main()
 {
 int i,j;
 // structure initialization
 emprec  Emp[3] ={
                         {6000.0,700.0,800.0,0.0},
                         {8000.0,980.0,650.0,0.0},
                         {9800.0,760.0,660.0,0.0}
                    };// total of 9 credits(3Employees x 3)

 for(i=0;i<3;i++)
  {
    for(j=0;j<3;j++)
    // we are totaling credits of i th employee
    Emp[i].total+=Emp[i].credits[j];
  }

  printf("Employee    Total \n\n");
```

```
        for(i=0;i<3;i++)
        printf("Employee[%d] %5.1f\n",i+1,Emp[i].total);
    }// end of main
    /*
    OUTPUT:
    Employee    Total
    Employee[1] 7500.0
    Employee[2] 9630.0
    Employee[3] 11220.0
    */
```

7.4 INPUT AND OUTPUT USING STRUCTURES

In the following example we will consider a structure called Account. We will write a program to read data of specified number of account holders data from key board and record them in to structure called account

Example 7.2 struct2.c to read data of specified number of account holders data from key board and record them in to structure called account

```
#include<stdio.h>
#include<stdlib.h>

// fn decl
void ReadInput(int n);
void WriteOutput(int n);
// struct declaration
struct date
{
 int dd;
 int mm;
 int yy;
};
struct Account
{
 int accNo;
 char accType;
 char name[20];
 float bal;
 struct date pdate; // date of payment
};
struct Account cust[100];// declare an array of 100 customers

void main()
{
 int n,i;
```

```
   printf("enter no of customers\n");
  scanf("%d",&n);
  // read data into structure
  for (i=0;i<n;i++)
   ReadInput(i);
  //write output
  for (i=0;i<n;i++)
   WriteOutput(i);
 }// end of main
 // fn definitions
 void ReadInput(int i)
 {
   float bal;
   printf("\n enter data for %d account holder",i+1);
   printf("\nEnter <name>:");scanf("%s",cust[i].name);
   printf("\nEnter <accNo>:");scanf("%d",&cust[i].accNo);
   printf("\nEnter <accType>:");scanf(" %c",&cust[i].accType);
   printf("\nEnter <balance>:");scanf("%f",&bal);cust[i].bal=bal;
   printf("\nEnter pdate<dd mm yy>:");
   scanf("%d%d%d",&cust[i].pdate.dd,&cust[i].pdate.mm,&cust[i].pdate.yy);
   printf("\n— — — — — — — — — — — — —");
}//end of ReadInput
void WriteOutput(int i)
{  printf("\n————————————");
   printf("\nname:");printf("%s",cust[i].name);
   printf("\naccNo:");printf("%d",cust[i].accNo);
   printf("\naccType:");printf("%c",cust[i].accType);
   printf("\nbalance:");printf("%f",cust[i].bal);
   printf("\npdate<ddmmyy>:");
   printf("%d/%d/%d",cust[i].pdate.dd,cust[i].pdate.mm,cust[i].pdate.yy);
}//end of WriteOutput

/*
OUTPUT:

enter no of customers
2
enter data for 1 account holder
Enter <name>: ram
Enter <accNo>: 1001
Enter<accType>: s
Enter <balance>: 3589.50
Enter pdate<dd mm yy>: 17 2 2003
— — — — — — — — — — — — —
```

```
enter data for 1 account holder
Enter <name>: kiran
Enter <accNo>: 1002
Enter<accType>: s
Enter <balance>: 2000
Enter pdate<dd mm yy>: 24 5 2002

-----------------------------------------
-----------------------------------------

name:ram
accNo:1001
accType:s
balance:3589.500000
pdate<ddmmyy>:17/2/2003
-----------------------------------------
name:kiran
accNo:1002
accType:s
balance:2000.000000
pdate<ddmmyy>:24/5/2002

*/
```

■■■ 7.5 PASSING OF STRUCTURE ELEMENTS AS ARGUMENTS TO A FUNCTION

In the following example, we will demonstrate the passing of arguments to a function. These arguments are members of structure.

Example 7.3 struct3.c Passing of members of structure as arguments to a function.

```
#include<stdio.h>
#define currentyear 2000
float Increment(float sal,int year,float inc);

typedef struct
   { int day;
     int month;
     int year;
   }date;
typedef struct
   { char name[20];
```

```
    date bdate;
    float sal;
   }emprec ;

void main()
{  float x=1000.00;
   emprec emp={"govind",10,11,54,6000.00};
   printf("\n name %s",emp.name);
   printf("\n sal prior increment %6.2f",emp.sal);
    emp.sal=Increment(emp.sal,1940,x);
   printf("\n sal after increment %6.2f",emp.sal);
  } // end of main

 float Increment(float sal,int year, float inc)
 {
   if ((currentyear-year)>40)
       sal+=inc;
  else
       sal+=500.00;
   return sal;
 }
/*
OUTPUT:
name govind
sal prior increment 6000.00
sal after increment 7000.00
```

7.6 PASS A STRUCTURE AS AN ARGUMENT TO A FUNCTION

In our next example you will learn how to pass a structure as an argument to a function. We will write a program to forward structure called account to a function. Update receives structure as an argument and returns structure to main function

Example 7.4 struct4.c Pass a structure as an argument to a function.

```
#include<stdio.h>
#include<stdlib.h>
// struct declaration
struct date
{
 int dd;
```

```
 int mm;
 int yy;
};
struct Account
{
 int accNo;
 char accType;
 char name[20];
 float bal;
 struct date pdate;  // date of payment
};

typedef struct Account acct;

// fn decl
acct ReadInput(acct cust);
acct Update(acct cust);
void WriteOutput(acct cust);

void main()
{
 acct cust;  // create an instance of structure acct

 // read data into structure by passing structure to ReadInput()
 // that returns structure filled with data
   cust=ReadInput(cust);
 // Update status of account
   cust=Update(cust);
 //write output
    WriteOutput(cust);
 }// end of main
// fn defenitions
acct ReadInput(acct cust)
{  printf("\n enter data for  account holder");
   printf("\nEnter <name>:");scanf("%s",cust.name);
   printf("\nEnter <accNo>:");scanf("%d",&cust.accNo);
   printf("\nEnter <accType>:");scanf(" %c",&cust.accType);
   printf("\nEnter <balance>:");scanf("%f",&cust.bal);
   printf("\nEnter pdate<dd mm yy>:");
   scanf("%d%d%d",&cust.pdate.dd,&cust.pdate.mm,&cust.pdate.yy);
   printf("\n——————————————————————");
   return cust;
}
```

```
void WriteOutput(acct cust)
{ printf("\n——————————————————");
  printf("\nname:");printf("%s",cust.name);
  printf("\naccNo:");printf("%d",cust.accNo);
  printf("\naccType:");printf("%c",cust.accType);
  printf("\nbalance:");printf("%g",cust.bal);
  printf("\npdate<ddmmyy>:");
  printf("%d-%d-%d",cust.pdate.dd,cust.pdate.mm,cust.pdate.yy);
}
acct Update(acct cust)
{
 //if the balance is more than 1000.00 set accType as current(c)
 // and add 10% of balance to balance amount as Interest. Else
 //classify the account as inactive(I)
 if(cust.bal>=1000.00)
  {
   cust.bal+=cust.bal*0.1;
   cust.accType='C';
  }
 else
   cust.accType='I';
 return cust;
}
/*
OUTPUT:

enter data for account holder
Enter <name>: ram
Enter <accNo>: 1001
Enter<accType>: C
Enter <balance>: 20000
Enter pdate<dd mm yy>: 17 2 2003
——————————————————
——————————————————

name:ram
accNo:1001
accType:C
balance:22000
pdate<ddmmyy>:17-2-2003
*/
```

7.7 PASS A POINTER TO A STRUCTURE AS AN ARGUMENT TO A FUNCTION.

Now let us learn how to pass a pointer to a structure as an argument. This is important because structure contains large amount of data and it is elegant and efficient to pass as pointer.

Example 7.5struct5.c. Pass a pointer to a structure as an argument to a function.

```
#include<stdio.h>
#include<stdlib.h>
// struct declaration
struct date
{
 int dd;
 int mm;
 int yy;
};
struct Account
{
  int accNo;
  char accType;
  char name[20];
  float bal;
  struct date pdate;  // date of payment
};

typedef struct Account acct;

// fn decl
void ReadInput(acct *cust);
void Update(acct *cust);
void WriteOutput(acct *cust);

void main()
{
 acct cust;  // create an instance of structure acct
 // read data into structure by passing a pointer to structure
 //to ReadInput().
   ReadInput(&cust);
 // Update status of account
   Update(&cust);
 //write output
   WriteOutput(&cust);
```

```
 getch();
}// end of main
// fn defenitions
void ReadInput(acct *cust)
{  float bal;
  printf("\n enter data for  account holder");
  printf("\nEnter <name>:");scanf("%s",cust->name);
  printf("\nEnter <accNo>:");scanf("%d",&cust->accNo);
  printf("\nEnter <accType>:");scanf(" %c",&cust->accType);
  printf("\nEnter <balance>:");scanf("%f",&bal);cust->bal=bal;
  printf("\nEnter pdate<dd mm yy>:");
  scanf("%d%d%d",&cust->pdate.dd,&cust->pdate.mm,&cust->pdate.yy);
  printf("\n————————————————");

}
 void WriteOutput(acct *cust)
{  printf("\n————————————————————");
  printf("\nname:");printf("%s",cust->name);
  printf("\naccNo:");printf("%d",cust->accNo);
  printf("\naccType:");printf("%c",cust->accType);
  printf("\nbalance:");printf("%g",cust->bal);
  printf("\npdate<ddmmyy>:");
  printf("%d-%d-%d",cust->pdate.dd,cust->pdate.mm,cust->pdate.yy);
}

void Update(acct *cust)
{
 //if the balance is more than 1000.00 set accType as current(c)
 // and add 10% of balance to balance amount as Interst. Else
 //classify the account as inactive(I)
 if(cust->bal>=1000.00)
  {
   cust->bal+=cust->bal*0.1;
   cust->accType='C';
  }
 else
   cust->accType='I';

 }
/*OUTPUT:
enter data for account holder
Enter <name>: ram
Enter <accNo>: 1001
```

```
Enter<accType>: C
Enter <balance>: 20000
Enter pdate<dd mm yy>: 17 2 2003
------------------------------------------
------------------------------------------
name:ram
accNo:1001
accType:C
balance:22000
pdate<ddmmyy>:17-2-2003*/
```

7.8 CREATE A POINTER TO A STRUCTURE

In the next program you will learn to create a pointer to structure. For example you can declare a pointer to structure as

```
            struct Account
            { int accNo;
    char accType;
    char name[20];
    float bal;
  };
typedef struct Account acct;
        acct    cust , * ptr ;   // ptr is a pointer to structure
```

Once created you can refer to variables in a structure

```
    cust. name    or    ptr -> name
    cust. acctype or    ptr -> acctype.
```

We will write a program to forward *pointer to structure* to a function. ReadInput and WriteOutput & Update receives pointer to structure as an argument..

Example 7.6 struct6.c to create a pointer to structure

```
//struct6.c

#include<stdio.h>
#include<stdlib.h>
// struct declaration
struct date
{
 int dd;
```

```
 int mm;
 int yy;
};
struct Account
{
 int accNo;
 char accType;
 char name[20];
 float bal;
 struct date pdate;
};
typedef struct Account acct;
acct cust,*ptr; // ptr is a pointer to structure
// fn decl
void ReadInput(acct *cust); // cust is a pointer to structure
void Update(acct *cust);
void WriteOutput(acct *cust);

void main()
{
 acct cust;  // create an instance of structure acct
  // read data into structure by passing a pointer to structure
 //to ReadInput().
  ReadInput(&cust); //&cust would imply address of cust i.e pointer
 // Update status of account
  Update(&cust); // we are again passing pointer
 //write output
  WriteOutput(&cust);
  }// end of main
// fn defenitions
void ReadInput(acct *cust)
{  float bal;
  printf("\n enter data for  account holder");
  printf("\nEnter <name>:");scanf("%s",cust->name);
  printf("\nEnter <accNo>:");scanf("%d",&cust->accNo);
  printf("\nEnter <accType>:");cust->accType=getche();
  printf("\nEnter <balance>:");scanf("%f",&bal);cust->bal=bal;
  printf("\nEnter pdate<dd mm yy>:");
  scanf("%d%d%d",&cust->pdate.dd,&cust->pdate.mm,&cust->pdate.yy);
  printf("\n——————————————————————");

}
```

```
void WriteOutput(acct *cust)
{ printf("\n--------------------------------");
  printf("\nname:");printf("%s",cust->name);
  printf("\naccNo:");printf("%d",cust->accNo);
  printf("\naccType:");printf("%c",cust->accType);
  printf("\nbalance:");printf("%g",cust->bal);
  printf("\npdate<ddmmyy>:");
  printf("%d-%d-%d",cust->pdate.dd,cust->pdate.mm,cust->pdate.yy);
}

void Update(acct *cust)
{
 //if the balance is more than 1000.00 set accType as current(c)
 // and add 10% of balance to balance amount as Interst. Else
 //classify the account as inactive(I)
 if(cust->bal>=1000.00)
  {
   cust->bal+=cust->bal*0.1;
   cust->accType='C';
  }
 else
   cust->accType='I';

}
/*
OUTPUT:

enter data for account holder
Enter <name>: ram
Enter <accNo>: 1001
Enter<accType>: C
Enter <balance>: 20000
Enter pdate<dd mm yy>: 17 2 2003
______________________________
output
______________________________
name:ram
naccNo:1001
accType:C
balance:22000
pdate<ddmmyy>:17-2-2003*/
```

7.9 PASSING ARRAY OF STRUCTURES TO A FUNCTION

In this program you will learn how to dispatch array of structures to a function ReadInput().Function FindMax() receives array of structures but returns a pointer to structure instance which has maximum balance. WriteOutput takes an instance of array of structure and prints the result. Function FindMax returns a pointer to structure

Example 7.7 struct7.c. Passing array of structures to a function

```
#include<stdio.h>
#include<stdlib.h>
#define MAX 3
// struct declaration
struct Account
{
 int accNo;
 char name[20];
 float bal;
};
typedef struct Account acct;

// fn decl
void ReadInput(acct cust[],int n);
acct * FindMax(acct cust[],int n); // fn returns a pointer
void WriteOutput(acct *cust);// writes account details of largest account

void main()
{  int n;
  // create an instance of structure acct
 acct *cust;
 acct *max; // hold details of largest account
  clrscr();
 // read data into structure by passing a pointer to structure
 //to ReadInput().
 printf("enter no of account holders<n>\n");
 scanf("%d",&n);
 cust=(acct*)malloc(n*sizeof(acct));
 ReadInput(cust,n);  // observe cust is a pointer
 // Find account holder whose balance is maximum
 max=FindMax(cust,n); // cust is a pointer
 //write output
 WriteOutput(max); // max is a pointer
}// end of main
// fn defenitions
```

```
void ReadInput(acct cust[],int n)
{ int i;
  float bal;
  for(i=0;i<n;i++)
  {printf("\n enter data for  customer[%d]",i+1);
   printf("\nEnter <name>:");scanf("%s",cust[i].name);
   printf("\nEnter <accNo>:");scanf("%d",&cust[i].accNo);
   printf("\nEnter <balance>:");scanf("%f",&bal);cust[i].bal=bal;
   printf("\n——————————————————————");
  }
}
 void WriteOutput(acct *cust)
{  printf("\nDetails of the account with maximum balance ");
   printf("\nname:");printf("%s",cust->name);
   printf("\naccNo:");printf("%d",cust->accNo);
   printf("\nbalance:");printf("%g",cust->bal);

}

acct * FindMax(acct cust[],int n)
{ // find index of customer whose balance is maximum
  int max=cust[0].bal;
  int i,j=0;

  for(i=1;i<n;i++)
  {
   if (max<cust[i].bal)
   {
    max=cust[i].bal;
    j=i;  // store the index
   }
  }
  // rerurn the pointer to account with max balance
  return &cust[j];
}
/*
OUTPUT:

enter no of account holders<n>
3
enter data for  customer[1]
Enter <name>:ram
Enter <accNo>:1001
Enter <balance>:2000
——————————————————————
```

```
enter data for  customer[2]
Enter <name>:suresh
Enter <accNo>: 1003
Enter <balance>:1000
---------------------------------
enter data for  customer[3]
Enter <name>:srinu
Enter <accNo>:1002
Enter <balance>:3000
---------------------------------
Details of the account with maximum balance
name:srinu
accNo:1002
alance:3000
*/
```

7.10 SORTING AN ARRAY OF STRUCTURES

In this program you will learn how to dispatch array of structures to a function ReadInput().Function SortStru() receives array of structures sort the elements by balance.
WriteOutput takes array of structure and prints the result.

Example 7.8 struct8.c. Sorting an array of structures

```
#include<stdio.h>
#include<stdlib.h>
#define MAX 3
struct Account
{
 int accNo;
 char name[20];
 float bal;
};
typedef struct Account acct;

// fn decl
void ReadInput(acct cust[],int n);
void SortStru(acct cust[],int n);
void WriteOutput(acct cust[],int n);// writes account details of largest account

void main()
{  int n;
 // create an instance of structure acct
```

```
acct *cust;
clrscr();
// read data into structure by passing a pointer to structure
//to ReadInput().
printf("enter no of account holders<n>\n");
scanf("%d",&n);
cust=(acct*)malloc(n*sizeof(acct));
ReadInput(cust,n); //cust is a pointer
// Sort array of structures based on balance
SortStru(cust,n);
//write output
WriteOutput(cust,n);
  getch();
}// end of main
// fn defenitions

void ReadInput(acct cust[],int n)
{ int i;
 float bal;
 for(i=0;i<n;i++)
 {printf("\n enter data for  customer[%d]",i+1);
  printf("\nEnter <name>:");scanf("%s",cust[i].name);
  printf("\nEnter <accNo>:");scanf("%d",&cust[i].accNo);
  printf("\nEnter <balance>:");scanf("%f",&bal);cust[i].bal=bal;
  printf("\n——————————————————————");
 }
}
void WriteOutput(acct cust[],int n)
{  int i;
  printf("\nDetails of the account sorted on balance ");
  for(i=0;i<n;i++)
  { printf("\n customer[%d]",i+1);
    printf("\nname:");printf("%s",cust[i].name);
    printf("\naccNo:");printf("%d",cust[i].accNo);
    printf("\nbalance:");printf("%g",cust[i].bal);
    printf("\n——————————————————————————");
  }
}

void  SortStru(acct cust[],int n)
{
 acct temp;
 int i,j;
```

```
for(i=0;i<n-1;i++)
 {
  for(j=i+1;j<n;j++)
  {
   if (cust[i].bal<cust[j].bal)
    { // swap cust[i] and cust[j]
       temp=cust[i];cust[i]=cust[j];cust[j]=temp;
    }
  }
 }
}
/*
OUTPUT:

enter no of account holders<n>
3
enter data for  customer[1]
Enter <name>:ram
Enter <accNo>:1001
Enter <balance>:2000
______________________________
enter data for  customer[2]
Enter <name>:suresh
Enter <accNo>: 1003
Enter <balance>:1000
______________________________
enter data for  customer[3]
Enter <name>:srinu
Enter <accNo>:1002
Enter <balance>:3000
______________________________
Details of the account sorted on balance
customer[1]
nname:srinu
naccNo:1002
balance:3000
______________________________
customer[2]
nname:ram
naccNo:1001
balance:2000
______________________________
customer[3]
nname:suresh
naccNo:1003
balance:1000 */
```

7.11 UNIONS

Unions are useful when memory conservation is the criteria. Union, like structure holds data types like *int, char, float etc.* However , the major difference is that union holds only one data object at a time. Union calculates which of its declarations require maximum storage requirements and allocates memory space accordingly. It means that all the variables declared in a Union share the same memory location.

Compiler handles different memory requirements of various data types automatically but it is users responsibility to keep track of which data type is stored at a particular instant of time. Otherwise garbage result. The general syntax of Union is

```
Storage class union  nametag
{
     data member 1;
          data member 2;
} var1, var2, var3;
```

Let us declare a union called details to make the working clear.

```
union details
{
 char country[12];
 float networth;
}indian, nri;
```

We have declared two variables resident and nri. They are of type details. Each of the variable resident and nri can represent either country or networth at any one particular instant of time. The country[25] requires more storage slot 25 bytes than a float value. Therefore union allocates a block memory space to each of the variable declared in the union. The union can be declared with in a structure. **we will write a program to declare a union within a structure.**

Note that we have to keep track of the data variable that is active in the memory. For example after ReadInput() function, the field, cust.id.accNo is active and similarly after update() again cust.id.accNo is active. That is why we could print the same in WriteOuntput2() function. If you try to print accNO it would print garbage. Try it out.

Methods of accessing union members are same as that of structure. As a matter of fact every thing we discussed about structures hold good for unions as well.

In the next example, we will demonstrate the use of unions.

Example 7.9 union1.c To demonstrate the use of unions.

```
#include<stdio.h>
// union declaration
union details
{
  int accNo;
  char accType;
};
//struct hold union
struct Account
{ char name[20];
  float bal;
  union details id;
};
typedef struct Account acct;
// fn decl
acct ReadInput(acct cust);
void WriteOutput1(acct cust);
acct Update(acct cust);
void WriteOutput2(acct cust);

void main()
{
  acct cust;  // create an instance of structure acct

 // read data into structure by passing structure to ReadInput()
 // that returns structure filled with data
  cust=ReadInput(cust);
 // after ReadInput cust.id.accNo is active
  WriteOutput1(cust);
 // Update status of account
  cust=Update(cust);
 //After Update() function only cust.id.accType is active.
 //write output void WriteOutput2(acct cust) prints only cust.id.accType.
  WriteOutput2(cust);
  getch();
}// end of main
// fn defenitions

acct ReadInput(acct cust)
{  printf("\n enter data for  account holder");
  printf("\nEnter <name>:");scanf("%s",cust.name);
```

```
   printf("\nEnter <balance>:");scanf("%f",&cust.bal);
   printf("\nEnter <accNo>:");scanf("%d",&cust.id.accNo);
  printf("\n————————————————————");
  return cust;
}
 void WriteOutput1(acct cust)
{  printf("\noutput after calling ReadInput()");
  printf("\n\nNow cust.id.accNo is active.....");
  printf("\noutput<name,cust.id.accN0,cust.bal>...");
  printf("\n\nname:");printf("%s",cust.name);
  printf("\naccNo:");printf("%d",cust.id.accNo);
  printf("\nbalance:");printf("%g",cust.bal);
}
void WriteOutput2(acct cust)
{  printf("\n\noutput after calling Update()");
  printf("\n\nNow cust.id.accType is active.....");
  // after update() only cust.id.accType is active. Next statement is correct
  printf("\naccType:");printf("%c",cust.id.accType);
  // Next statement prints garbage as cust.id.accNo is not active after updtae()
  printf("\n<accNo> is not active. Hence garbage out");printf("%d",cust.id.accNo);
 }
acct Update(acct cust)
{
 //if the balance is more than 1000.00 add 10% of balance
 //to balance amount as Interst. Else add 20 % to balance
 if(cust.bal>=1000.00)
  {
   cust.bal+=cust.bal*0.1;
   cust.id.accType='C';
  }
 else
  {
   cust.bal+=cust.bal*0.2;
   cust.id.accType='D';
  }
 return cust;
}
/*output

 enter data for  account holder
Enter <name>:ramesh

Enter <balance>:2000.00

Enter <accNo>:5050

————————————————————
```

output after calling ReadInput()

Now cust.id.accNo is active.....
output<name,cust.id.accN0,cust.bal>...

name:ramesh
accNo:5050
balance:2000

output after calling Update()

Now cust.id.accType is active.....
accType:C
<accNo> is not active. Hence garbage out4931*/

OBJECTIVE QUESTION

1. If we declare the structure inside main, then we have to specify the storage class as static True/Fale
2. `Structures are passed to functions only by pass by reference method True/False
3. A structure can be declared with in another structure True/False
4. If function is defined as void ReadInput(acct *cust), the while passing arguments in main program, we would write
   a) ReadInput(cust); b) ReadInput(&cust);
   c) ReadInput(*cust); d) ReadInput(**cust);
5 struct Account

```
{ int accNo;
  char accType;
  char name[20];
  float bal;
};
typedef struct Account acct;
  acct  cust , * ptr ;  // ptr is a pointer to structure
```

for referring to name using pointer ptr, we would write
   a) ptr.name b) ptr->name
   c) ptr.name[20] d) ptr->name[20]

6 In structure definition

```
struct Account
    { int accNo;
    };
typedef struct Account acct;
    acct   cust , * ptr ;   // ptr is a pointer to structure
```

for referring to accNo using pointer reference to structure cust, we would write

a) cust.name   b) cust->name
c) cust.name[20]   d) cust->name[20]

7. Union can hold as many data objects at a time as declared in union   True/false
8. In union the variable share the memory space   True/false
9. Structure contains similar data types   True/false
10. A variable inside a function is defined as an object of structure. Then the structure is required to be defined as
    a) external b) static
    c) stack d) heap

REVIEW QUESTIONS

1. *What is a structure? Describe the governing rules for declaring a structure.*
2. *When are array of structures used ? Declare a variable as array of structures and initialize it?*
3. *List out the similarities and differences between structures and unions.*
4. *What is the general format of a union ? Declare a union and assign values to it. Explain the process of accessing the union members.*
5. *What is the structure keyword? Explain the use of dot operator? Give an example for each.*
6. *How are structure elements accessed using pointer ? Which operator is used? Give an example.*
7. *Explain the method of passing structures as arguments in functions.*
8. *What is structure with in structure ? Give an example for it.*

SOLVED PROBLEMS

1. Write a program to read data into a structure using. operator and print the data using indirection operator.

```
//indirection.c to read data into a structure using. operator and print the data using //indirection operator.
#include<stdio.h>

struct account
{char name[10];
```

```
 char acctype[8];
 int accno;
 float balance;
};
typedef struct account acc;

void main()
{
 acc cust,*p;
 p=&cust;
   printf("\nEnter name:");
        scanf("%s",cust.name);
        printf("Enter account number:");
        scanf("%d",&cust.accno);
        printf("Enter account type:");
        scanf("%s",cust.acctype);
        printf("Enter Balnce:");
        scanf("%f",&cust.balance);

   printf("\nName=%s\tAccountNo=%d\tAccount Type=%s",p->name,cust.accno,p->acctype);
   printf("\nBalane=%.2f",p->balance);
}
/*Output:
Enter name:Shankar
Enter account number:1234
Enter account type:Savings
Enter Balnce:340000

Name=Shankar    AccountNo=1234  Account Type=Savings
Balance=340000.00 */
```

2 Write a program to compute tax payable by a person as per following chart

upto 100000	nil
1,00001 to 150000	10% of amount that exceeds 100000
1,50001 to 300000	20% of amount that exceeds 150000
>300000	30 % of amount that exceeds 300000

```
//taxstruct.c
#include<stdio.h>

struct tax{
 char name[10];
 float salary;
 float tax;
};
```

```
typedef struct tax account;
account acc[3]; //create 3 instances of the above structure

void computetax();

void main()
{
  int i;
  for(i=0;i<3;i++)
  {
    printf("\nEnter name:");
   scanf("%s",acc[i].name);
   printf("\nEnter yearly salary:");
          scanf("%f",&acc[i].salary);
  }

 computetax();
 for(i=0;i<3;i++)
  printf("\nTax to be paid by %s=%.2f",acc[i].name,acc[i].tax);
}

void computetax()
{
 int i;
 for(i=0;i<3;i++)
 {
   if(acc[i].salary<=100000)
                    acc[i].tax=0;
          else
          if(acc[i].salary>100000 && acc[i].salary<=150000)
      acc[i].tax=acc[i].salary*10/100;
          else
          if(acc[i].salary>150000 && acc[i].salary<=300000)
      acc[i].tax=acc[i].salary*20/100;
          else
      acc[i].tax=acc[i].salary*30/100;
 }//end of for
}

/*Output:
Enter name:Rahul
Enter yearly salary:350000

Enter name:Ravi
Enter yearly salary:96000
```

Enter name:Srinivas
Enter yearly salary:165000

Tax to be paid by Rahul=105000.00
Tax to be paid by Ravi=0.00
Tax to be paid by Srinivas=33000.00*/

ASSIGNMENT QUESTIONS

1 Write a c program to calculate student-wise total for three students using an array of structures.

2 Write a c program to add the two given complex numbers. Define function add a print with pointers as arguments. The complex number is a structure object with real and image fields.

3 Write a C program to accept records of different states using array of structures.
The structure should contain char state, population, literary rate, and income.
Display the state whose literary rate is highest and whose income is highest.

4. The annual examination is conducted for 50 students for three subjects. Write a program to read the data and determine the following:

a. Total marks obtained by each student.

b. The highest marks in each subject and the roll no of the student who secured it.

c. The student who obtained the highest total marks.

5. Write a C program to illustrate the comparison of structure variables.

6. Define a structure to represent a data. Use your structure that accepts two different dates in the format mm dd of the same year. And do the following:

7. Write a C program to display the month names of both dates. Write a program to use structure within union. Display the contents of structure elements.

8. Write a C program to illustrate the method of sending an entire structure as a parameter to a function.

9. Write a C program to prepare marks memo of a class of students using structures.

10. Write a C program to print maximum marks in each subject along with the name of the student by using structures. Take 3 subjects and 3 student records.

11. Write a program to read n records of students and find out how many of them have passed. The fields are students roll-no, name, mark and Result. Evaluate the result as follows

If marks > 35 then
Result = "pass"
Else
Result="fail".

12 Write a C program to illustrate the concept of structure within structure.

You will do well to understand the concepts and acquire the necessary programming skills. We would like to remind the reader that any thing in ***italics in this text*** means it has been asked in the past by University

Solutions to Objective Questions

1) true 2) false 3) True 4) b 5) b 6) a 7) False
8) True 9) True 10) a

CHAPTER 8

FILES

8.1 INTRODUCTION TO FILES

We would come across files everywhere we go. For example, college holds a file for each of their students. Similarly municipality, holds file, containing details of taxes to be paid by citizens. Indeed files are so common to our lives, C language and other languages support files.

What is a file ?: File is collection of records. Fig. 8.1 shows a file named student.dat with **n** records belonging to n number of students.

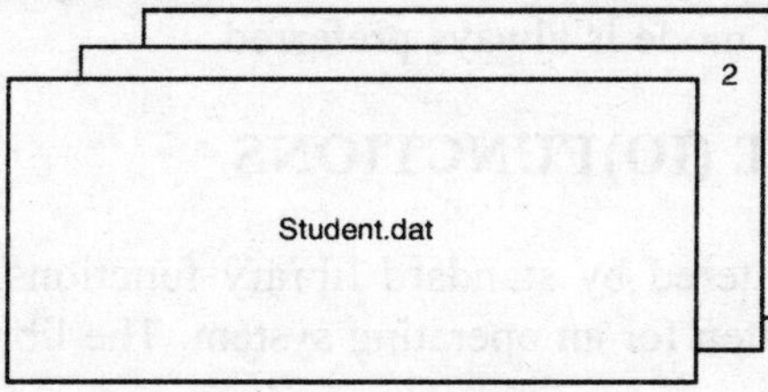

Fig. 8.1

A record, in a physical file is a data sheet, where in details of a student are recorded. There will be as many records as there are students. In a c file too, there will be records, again one each for a student. Fig. 8.2 shows a record.

A record in turn contains fields. Fig. 8.2 shows a record and fields contained therein.

Student Record **1**

Name:…………… rollNo:………..
marks[1]:… marks[1]:… …..marks[5]:…
Total:……. Grade:…….

```
char  name[20]; // array of name with  space for 20 characters
int rollNo;
float marks[5]; //marks as array for 5 subjects
 float total;
 char grade;
```

Fig. 8.2 Record and fields

8.2 FILE TYPES

Files can be classified based on the way they are accessed from the memory as

Sequential File : All records are stored sequentially as they are entered. This type of file is best suited, when we have to access all the records in sequence one after the other. Marks processing of a class is an example.

Random Acces File : In this mode of access, a record is accessed using index maintained for this purpose. Its like going to chapter and with in the chapter a point of interest, using Index provide at the beginning of the book.

Direct Access File : In this mode, the records are stored based on their relative position with respect to first record. For example, record 50 will be 50 lengths away from the address of record 1. The main advantage of this mode of access is there is no need to maintain indexes that would result in memory over head. The disadvantage is that memory locations gets blocked.

C language supports both sequential and random/direct access mode.
Files can be further classified as ***text files*** or ***binary file***. Normally, in a text file data is stored using Ascii character code. Thus to store 1234.5, in text mode, we would need 6 character spaces i.e 48 bits, where as if you store it in binary mode, one would save lot of memory. Hence for storing intrinsic data of large numbers and sizes, binary mode is always preferred.

8.3 INPUT-OUTPUT (IO)FUNCTIONS

Input and output functions are catered by standard library functions,like stdio.h, provided by the suppliers. These functions are written for an operating system. The library functions are classified as

a) Console IO
b) Disk IO
c) Port IO

Port IO are used for input and output programming when we want to use ports for data input and output. We will discuss in detail about high level DiskIO in the subsequent sections.
console IO : All the input and out put functions control the way input has to be fed and the way output looks on standard output device i.e screen These IO statements are further classified as formatted and un formatted.

Formatted IO : printf() and scanf(). We specify the format through % and escape sequences like \n. Conversion and escape sequences have been dealt in chapter 2.

Unformatted IO : The unformatted category for input and output are shown below

Input :

getch() : gets a char from keyboard the moment its entered. We have used this feature to make computer wait for us to enter input so that we can view the out put in Turbo compilers.

getche() : Same as that of getch() but the character is echoed on the screen as well.

getchar(): Gets a character and displays on to screen on pressing of the <enter> key

gets() : **Inputs the string till enter key is pressed.**

Output

putch() : prints a character on to screen.
putchar() : same as putch()
puts() : displays a string.

Disk IO: This mode of operations are performed on entities called files. Usually writing on to files and reading from the files are never done directly on to disk. Instead a buffer (a memory) is used to store prior to writing on to file and after reading from the file. Buffering in case of Disk IO is essential for saving access time required to access memory. DiskIO is of two types:

a) High level disk IO also called ***standard IO/Stream IO:*** Buffer management is done by the compiler / operating system.
b) Low level disk IO also called ***system IO :*** Buffer management is to be taken care by the programmer.

Standard IO refers to standard input and output functions. The functions supported by C language under standard IO are objects called stdin and stdout.

Important streaming functions available under standard IO are listed in Table 8.1.The different access modes available under text and binary modes are listed in Table 8.2. We will explain the function, usage, and syntax through examples.

File Handling in C. Important modes and standard Library functions

Like a normal physical file, a computer file needs to be opened, accessed(reading and writing) and closed after use.

Table 8.1 Important streaming functions

Functions	Operations
fopen()	Opens a file in the mode and name specified as arguments and returns a pointer
flcose()	Closes file listed in the argument
fgetc()	Gets a character from file and advances pointer to next character.
getc()	Gets a character from file and advances pointer
fputc()	writes a character to a file character by character.
fputs()	Writes the string on to file specified by arguments
fgets()	Reads the string from the file
fprintf()	Writes data type to file
fscanf()	Reads data types from file
getw()	Read an integer from file
putw()	Writes an integer from a file.
fwrite()	Writes a structured data specified by format to a file

Contd...

fread()	Reads a structured data specified by format from the file.
fseek()	Stes the pointer to location specified in the argument.
ftell()	Returns current pointer's position
ferror()	Reports errors encountered while read or write in progress
feof()	Detects an end of file marker
rewind()	Set the pointer to beginning of the file
rename()	Renames the file specified in th eargument
remove()	Removes the file

Table 8.2 Modes in file access and operations

Mode	Meaning Stream file
w	Open in write mode. If the file already exists it will be over writtenElse a new file will be created .
r	Open in read mode. If the file does not exist it will return a NULL pointer
a	Open an existing file and append at the end .Else a new file will be created .
w+	Open in write and read mode. If the file already exists it will be over written. You can also read the file after write.
r+	Open in read and write mode. If the file does not exist it will return a NULL pointer
a+	Open an existing file and append at the end . You can also read the file after append.Else a new file will be created .
Mode	**Meaning Binary File**
wb	Open a binary filecwrite mode. If the file already exists it will be over written.Else a new file will be created .
rb	Open a binary file in read mode. If the file does not exist it will return a NULL pointer
ab	Open an existing binary file and append at the end .Else a new file will be created .
r+b	Open in binary mode for read and write. If the file does not exist it will return a NULL pointer
w+b	Open a binary file in write and read mode. If the file already exists it will be over written. You can also read the file after write.
a+b	Open an existing binary file and append at the end You can also read the file after append.Else a new file will be created .

Stream means reading and writing data onto and from files. These function are also called file input and output functions. These operations and supporting functions are provided by an object called FILE. We have to create a pointer to FILE object to access functionality.

```
FILE *fp; // fp is a pointer to data object called FILE
```

. We will accept file name from the user interactively using the commands

```
printf("\nEnter the filename:");
scanf("%s",fname);
```

To ***open*** a file we would use a function fopen (). The syntax and example is shown below:

fp= fopen("filename","***mode***");
fp = fopen("student.dat", "w").

This statement opens file named student.dat in write mode. To close a file after use we use flcose(file pointer) function as shown below

fclose(fp); // closes the file student.dat

fcloseall() closes all the files.

8.3.1 Errors while Opening Files

You have to take care of errors that can surface while opening file. These are:

(If fp == NULL) ; //it means file has not been opened successfully

or

if(ferror(fp)) ;

ferror is an object that would capture errorr and exceptions while opening the file in any of the modes. It returns a 0 if the operation is successful. Else it returns a 1

perror("error message") ; It is also an object of standard IO and you can use it to display error messages.

8.3.2 Checking for End of File

We can check the end of file by calling a function feof() which will return a 1 when end of file is reached.

while(!feof(fp))

We can also check the end of file using a macro EOF as follows

while(!EOF)

Example 8.1 fileop.c . This program demonstrates the various file operations like creating a file, entering data on to file, then reading it back. in r and w modes. The functions used are are fopen,, fclose, fopen etc.. We have also shown how to detect end of file through feof() function and error handling while trying to open the file*/

```
#include<stdio.h>
#include<stdlib.h>
#include<conio.h>
#include<process.h>
void main()
{   FILE *fp;   // fp is a pointer to FILE object
    char c=' ';
    char fname[10];
    printf("\nEnter the filename:");
    scanf("%s",fname);
    fp = fopen(fname,"w"); // open in write mode
    if (fp==NULL)
    {   printf("\nCould not open the file. \n");
        exit(1);
    }
```

```
        else
          { printf("\nEnter data.\n");
            while((c=getchar())!='.')
                    fputc(c,fp);
          }
        fclose(fp); // close the file pointed by fp
        // now let us read
        printf("\n\n"); // new line
        printf("\n Data being read from file......\n");
        fp=fopen(fname,"r");
        if(ferror(fp))
          printf("\nUnable to open  file");
        printf("\n\n"); // new line
        while(!feof(fp))                    // foef() function detects the end of file
                printf("%c",getc(fp));
        fclose(fp);
}//end of main
```

```
OUTPUT
Enter the filename:ramesh
Enter data.
hello ramesh.
 Data being read from file......
hello ramesh
```

fgetc() and getc() achieve same functionality. Similarly fputc() and putc() are also interchangeable. The statements shown below : fputs() and fgets() are used to write and read strings directly. As gets() does not add end of line,wee add a new line character at the end of string so that it can be easily read from the file.

```
        int fputs( const char * stg, FILE *fp);
        char * fgets(char *stg, int len, FILE *fp);
Example of usage is :  fputs(stg,fp);
                       fgets(stg ,80,fp);
```

Example 8.2 fconcat.c This program concatenates 2 files and generates a third file. The example uses characters as data, however it can be extended to other datatypes.*/. We have used the function to write character by character on to file using fputc(c,fp) and read from file again character by character using a function fgetc(c,fp); getchar() and putchar() are the functions we would use for getting information from keyboard and printing on to screen.

```
#include<stdio.h>
#include<conio.h>
void main()
{
        FILE *f1,*f2,*f3;
```

```
char z;
char c;
int i,n;
char f1nm[10],f2nm[10],f3nm[10];
printf("Enter the name of the first file:");
fflush(stdin);
scanf("%s",f1nm);
f1 = fopen(f1nm,"w");
printf("\nEnter data on to file 1.\n");
while((c=getchar())!='.')
 fputc(c,f1);
fclose(f1);
printf("Enter the name of the second file:");
fflush(stdin);
scanf("%s",f2nm);
f2 = fopen(f2nm,"w");
printf("\nEnter data on to file 2.\n");
while((c=getchar())!='.')
 fputc(c,f1);
fclose(f2);
printf("Enter the name of the destination file:");
fflush(stdin);
scanf("%s",f3nm);
f3 = fopen(f3nm,"w");
f1 = fopen(f1nm,"r");
f2 = fopen(f2nm,"r");
while(!feof(f1))
{
        z=fgetc(f1);
        fputc(z,f3);
}
while(!feof(f2))
{
        z=fgetc(f2);
        fputc(z,f3);
}
fclose(f1);
fclose(f2);
fclose(f3);
f3 = fopen(f3nm,"r");
while(!feof(f3))
{       z=fgetc(f3);
        putchar(z);
}
```

```
        fclose(f3);
        getch();
}
```

output
Enter the name of the first file:ramesh
Enter data on to file 1.
hello students.
Enter the name of the second file:usha
Enter data on to file 2.
how are you.
Enter the name of the destination file:gautam

hello students
how are you

Example8.3 fileop1.c. We will show you some more file operations like create for the first time, enter data and read subsequently, rename and remove operations. It may be noted that remove() and delete() function demonstrated in the next example is for DOS/Linux systems only and do not work for Windows XP

```
#include<stdio.h>
#include<string.h>
#include<stdlib.h>
void main()
{
        FILE *fp; // fp is a pointer to FILE object
        int ch;
        char c=' ';
        char fname[10],oldname[10],newname[10];

        do
        {
        printf("\n**************************************************");
        printf("\n MENU ");
        printf("\n 1.Create a file\n");
        printf("\n 2.Enter data on to file and read the contents after entry\n");
        printf("\n 3.Rename a file\n");
        printf("\n 4.Remove a file\n");
        printf("\n 5.Exit ");
        printf("\n**************************************************");
        printf("\n Enter choice of operation: ");
        scanf("%d",&ch);
```

```
switch(ch)
{
        case 1: printf("\nEnter the filename:");
                scanf("%s",fname);
                strcat(fname,".txt");
                fp = fopen(fname,"r"); // open in read mode
                if(fp!=NULL) // read operation successful
                {
                        printf("\nFile exists..Overwrite y/n ? ");
                        fflush(stdin);
                        scanf("%c",&c);
                        if(c=='n')
                                break;
                }
                fp = fopen(fname,"w");  //open in write mode
                if(ferror(fp))
                        printf("\nUnable to create new file");
                else
                        printf("\nNew file created");
                fclose(fp);
                break;

        case 2: printf("\nEnter the filename:");
                scanf("%s",fname);
                strcat(fname,".txt");
                fp = fopen(fname,"w");  //open in write mode
                if(ferror(fp))
                        printf("\nUnable to create new file");
                else
                        printf("\nNew file created");

                printf("Enter the characters:\n");
                while((c=getchar())!='.')
                fputc(c,fp);
               fclose(fp);
                fp = fopen(fname,"r");
                while(!feof(fp))
                 {
                    printf("%c",getc(fp));
                 }
                fclose(fp);
                break;
        case 3: printf("\nEnter the old filename: ");
                scanf("%s",oldname);
```

```
                strcat(oldname,".txt");
                fp = fopen(oldname,"r");
                if(fp==NULL)
                {   printf("\nFile does not exist");
                    break;
                }
                printf("\nEnter the new filename: ");
                scanf("%s",newname);
                strcat(newname,".txt");
                if (rename(oldname, newname) == 0)
                        printf("Renamed %s to %s.\n", oldname, newname);
                else
                        perror("rename");
                break;

        case 4: printf("\nEnter the filename to be removed:");
                scanf("%s",fname);
                strcat(fname,".txt");
                fp = fopen(fname,"r");
                if(fp==NULL)
                        printf("\nFile does not exist");
                else
                {
                        remove(fname);
                        printf("\nFile deleted");
                }
                break;
        case 5: exit(1);
    }
    }while (1);
}
```

OUTPUT

```
*********************************************************
 MENU
 1.Create a file
 2.Enter data on to file and read the contents after entry
 3.Rename a file
 4.Remove a file
 5.Exit
*********************************************************
 Enter choice of operation: 1
Enter the filename:file1
File exists..Overwrite y/n ? y
New file created
```

```
************************************************************
 MENU
 1.Create a file
 2.Enter data on to file and read the contents after entry
 3.Rename a file
 4.Remove a file
 5.Exit
************************************************************
 Enter choice of operation: 2
Enter the filename:file1
New file createdEnter the characters:
hello world.
hello world
```

It may be noted that for streaming input and output the object that are use are stdin and stdout. To flush out last in character during read or write operations. we need to statement for flushing the stream pipes. For example. for flushing input stream pipe

```
fflush(stdin);
scanf("%c",&c);
```

You can record the exception and errors occurring during and operation using

```
perror("exception during rename operation");
```

8.3.3 More Streaming Functions

fprintf() : This function writes formatted data to file. The format is given as agument. The syntax and example is shown below

fprintf(file pointer, "controlling format", data);

fprintf(fp,"%s",line);

fscanf() : This function reads data written on to file using fwrite(). The format is given as agument. The syntax and example is shown below

fscanf(file pointer, "controlling format", data);

fscanf(fp,"%d%s",&no, line); // reads data on to no & line.

fseek() : This function positions file pointer to a particular position, as dictated by the arguments. The syntax is

fseek(filepointer, offset, location);

file pointer : fp

offset in bytes : +m or −m

location :

SEEK_SET : BEGINNING OF THE FILE

SEEK_CUR : CURRENT POSITION

SEEK_END: END OF FILE

Example : fseek(fp, -5, SEEK_CUR); // pointer is positioned – m bytes from current location.

ftell() : This function returns current position in bytes on the stream file. The syntax is
int len = ftell(fp); // returns the bytes before current pointer.

Example 8.4 fuppercase.c. This program demonstrates the use of fprintf, fscanf, fseek, functions. It converts all the characters entered to uppercase and writes to the same file*/

```
#include<stdio.h>
#include<conio.h>
void main()
{
        FILE *f1;
        int i,n,j;
        char z,f1nm[10];
        clrscr();
        printf("Enter the name of the file:");
        fflush(stdin);
        scanf("%s",f1nm);
        printf("How many characters do you want to write:");
        scanf("%d",&n);
        f1 = fopen(f1nm,"w");
        for(i=0;i<n;i++)
        {
                fflush(stdin);
                z = getchar();
                fprintf(f1,"%c",z);
        }
        fclose(f1);
        f1 = fopen(f1nm,"r+");
        for(i=0;i<n;i++)
        {
                fscanf(f1,"%c",&z);
                if(z>=97 && z<=122)  z=z-32;
                fseek(f1,-1,1);
                fputc(z,f1);
                fseek(f1,0,1); //fp,current position, seek set)
        }
        fclose(f1);
        f1 = fopen(f1nm,"r");
        printf("\n");
        for(i=0;i<n;i++)
        {
```

```
            fscanf(f1,"%c",&z);
            putchar(z);
        }
        fclose(f1);
        getch();
}
```

Example 8.5 charstofile.c. This program copies a character array to a file. We open the file in w+

```
//This program reads the content of file character by character.
#include <stdio.h>
#include <conio.h>
#include <string.h>
void main()
{
  FILE *fp;
  char str1[] = "I love India";
  char ch;
  fp = fopen("tmp.txt", "w+");
  fwrite(str1, strlen(str1), 1, fp);//write a string into the file
  rewind(fp);
  do
  {
    ch = fgetc(fp);// read a char from the file
    putch(ch);
  } while (ch != EOF);
  printf("\n");
  fclose(fp);
}
/*output
I love India*/
```

Example 8.6 intar2file.c. A program to write and read an array of integer values to a file

```
#include <stdio.h>
#include <stdlib.h>

void main()
{  FILE *fp;
  int a[5]={10,20,30,40,50},b[5],i;
  char file[10];
  printf("Enter a file name: ");
  scanf("%s",file);
```

```
fp = fopen(file, "wb");
if (fp == NULL)
{ printf("Error opening file %s\n", file);
  exit(1);
}
for(i=0;i<5;i++)
        putw(a[i],fp);//puts an integer on file stream
if (ferror(fp))
   printf("Error writing to file\n");
else
   printf("Successful write\n");
fclose(fp);
fp = fopen(file, "rb");
if (fp == NULL)
{ printf("Error opening file %s\n", file);
  exit(1);
}
i=0;
b[i++] = getw(fp); // gets the integer
while(!feof(fp))
{
  b[i++] = getw(fp);//gets an integer from file stream
}
if (ferror(fp))
   printf("Error reading file\n");
else
{ printf("Successful read of the file and the contents are: \n");
   for(i=0;i<5;i++)
   printf("%d ",b[i]);
}
fclose(fp);
}// end of main
/* OUTPUT
Enter a file name: file1
Successful write
Successful read of the file and the contents are:
10 20 30 40 50 */
```

8.3.4 Stream Functions for Writing Structures on to File

fwrite() and fread() : The structure usually comprises several type of data, like integer, char and string etc , and storing them directly is expensive in terms of storage space requirements. Hence we will use only binary mode only. This mode is ensured by fread() and fwrite() commands. The syntax is

fwrite(&structobject, sizeof(sructobject), number of blocks of structobject, filepointer);
fwrite(&std, sizeof(std),1, fp);

Similarly for reading on to structure object std, we can use
fread(&std, sizeof(std),1, fp);

Example 8.7 struct2file.c This program demonstrates the usage of fread and fwrite functions, which are used to read and write structured data respectively. It also demonstrates the operations of functions like fseek, rewind,ferror. The programs starts by giving two options. One is to add a record to a file. This can be done by entering the student name and marks in 3 subjects. The second option is to display a particular record given the index value. It does ask for the filename. The filename "student.c" is used here.*/

```
/*This program demonstrates the usage of fread and fwrite functions,
which are used to read and write structured data respectively.
It also demonstrates the operations of functions like fseek, rewind,ferror*/
#include<stdio.h>
#include<stdlib.h>
struct   student
{
        char name[20];
        float mat,sci,eng,total,avg;
};
void main()
{
        FILE *fp;
        struct student s1,s2;
        int ch,pos,p,sz=0;

        fp = fopen("student.c","w");
        fclose(fp);
   while(1)
        {
                printf("\n  MENU ");
          printf("\n 1.Add a record\n 2.Display nth record\n 3.Exit\n");
          printf(" Enter choice of operation: ");
          scanf("%d",&ch);

                switch(ch)
                {
            case 1: fp = fopen("student.c","a");
                  printf("\nEnter student name:");
                  scanf("%s",s1.name);
```

```
            printf("\nEnter student marks in the 3 subjects - maths, science and english :");
            scanf("%f%f%f",&s1.mat,&s1.sci,&s1.eng);
            s1.total = s1.mat + s1.sci + s1.eng;
            s1.avg = s1.total/3;
            fwrite(&s1,sizeof(s1),1,fp);
            if(ferror(fp))
                printf("\nError occured");
            else
                {
                printf("\nAction successful");
                sz++;
                }
            fclose(fp);
            break;
    case 2: fp = fopen("student.c","r");
            printf("\nEnter the position of the record to be displayed : ");
            scanf("%d",&p);
            if(p>sz)
                    {printf("\nPosition out of bounds");
                break;
                    }
            pos = (p-1) * sizeof(s2) ;
            rewind(fp);
            fseek(fp,pos,SEEK_SET);
            fread(&s2,sizeof(s2),1,fp);
            printf("\nDetails of record %d : \n",p);
                printf("\nName of the student :\t%s\nMarks in each subject\n\tMaths :
\t%f\n\tScience :\t%f\n\tEnglish :\t%f",s2.name,s2.mat,s2.sci,s2.eng);
            fclose(fp);
            break;
    case 3:     exit(1);
        }//end of switch
    }//end of while
}//end of main

/*output


 MENU
 1.Add a record
 2.Display nth record
 3.Exit
 Enter choice of operation: 1
```

```
Enter student name:govind

Enter student marks in the 3 subjects - maths, science and english :70 80 90

Action successful
 MENU
 1.Add a record
 2.Display nth record
 3.Exit
 Enter choice of operation: 2

Enter the position of the record to be displayed : 1

Details of record 1 :

Name of the student :   govind
Marks in each subject
      Maths :        70.000000
      Science :      80.000000
      English :      90.000000
Total marks :  240.000000
Average Marks : 80.000000
  MENU
 1.Add a record
 2.Display nth record
 3.Exit
 Enter choice of operation: 3*/
```

Example 8.8 sortfile.c This program shows you how you can sort a file.. We have defined a structure for students and filed in the data in to structure. We have written this to file. Later, we have copied this file into an array of student structure. We have dispatched the structure of students to a function sortstruct to sort the structure. Finally we have written on to file, resulting in a sorted file.

```
/*struct to file,read the file, file to struct, struct to sort
sorted struct to file, read file*/
#include<stdio.h>
struct   student
{        char name[20];
         float mat,sci,eng,total,avg;
};
typedef struct student std;
std s1,s2[5];
void sortstruct(std s[],int n);
```

```
void disprecords(int n);
void main()
{       FILE *fp;
        int ch,p,sz=0,i,pos;
       float a[50]; // we need this array for sorting on average marks
        fp = fopen("student.c","w");
        fclose(fp);
        do
         {  printf("\n  MENU ");
          printf("\n 1.Add a record\n ");
          printf("\n 2.Display nth record\n");
          printf("\n 3.Display all the records\n");
          printf("\n 4.Sort the records\n");
          printf("\n 5.Exit\n");
           printf(" Enter choice of operation: ");
           scanf("%d",&ch);
           switch(ch)
           { case 1:  fp = fopen("student.c","a");
                      printf("\nEnter student name:");
             scanf("%s",s1.name);
                      printf("\nEnter marks in : maths, science and english :");
                      scanf("%f%f%f",&s1.mat,&s1.sci,&s1.eng);
                      s1.total = s1.mat + s1.sci + s1.eng;
                      s1.avg = s1.total/3;
                      fwrite(&s1,sizeof(s1),1,fp);
                      if(ferror(fp))
                              printf("\nError occured");
                      else
                        { printf("\nAction successful");
                          sz++; // keep the count
                        }
                      fclose(fp);
                      break;
             case 2:  fp = fopen("student.c","r");
                      printf("\nEnter the position of the record to be displayed : ");
                      scanf("%d",&p);
                       if(p>sz)
                        { printf("\nPosition is out of bound");
                          break;
                        }
                       pos = (p-1) * sizeof(s2) ;
                       rewind(fp);
                      fseek(fp,pos,SEEK_SET);
```

```
                        fread(&s1,sizeof(s1),1,fp);
                        printf("\nDetails of record %d : \n",p);
                           printf("\nName of the student :\t%s\nMarks in each subject\n\tMaths :
\t%f\n\tScience :\t%f\n\tEnglish :\t%f",s1.name,s1.mat,s1.sci,s1.eng);
                        printf("\nTotal marks :\t%f\nAverage Marks :\t%f",s1.total,s1.avg);
                        fclose(fp);
                        break;
            case 3: disprecords(sz);
                        break;
            case 4:
                        printf("\nSorting by average....\n");
                       fp = fopen("student.c","r");
                       for(i=0;i<sz;i++)
                       fread(&s2[i],sizeof(s1),1,fp);
                       fclose(fp);
                      sortstruct(s2,sz);
                      // write the sorted structure on to file
                     fp = fopen("student.c","w");
                     for (i=0;i<sz;i++)
                            fwrite(&s2[i],sizeof(s1),1,fp);

                     fclose(fp);
                     // now read and display
                   disprecords(sz);
                     break;
            case 5:        exit(0);
           }
      } while (ch<ch<1 || ch>5);
}// end of main
// function definitions
void sortstruct(std s[],int n)
{  std temp;
  int i,j;
  for(i=0;i<n-1;i++)
  {
   for(j=i+1;j<n;j++)
    {
     if (s[i].avg<s[j].avg)
            { // swap s[i] and s[j]
          temp=s[i];s[i]=s[j];s[j]=temp;
            }
       }
  }
}// end of sortstruct
```

```
void disprecords(int n)
{  FILE *fp1;
   int i;
   fp1 = fopen("student.c","r");
   printf("\nName  Mathematics  Science  English  Total  Average");
   for(i=0;i<n;i++)
   {  fread(&s1,sizeof(s1),1,fp1);
      printf("\n%s     %5.2f   %5.2f %5.2f   %5.2f
              %5.2f",s1.name,s1.mat,s1.sci,s1.eng,s1.total,s1.avg);
   }
   fclose(fp1);
}
```

```
OUTPUT
 MENU
 1.Add a record
 2.Display nth record
 3.Display all the records
 4.Sort the records
 5.Exit
 Enter choice of operation: 1
Enter student name:s1
Enter student marks in the 3 subjects - maths, science and english :67 77 87
Action successful
 MENU
 1.Add a record
 2.Display nth record
 3.Display all the records
 4.Sort the records
 5.Exit
 Enter choice of operation: 1
Enter student name:s2
Enter student marks in the 3 subjects - maths, science and english :77 88 98
Action successful
 < MENU>
Enter choice of operation: 2
Enter the position of the record to be displayed : 2
Details of record 2 :
Name of the student :   s2
Marks in each subject
     Maths :        77.000000
     Science :      88.000000
      English :       98.000000
Total marks :   263.000000
```

Average Marks : 87.666664
<MENU>
Enter choice of operation: 3

Name	Mathematics	Science	English	Total	Average
s1	67.00	77.00	87.00	231.00	77.00
s2	77.00	88.00	98.00	263.00	87.67

<MENU>
Enter choice of operation: 4
Sorting by average....

Name	Mathematics	Science	English	Total	Average
s2	77.00	88.00	98.00	263.00	87.67
s1	67.00	77.00	87.00	231.00	77.00

■■■ 8.4 COMMAND LINE ARGUMENTS

We have learnt how to pass the values to a function through the arguments. But how do we pass arguments to void main() i.e our main function. It is through command line arguments. Till now, we have been obtaining the file names from the user with statement

printf("\enter file name"); and scanf("%s",filename);

Now suppose, we have two files with names BTech.dat and MTech.dat with students marks. Further, a source program, say ***process.c*** is available that can process the either of data files BTech.dat and MTech.dat as required and declare results through a file called resuts.dat. Then we can use command line arguments as shown below:

```
C:>\tc\bin>process MTech.dat result.dat
                    Or
C:>\tc\bin>process BTech.dat result.dat
```

For command line arguments to wotk:

```
void main( argc, argv[])
{
   int argc;        // counter for arguments
   int *argv[]; // arguments list.
   ......
   ..........
}
```

In the example shown :argc = 3
argv[0] = process   argv[1] = MTech.dat   argv[2] = result.dat

Command line arguments facilitate us o use program name i.e process directly from command prompt instead of from C language development environment called integrated development environment(IDE). for this facility, compile the program and use ***build*** option or ***mak*** option. With this we will be making a exe version or mak version i.e process.exe or process.mak. Then use C:>\tc\bin>process MTech.dat result.dat

Example 8.9 cmdline.c. In this example, we would accept program name, input file name and output file name as arguments. We would copy the input file to out put file after conversion of each character to an upper case.

```
//cmdline.c A program to copy from a source text to destinations
//after converting to upper casetext
#include<stdio.h>
#include<stdlib.h>
#include<ctype.h>
void main(int argc,char * argv[])
{
        char c;
        FILE *fp1,*fp2;
        printf("file1=%s\n",argv[1]);
        printf("file2=%s\n",argv[2]);
        fp1 = fopen(argv[1],"r");
        if (fp1 == NULL)
        {
                printf(" 1 Error opening file \n");
                exit(1);
        }
        else
        {
                fp2=fopen(argv[2],"w");
                if (fp2 == NULL)
                {
                        printf("2 Error opening file\n");
                        exit(1);
                }
                else
                   while( ( c=fgetc(fp1))!=EOF)
                        putc(toupper(c),fp2);
                printf("successful copy operation\n");
        }
} // end of main

 /*
 Execution:
 In the command prompt
 C:\TC> cmdline a.c b.c

 OUTPUT:
 file1 = a.c
 file2 = b.c
 Successful copy operation.
 */
```

OBJECTIVE QUESTIONS

1 Based on the access technique Files in C language can be classified as ______ ______ ______ files.

2 Text mode file takes ______ many bytes to store a number 12345.6
a) 5 b) 6
c) 7 d) 8

3. The library file are classified as ______, ______ and ______.

4. getchar() reads data from
a) file b) keyboard as soon as it is entered
c) keyboard but on enter d) file till EOF

5. fscanf () read data from
a) file b) disk
c) keyboard

6. EOF marker can be used to check end of file while reading
a) integer data types b) character based IO
c) float data types d) all data types

7. fopen returns on failure to read a) 0 b) 1 c) -1 d) NULL.

8. A file with a+ mode can be
a) only append b) read and write at end
c) only read d) only write

9 EOF returns
a) 1 b) -1
c) 0 d) none of the above

10. In command line arguments char *argv[] is
a) list of arguments b) count of arguments
c) program name d) command

11 To capture errors during file operations the function that can be used
a) ferror() b) fgets
c) perror d) feof()

12 To detect end of file marker for formatted file the function that can be used is
a) ferror() b) fgets
c) perror d) feof()

13 fread and fwrite function can be used for writing data in
a) text files b) binary files
c) both a & b d) Ascii files

14 In a file opened with r + mode, if fopen is unable to open file it will return
a) 1 b) -1
c) NULL d) 0

15 File opened with w+b mode is for
a) binary and read write b) read write
c) binary and write b) none

REVIEW QUESTIONS

1. *What are files and why they are required?*
2. *What are formatted and unformatted IO?*
3. *How do you use feof() and EOF functions to detect the end of file*
4. *Explain input and output statements available in unformatted segment*
5. *Explain input and output statements available in formatted segment*
6. *What is consoleIO?.*
7. *What is dic IO?*
8. *Explain syntax and working of string handling functions available in standard library.*
9. *Explain the character handling functions in standard library.*
10. *Explain getw() and putw() statements.*
11 *Describe w and w+ and w+b modes.*
12 *Why binary files occupy less memory space.*
13 *Explain fseek() and ftell() functions.*
14 *What are the likely errors while file handling. Explain the statements with syntax.*
15 *Explain fwrite() and fread() statement.*
16. *Explain fprintf() and fscanf() statement*
17. *Explain usage of command line arguments with* example.

SOLVED EXAMPLES

1. Write a program to count the words in a file and list them

//fstring.c. This program list words from the file and gives a count of word.

```
#include<stdio.h>
void main()
{       FILE *fp;
        int i,j,k,count=0;
        char c;
        char str[50][20];
        char stg[]="HELLO WORLD HOW ARE WE TODAY";
        fp=fopen("thunder.txt","w");
        fputs(stg,fp);
        i=0;
        j=0;
        fclose(fp);
        fp=fopen("thunder.txt","r");
```

```
        fseek(fp,0,SEEK_END);
        k=ftell(fp);
       printf("size of file in bytes is=%d",k);
        rewind(fp);
        while((c=fgetc(fp))!=EOF)
         {   if(c!=' '&& c!='\n' && c!=';')
                  {  str[i][j]=c;
                     j++;
                  }
             else
                  { str[i][j]='\0';
                    j=0;
                    i++;
                  }
         }
         count=i;
        for(j=0;j<i;j++)
         {          printf("\n");
                    printf("%s",str[j]);
         }
        printf("\n Number of words : %d\n",count);
}// end of main
/*Output:
size of file in bytes is=28
HELLO
WORLD
HOW
ARE
WE
Number of words : 5*/
```

2. Write a program to count the number of vowels in a file

```
//fvowels.c This program counts the number of vowels in a file
#include<stdio.h>
#include<ctype.h>
void main()
{  FILE *fp;
  char c;
  int k=0;
  char stg[]="be kind to human beings and animals";
   fp=fopen("thunder.txt","w");
  fputs(stg,fp);
  fclose(fp);
```

```
  fp=fopen("thunder.txt","r");
  while((c=fgetc(fp))!=EOF)
        {   c=toupper(c);
            if(c=='A'||c=='E'||c=='I'||c=='O'||c=='U')
                        k++;
        }
  printf("Number of vowels in the file =%d\n",k);
  fclose(fp);
}// end of main
/*Output:
Number of vowels in the file =11*/
```

3. Write a program to copy a file from source to destinations.

```
//fcopy.c
#include<stdio.h>
#include<stdlib.h>
void main()
{       char c;
        char file1[10],file2[10];
        FILE *fp1,*fp2;
        printf("Enter input file name: ");
       scanf("%s",file1);
        printf("Enter output file name: ");
      scanf("%s",file2);
      fp1 = fopen(file1, "r");
       if (fp1 == NULL)
        { printf("Error opening file \n");
         exit(1);
       }
        else
        {       fp2=fopen(file2,"w");
                if (fp2 == NULL)
                { printf("Error opening file\n");
                 exit(1);
                }
              else
                  while( ( c=getc(fp1))!=EOF)
                      putc(c,fp2);
              printf("successful copy operation\n");
        }
} // end of main
OUTPUT
Enter a input file name: file2filecopy.c
```

Enter output file name: f1.c
successful copy operation
Press any key to continue

4. Write a program to copy a two dimensional matrix on to file and read and display the matrix.

```
//intarrasfile.c. A program to write an array of integer
//values to a file and reads it back
#include <stdio.h>
#include <stdlib.h>
void main()
{  FILE *fp;
  int a[2][5]={10,20,30,40,50,
                  60,70,80,90,100}; // a ia a 2x5 matrix
  int i,j,temp;
  char file[10];
  printf("Enter a file name: ");
  scanf("%s",file);
  fp = fopen(file, "w+");
  if (fp == NULL)
  {  printf("Error opening file %s\n", file);
     exit(1);
  }
  for(i=0;i<2;i++)
          for(j=0;j<5;j++)
             putw(a[i][j],fp);//puts an integer on file stream
  if (ferror(fp))
     printf("Error writing to file\n");
  else
     printf("Successful write\n");
  fclose(fp);
  fp = fopen(file, "r");
  if (fp == NULL)
  {
    printf("Error opening file %s\n", file);
    exit(1);
  }
  printf("Successful read of the file and the contents are: \n");
  for(i=0;i<2;i++)
  {
        for(j=0;j<5;j++)
            {  temp = getw(fp);
               printf("%d ", temp);
            }
```

```
            printf("\n");
   }
   fclose(fp);
}// end of main
/* OUTPUT
Enter a file name: file1
Successful write
Successful read of the file and the contents are:
10 20 30 40 50
60 70 80 90 100
Press any key to continue
*/
```

5. **Write a program to copy array of characters (n number of strings) on to file. Also display the contents of file.**

```
//stgfile.c. This program reads the content of file character by character.
#include <stdio.h>
#include <conio.h>
#include <string.h>
void main()
{  FILE *fp;
  char stg[20];
  fp = fopen("stg.dat", "w+");
  if ( fp==NULL)
  { printf("\n Sorry could not open stg.dat");
   exit(1);
  }
  printf("\n Enter a string <END> to stop\n");
  gets(stg);
  while(strcmp(stg,"END"))
        { //strcat(stg,"\n"); // add a new line character
         fputs(stg,fp);
         //  fwrite(stg, strlen(stg), 1, fp);//write a string into the file
        printf("\n Enter a string <END> to stop\n");
         gets(stg);
        }
  // now read and display the file
  rewind(fp);
  while(!feof(fp))
        {          fgets(stg,19,fp);
                   printf("\n%s\n ", stg);
        }
  fclose(fp);
}// end of main
```

```
/*output
 Enter a string <END> to stop:HELLO
 Enter a string <END> to stopHOW
 Enter a string <END> to stopARE
 Enter a string <END> to stopYOU?
 Enter a string <END> to stopEND
HELLOHOWAREYOU?*/
```

6. Write a program to update Inventory record on a file. Use structure to write on to file and updating the file. Inventory record contains part name and value

```
// fileupdate.c. A program to update record
#include<stdio.h>
#include<stdlib.h>
struct    Inventory
{         char name[20];
          float val;
};
typedef struct Inventory item;
item part;
// fn prototypes
void disprecords(int n);
void main()
{         FILE *fp;
          int ch,p,sz=0,pos;
          fp = fopen("inventory.dat","w");
          fclose(fp);
          do
          { printf("\n MENU ");
            printf("\n 1.Add a record\n ");
           printf("\n 2.Display nth record\n");
           printf("\n 3.Display all the records\n");
           printf("\n 4.Update the records\n");
           printf("\n 5.Exit\n");
            printf(" Enter choice of operation: ");
            scanf("%d",&ch);
            switch(ch)
            {
            case 1:
             fp = fopen("inventory.dat","a");
             printf("\nEnter item name:");
             scanf("%s",part.name);
             printf("\nEnter value of item:");
             scanf("%f",&part.val);
```

```
    fwrite(&part,sizeof(part),1,fp);
  if(ferror(fp))
        printf("\nError occured");
  else
        {
         printf("\nAction successful");
         sz++;
        }
        fclose(fp);
        break;
  case 2:
        fp = fopen("inventory.dat","r");
        printf("\nEnter the position of the record to be displayed : ");
        scanf("%d",&p);
        if(p>sz)
        {     printf("\nPosition is out of bound");
               break;
        }
        pos = (p-1) * sizeof(part) ;
        rewind(fp);
        fseek(fp,pos,SEEK_SET);
        fread(&part,sizeof(part),1,fp);
        printf("\nDetails of record......");
        printf("\n%s\t%5.2f\n",part.name,part.val);
        fclose(fp);
        break;
  case 3:
        disprecords(sz);
        break;
  case 4:
        printf("\nupdating record....\n");
        fp = fopen("Inventory.dat","r+");
        printf("\nEnter the position of the record to be updated: ");
        scanf("%d",&p);
        if(p>sz)
        {     printf("\nPosition is out of bound");
               break;
        }
        pos = (p-1) * sizeof(part) ;
        rewind(fp);
        fseek(fp,pos,SEEK_SET);
        // now read the record
        fread(&part,sizeof(part),1,fp);
```

```
            printf("\nbefore update %s\t%5.2f\n",part.name,part.val);
            // get updated details from the user
            printf("\nEnter item name:");
          scanf("%s",part.name);
          printf("\nEnter value of item:");
          scanf("%f",&part.val);

            // now we have to write on to same position
          rewind(fp);
            fseek(fp,pos,SEEK_SET);
            fwrite(&part,sizeof(part),1,fp);
           if(ferror(fp))
                printf("\nError occured");
           else
                printf("\nUpdate action successful");
            fclose(fp);
            disprecords(sz);
            break;
      case 5:  exit(0);
            }
  } while (ch<ch<1 || ch>5);
}
// function definitions
void disprecords(int n)
{   FILE *fp1;
        int i;
   fp1 = fopen("inventory.dat","r+");
        fseek(fp1,0,SEEK_SET);
        printf("\nPart Name      value\n");
        for(i=0;i<n;i++)
        {    fread(&part,sizeof(part),1,fp1);
             printf("\n%s       %5.2f\n",part.name,part.val);
        }
        fclose(fp1);
}
/*output
 <MENU>
 1.Add a record
 2.Display nth record
 3.Display all the records
 4.update the record
 5.Exit
 Enter choice of operation: 1
Enter item name:motor
```

```
Enter value of item:1000.00
Action successful
<MENU>
 Enter choice of operation: 1
Enter item name:pump
Enter value of item:1500.00
Action successful
<MENU>
 Enter choice of operation: 1
Enter item name:pipes
Enter value of item:1700.00
Action successful
<MENU>
 Enter choice of operation: 2
Enter the position of the record to be displayed : 2
Details of record......
pump   1500.00
<MENU>
 Enter choice of operation: 3
Part Name     value
motor     1000.00
pump     1500.00
pipes     1700.00
<MENU>
 Enter choice of operation: 4
updating record....
Enter the position of the record to be updated: 2
before update pump     1500.00
Enter item name:monopump
Enter value of item:2000.00
Update action successful
Part Name     value
motor     1000.00
monopump     2000.00
pipes     1700.00
 */
```

ASSIGNMENT PROBLEMS

1 Write a program to merge two files into a third file. Each file holds specified number of strings.

2 Write a program to print telephone directory. Use structure to create the directory and the file.

3. Write a program to sort the file that holds a specified number of integers.

4. Develop a C program that would store the details of electrical consumption by a customer in two files, namely customer.dat that stores id number, name,poll no, address and a second file that stores id number,custbill no, dtae and amount. The program must have facilities for
   a) data entry on to rwo file.
   b) display the full details on customer id number.
   c) display all records.
   d) Update a record
   e) delete a record. (Hint : mark a flag field to 1 to indicate that its deleted)
5. Write a c program to encode the file. Read input from a file1.Encode the text replacing the character with next character. For example a will be replaced by b and z will be replaced with A. Similar scheme can be used for capitals and numbers form 0 to 9.

   a) Write code for encoding and writing on to a file.
   b) decode and read the file.
   c) Compare with the original file and say if decoding is indeed correct.
      (hint : check bytes and character by character

Solutions to Objective Questions

1) sequential random direct			2) c	3) consoleIO,DiskIO,and portIO.		
4) c	5) a	6) b	7) d	8) b	9) b	10) a
11) a	12) d	13) b	14) c	15) a		

CHAPTER 9

LINEAR DATA STRUCTURES

9.1 INTRODUCTION TO DATA STRUCTURES

What is a data structure? Why we have to use data structures ? These questions often trouble many a student. We intend in this chapter, to give you basic understanding concepts behind data types, data structures, prior to taking up linear data structures called linked lists.

Why use data structure?

Many of the operations and data encountered in daily life can not be directly mapped to digital computer so that programmers can develop solutions. For example consider students record held at college administration, that contain several data values such as name, number, and attendance etc. Data structure called structure afforded by C language solves this problem efficiently. Similarly problem of finding shortest path amongst cities can best be solved when graph theory, a mathematical tool is employed. This problem can best be solved when Graph can be viewed as Adjacency Matrix, a two dimensional data structure. Therefore, we can say that programmers ability to convert a concept in to data structure is of paramount important for efficiency.

What are data structures?

Firstly you are aware that when you write a code and declare variables, these variables are stored in program's temporary storage (stack area) and permanent values are committed to files. Often, program has to refer to these variable while executing the program and hence they are to be accessed from the memory efficiently. *So how they are stored organized in memory is important to us.*

Secondly, you are familiar with data types a language uses. For example *int, float, double* are some of the data types you have been using in the code you have developed. We have further learnt that a data type has a permitted range. For example *unsigned int has a range of 0 to 65535.* In addition, operations allowed on int data types such as addition, subtraction, multiplication etc have been explored by you. *Hence we can define data type as permitted data values and allowable operations on these variable.* Simple data types can be used to build new data types, for example enumerated data types.

Now, we are ready to define data structure as ***organized data and allowed operations***. Array is one of the standard data structure provide by the language and it can be used to define more complex data structures for example a data structure called structure provided by C language.. Array allows us to define memory allocation and storing of data values a type, where as structures allows us to store data values of different data type as a single storage unit. Both arrays and structures are static in nature in that storage is required to be defined prior to compilation stage it self and actual exploitation of memory becomes evident only at the time of execution time. Thus we need data structures that are more suitable for handling dynamic data collections.

We can classify the data structures in several ways

a) Linear / Non linear data structures. Linear data structures organize the data in a sequential order, like you store data on to arrays. Non Linear data types store the data values in such a fashion so that relation ships can be exhibited. Trees and Graphs are examples of non linear data structures. In trees, for example, we can depict an organizations hierarchy.

b) Homogenous/Non homogenous data structures. Arrays which store same data types are called homogenous data structures while structures of C language can be called non homogenous data structures.

c) Static and dynamic data structures. The memory locations and sizes of static data structures are fixed at compile time itself while they are dynamically allotted at run time in case of dynamic data structures.

The type of data structure to be used in a program depends on factors such as program execution time and storage space. We will learn more about complexity of algorithms in chapter on Searching and Sorting. Several of day to day problems can be solved by using abstract data types such as linkèd lists, queues, stacks etc. In this chapter linear data structures called linked lists are introduced.

■■■ 9.2 SINGLE LINKED LISTS

9.1 Linked List are used extensively in Computer Science applications, for example, in maintaining databases, operating system etc. Linked Lists use dynamic storage i.e instead of allocating space at compile time, as is done in the case of arrays, while using Linked Lists you can allocate space at run time depending on actual need. Thus linked list is a superior data structure.

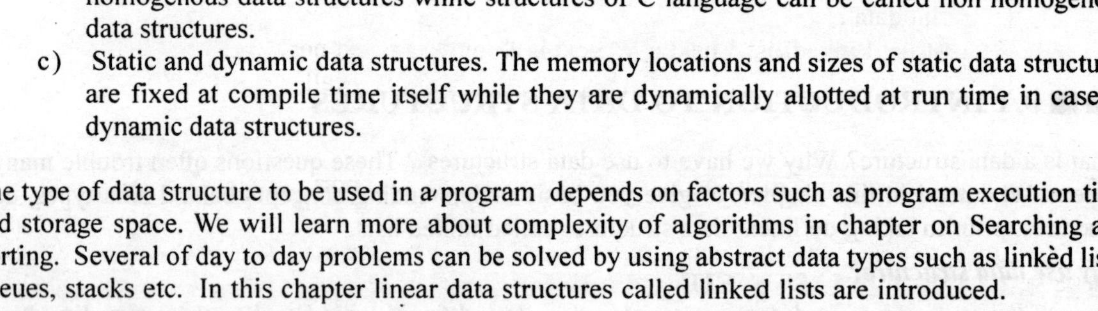

Fig. 9.1 Linear linked list

In the above Fig. A is header node and is predecessor of B.C is a successor of B D is a tail node.

9.2.1 How to Define a Node

A node will have data assigned to it and a pointer to its successor.
Newnode is the name of the node.

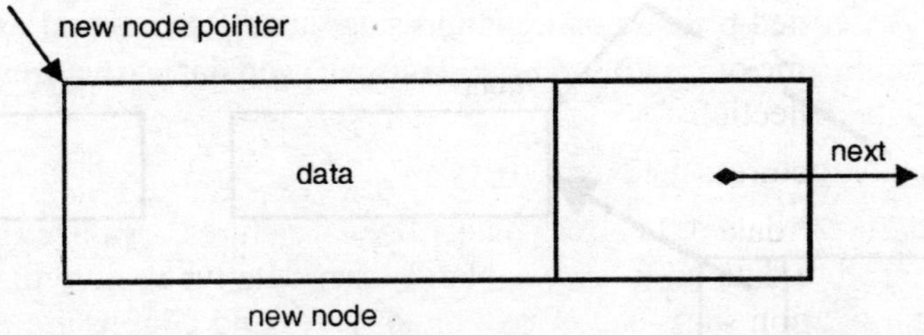

Fig. 9.2 New node structure

```
struct LinkedList
{       int data ;
        struct LinkedList * next ;  // *next is a pointer to next node
};                                  // This type of definition is called self
                                       referential structure.

typedef struct LinkedList node; // we will be able to use short name "node"
```

■■■ 9.3 LINKED LISTS FUNCTIONS

9.3.1 How to Create a New Node? We want to create a new node with name newnode and assign data and next pointer pointing to null. This newnode thus created will be passed as an argument to function to create linked list. Obtain data for new node and assign data and next pointer to NULL.

C module is given below:

```
node *newnode;  // declaration of newnode of structure node
 printf ("enter new node data\n");
 scanf("%d", & data);
 // allocate space for new node. malloc ( ) allocates space of size of node and
 // returns a pointer of type node to newnode
 newnode= (node*) malloc (size of (node));
 newnode → data = data ; // you have assigned data
 new node → next = NULL ; // assign next to NULL
// now we will call our AddFront function which will add newnode in
//linkedlist.
```

9.3.2 Function AddFront (node ** font, node *newnode) accepts newnode and data as arguments and adds it in the front of the list. If the list is empty it will add as first element. Observe that we have passed ** front, which is a pointer to pointer because we are adding newnode as first node and we may be required to delete first node as well. As the first node is address for the entire Linked List, addition or deletion of as first element would change address. Hence we have chosen a pointer-to-pointer. Further as a learning exercise pointer to pointer concept is worth mastering.

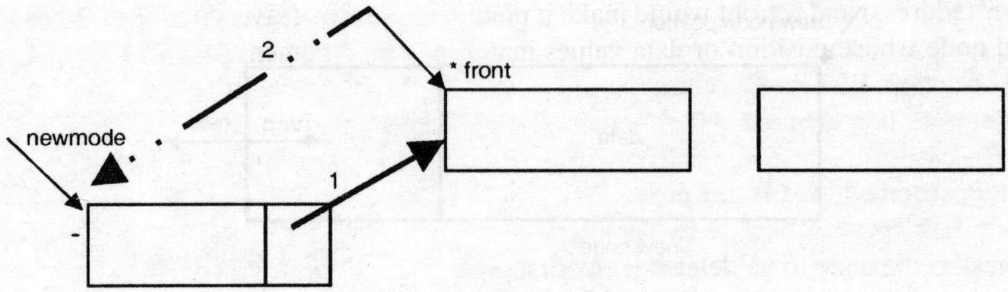

Fig. 9.3 Adding a node in the front of a linked list

```
void AddFront (node ** front, node *new node)
   {
     // make new node  as fist node. // next to point to  * front
    newnode → next = * front ; // ref 1 in above fig
    * front = newnode ; // ref 2. Now you made newnode to be known as * front.
   }
```

9.3.3 In this module functions, **int DeletePos (node ** front, int pos) and int DeleteElm(node ** front, int data),** we will delete node from linked list given a position. Function will return 1 if successful in deleting else it will return 0 to main function.

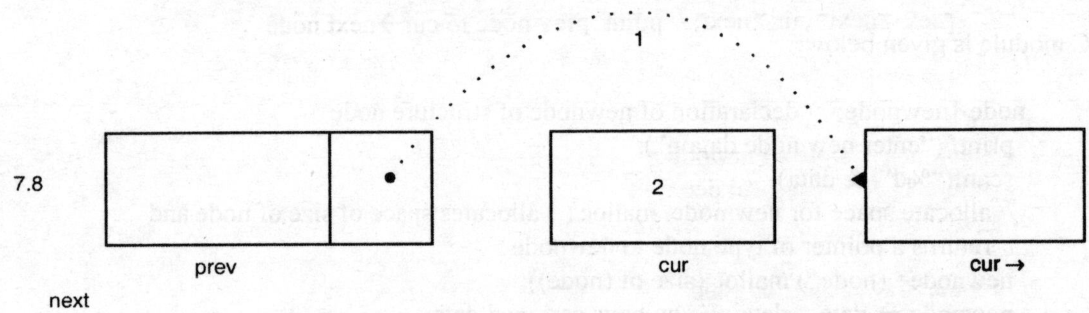

Fig. 9.4 Linked list showing prev,cur,cur->next nodes

01. Locate the position to be deleted by traversing the List. Traversal can be based on finding position or finding a value of a node to be deleted. Cur is the node to be deleted.
02. Point prev → next to current → next. Refer 1 in fig 9.4
03. Delete current node. We have to check if the node we are deleting is the first node. If yes we have to readjust the front pointer.

Now we will write a function modules **int DeletePos** and **int DeleteElm.** Both functions accept **node ** font and, pos/data.** Remember front is a pointer to pointer. Hence we will pass it as &front i.e front is a pointer (address) and &front would make it pointer to pointer. Traversal of the Linked List takes us to desired node whose position or data values matches with argument passed. Function returns 1 on successful deletion. Else it will return a 0.

```
/* deletes at pos.  first element is 0. fn returns 0 if no element at given pos*/

int DeletePos(node ** front, int pos)
  { node *cur,*prev; // declare two pointers
   //check if the node to be deleted is the first node
   i f (pos==0)  // delete first node
     { cur= * front; // store first node in cur for deletion later.
      * front=(*front)->next; // shift header to next node
     }
   else
     { int i=0;
       cur=* front; // store  in cur. We will use cur for traversal.
       while( i< pos && cur)   //| cur!=NULL
       {
           prev=cur;  //store it in prev. You will need prev for pointer readjustment
           cur=cur->next; // go to next node
           i++;
       }
       /* check if element at given pos exists*/
       if(cur)
           prev->next=cur->next; // point  prev node to cur→next node
     }

    if (cur)
     { free(cur); // delete cur node
       return 1;  // successful deletion
     }
    else
      return 0;  // deletion failed
  }// end of DeletePos ( )
```

9.3.4 DeleteElm deletes a node whose data field is given returns 0 if no element is found

```
int DeleteElm(node ** front, int data)
{  node *cur,* prev;
  // traverse to find required node
  cur=*front;
  while(cur&& cur->data!=data)
  {     prev=cur; // save cur in prev
   cur=cur->next;
```

```
}
//if the element  is found
if (cur)
{ // if its first element
    if(cur==*front)
      *front=(*front)->next;
    else
      prev->next=cur->next;
    free(cur);
    return 1;
}
else
    return 0;
}// end of DeleteElm
```

9.3.5 Erasing of Linked List. We will write a module to erase the linked list completely. We will pass *front as argument because we are erasing the Linked list totally.

```
void EraseList( node * front)
  {
    node *cur = front; // cur, we will use for traversal
    while(cur)
      {   front=front->next; // front points to next node in the list
          free(cur);  //delete the node
      }
  }// end of erase list
```

9.3.6 GetChoice ( ) Many a time, we will need a function to get choice from the user. You will also need a function to obtain data for a new node. Further you will need to display the Linked List. Use these modules.

```
int GetChoice ( )
{ int choice ;
   do
     { printf("1. Insert at beginning of the Linked  List \nx");
       printf("2  Delete an element at given position \n");
      printf ("3  Delete an element at given position \n");
     printf ("4  Display the Linked List \n");
     printf ("5  Quit \n");
     printf ("\n Enter your choice.. \n);
     scanf("%d", &choice);
      } while(choice <1 || choice >6); // continue loop
}//end of GetChoice
```

9.3.7 int GetData ( )

```
{  int data;
```

```
    printf(" Enter data for the node\n");
    scanf( "%d", & data);
     return data;
  }//end of GetData( )
```

9.3.8 void DispalyList (node * front)

```
    { node * cur;
      cur = front ; // cur is the node for traversal
      printf("\u  the list is ......\n");
      if (!cur)
         printf("the list is empty ln");
      else
         {
              while (cur)
                 { printf ("%d", cur → data);
                   if (cur → next) ; next node exists
                       print f(" → ");
                   cur= cur → next ; // go to next node
                 }
         }
    } // end of DisplayList( )
```

Example 9.1 list1.c Here comes the complete program.

```
// single Linked List
#include<stdio.h>
#include<stdlib.h>
struct LinkedList
{  int data;
   struct LinkedList * next;
};
typedef struct LinkedList node;
// declarations of function prototypes
void AddFront(node **front,  node  *newnode);
int DeletePos( node **front, int pos);
int DeleteElm( node **front, int data);
void EraseList(node *front);
int GetData();
int GetChoice();
void DisplayList(node *front);

int main()
 {
   node* front =  NULL;
```

```
 node *newnode;
 int data,pos;
while(1)
    {  switch(GetChoice())
       {            case 1:
                      {
                    data=GetData();
                      newnode=( node*) malloc(sizeof(node));
                      newnode->data=data;
                      AddFront(&front,newnode); //&front is a pointer to pointer
                      DisplayList(front);  // front is a pointer to list
                      break;
                    }
                    case 2:
                      {
                           printf("\n Enter the position : ");
                           fflush(NULL);
                           scanf("%d",&pos);
                           if(DeletePos (&front,pos)==0)
                             printf("\n there is no element to delete\n");
                           else
                             {printf("the Linked List after deletion is....\n");
                             DisplayList(front);  // display the list
                             }
                             break;
                    }
                     case 3:
                      {          data=GetData();
                                   if(DeleteElm(&front,data)==0)
                                    printf("no element whose value is %d\n ", data);
                                   else
                                   {
                                    printf(" the Linked List after deletion is....\n");
                                    DisplayList(front);  // display the list
                                   }
                                   break;
                      }
                      case 4:
                           {       DisplayList(front);  // display the list
                                   break;
                           }
                      case 5:
                           {
```

```
                                EraseList(front);
                                break;
                           }
                   case 6:  exit(0);

            } // end of switch
        } // end of while

  }// end of main

//* AddFront adds  node pointed by new node in thebegining
void AddFront (node **front, node *newnode)
 {
   // make new node  as first node.  // next to point to  * front
     newnode->next =*front ;
    *front = newnode ; // ref 2. Now you made newnode to be known as * front.
 }
/* deletes at pos.  first element is 0. fn returns 0 if no element at given pos*/

int DeletePos( node ** front, int pos)
    {      node *cur,*prev; // declare two pointers
           //check if the node to be deleted is the first node

           if (pos==0)   // delete first node
               {
                 cur= * front; // store first node in cur for deletion later.
                 *front=(*front)->next; // shift header to next node
               }
               else
               {
                 int  i=0;
                 cur=*front; // store  in cur. We will use cur for traversal.
                 while( i< pos && cur)    //| cur!=NULL
                   {
                       prev=cur;  //store it in prev. You will need prev for pointer
                                             //readjustment.
                       cur=cur->next; // go to next node
                       i++;
                   }
                 /* check if element at given pos exists*/
                 if(cur)
                 prev->next=cur->next; // point  prev node to cur—>next node
               }
```

```
            if (cur)
            { free(cur); // delete cur node
              return 1;  // successful deletion
            }
            else
              return 0;  // deletion failed
      }// end of DeletePos ( )

/* DeleteElm deletes a node whose data field is given
returns 0 if no element is found*/

int DeleteElm( node **front, int data)
{
  node *cur,* prev;
  // traverse to find required node
  cur=*front;
  while(cur&& cur->data!=data)
  {
    prev=cur; // save cur in prev
    cur=cur->next;
  }
  // if the element  is found
  if (cur)
    { // if its first element
        if(cur==*front)
          *front=(*front)->next;
        else
          prev->next=cur->next;
        free(cur);
        return 1;
    }
    else
        return 0;
}// end of DeleteElm

int GetChoice ( )
      { int choice ;
          do
              { printf("\n1 Insert at beginning of the Linked  List \n");
                printf("2  Delete an element at given position \n");
                printf ("3  Delete an element of given data \n");
                printf ("4  Display the Linked List \n");
                printf ("5  Erase the Linked List \n");
```

```
            printf ("6  Quit \n");
            printf ("\n Enter your choice.. : ");
            fflush(NULL);
            scanf("%d", &choice);
           } while(choice <1 || choice >6); // continue loop
       return (choice);

     }//end of GetChoice()

 int  GetData ( )
   { int data;
    printf("\n Enter data for the node :  ");
    fflush(NULL);
    scanf( "%d", & data);
    return data;
   }//end of GetData( )

void DisplayList (node *front)
     { node * cur;
         cur = front ; // cur is the node for traversal
         if (!cur)
            printf("\n the list is empty \n ");
         else
           {
                 printf("\n the list is......\n");
                 while (cur)
                 { printf ("%d", cur->data);
                    if (cur->next) ;// next node exists
                    printf(" —> ");
                    cur = cur->next ; // go to next node
                 }
           }
} // end of DisplayList( )

void EraseList(node *front)
{
        node *cur;
        cur = front;
        while(cur)
        {
         front = cur -> next;
         free(cur);
         cur = front;
```

```
        DisplayList(front);
    }
    return;
}
/*output
1 Insert at beginning of the Linked  List
2  Delete an element at given position
3  Delete an element of given data
4  Display the Linked List
5   Erase the Linked List
6  Quit

 Enter your choice.. : 1
 Enter data for the node :  10
 the list is......
10 —>
 Enter your choice.. : 1
 Enter data for the node :  20
 the list is......
20 —> 10 —>

 Enter your choice.. : 1
 Enter data for the node :  30
 the list is......
30 —> 20 —> 10 —>
 Enter your choice.. : 3
 Enter data for the node :  20
 the Linked List after deletion is....
 the list is......
30 —> 10 —>

 Enter your choice.. : 1
 Enter data for the node :  50
 the list is......
50 —> 30 —> 10 —>

 Enter your choice.. : 2
 Enter the position : 1
the Linked List after deletion is....
 the list is......
50 —> 10 —>

 Enter your choice.. : 5
 the list is......
10 —>
 the list is empty

 Enter your choice.. : 6 */
```

9.4 REVERSE LIST

In this module functions, void ReverseList (node ** front) we would reverse the list. The lists are shown in 9.5. The reversed list appears at Fig. 9.5b

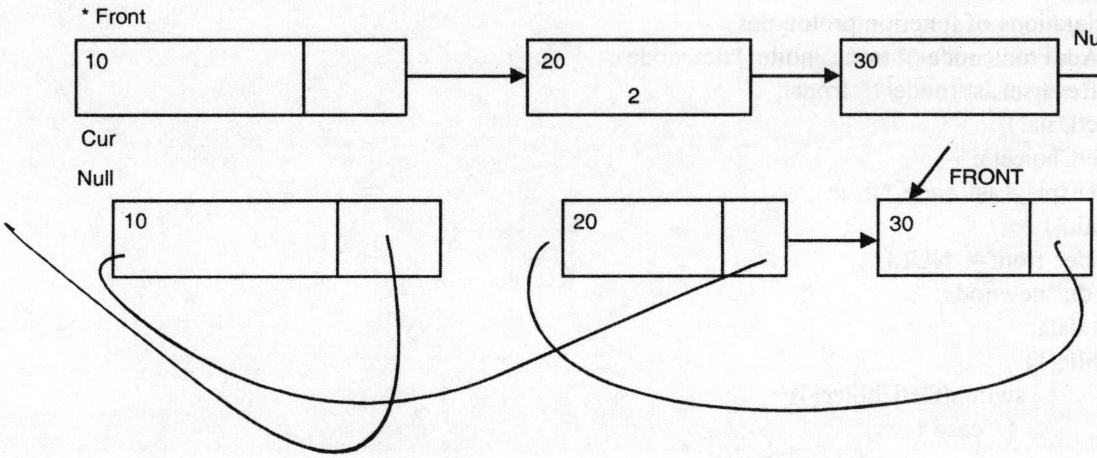

Fig. 9.5 a& b Original linked list and the reversed

```
void ReverseList (node ** front)
 {
       node *cur,*prev, *temp; // declare three  pointers
       cur=*front;
       prev=NULL;
       while ( cur !=NULL)
        {
             temp=prev;
             prev=cur;
             cur=cur->next;
             prev->next=temp;
        }
       *front= prev;
}
```

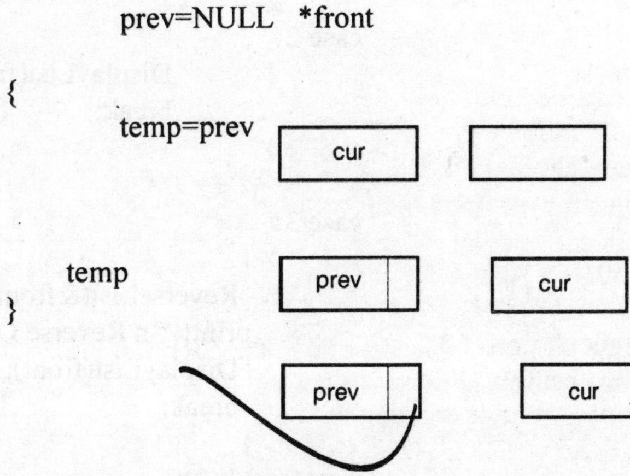

Example 9.2 reverselist.c. Here is the complete listing of the program.

```
//reverselist.c a program to reverse the list.
// single Linked List
#include<stdio.h>
#include<stdlib.h>
```

```
struct LinkedList
{   int data;
    struct LinkedList * next;
};
typedef struct LinkedList node;
// declarations of function prototypes
void AddFront(node **front,  node  *newnode);
void ReverseList (node ** front);
int GetData();
int GetChoice();
void DisplayList(node *front);
int main()
  { node* front =  NULL;
    node *newnode;
    int data;
    while(1)
         {   switch(GetChoice())
             {   case 1:
                     { data=GetData();
                          newnode=( node*) malloc(sizeof(node));
                          newnode->data=data;
                          AddFront(&front,newnode); //&front is a pointer to pointer
                          DisplayList(front);  // front is a pointer to list
                          break;
                     }

                 case 2:
                        {        DisplayList(front);  // display the list
                                 break;
                        }

                 case 3:
                        {
                         ReverseList(&front); //&front is a pointer to pointer
                        printf("\n Reverse Order.....\n");
                         DisplayList(front);  // front is a pointer to list
                         break;
                        }
                case 4:  exit(0);
             } // end of switch
         } // end of while
  }// end of main
```

```
//* AddFront adds  node pointed by new node in thebegining
void AddFront (node **front, node *newnode)
 {
    // make new node  as first node. // next to point to * front
     newnode->next =*front ;
    *front = newnode ; // ref 2. Now you made newnode to be known as * front.
 }
int GetChoice ( )
        { int choice ;
          do
                    { printf("\n1 Insert at beginning of the Linked  List \n");
                      printf ("2  Display the Linked List \n");
                      printf ("3   Reverse the Linked List \n");
      printf ("4  Quit \n");
                      printf ("\n Enter your choice.. : ");
                      fflush(NULL);
                      scanf("%d", &choice);
                    } while(choice <1 || choice >4);  // continue loop
          return (choice);

        }//end of GetChoice()

 int  GetData ( )
   { int data;
    printf("\n Enter data for the node :  ");
    fflush(NULL);
    scanf( "%d", & data);
    return data;
   }//end of GetData( )
void DisplayList (node *front)
    { node * cur;
         cur = front ; // cur is the node for traversal
         if (!cur)
            printf("\n the list is empty \n ");
         else
           {
                 printf("\n the list is......\n");
                 while (cur)
                 { printf ("%d", cur->data);
                    if (cur->next) ;// next node exists
                    printf(" —> ");
                    cur = cur->next ; // go to next node
                 }
           }
```

```
} // end of DisplayList( )
void ReverseList (node ** front)
 {
      node *cur,*prev, *temp; // declare three  pointers
      cur=*front;
      prev=NULL;
      while ( cur !=NULL)
       {
           temp=prev;
           prev=cur;
           cur=cur->next;
           prev->next=temp;
       }
      *front= prev;
}
/*output
1 Insert at beginning of the Linked  List
2  Display the Linked List
3   Reverse the Linked List
4  Quit
Enter your choice.. : 1
Enter data for the node :  10
the list is......
10 —>
Enter your choice.. : 1
Enter data for the node :  20
the list is......
20 —> 10 —>
Enter your choice.. : 1
Enter data for the node :  30
the list is......
30 —> 20 —> 10 —>
Enter your choice.. : 3
Reverse Order.....
 the list is......
10 —> 20 —> 30 —>
*/
```

A note on why we have used **front instead of *front to indicate first node is appropriate here. The idea is two fold. First is to teach you how to handle pointer to pointer in a major application. Secondly **front is affording us to add in the front of the list. In the subsequent applications we would show you how to use *front and still get the result, obviously with much less complexity. Solved Problems also demonstrate the use of a pointer to handle single linked list.

```
node *createlist(node *front)
{   node *temp,*p;
    int dat;
```

```
printf("\nenter data<9999 to stop>:");
scanf("%d",&dat);
while(dat!=9999)
    {  // check if list is empty
     if(front==NULL)
       {front=(node*)malloc(sizeof(node));
        front->data=dat;
        front->next=NULL;
       }
      else
      { temp=front;  //  temp will be use for traversing
      // traverse the list till the end
       while(temp->next!=NULL)
            temp=temp->next;  //now temp points to the last element of the list
      // get a new node and assign data and next to point to NULL
       p=(node*)malloc(sizeof(node));
        p->data=dat;
        p->next=NULL;
        temp->next=p;   // assign prev node to just added node p
       }
       printf("\nenter data<9999 to stop>:");
     scanf("%d",&dat);
    }//end of while
    return(front);
}//end of create list
```

9.5 DOUBLE LINKED LISTS

A single linked list with a pointer to next node, is efficient and fast only when the linked list is small. But for large size linked lists, it is inefficient. Consider for example if you have 1000 nodes and you are currently at 800th node and your destination node is 400. Then, traversal to end of the list takes 200 nodes and a further nodes of 400, making a total of 600 nodes.

In double linked list an additional pointer to previous node is provided so that traversal can be in any direction to the left of current node or to the right of current node.

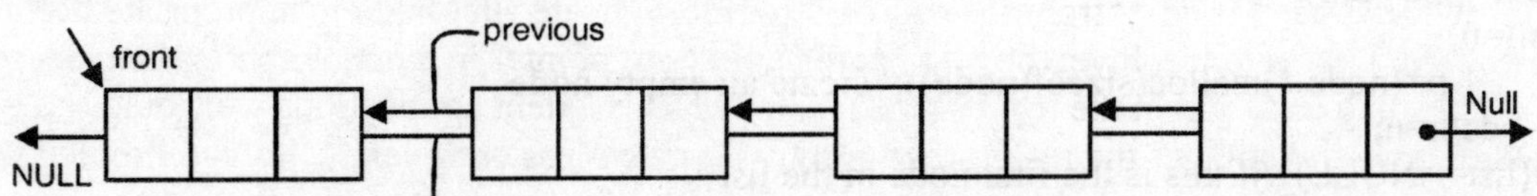

Fig. 9.6 A double linked list with next and previous pointers

Example 9.3 Double Linked List.

```
// dllist.c.double linked list
//dllist.c
#include<stdio.h>
#include<stdlib.h>

struct doublellist
{ int data;
  struct doublellist *left;
  struct doublellist *right;
};
typedef struct doublellist node;

node *createlist(node *list);
node *insert(int n,int val,node *list);//insert node with data=val to the right of node with data=n;
node *delet(int n,node *list);
void printlist(node *list);
void main()
{  int val,n;
   node *list=NULL;
   list=createlist(list);
   printlist(list);
   printf("\nEnter value to be inserted:");
   scanf("%d",&val);
   printf("Node after which value has to be inserted<0 for starting>:");
   scanf("%d",&n);
   list=insert(n,val,list);
   printlist(list);
   printf("\nEnter value to be deleted:");
   scanf("%d",&n);
   list=delet(n,list);
   printlist(list);
}
node *createlist(node *list)
{ int n;
  node *p,*temp;
  do{ printf("Enter value<0 to stop>:");
     scanf("%d",&n);
     if(n!=0)
           { p=(node *)malloc(sizeof(node));//create an empty node
       p->data=n;
       if(list==NULL) //if this is the first node in the list
                      {list=p;
                       p->left=NULL;
                       p->right=NULL;
                      }
       else
```

```
            { temp=list;
             while(temp->left!=NULL)
             temp=temp->left; //traverse to the end of the list
    //now add the new node at the end
             temp->left=p;
             p->right=temp;
             p->left=NULL;
            }
        }
  }while(n!=0);
  return(list);
}//end of createlist
node *insert(int n,int val,node *list)
{ node *p,*temp;
 temp=list;
 p=(node *)malloc(sizeof(node));
 p->data=val;
 if(n==0)
  {p->right=NULL;
  p->left=list;
  list->right=p;
  list=p;
  }
  else
  { while(temp->data!=n && temp->left!=NULL)
    temp=temp->left;  //find location oh n in the list
   if(temp->data!=n)
        {printf("node does not exist in list\n");
    exit(1);
        }
   else
        { p->left=temp->left;
     temp->left=p;
         p->right=temp;
   if(p->left!=NULL) //check if the node is to be added in the end
         (p->left)->right=p;
        }
  }
 return(list);
}
node *delet(int n,node *list)
{ node *temp=list;
 while(temp->data!=n && temp->left!=NULL)
  temp=temp->left;  //find location oh n in the list
```

```
 if(temp->data!=n)
 {printf("node does not exist in list\n");
  exit(1);
 }
 else
 { //case 1:deletion of starting node
        if(temp->right==NULL)//check if it is the staring node
        {list=temp->left;
         list->right=NULL;
         free(temp);
        }
       //case 2:node is general node with left and right nodes
        else
        {(temp->right)->left=temp->left;
         if(temp->left!=NULL) //check if node is last node
    (temp->left)->right=temp->right;
         free(temp);
        }
 }
 return(list);
}
void printlist(node *list)
{  node *temp=list;
   printf("list:");
       if(list==NULL)
       {printf("Empty list");
        exit(1);
       }
       else
       {
        while(temp!=NULL)
        {printf("%5d",temp->data);
         temp=temp->left;
        }
       }
}
/*Output:
Enter value<0 to stop>:34
Enter value<0 to stop>:56
Enter value<0 to stop>:23
Enter value<0 to stop>:67
Enter value<0 to stop>:0
list:  34  56  23  67
```

Enter value to be inserted:55
Node after which value has to be inserted<0 for starting>:0
list: 55 34 56 23 67
Enter value to be deleted:56
list: 55 34 23 67 */

OBJECTIVE QUESTIONS

1. Linked List is dynamic and linear data structure True/False
2. The declaration shown below refers to

```
        struct list
        {
int info;
struct list *next;
};
```

a) Doubly-linked list b) Circular linked list
c) Singly linked list d) Stack

3. In a linear linked list the nodes are linked sequentially True/False
4. If the next pointer is made to point to the first node of the list, the the list can be called as

a) Single linked list b) Circular Linked List
c) double linked list c) circular queue

5. Array is a dynaic data structure True/False
6. In linked Lists, each node contains a pointer that points to

a) instance of same structure that is next to current node
b) Value of next component
c) Pointer to next component
d) None of the above

7. Last node in a linked list points to

a) FIRST node b) Last node
c) NULL d) Previous

8. An abstract data type hides the implementation details True/false
9. Calloc() requires arguments

a) one b) two arguments
c) 0 d) 3

10. Calloc() allocates memory that contain garbage value True/False
11. Malloc() allocates memory that contain garbage value True/False

REVIEW QUESTIONS

1. What is a data structure? Explain the various types of data structures with suitable example?
2. Write the routines to
   a. Insert element at nth position.
   b. Delete element at nth position in double linked list.
3. What is the difference between linked list and an array?
4. What is circular doubly linked list? Explain the various operations on circular doubly linked list with suitable algorithms?
5. Write a function in 'c' to remove duplicate elements in a single linked list?
6. Write a function in 'c' to combine two ordered lists in to a single ordered list?
7. What is single list ? Explain various operations on single linked list with algorithms?

SOLVED PROBLEMS

1. Write a program to concatenate two linked lists. List2 to be attached at the end of list1.

```
//concatlist.c
#include<stdio.h>
#include<stdlib.h>
struct linkedlist
{ int data;
  struct linkedlist *next;
};
typedef struct linkedlist node;
node *createlist(node *front);
node *concatlist(node *front1,node *front2);
void printlist(node *front);
void main()
{ node *front1=NULL;
  node *front2=NULL;
  printf("create first list........\n");
  front1=createlist(front1);
  printlist(front1);
  printf("\ncreate second list.......\n");
  front2=createlist(front2);
  printlist(front2);
  front1=concatlist(front1,front2);
  printlist(front1);
}
node *createlist(node *front)
{   node *temp,*p;
    int dat;
```

```
    printf("\nenter data<0 to stop>:");
   scanf("%d",&dat);
   while(dat!=0)
        {
         if(front==NULL)
           {front=(node*)malloc(sizeof(node));
            front->data=dat;
           front->next=NULL;
        }
          else
          { temp=front;
           while(temp->next!=NULL)
                 temp=temp->next;  //now temp points to the last elemnt of the list
           p=(node*)malloc(sizeof(node));
            p->data=dat;
            p->next=NULL;
            temp->next=p;
           }
           printf("\nenter data<0 to stop>:");
          scanf("%d",&dat);
        }//end of while
        return(front);
}//end of create list
node *concatlist(node *front1,node *front2)
{       node *temp;
        temp=front1;
         while(temp->next!=NULL)
                  temp=temp->next;
         temp->next=front2;
         return(front1);
}
void printlist(node *front)
{  node *temp;
   temp=front;
   printf("\nPrinting list........\n");
   while(temp->next!=NULL)
        { printf("%d\t",temp->data);
          temp=temp->next;
        }
  printf("%d",temp->data);
}
/*output
create first list........
```

```
enter data<0 to stop>:76
enter data<0 to stop>:279
enter data<0 to stop>:90
enter data<0 to stop>:0
Printing list........
76      279     90
create second list.......
enter data<0 to stop>:34
enter data<0 to stop>:67
enter data<0 to stop>:98
enter data<0 to stop>:0
Printing list........
34      67      98
Printing list........
76      279     90      34      67      98*/
```

2 Write a program to sort a linked list

```
#include<stdio.h>
#include<stdlib.h>

struct linkedlist
{ int data;
  struct linkedlist *next;
};
typedef struct linkedlist node;
 node *createlist(node *front);
 node *llsort(node *front);
 void printlist(node *front);

void main()
{node *front=NULL;
  printf("create list........\n");
   front=createlist(front);
  printlist(front);
   front=llsort(front);
  printf("\nsorted linked list.......\n");
   printlist(front);
}

 node *createlist(node *front)
 { node *temp,*p;
   int dat;
```

```
printf("\nenter data<0 to stop>:");
scanf("%d",&dat);
    while(dat!=0)
        { if(front==NULL) //if the new node to be created is the first node in the list
                {front=(node*)malloc(sizeof(node)); //create newnode and store address as
in front
                 front->data=dat; //assign data to the first node
                 front->next=NULL;
                }
      else
                { temp=front;
      while(temp->next!=NULL)//traverse the list till you reach the last node
                        temp=temp->next; //now temp points to the last element of the list
       p=(node*)malloc(sizeof(node));//create new node
                        p->data=dat; //assign data to the new node
                        p->next=NULL;
                        temp->next=p; //make the last node point to the new node
                }
                printf("\nenter data<0 to stop>:");
      scanf("%d",&dat);
          }//end of while
          return(front);
}

node *llsort(node *front)
{  node *temp,*min,*p,*q,*r,*previous;//create theree pointers
   int val;
       min=front;
       r=front;
       while(min!=NULL)
       { temp=min->next;
            previous=min;
             val=min->data;
             while(temp!=NULL)
                { while(val<temp->data)
                      { previous=temp;
                    temp=temp->next;
                       if(temp==NULL)
                        break;
                      }
                 if(temp!=NULL)
                 { if(min->next==temp)
                       { min->next=temp->next;
```

```
temp->next=min;
                                if(min==front)
                                      front=temp;
                                else
                                r->next=temp;
                        }
                        else
                        { p=temp->next;
                          previous->next=min;
                              temp->next=min->next;
                          min->next=p;
                        if(min==front)
                         front=temp;
        else
          r->next=temp;
                        }
                        q=temp; //swap temp and min
                        temp=min;
                        min=q;
                  val=min->data;//set val to newmin
                                if(min==front)
                                r=min;
                            previous=temp;
                            temp=temp->next;
                     }//end of if
                    }//end of while
     r=min;
                    min=min->next;
   }//end of while
  return(front);
}
void printlist(node *front)
{ node *temp;
  temp=front;
  printf("\nPrinting list........\n");
   while(temp->next!=NULL)
        { printf("%d\t",temp->data);
          temp=temp->next;
        }
  printf("%d",temp->data);
}
```

```
/*Output:
create list........
enter data<0 to stop>:34
enter data<0 to stop>:56
enter data<0 to stop>:12
enter data<0 to stop>:78
enter data<0 to stop>:93
enter data<0 to stop>:100
enter data<0 to stop>:3
enter data<0 to stop>:59
enter data<0 to stop>:67
enter data<0 to stop>:0

Printing list........
34    56    12    78    93    100   3     59    67
sorted linked list.......
Printing list........
3     12    34    56    59    67    78    93    100*/
```

3. Write a program to merge two sorted linked lists

```
#include<stdio.h>
#include<stdlib.h>

struct linkedlist
{       int data;
struct linkedlist *next;
};
typedef struct linkedlist node;
node *createlist(node *front,int dat);
node *llmerge(node *front1,node *front2);
void printlist(node *front);
void main()
{ node *front1=NULL;
  node *front2=NULL;
  node *front3=NULL;
  int dat;
  printf("create first list........\n");
  do{ printf("\nenter data<0 to stop>:");
     scanf("%d",&dat);
     if(dat!=0)
          front1=createlist(front1,dat);
  }while(dat!=0);
```

```
  printlist(front1);
  printf("\ncreate second list.......\n");
  do{
   printf("\nenter data<0 to stop>:");
   scanf("%d",&dat);
   if(dat!=0)
                    front2=createlist(front2,dat);
  }while(dat!=0);
          printlist(front2);
  front3=llmerge(front1,front2);
  printlist(front3);
}
node *createlist(node *front,int dat)
{  node *temp,*p;
  if(front==NULL)
  {  front=(node*)malloc(sizeof(node));
         front->data=dat;
         front->next=NULL;
  }
  else
         { temp=front;
   while(temp->next!=NULL)
                  temp=temp->next;  //now temp points to the last element of the list
   p=(node*)malloc(sizeof(node));
         p->data=dat;
         p->next=NULL;
         temp->next=p;
  }
  return(front);
}
node *llmerge(node *front1,node *front2)
{
        node *temp1,*temp2;
        node *front3=NULL;
        temp1=front1;
         temp2=front2;
          while(temp1!=NULL && temp2!=NULL)
          { if(temp1->data>temp2->data)
                 {      front3=createlist(front3,temp2->data);
                            temp2=temp2->next;
                 }
      else
       {
```

```
                    front3=createlist(front3,temp1->data);
                    temp1=temp1->next;
            }
    }//end of while
        if(temp1==NULL)
        {  while(temp2!=NULL)
            {
       front3=createlist(front3,temp2->data);
                    temp2=temp2->next;
            }
    }
    else
        {  while(temp1!=NULL)
            {   front3=createlist(front3,temp1->data);
                  temp1=temp1->next;
            }
        }
    return(front3);
}
void printlist(node *front)
{
        node *temp;
        temp=front;
  printf("\nPrinting list........\n");
        while(temp->next!=NULL)
        {  printf("%d\t",temp->data);
           temp=temp->next;
        }
  printf("%d",temp->data);
}
/* output
create first list........
enter data<0 to stop>:1
enter data<0 to stop>:3
enter data<0 to stop>:4
enter data<0 to stop>:7
enter data<0 to stop>:9
enter data<0 to stop>:0
Printing list........
1    3    4    7    9
create second list.......
enter data<0 to stop>:2
enter data<0 to stop>:4
```

enter data<0 to stop>:6
enter data<0 to stop>:8
enter data<0 to stop>:0
Printing list........
2 4 6 8
Printing list........
1 2 3 4 6 7 8 9*/

ASSIGNMENT PROBLEMS

1. Write a "C" program to reverse the elements in a single linked list.
2. How can a polynomial in three variables(x,y&z)be represented by a singly linked list? Each node should represent a term and should contain the power of x,y,z as well as coefficient of that term. write a "C" program to add two such polynomials.
3. Write a "C" program to exchange two nodes of a singly linked list.
4. Write a "C" program to create a singly linked list and split it at the middle and make the second hay as the first and make the second hay as the first and vise-versa display the final list.
5. Write a "C" program to multiply two polynomials

Solutions to Objective Questions

1) True	2) c	3) true	4) b	5) False	6) a
7) c	8) True	9) b	10) False	11) True	

CHAPTER 10

STACKS

10.1 INTRODUCTION

We have seen linked lists, linear, double, and circular linked lists and seen how they are useful data structures. In this chapter, we will study one of the most frequently used data structure, called stacks. Stack is a linear data structure. Data is inserted and extracted based on a technique called Last in first Out. As an example think of an activity of students submitting assignments to teacher. The teacher will receive and pile them in a stack on the table, and starts corrections from the top. Therefore, last in assignment gets service first. As you will see computer system depends on stack structure to solve several of the problems.

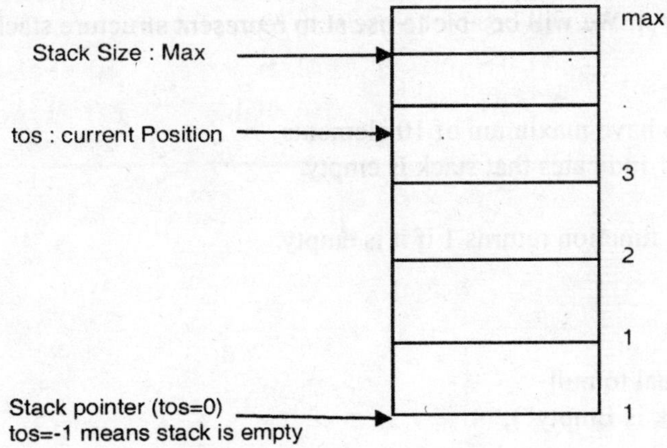

Fig. 10.1 Stack representation and terms

10.2 STACK OPERATIONS

We can perform following operations on a stack:

1. Create a stack.
2. Check if stack is full or empty. We can not insert into a full stack. Neither we can extract from empty stack.

3. Initialize the stack. For example, SP = -1, and tos = max - 1; are initialization commands. Stack extends from 0 to (max –1).
4. Push (insert) an element onto stack, if it is not full.
5. Pop(extract) an element from the stack, if it is not empty.
6. Read from top of stack.
7. Display / Print the entire stack.

Stack can be implemented using array or linked lists. We will learn the theory of stacks using arrays and later on show how it is implemented using linked lists.

10.3 ARRAY IMPLEMENTATION OF STACK DATA STRUCTURE

We can define data structure for stack as follows:

```
struct stack //implement stack as a structure
{
        int s[10]; // 10 elements in the stack
        int sp;   // top of stack
};
typedef struct stack st;
```

We have typecasted stack as st. We will be able to use st to represent structure stack. We can initialize the stack using

```
#define max = 10 ; stack to have maximum of 10 elements
st.sp = -1 ; // assigning to –1 indicates that stack is empty.
```

Check if stack is Empty. The function returns 1 if it is empty.

```
int isEmpty()

{  if(st.sp==-1) //if top is equal to null
        {       printf("Stack is Empty");
                return 1;
        }
 else
    return 0;
}// end of isEmpty()
```

Check if stack is full; The function returns 1 if it is full.

```
int isFull ()
{  if(st.sp==max-1) //if top is equal to max position
```

```
        {       printf("Stack is overflow");
                return 1;
        } .
  else
    Return 0;
 } // end of isFull()
```

Push Operation : Check if stack is full. If not full push the element to stack using 'push' instruction. Then increment sp pointer by 1.

```
int push(int val)
{   /* data item to be pushed onto stack. Ans holds information if stack
  is full or empty returned by function isFull()*/
  int ans;
  ans = st.isFull(); // we have invoked isFull()
  if ( ans == 0)   // stack is not full
          { st.sp++;//increment sp to next position
            st.s[st.sp]=val;//assigning vai to st[sp]
    }
    else
    { printf("Stack is overflow");
    }
    return 0;
} // end of int push ().
```

Pop Operation : Check if stack is empty. If not empty the pop the element. Decrement the stack pointer SP by 1.

```
int pop()
{
        int ans ; // ans hold the return value from isEMpty(). 1 if it is
          // empty. Else it holds 0.

    ans = st.isEmpty();
    if (ans == 0) // The stack is not empty
     {
      //print popped item
      printf("The pop element is \t%d",st.s[st.sp]);
      st.sp—; //decrement stack[sp]
     }
    else
     {
      printf( "\n Stack is Empty");
     }
}// end of int pop
```

Display operation: This operation is simple and straight forward. In fact by now you should be comfortable with these kind of modules. We are displaying the stack from top to bottom to reflect its LIFO structure, i.e from current sp to beginning of stack.

```
int disp()//display function
{       int i, ans ;
        printf("\n");

        if (st.isEmpty()= 0) // function returns 0 i.e stack is not empty
         {   for(i=st.sp;i>=0;i—) //display stack items
             printf("%d\t",st.s[i]);
         }
    else
      {      printf("\n stack is Empty.");
      }
    return 0;
}//end disp()
```

Now, we present full program for implementation of stack data structure using arrays.

Example 10.1 stackarray.c

```
/* program to implement stack operations using arrays */
//stackarr.c
#include<stdio.h>
#define max 10 //assign variable max to 10. Number of stack array

// Prototype Declarations

int push(int val);
int pop();
int disp();
int isEmpty();
int isFull();

// Stack structure declaration.

struct stack //implement stack as a structure
{
        int s[10];
        int sp;
};
typedef struct stack stk; // typedefining structure stk as st.
stk st;

int main()
{
```

```
        int choice,item; // item is data to be pushed on to stack
        st.sp=-1; // Initialization command. -1 indicates stack is empty.

        do
        {
                printf("\n\n");
                printf("\n menu");
                printf("\n 1:push");
                printf("\n 2:pop");
                printf("\n 3:display");
                printf("\n 4:exit\t\t");
                printf("\n Enter your choice:");
                scanf("%d",&choice);
                switch(choice)

                {
                        case 1:
            printf("\nEnter an element to push: ");
                  scanf("%d",&item); //scan item
                                        push(item);
                                        disp();
                                        break;
                        case 2:
                                        pop();
                                        disp();
                                        break;
                        case 3:
                                        disp();
                                        break;
                }

        }while(choice !=4);
    return 0;
}// end of main

// Function Declarations

int isEmpty()

{
 if(st.sp==-1) //if top is equals to null
        {
                //printf("Stack is Empty");
```

```
                return 1;
        }
 else
    return 0;
}// end of isEmpty()

int isFull ()
 {
   if(st.sp==max-1) //if top is equals to max position
        {
        //          printf("Stack overflow");
                    return 1;
        }
   else
     return 0;
  } // end of isFull()

int push(int val)
{
  /* data item to be pushed onto stack. Ans holds information if stack
  is full or empty returned by function isFull()*/
  int ans;
  ans = isFull(); // we have invoke isFull()
  if ( ans == 0)  // stack is not full
        {

          st.sp++;//increment sp to next position
          st.s[st.sp]=val;//assigning val to st[sp]
   }
   else
    {
      printf("Stack overflow");
        }
    return 0;
} // end of int push ().

int pop()
{
        int ans ; // ans hold the return value from isEMpty(). 1 if it is
          // empty. Else it hold 0.
    ans = isEmpty();
    if (ans == 0) // The stack is not empty
     {
```

```
//print popped item
printf("\nThe pop element is \t%d",st.s[st.sp]);
st.sp—; //decrement stack[sp]

        }
    else
    {
    printf( "\n Stack is Empty no items to pop");
    }
        return 0;
}// end of int pop

    int disp()//display function
    {
            int i ;
            printf("\n");

            if (isEmpty()== 0)
            {

                        printf("\n ****elements of stack****");
                        for(i=st.sp;i>=0;i—) //display stack items
                printf("\n %d\t",st.s[i]);
        }
        else
        {
        printf("\n stack is Empty.");
        }
    return 0;
    }//end disp()
/*output
 menu
 1:push
 2:pop
 3:display
 4:exit
 Enter your choice:1
Enter an element to push: 10
 ****elements of stack****
 10
 menu
 Enter your choice:1
Enter an element to push: 20
```

```
****elements of stack****
20
10
menu
Enter your choice:1
Enter an element to push: 30
****elements of stack****
30
20
10
menu
Enter your choice:3
****elements of stack****
30
20
10
menu
Enter your choice:2
The pop element is      30
****elements of stack****
20
10
menu
Enter your choice:4 */
```

Compile and run. Push and pop operations are important. Get acquainted well with basic functions presented here. In subsequent sections we will concentrate only on main functionality. You should be able to build full programme by using functions described in this section. Let us turn our attention to stack implementation using linked list.

■■■ 10.4 STACK IMPLEMENTATION USING LINKED LISTS

Example 10.2 stacklist.c

```
/*Implementation of stack data structure using Linked List
  stackll.c*/
  # include<stdio.h>
  # include<stdlib.h>
  #define size 10

  struct stack
  {     int data;
        struct stack *next; // self referential structure
  };
```

```
typedef struct stack stk;
stk *tos=NULL;
void push();
int pop();
void display();
void main()
{int choice=0;
 int val;
 do
 {       printf("\n  Menu Details........ \n");
         printf("\n 1.  push a data item onto stack and display");
         printf("\n 2.  pop a data item from stack and display");
         printf("\n 3.  display stack");
         printf("\n 4.  exit");
        printf("\n enter your choice:");
        scanf("%d",&choice);
        switch(choice)
         {
          case 1:
                        push();
                        display();
                        break;
          case 2:  val=pop();
                        printf("\n pop up value= %d",val);
                        printf("\n stack after pop up");
                        display();
                        break;
          case 3:  display();
                        break;
          case 4:  printf("exiting from the programme");
                        break;
         default: printf("\nwrong choice<enter between 1 & 4 only");
                  }
        }while(choice!=4);
}//end of main

// Function definitions
 void push()
  {       stk *node; // node is new node to be pushed as first node
          node=(stk*)malloc(sizeof(stk));
          printf("\n enter data to be pushed on to stack:");
          scanf("%d",&node->data);
          //make node as first node of stack
```

```
        node->next=tos;
      tos=node; // now tos points to new node inserted
}
int pop()
{  int val; // val returns data item from top of stack
        // store first node in temp
        stk *temp;
        temp=tos;
   //check if stack is empty
        if (tos==NULL)
        { printf("\n stack is empty");
          exit(0);
       }
        else
        { val=tos->data;
          // shift tos to next element
          tos=tos->next;
        free(temp); // release temp
        }
        return val;
}
void display()
 {      stk *temp;
        temp=tos; // we will use temp for traversing the stack
        printf("\n Stack elements are....\n");
        if (temp == NULL)
          printf("\n stack is empty");
        else
        { while (temp->next!=NULL)
          {          printf(" %d \n",temp->data);
                     temp=temp->next;
           } //end of while
       //now last element still left for display
        printf("%d",temp->data);
      }//end of if
}
/*output

 Menu Details........

      1.  push a data item onto stack and display
      2.  pop a data item from stack and display
      3.  display stack
      4.  exit
```

```
enter your choice:1
enter data to be pushed on to stack:100
Stack elements are....
100
 Menu Details........
enter your choice:1
enter data to be pushed on to stack:200
Stack elements are....
200
100
 Menu Details........
enter your choice:1
enter data to be pushed on to stack:300
Stack elements are....
300
200
100
 Menu Details........
 enter your choice:3
Stack elements are....
300
200
100
 Menu Details........
enter your choice:2
pop up value= 300
stack after pop up
Stack elements are....
200
100
 Menu Details........
```

10.5 APPLICATIONS OF STACK

10.5.1 Infix to Postfix Notation. Normally you will code your expressions in the programmes using infix notation, but compiler understands and uses only postfix notation and hence it has to convert infix notation to post fix notation. For this activity, stack data structure is used. We will consider following binary operators and their precedence rules:

^ Exponentiation

****/ Multiplication and Division. Both have same priority***
Execution is from left to right.

+- Addition and Subtraction. Both have same priority
Execution is from left to right.

When un parenthesized operators are encountered
Exponentiation : order is from right to left
Example A^B^C means A^(B^C)
Other Operators : order is from left to right
Example D+E-G means (D+E)-G

Let us solve a problem

Infix notation : A +B * C – D

Step 1 : Based on priorities of operators, parenthesize the expression. You know, the priority for the expression given is (* or /) and followed by (+ or -).

((A + (B * C)) – D)

Step 2. Check your brackets are correct and opening and closing brackets match.

Opening brackets = closing brackets = 3

Step 3. Number your brackets starting from Right Hand side. Give the same number to governing bracket on left hand side.

```
( ( A +  ( B *  C ) ) – D )
1 2      3       3 2    1          start ←
```

Step 4 : Start scanning from RHS and when you encounter a closed bracket (for example 1), identify opening bracket with the same number and putdown the governing operator for the pair (in this case it is '–'. We can store it on a stack by push command. Continue till you encounter next closing bracket (2), pushing variable or symbols on to stack (for example D). Stack, now holds D -.

```
( ( A +  ( B *  C ) ) – D )
1 2      3       3 2    1          start ←
```

For closing and opening bracket pair numbered 2, the governing operator is '+'. Push it on to stack : Stack now is + D -. Next, you encounter bracket pair 3 and governing operator is *. Push it on to stack ; stack now holds * + D -. Continue scanning and you will encounter variables C B, and A. Push them on to stack. The stack at the end of conversion A B C * + D -.

Post Fix Notation : A B C * + D -

Now attempt all the problems in the exercise before you proceed to analyze the c code. The algorithm is presented below:

Step 1 : Do for each character in the infix string repeat steps 2 to 5
Step 2 : if (character = = operand)
        Append to postfix string
Step 3 : If (character == "(")
        Push it on to stack.
Step 4: If (character == operator)

```
{ While (priority of operator on tos >= priority of Operator)
    { pop()
      append to postfix string
    }
    push(operator)
}
```

Step 5: If (symbol == ")")

```
{ while( pop()!="(")
    {
     pop()
     append to postfix string
    }
   // drop "(" parenthesis
}
```

Step 6 : if input string ends then pop and append the stack contents to output string.
Step 7 : Exit

Example 10.3 Infix to post fix notation
//in2post.c

```
#include<stdio.h>//preprocessor
#include<string.h>//preprocessor
#include<stdlib.h>//preprocessor

 int preceed(char c);
 void push(char c);
 char pop();
 char stk[30];
 int tos =-1;
void main()
{       int i,j=0,n,u,v;
        char infix[30],postfix[30];
  char c;

  printf("\n enter the infix expression:");
```

```
    scanf("%s",infix);
    n=strlen(infix);
  for(i=0;i<n;i++)
          {
                  if((infix[i]>= 'a' && infix[i]<= 'z') || (infix[i]>= 'A' && infix[i]<= 'Z'))
                  {  postfix[j] = infix[i];
                     j=j+1;
   } //end of if
   else
    if( infix[i]=='^'||infix[i]=='*'||infix[i]=='/' ||infix[i]=='+'||infix[i]=='-')
                  {           u = preceed(stk[tos]);
                              v = preceed(infix[i]);
                     while(v<= u && stk[tos]!= '(')
                         {           postfix[j]=pop();
                                     j=j+1;
                                     u = preceed(stk[tos]);

      }
     push(infix[i]);
   }//end of else if 1
   else
                  if( infix [i] == '(')
                  { push(infix[i]);
                  } // end of else if 2
else
              if (infix[i] == ')')
              { c = pop();
               while(c != '(')
                            { postfix[j]= c;
                              j=j+1;
      c= pop();
    } // end of while
                  }// end of if else 3
              else
                   {
                   printf("\n\tTHE EQUATION HAS ERROR");
                   exit(0);
                  }//end else

            } // end of for
            while(tos!=-1)
            {  postfix[j]= pop();
   j=j+1;
            }
```

```
            postfix[j]='\0';
      printf("\nThe equation in POSTFIX notation is: %s\n",postfix);
}//end main

int preceed(char c)//preceed function
{  int v;
      switch(c)
      {
            case '^': v=3;
                  break;
            case '*':
            case '/': v=2;
                  break;
            case '+':
            case '-': v=1;
                  break;
            default : v=0;
                  break;
      }//end switch
      return(v);
}//end preced()


void push(char c)
 { tos++;
  stk[tos] = c;
 }


char pop()
{ char val;
 val = stk[tos];
 tos—;
 return(val);
}
/*output
 enter the infix expression:A+B*C-D
The equation in POSTFIX notation is: ABC*+D-*/
```

10.5.2 Evaluation of Postfix Expression. Stack data structure can be employed to evaluate post fix notation expression. We provide the example, algorithm and code. Analyze and understand the algorithm and code. Be advised that these kind of algorithms are used by compilers to evaluate expressions written in your code.

Algorithm

1 Scan the input symbol from a given input string

If (symbol = = operand)
Push it on to stack.
2 Else
{
if (symbol = = operator)
apply operation on two operands
obtained by two successive stack pop operations

Push the result on to stack.
}
3. Continue steps 1 & 2 till end of input string

Example for evlaution of a postfix notation expression

Infix notation : A +B * C – D

Post Fix notation : A B C * + D -

For A = 2, B = 3, C = 4, and D = 5 ; the above infix expression would yield 2 + 3 * 4 – 5 = 9. Let us see how our stack goes around doing its job

Step 1 : first 3 symbols are operands A B C i.e 2, 3,4 ; hence they are pushed on to stack. Stack entries are :

→ C B A i.e 4 3 2

Step 2 : Now you will encounter *. Therefore pop two top most operands from stack and perform the operation and push the result on to stack.

Operands popped : C & B i.e 4 * 3 = 12
Push result on to stack.
Stack entries at this stage are : **→ 12 2**

Step 3 : Now you will encounter +
POP 12 & 2 and Result = 12 + 2
Push on to stack. Stack entry now will be : 14

Step 4 : Next encounter is D. Push it on to stack. Stack entries at this stage :
→ 5 14

Step 5 : Next to encounter is - . Therefore pop two entries from stack i.e 5 & 14. Perform the operation 14 – 5 = 9.

Push the result on to stack : ⟶ 9

We provide the code in the next sub section. However, we encourage you to write the code yourself by looking at the algorithm. That is how good programmers take shape.

Example 10.4 eval.c

```
/* program for evaluation of a post fix expression. */

#include<stdio.h>//preprocessor
#include<string.h>//preprocessor
#include<stdlib.h>//preprocessor
#include<math.h>//preprocessor
char p[20]; //input string
float s[10];// stack
signed int top=-1,i=0,j=0,n;
float a,b,c,x;
//function declarations
signed int push(float);
float pop();
float pow1(float,float);
void main()//main function
 {
        printf("\n\tEnter An expression in post fix notation\n\t");
        scanf("%s",p);
        n=strlen(p);//find length of expression
        // we are inserting ")" because we can check end of expression
   // and '\0' to denote end of string
   p[n]=')';
   p[n+1]='\0';
        n=n+2;
        while(p[i]!=')')
        {
                switch(p[i])
                {
                        case '+':
                                        b=pop();
                                        a=pop();
                                        c=a+b;
                                        push(c);
                                        break;
                        case '-':
                                        b=pop();
                                        a=pop();
                                        c=a-b;
```

```
                                push(c);
                                break;
                case '*':
                                a=pop();
                        b=pop();
                                c=a*b;
                                push(c);
                                break;
                case '/':

                                b=pop();
                                a=pop();
                                c=a/b;
                                push(c);
                                break;
                case '^':
                                b=pop();
                                a=pop();
                                c=pow1(a,b);
                                push(c);
                                break;
                default :
        /*we have to typecast p[i] which is character
        to float so that we can push it on to float
        type stack*/
                            x = float(p[i]-'0');
                                push(x);
                                break;

            }
            i++;
    }
 printf("\n\tThe evaluation of given expression is %8.4f\n\t",s[top]);
}//end main

//function definitions
int push(float x)//push function
{
        top++;//increment top
        s[top]=x;//assign x to stack of top
        s[top+1]='\0';
        return 0;
}//end push
float pop()//pop function
```

```
{
        float item;
        item=s[top];//assign stack of top to item
        s[top]='\0';
        top--;//decrement top
        return (item);
}//end pop

float pow1(float a, float b)//power function
{
        int i;
        float n =1;
        for(i=1;i<=b;i++)
        {
        n=n*a;
        }//end for
        return n;
}//end pow1()
```

Output :

Infix Expression : A - B/(C * D ^ E)
Postfix Expression :ABCDE^*/-. values for ABCDE are : 5 4 3 2 1

Enter An expression in post fix notation
54321^*/-

The evaluation of given expression is 4.3333
Press any key to continue

OBJECTIVE QUESTIONS

1) Which of the following mechanism is followed by stack:
   a) LILO b) FIFO
   c) LIFO d) None of the above
2. Automatic variables are stored in
   a) Stack b) Queues
   c) static d) heap memory
3. Stack using a linked list is better than a stack using array implementation because memory size is fixed True/False
4. To remove an item fron the stack, we use
   a) push b) pop
   c) tos d) top

5 To insert an item fron the stack, we use

a) push b) pop

c) tos d) top

6. An empty stack is denoted by

a) tos=0 b) tos=1

c) tos=-1 d) tos=max+1

7. A stack linear data structure True/False

8 A stack is static data structure True/False

9 pop() operation

a) displays the value popped on the screen

b) value is removed from top of stack and stored in a variable.

c) value is popped but lost.

d) none of the above.

10 top of stack pointer is incremented before push operation True/False

REVIEW QUESTIONS

1) Declare two stacks of varying length in a single array. Write c routines push1, push2, pop1and pop2 to manipulate the two stacks.

2) Discuss two applications of the stack.

3 Use the operations push, pop, stacktop, and empty to construct operations on stack, which do each of the following.

a) Given an integer n, set i to the n the element from the top of stack, leaving the stack unchanged ans

b) set i to the bottom elements of stack, leaving stack empty.

SOLVED PROBLEMS

1. Convert following infix expression to postfix expression.

A ^ B * C – D + E / F/ (G + H)

Step 1: Parenthesize

$$\Big(\Big(\big((A \wedge B) * C\big) - D\Big) + \big((E / F) / (G + H)\big)\Big)$$

1 5 6 7 7 6 5 2 4 4 3 3 2 1

Step 2: Check the correctness of parenthesizing by numbering

No. of open braces and closed braces

open braces=7 Close braces = 7

Step 3: Number the braces from right to left with Gove ring operator is +

Step 4: In postfix operators are placed after the operand and we will scan from right to left. Here is the post fix expression.

AB ^ C * D – E F / G H + / +

How did we put the postfix expression

Scan from right to left i.e follow

Scan from right to left i.e follow ←

Symbol	Gove ring operator	Output
Closed brace 1	+	+
Closed brace 2	/	/
Closed brace 3	+	+
H		H
G		G
Closed brace 4	/	/
Closed brace 5	-	-
D		D
Closed brace 6	*	*
Closed brace 7		^
B		B
A		A

Solution :

A B ^ C * D –EF/GH+/

2. Convert following infix expression to postfix expression.

((A + B) * C – (D – E)) ^ (F + G)

Parenthesize, number the braces and scan from right to left

((((A + B) * C) – (D – E)) ^ (F + G)) ←

1 3 5 6 6 5 4 4 3 2 2 1

A B + C * D E – – F G + ^

3. Convert following infix expression to postfix expression.

(A + B) * ((C + D) – E) * F ←

Parenthesize, number braces . Scan from right to left

(((A + B) * ((C + D) – E)) * F) ←

1 2 5 5 3 4 4 3 2 1

A B + C D + E – * F *

4. Convert following infix expression to postfix expression.

A + B * C + D – E * F

Parenthesize, number braces . Scan from right to left

```
( ( (A+(B * C))+D)-(E* F))   <----
1 3 4    5        5 4   3  2       2 1
```

ABC*+D+EF*-

5. Convert following infix expression to postfix expression.

A - B / (C * D ^ E)

Parenthesize, number braces . Scan from right to left

```
( A - ( B / ( C * ( D ^ E ) ) ) )   <----
1       2     3       4      4 3 2 1
```

ABCDE^*/-

Now let us convert infix to prefix. The rules are same as postfix but we will scan from right to left and place operators in front of operands

6. Convert following infix expression to prefix expression.

A ^ B * C - D + E / F / (G + H)

Step 1: The prefix form of the given expression is

+-*^ABCD//EF+GH

How did we get the expression

Insert brace brackets to get the desired operations

Check the correctness of brace brackets

Scan from right to left & place the operators in front of operands

```
---->  ( ( ( ( A ^ B ) * C ) - D ) + ( ( E / F ) / ( G + H ) ) )
       1 5 6 7         7     6     5  2 4         4   3         3 2 1
```

Operator / Operand	Governing operator	Output
open brace 1	+	+
open brace 5	-	-
open brace 6	*	*
open brace 7	^	^
A		A
B		B
C		C
D	/	D
open brace 2	/	/
open brace 4		/
E		E
F		F
open brace 3	+	+
G		G
H		H

7. Convert ((A + B) * C – (D – E)) ^ (F + G) to prefix expression

Parenthesize

Scan right to left

Place operators before operand

^ - * + A B C - D E + F G

We have put it directly we advise you to go through all the steps till the process is clear.

7. Convert (A + B) * ((C + D) – E) * F to prefix expression

* * + A B - + C D E F

8. Convert A + B * C + D – E * F to prefix expression

- + + A * B C D * E F

9. Convert A - B / (C * D ^ E) to prefix expression

- A / B * C ^ D E

10. Apply evaluation algorithm and evaluate following postfix expression

A- (B+C) for A = 1, B =2, C = 3, D = 4

Given post fix expression :B C + A -

Infix = ((B + C) – A)

1 2 2 1 ←

a) A B C + -

Step 1: First three symbols are operands. So push them on to stack

→ 3 2 1

Step 2: Now you will encounter '+' pop two upper most entries 3,2 and perform operations i.e. 3 + 2 = 5. Push it on to stack

→ 5 1

Step 3: Now you will encounter - . Pop two from Stack and perform output : 1 – 5 = - 4. Note that when we pop two elements b & a. Then we have to perform a operator b. Hence it will be 1 - 5

Answer = 4

11. Apply evaluation algorithm and evaluate following postfix expression

A B C + * C B A - + * for A = 1, B =2, C = 3

1) ABC are operands. Therefore Push → 3 2 1
2) +. Therefore Pop two elements from stack 2 + 3 = 5 & Push → 5 1
3) *. Therefore Pop two elements from stack 5 * 1 = 5 & Push → 5
4) C B A are operand. Therefore Push → 1 2 3 5
5) -. Therefore Pop two elements from Stack (2 – 1) = 1 Push → 1 3 5
6) +. Therefore Pop two elements from Stack (3 + 1) = 4 Push → 4 5
7) *. Therefore Pop two elements from Stack (4 * 5) = 20 Push → 20

Result = 20

12. Write a program to convert of a number from one base to another using Stack data structure.

We will use stack data structure to convert a number from one base to another base. For example decimal to binary. Algorithm and code are given below. We are providing a function call to a function void Convert(int num1, int base1,int base2). We encourage you to build the complete program and test it to convert it to number of required base.

Algorithm:

Step1: Obtain inputs viz num,base
Step2: rem = num1%base
Step3: push(rem)
Step4: num1= num1/base
Step5: repeat steps 2 to 4 till num ! = 0
Step6: display stack items on LIFO basis

```
//numconver.c
#include<stdio.h>
#include<conio.h>
#define max 12 //assign varriable max to 10. Number of stack array
// Prototype Declarations
void push(int val);//pushes val on to top of stack
int pop();
int disp();
int isEmpty();
int isFull();
/* NumConvert takes num converts a equivalent binary number. For this activity the function uses a
stack data structure.*/
```

```
void NumConvert(int num );
// Stack structure declaration.
struct stack //implement stack as a structure
{       int s[20];
        int tos;
};
typedef struct stack stk; // typedefining structure stk as st.
stk st;
void main()
{       int choice,num;
        st.tos=-1; // -1 indicates stack is empty.
                printf("\n\tEnter base of source number n\n");
                printf("\n\t1:decimal number");
    printf("\n\t2:octal number");
                printf("\n\t3:hexa number");
                printf("\n\t4:exit\n\t");
                scanf("%d",&choice);
                switch(choice)
                {  case 1:
                      printf("\n\tEnter decimal number \t");
                   scanf("%d",&num);
                      NumConvert(num);
                   break;
                   case 2:
                      printf("\n\tEnter octal number \t");
                   scanf("%o",&num);
                   NumConvert(num);
                      break;
                   case 3:
                      printf("\n\tEnter hexa number \t");
                  scanf("%x",&num);
                      NumConvert(num);
                   break;
      }
   //Stack now contains converted number. Remember Stack is a Last
   //in First out structure.
   disp();
}// end of main
// Function definitions
void NumConvert(int num)
{  int rem; // remainder
   do
   {
    rem=num%2;// % operator directly gives the remainder
     push(rem);
```

```
        num=num/2;
    }while (num >1);
    if(num == 1)
    {       rem=1;
            push(rem);
    }
}
void push(int val)
  { st.tos++;//increment sp to next position
    st.s[st.tos]=val;//assigning item to st[st.tos]
  } // end of int push(val).
int disp()//display function
     {      int i;
            printf("\n");
            if (isEmpty()== 0)
            { printf("\tbinary equivalent number is....\n\n");
              for(i=st.tos;i>=0;i—) //display stack items
                     printf("\t%d",st.s[i]);
            printf("\n");
            }
       else
         { printf("\n stack is Empty.");
         }
       return 0;
       }//end disp()
int isEmpty()
{   if(st.tos==-1) //if top is equals to null
        {           //printf("Stack is Empty");
                    return 1;
        }
 else
    return 0;
}// end of isEmpty()

int isFull ()
{   if(st.tos==max-1) //if top is equals to max position
        {           printf("Stack overflow");
                    return 1;
        }
  else
    return 0;
  } // end of isFull()*/
```

Output

Enter base of source number n

```
1:decimal number
2:octal number
3:hexa number
4:exit
 1
Enter decimal number    20
binary equivalent number is....
1    0    1    0    0
<menu>
2
Enter octal number     116
binary equivalent number is....
1    0    0    1    1    1    0
<menu>
3
Enter hexa number      3f
binary equivalent number is....

1    1    1    1    1    1
```

13. Write an algorithm for conversion of Infix to Prefix Notation:

Algorithm:

Step 1 : Do for each character in the infix string repeat steps 2 to 5,start from the RHS of the equation i.e starting with the last character and proceed to the first

Step 2 : if (character = = operand)
Append to postfix string

Step 3 : If (character == ')')
Push it on to stack.

```
Step 4:  If ( character == operator )
      {
        While (priority of operator on tos > priority of
                            Operator)
          {
            pop()
            append to prefix string
          }
          push(operator)
      }
```

```
Step 5: If ( symbol == '(' )
        {
          while( pop()!=')')
          {
            pop()
            append to postfix string
          }
          drop ")" parenthesis
        }
```

Step 6 : if input string ends then pop and append the stack contents to output string.

Step 7 : Exit

14. Write a c program to convert from infix to prefix.c

```
//in2prefix.c
#include<stdio.h>//preprocessor
#include<string.h>//preprocessor
#include<stdlib.h>//preprocessor
  int preceed(char c);
  void push(char c);
  char pop();
   char stk[30];
   int tos =-1;
 void main()
 { int i,j=0,n,u,v,k;
   char infix[30],postfix[30];
   char c;
   printf("\n enter the infix expression:");
   scanf("%s",infix);
   n=strlen(infix);
   k=n-1;
   for(i=k;i>=0;i--)
 { if((infix[i]>= 'a' && infix[i]<= 'z') || (infix[i]>= 'A' && infix[i]<= 'Z'))
   {  postfix[j] = infix[i];
      j=j+1;
   } //end of if
   else
     if( infix[i]=='^'||infix[i]=='*'||infix[i]=='/' ||infix[i]=='+'||infix[i]=='-')
       {   u = preceed(stk[tos]);
```

```
      v = preceed(infix[i]);
      while(v< u && stk[tos]!= '(')
      {  postfix[j]=pop();
       j=j+1;
       u = preceed(stk[tos]);
      }
      push(infix[i]);
    }//end of else if 1
    else
      if( infix [i] == ')')
       {push(infix[i]);
       } // end of else if 2
     else
       if (infix[i] == '(')
       { c = pop();
         while(c != ')')
          { postfix[j]= c;
              j=j+1;
            c= pop();
          } // end of while
     }// end of if else 3
    else
       {  printf("\n\tTHE EQUATION HAS ERROR");
         exit(0);
       }//end else
 } // end of for
 while(tos!=-1)
  {  postfix[j]=  pop();
    j=j+1;
  }
  k=j;
  printf("\nThe equation in PREFIX notation is:");
 for(i=k-1;i>=0;i—)
   printf("%c",postfix[i]);
           printf("\n");
}//end main

int preceed(char c)//preceed function
{  int v;
  switch(c)
   { case '^': v=3;
          break;
```

```
        case '*':
            case '/': v=2;
                      break;
            case '+':
            case '-': v=1;
                      break;
            default : v=0;
                      break;
        }//end switch
        return(v);
}//end preceed()

void push(char c)
{ tos++;
  stk[tos] = c;
}
char pop()
{ char val;
  val = stk[tos];
  tos—;
   return(val);
}
/*output
 enter the infix expression:((a+(b*c))-d)
The equation in PREFIX notation is:-+a*bcd*/
```

ASSIGNMENT PROBLEMS

1. Write a C program using pointers to implement a stack with all the operations.
2. Write a program to convert a given prefix expressions to postfix expression using stacks
3. Write a program to evaluate a postfix expression using stack.
4. Convert following infix expressions to prefix and post fix expressions.
   a) A-B+C
   b) A*B+C
   c) A+B*C
   d) A*(B+C)
   e) (A-B)*)*(C+D)^E/F
   f) (A+B)/(C^ (D-E)+F)- G
   g) A + (((B + C) * (D – E) – F) / G) ^ (H – J)
5. Convert following prefix expressions in to infix expression.
   a) + - * ^ ABCD / / EF+GH
   b) ^ - * + ABC – DE + FG
   c) * * + AB - + CDEF

d) - + + A * BCD * EF

6. Convert following post fix expressions to infix expression
   a) AB ^ C * D - EF / GH + / +
   b) AB + C * DE - - FG + ^
   c) AB + CD + E - * F *
   d) ABC * + D + EF * -
7. With A =1, B =2, C=3, and D = 4 evaluate following post fix expressions
   a) AB+C-
   b) AB-C+DEF- + *
   c) AB + C – BA + C / -
   d) ABCDE - + * * EF * -

Solutions to Objective Questions

1) a	2) a	3) False	4) b	5) a	6) c
7) True	8) False	9) c	10) True		

CHAPTER 11

QUEUES

■■■ 11.1 INTRODUCTION TO QUEUES

In our daily life, to catch a bus, to with draw money from ATM or to buy a cinema ticket, we form a queue. Queue is a ***first in first out FIFO*** linear data structure Queue is an important data structure for computer applications even.

Look at the Fig. 11.1a.Initially the queue is empty. Element is serviced (deleted) from the front. An element is added to the queue at the rear. Condition q.front =0 & q.rear= -1 initially implies that queue is empty. In 11.1 b arrival of element 25 as first element means both front and rear are assigned to first position. Fig. 11.1c & 11.1 d show the position of rear and front with each addition to queue. Note that in Fig. 11.1b, when first element is entered, we have incremented front by 1. After that front is never changed during addition to queue process. Observe that rear is incremented by one prior to adding an element to the queue. We will call this process as ***enque.*** However to ensure that we do not exceed the Max length of the queue, prior to incrementing rear we have to check if the queue is full. This can be easily achieved by checking the condition *if (q.rear = = MAX-1)*

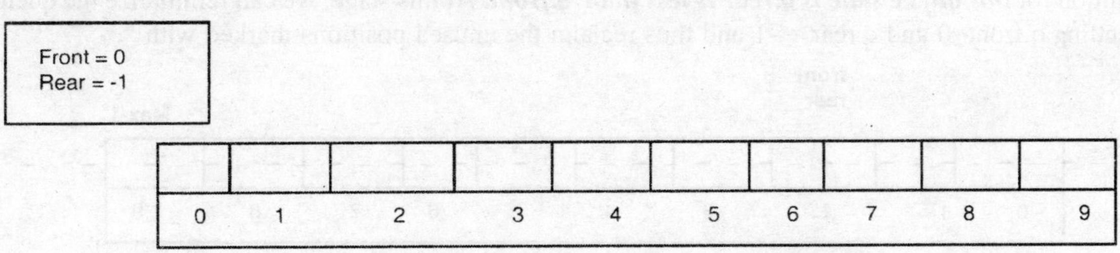

Fig. 11.1a *An Empty Queue . MAX= 10 , numbered 0 to 9*

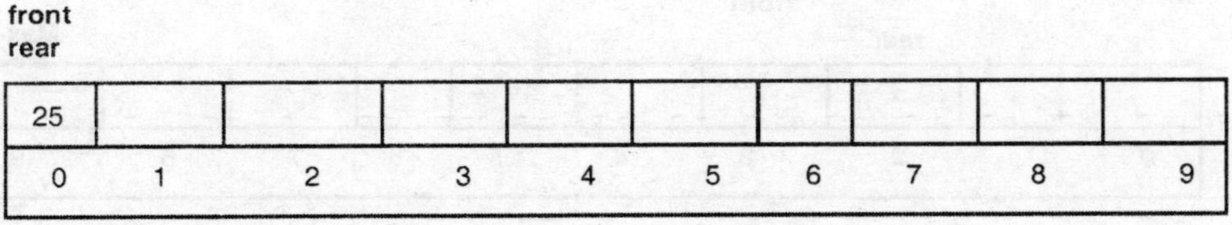

Fig. 11.1b *Queue with arrival of first element* 2225

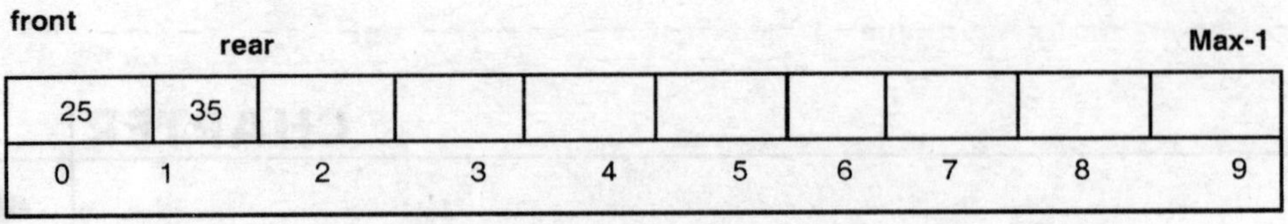

Fig.. 11.1c Queue with arrival of second element. Rear is incremented by 1

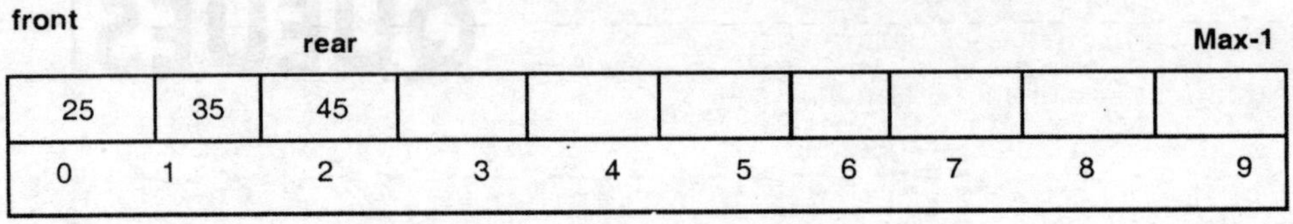

Fig. 11.1d Queue with arrival of 3rd element

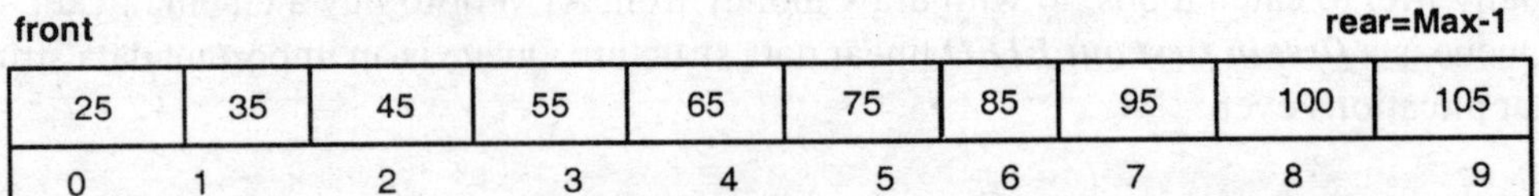

Fig. 11.1e Queue full i.e. q.rear = = Max -1

Deleting an Element from the Queue : Elements are always removed from the front. **After removing the element, front is incremented by one.** Fig. 11.1 f shows status of front and rear after two deletions from Fig. 11.1d. Observe that positions vacated by front marked as * are unusable by queue any further. This is one of the major draw back of linear queue array representation. In Fig. 11.1 g, we have carried out three deletions for 25,35,and 45. after deleting 45, we find queue is empty and the condition for ***this queue state is q.rear is less than q.front.*** At this stage, we can reinitialize the queue by setting q.front=0 and q.rear = -1 and thus reclaim the unused positions marked with *.

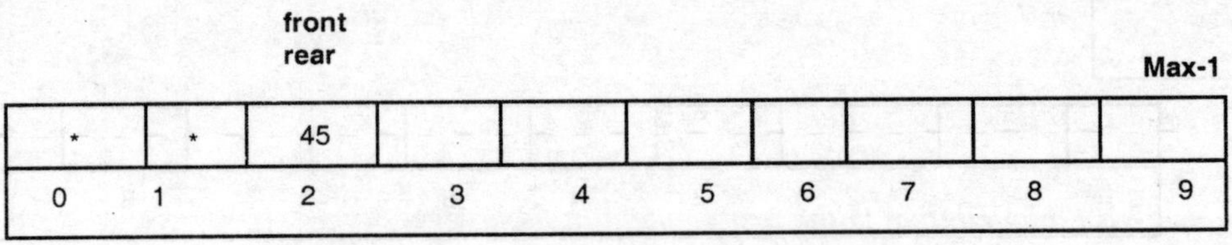

Fig. 11.1f Queue after two deletions 25 & 35 from Fig. 11.1d

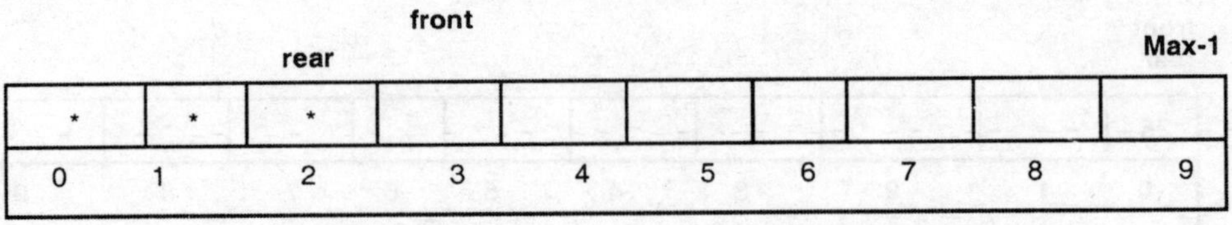

Fig. 11.1g Queue after deletions of 25, 35, and 45 from Fig. 11.1d

Number of elements in the queue: At any instance rear – front + 1

Queues can be represented in the following ways

Static implementation using array representation.

Dynamic implementation using Linked List representation

Operations available on the Queue are

Addition of an element – Enque

Deletion of an element - dequeue

11.2 ARRAY REPRESENTATION OF QUEUE

Queue is defined as array of maximum size MAX. While inserting and deleting elements from the queue, we have to check for empty and full conditions.

11.2.1 Algorithm for Addition of An Element to the Queue

Initialize the que q.front = 0 and q.rear = -1

Step1 : Check if queue is full by calling isFull()

i.e. if q.rear =MAX-1 declare queue as full & exit

Step3 : Else

Rear=Rear +1

q.rear=val; // insert value on to queue

11.2.2 Algorithm for Deletion of An Element to the Queue

Step 1: Check if queue is empty by checking the condition

If ((q.rear < q.front) then declare queue is empty and exit

Step 2.Else

Item = q.front ; display item

Front = front +1

Step 3: // check if removed item is the last element in the queue

If (q.rear < q.front)

// all items removed. Hence re-initialize the queue

q.front =0;

q. rear = -1

Example 11.1 QueArray.c for array implementation of Queue

```
//queuearr.c
#include<stdio.h>
#define MAX 20
  void enqueue(int val);
  int dequeue();
  int isEmpty();
  void display();
  void exit();
 struct queue
  {  int data[MAX];
          int front,rear;
  };
  typedef struct queue que;
  que q;

void main()
{         int ch,val,x;
          q.rear=-1;
          q.front=0;
          do
  {
   printf("\n\t\t\t QUEUE  USING ARRAYS  ");
   printf("\n\t\t\t ----- ----- ------\n");
   printf("\n\t1.ENQUEUE");
   printf("\n\t2.DEQUEUE");
   printf("\n\t3.DISPLAY");
   printf("\n\t4.EXIT\n");
   printf("\nEnter your choice:\t");
   scanf("%d",&ch);
   switch(ch)
   {      case 1:
                    printf("enter value:");
                    scanf("%d",&val);
                    enqueue(val);
      display();
                    break;
            case 2:
                    x=dequeue();
                    if(x!=-1)
                      printf("dequed value=%d\n",x);
```

```
                    display();
                    break;
            case 3:display();
                    break;
            case 4:exit();
            default:printf("INVALID  CHOICE!!\n");
                        break;
    }//end of switch
  }while(ch!=4);
}
void enqueue(int val)
{ q.rear++;//increment rear to point to next empty slot
  q.data[q.rear]=val;
}

int dequeue()
{ int k,ans;
  k=isEmpty();
  if(k==0)//queue is not empty
  { ans=q.data[q.front];
        q.front++;
  }
  else
  {       printf("Queue is empty\n");
   ans=-1;
  }
  return(ans);
}

int isEmpty()
{  int ans;
  if(q.rear<q.front)
                ans=1;
  else
                ans=0;
  return(ans);
}

void display()
{          int ans,i;
           printf("****data elements in queue****\n");
    ans=isEmpty();
```

```
        if(ans ==0)
        {  for(i=q.front;i<=q.rear;i++)
             printf("%d\n",q.data[i]);
        }
        else
                    printf("queue is empty\n");
}
/*output
                QUEUE  USING ARRAYS
                -----  --------  ----------
        1.  ENQUEUE
        2.  DEQUEUE
        3.  DISPLAY
        4.  EXIT

Enter your choice:    1
enter value:10
****data elements in queue****
10

Enter your choice:    1
enter value:20
****data elements in queue****
10
20

Enter your choice:    1
enter value:30
****data elements in queue****
10
20
30

Enter your choice:    3
****data elements in queue****
10
20
30

Enter your choice:    2
dequed value=10
****data elements in queue****
20
```

30

Enter your choice: 4*/

11.3 DYNAMIC REPRESENTATION OF QUEUES USING LINKED LISTS

11.3.1 Create A New Node: A node will have data assigned to it and a pointer to its successor. Node is the name of the new node we are going to insert.

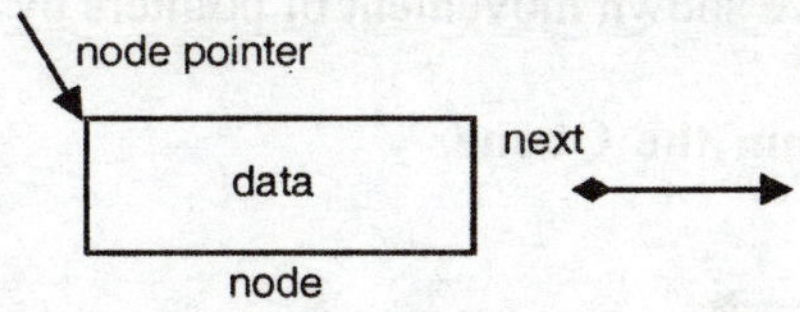

Fig. 11.2 Node structure

```
struct queue
        {      int data
              struct queue * next ;  // *next is a pointer to next node
        };                                          // This type if definition is called self
                                                          referential structure.
        typedef struct queue que; // we will be able to use short name que
```

We also need two pointers called front and rear. Create them using statements

```
   que *front =NULL
   que *rear  =NULL
```

11.3.2 Adding Node to Empty Queue

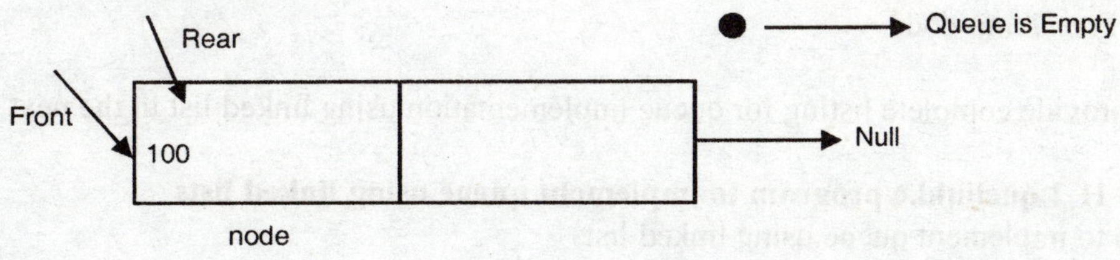

Fig. 11.3a Addition of first element to queue

Queue is empty and node to be inserted is the first node. Therefore assign front and rear to node

Adding node to queue.

rear

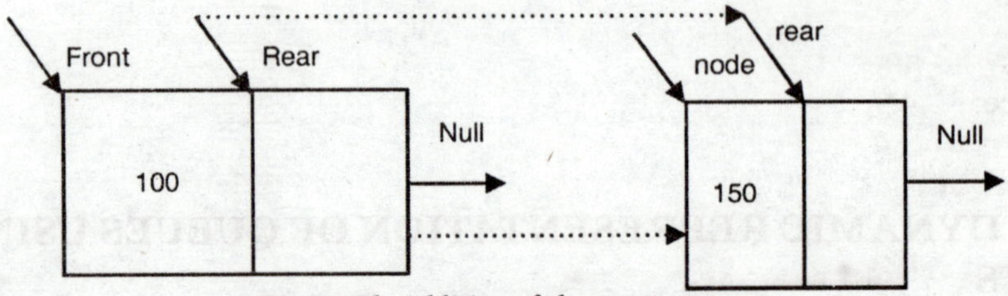

Fig. 11.3b Addition of element to queue

Step 1: rearànext = node ; assign node to rear ->next
Step 2: rear = node // we have shown movement of pointers by .... line.

11.3.3 Deleting An Element from the Queue.

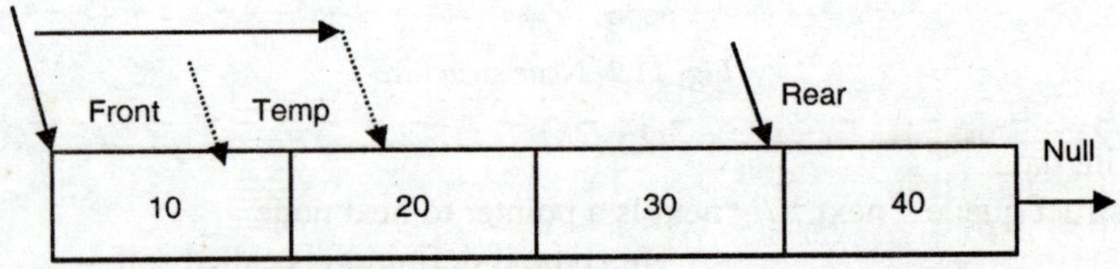

Fig. 11.4 Deleting a node from queue

Step 1 : Store Front in Temp pointer
Step 2 : Move Front to next node
Front=Front->next
Step 3 : Remove temp->data and display to user
Step 4 : If Front = = NULL, set Rear = NULL. Front=Null means queue is empty
Step 5 : Free Temp node.

We now provide complete listing for queue implementation using linked list in the next section.

Example 11.2 quelinkl.c program to implement queue using linked lists

```
//program to implement queue using linked lists
//qinkl.c
# include<stdio.h>
# include<stdlib.h>

struct queue
{ int data;
  struct queue *next;
 // struct quueue *front;
      // struct queue *rear;
```

```
};
typedef struct queue que;

    que *front=NULL;
    que *rear =NULL;

  void enqueue(int val);
  int dequeue();
//  int isEmpty();
  void display();
//  void exit();

void main()
{
 int ch,val,x;
  do
  { printf("\n\t\t\t QUEUE  USING LINKED LISTS  ");
    printf("\n\t\t\t ----- ---- ------ -----\n");
    printf("\n\t1.ENQUEUE");
    printf("\n\t2.DEQUEUE");
    printf("\n\t3.DISPLAY");
    printf("\n\t4.EXIT\n");
    printf("\nEnter your choice:");
    scanf("%d",&ch);
    switch(ch)
    {    case 1:
                    printf("\nenter value:");
                    scanf("%d",&val);
                    enqueue(val);
                  display();
                    break;
         case 2:
                    x=dequeue();
                    if(x!=-1)
                       printf("dequed value=%d\n",x);
                    display();
                    break;
         case 3:display();
                  break;
         case 4:exit(1);

         default:printf("INVALID  CHOICE!!\n");
                  break;
    }
  }while(ch!=4);
```

```
}

void enqueue(int val)
{   que *node;
    node=(que *)malloc(sizeof(que));//creation of new node
    node->data=val;
    node->next=NULL;
    if(front==NULL)//check if initially empty
        front=node;  //if empty assign front to newly created node
    else
          rear->next=node;
    rear=node;
}
int dequeue()
{   int val;
   que *p;
   if(front==NULL)//check if initially empty
         {
           printf(" list is empty\n");
            val=-1;      //if queue is empty return -1 as answer
           }
    else
         {  p=front;
           front=p->next;   //make front point to the next element
           val= p->data;
            if(front==NULL)  //if front now points to null it means an empty queue
                    rear=NULL;  //so make rear also to point to null
            free(p);          //now free p i.e. release the mem location for reuse
         }
     return(val);
}

void display()
{         que *temp;
          temp=front; // we will use temp for traversing the queue
          printf("\n ****queue elements are****\n");
         if (temp == NULL)
                   printf("\n queue is empty");
          else
          {
             while (temp->next!=NULL)
             {       printf("\n %d",temp->data);
                     temp=temp->next;
```

```
        } //end of while
      //now last element stiil left for display
        printf("\n %d",temp->data);
      }//end of if
}
/*output          QUEUE  USING LINKED LISTS

    1.ENQUEUE
    2.DEQUEUE
    3.DISPLAY
    4.EXIT

Enter your choice:1
enter value:10
 ****queue elements are****
 10

Enter your choice:1
enter value:20
 ****queue elements are****
 10
 20

 Enter your choice:1
enter value:30
 ****queue elements are****
 10
 20
 30
Enter your choice:3
 ****queue elements are****
 10
 20
 30
Enter your choice:2
dequed value=10
 ****queue elements are****
 20
 30
Enter your choice:4*/
```

11.4 CIRCULAR QUEUE-ARRAY REPRESENTATION

Linear queue discussed so far in section 11.2 suffers from one major drawback. When the first element is serviced, the front is moved to next element. However, the position vacated is not available for further use. Thus, we may encounter a situation, wherein program shows that queue is full, while all the whose elements have been deleted are available but unusable, though empty. The situation is shown in fig 11.5 As a solution, we would consider a superior data structure called circular queue. Look at the fig 11.6.showing an empty circular queue. Observe that both front and rear are initialized to the same position MAX-1 i.e. position9. For programmer only positions available are from 0 to 8. W have sacrificed one position, shown as * in the diagram, in order that we could identify the conditions empty and full for circular queue. Consider following two statements

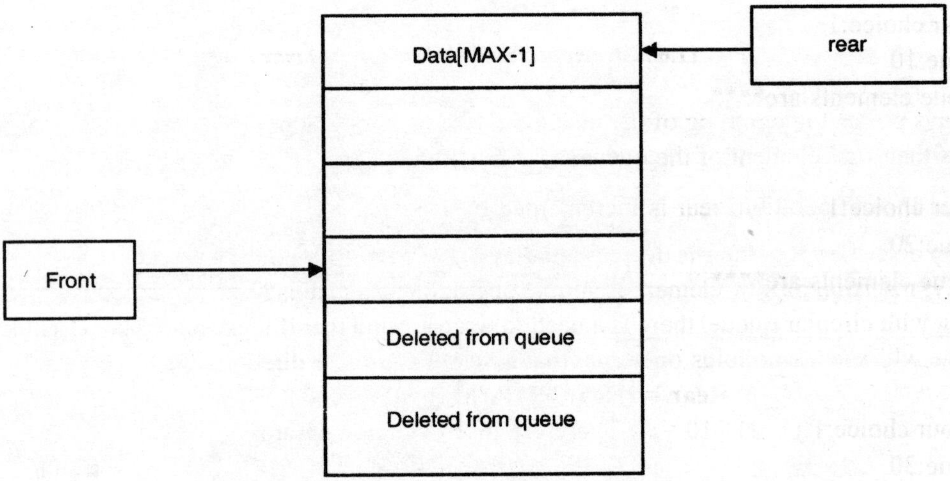

Fig. 11.5 Linear queue–major drawback

Circular queue is empty if q.rear = = q.front

For checking Full condition, we will increment q.rear and then check if q.rear= = q.front

In a circular queue, there is no fixed positions for front and rear.

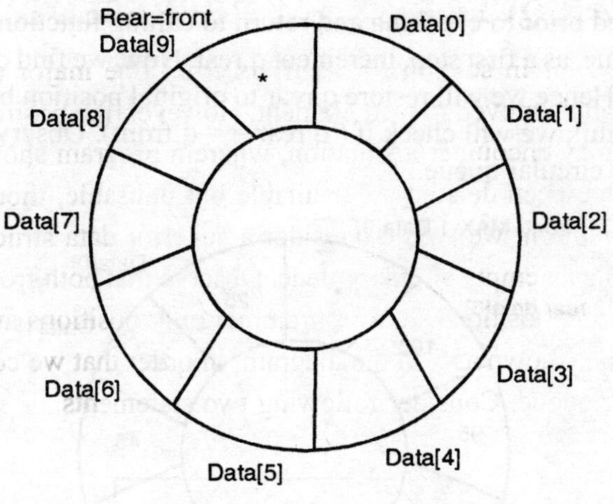

Fig. 11.6 : An empty circular queue capacity max = 12.

Front always points to beginning of the queue but it does not point to first element. It is always point to one less than first element of the queue.

On Insert operation, rear is incremented by 1.

On delete front pointer is decremented by 1 and front now points to next element in the queue. In Fig. 11.7, insertion of new element is simple operation as queue is NOT full i.e. rear != front. As we are dealing with circular queue, there is a need to wrap around rear if it exceeds Max -1 value. For this activity, we will use %(modulus operator) that give us remainder directly.

Rear = (Rear +1)%(Max)

Rear = (1+1)%10 = 2. Therefore insert element 45 at rear =2

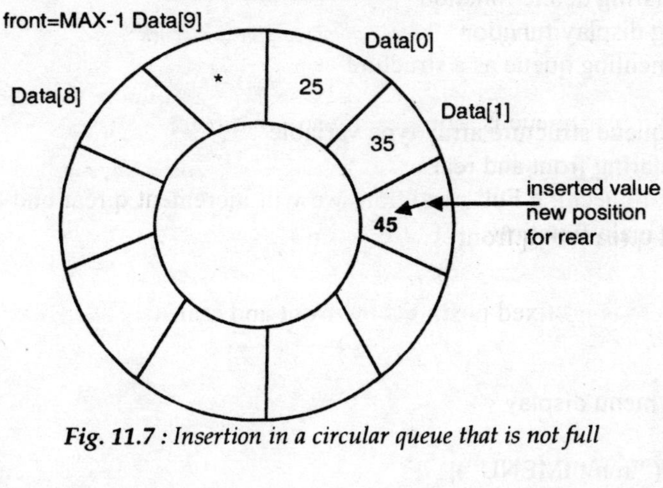

Fig. 11.7 : Insertion in a circular queue that is not full

For checking overflow condition, shown in Fig. 11.8 we will first increment q.rear and check if q.rear = = q.front. If condition is true, it implies that queue is full. Then we will decrement q.rear by one, which we have incremented prior to checking and return to calling function. For example, we want to add element 105 to the queue. as a first step, increment q.rear. Now, we find q.rear is equal to q.front.(9). It means that queue is full Hence we will restore q.rear to original position by decrementing by one. To check if circular queue is full, we will check if (q.rear = = q.front). Observe that condition is same as that of checking for empty circular queue.

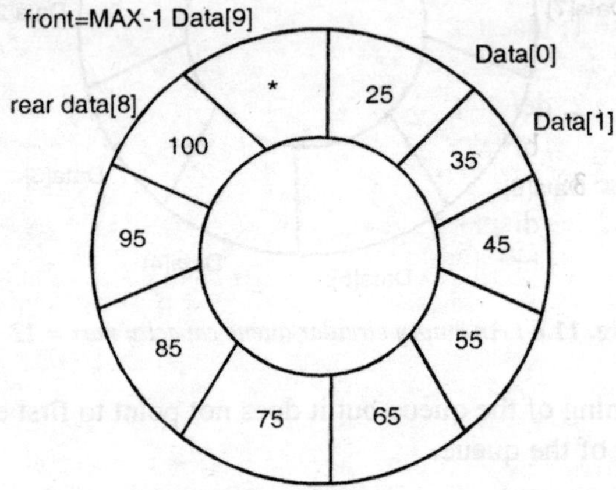

Fig. 11.8 Insertion in a circular queue that is full

Example 11.3. cirque.c Circular Queue implementación.

```
//PROgram for cirqular queue operations using arrays
#include<stdio.h> //preprocessor
# define max 5   //define varriable max = 5
int insert();    //declaring insert function
int delet();          //declaring delete function
int disp();    //declaring display function
struct queue   //implementing queue as a structure
{
        int q[max]; //queue structure array type variable
        int f,r;    //declaring front and rear
}qu;
int main() //initializing main function
{
        int ch=0;
        qu.f=0;
        qu.r=0;
        while(ch!=4)//menu display
        {
                printf("\n\n\t\tMENU");
                printf("\n\n\t1: INSERTION");
                printf("\n\t2: DELETION");
```

```
                printf("\n\t3: DISPLAY");
                printf("\n\t4: EXIT");
                printf("\n\n\tEnter your choice\t");
                scanf("%d",&ch);//scan your choice
                switch(ch)
                {
                        case 1: insert();
                                break;
                        case 2: delet();
                                break;
                        case 3:
                                disp();
                                break;
                }//end switch
        }//end while
return 0;
}//end main
//function definitions
int insert()//insert function
{
        int item;
        if((qu.r+1)%max==qu.f) //check for queue overflow
        {
                printf("\n\n\tQueue is overflow");
                return 0;
        }//end if
        else
        {
        /*      if(qu.r==max)       //if the entered position is last then
                                qu.r=0;*/

                qu.r=(qu.r+1)%max; //increment next position
                printf("\n\n\tEnter an element to insert");
                scanf("%d",&item); //scan item
                qu.q[qu.r]=item;    //assign the item to given position
                            /*if(qu.f==-1) qu.f++;*/
      }//end else
return 0;
}//end insert function
int delet()//delete function
{
        int item;
        if(qu.f==qu.r)
```

```
        {
                printf("\n\n\tThe queue is Underflow");
                return 0;
        }//end if

        qu.f=(qu.f+1)%max;//in circular queue front is always empty
        item=qu.q[qu.f]; //assign queue[front] to item
        if(qu.f==qu.r)  //front is equal to rear
        {
                qu.r=0;
                qu.f=0;
        }//end if()
        /*if(max==qu.f)
                qu.f=1;
        else
                qu.f++;*/
        printf("\n\n\tThe deleted item is %d",item);
return 0;
}//end delete()
int disp()//display function
{
        int i;
        printf("\n\n");
        if(qu.f==0 && qu.r==0) //front = -1 and rear = -1
        {
                printf("\n\n\tThe queue is Empty");
                return 0;
        }//end if()
        printf("\n\n\tThe elements in the queue are");
        if(qu.r < qu.f) //if rear is less than front
        {
          for(i=qu.f+1;i<max;i++)//print the values from front to queue max
                        printf("\n\t%d",qu.q[i]);
          for(i=0;i<=qu.r;i++) //print the values from 0th position to rear
                        printf("\n\t%d",qu.q[i]);
        }//end if
        else
        for(i=qu.f+1;i<=qu.r;i++)//print the values from front to rear
        printf("\n\t%d",qu.q[i]);
    return 0;
}//end display

/* output
        MENU
```

```
 1: INSERTION
 2: DELETION
 3: DISPLAY
 4: EXIT
 Enter your choice       1
 Enter an element to insert10

 Enter your choice       1

 Enter an element to insert20

 Enter your choice       1

 Enter an element to insert40

 Enter your choice       3

 The elements in the queue are
 10
 20
 40

 Enter your choice       2

 The deleted item is 10

 Enter your choice       3

 The elements in the queue are
 20
 40
*/
```

OBJECTIVE QUESTIONS

1. Queue follows which of the following
   a) LILO   b) FIFO
   c) LIFO   d) None of the above
2. Queue what type of data structures
   a) Static   b) Dynamic
   c) Linear   d) None

3. Queue empty condition is checked by
   a) rear<front b) front<rear
   c) rear=front d) rear=0
4. The no. of elements in a queue at any given time will be equal to
   a) rear-front+1 b) rear-front-1
   c) rear-front+2 d) rear-front-2
5. The order of storage in a queue is sequential True/fasle
6. Abstract data type implies that it is independent of implementation True/False
7. Queue is static data structure True/False
8. A self referential structure holds
   a) pointer to next structure of same type b) pointer to data of next
   c) next node d) pointer to next node
9. After inserting an element in the queue, the rear is
   a) incremented b) decrèmented
   c) no change d) made = front
10. Queue empty condition is checked by
   a) rear<front b) front<rear
   c) rear=Max d) rear=0

REVIEW QUESTIONS

1. What is a queue? Explain the various operations performed on queues with suitable algorithms.(i.e. insertion, deletion).
2. Write in detail Circular queue.
3. Explain how do you check if the queue is full or empty.
2. Explain two major applications of queue.
4. What are the advantages of a circular queue over a linear queue?

SOLVED EXAMPLES

1. Write a program to perform operations on circular queues using linked lists

```
#include<stdio.h>
/*
 Create a structure named "qlinklist" using a pointer link
 for creating a link between two successive nodes
 Declare two pointers for this: front and rear for moving through the queue
```

```
 A temporary pointer: temp
*/
struct qlinklist
{
 int data;
 struct qlinklist *link;
}*front,*rear,*temp;

/*
 A function for inserting a node into the queue using linked list
*/
int enqueue()
{
 printf("Give data to be inserted:\t");
 temp=(struct qlinklist*)malloc(sizeof(struct qlinklist));
 scanf("%d",&temp->data);
 /*
  The above three steps insert a value into the temporary pointer's memory
 */

 printf("%d IS INSERTED!!",temp->data);
 /*
  If no node exists then both rear and front are NULL
        Hence,it will be the first node in the queue
        So,make its front's link as NULL
  Else
        Make rear to be consisting of the data inserted
        and then make its rear link to NULL
 */
 if(rear==NULL&&front==NULL)
 {
  rear=temp;
  front=temp;
  rear->link=front;
  //To create a circular link for the first node
 }
 else
 {
  rear->link=temp;
  rear=temp;
  rear->link=front;
  //To create a circular link for the last created node
 }return 0;
}
```

```
/*
  A function for deleting a node from the circular queue using linked list
*/
int dequeue()
{
 /*
  Check if front is NULL and the rear is NULL
  If NULL then the queue would be empty
  If not so,if rear is equal to front
  Make them NULL
  Else
  Delete the temporary node pointing to front and make its link
  as front
  and then free the pointer containing this temporary value
  and link the last node to front
 */
 if(front==NULL&&rear==NULL)
 {
  printf("Cannot delete from empty list!!!\n");
 }
 else if(front==rear)
 {
  printf("%d IS DELETED!!!\n",front->data);
  front=rear=NULL;
 }
 else
 {
  printf("%d IS DELETED!!!\n",front->data);
  temp=front;
  front=front->link;
  rear->link=front;
  free(temp);
 }return 0;
}

/*
 A function to display the queue
*/
int display()
{
 /*
   If front and rear are not existing then the list is empty
   Else display the queue from front till temporary pointer points to front
```

```
 */
 if(front==NULL&&rear==NULL)
 {
   printf("Cannot display empty list!!!\n");
 }
 else
 {
  printf("DATA IN QUEUE IS:\n");
  temp=front;
  do
  {
   printf("%d\t",temp->data);
   temp=temp->link;
  }while(temp!=front);
 }return 0;
}

int main()
{
 int ch;
 do
 { printf("\n\t\t\t CIRCULAR QUEUE  USING LINKED-LISTS  ");
   printf("\n\t\t\t ———— ——— ——— ———————\n");
   printf("\n\t1.ENQUEUE");
   printf("\n\t2.DEQUEUE");
   printf("\n\t3.DISPLAY");
   printf("\n\t4.EXIT\n");
   printf("\nEnter your choice:\t\n");
   scanf("%d",&ch);
   switch(ch)
   {
        case 1:enqueue();
               break;
        case 2:dequeue();
               break;
        case 3:display();
               break;
        case 4:exit();
        default:printf("INVALID  CHOICE!!\n");
               break;
   }
 }while(1);
return 0;
}
/*output
```

```
                 CIRCULAR QUEUE  USING LINKED-LISTS
                 ---------  ------------  -----------------

        1.ENQUEUE
        2.DEQUEUE
        3.DISPLAY
        4.EXIT

Enter your choice: 1
Give data to be inserted:     200
200  IS  INSERTED!!

Enter your choice:1
Give data to be inserted:     300
300  IS  INSERTED!!

Enter your choice:1
Give data to be inserted:     400
400  IS  INSERTED!!

Enter your choice:3
DATA IN QUEUE IS:
200    300    400
Enter your choice:2
200  IS  DELETED!!!

Enter your choice:3
DATA IN QUEUE IS:
300    400         */
```

2. Represent a linked list as an array and build routines and program for all basic operations like create, insert and delete.

//clistarr.c

```
/program to implement circular linked list using an array
//and demonstrate insertion and deletion operations
#include<stdio.h>
struct clist
{ int data;
  int next; //index of next element in the list
};
typedef struct clist nodes;
nodes node[100]; //create 100 instances of the above structure
int curr=0;  //index of the current node which is free
```

```
int head=0;  //points to the start of the list initially 0 but could change
         //based on insertions and deletions
void createlist();
void insert(int n,int val);//inserts val to the right of n in the list
void delet(int val);
void printlist();

void main()
{
        int i,val,n;
        for(i=0;i<100;i++)
         node[i].next=i+1; //link all nodes n their natural order
   node[99].next=0;  //make the last node point to the first node in the list

  createlist();
  printlist();
        printf("\nEnter value to insert and vlaue of node after which it has to be inserted");
        scanf("%d%d",&val,&n);
        insert(n,val);
  printlist();
        printf("\nEnter value to be deleted:");
        scanf("%d",&val);
  delet(val);
  printlist();
}
void createlist()
{ int i,n;
 printf("Enter no of elements<maximum of 100>");
 scanf("%d",&n);
  for(i=0;i<n;i++)
  {printf("Enter element:");
  scanf("%d",&node[i].data);
  }
 node[i-1].next=0; //make the last node of list point to first node
 curr=i; //set current node to i as this the next free node
}
void insert(int n,int val)
{ int i=head;
 int p;
 while(node[i].data!=n) //search for node with value n
 { i=node[i].next;
  if(i==head)
```

```
 break;
 }
 if(node[i].data!=n)
 printf("Not a valid insertion as %d is not in the list\n",n);
 else
 { p=curr;   //get the next available free node
        curr=node[p].next; //assign curr to the next free node
  node[p].data=val;
  node[p].next=node[i].next;
        node[i].next=p;
 }
}
void delet(int val)
{ int i,j,previous;
 i=head;//initialize to start of list
  while(node[i].data!=val) //search for the node
  { previous=i;
         i=node[i].next;
         if(i==head)
         break;
  }
  if(node[i].data!=val)
        printf("Not a valid deletion as %d is not in the list\n",val);
  else
  if(i==head)  //if node to be deleted is the starting node
  { head=node[i].next; //shift head to the next element
         j=head;
         while(node[j].next!=i) //search for the last element in list
         j=node[j].next;
    node[j].next=head;  //make the last node point to the new head
  }
  else        //if node to be delted is between two nodes
  { node[previous].next=node[i].next;
   node[i].next=curr;
         curr=i;     //the last two operations return the deleted node to empty pool
                     //so that it can be used again
  }
```

```
}
void printlist()
{ int i=head;
 while(node[i].next!=head)
 {printf("%5d",node[i].data);
  i=node[i].next;
 }
 printf("%5d",node[i].data);
}
/*Output:
Enter no of elements<maximum of 100>5
Enter element:23
Enter element:67
Enter element:54
Enter element:12
Enter element:89
  23  67  54  12  89
Enter value to insert and vlaue of node after which it has to be inserted34 67
  23  67  34  54  12  89
Enter value to be deleted54
  23  67  34  12  89 */
```

ASSIGNMENT PROBLEMS

1. Show how to implement a queue of integers in c by using an array int Q[queuesize],where Q[0] is used to indicate the front of queue, Q[1] is used to indicate rear and where Q[2] through Q[queuesize-1] contain elements on the queue.. show how to initialize such on array to represent the empty queue and write routines remove, insert and empty for such as implementation.
2. Implement priority queue using array implementation. We need to provide 3 buffers(arrays). Array 1 stores highest priority elements, array 2 stores second priority elements, and array3 stores least priority elements. Write a program to display the queues as per following schedule

   Display array2 for after 3elements of array 1 are displayed.

   Display array3 for after 3elements of array 2 are displayed.

Solutions to Objective Questions

1) b	2) c	3) a	4) a	5) True	6) True
7) False	8) a	9) a	10) c		

CHAPTER 12

NON LINEAR DATA STRUCTURES—TREES

■■■ 12.1 TREES WHY – WHAT – HOW

The data structures like stack, linked lists etc are linear data structures, where as in real life, we will come across non linear structures like hierarchical data structure. For Example like Grand Father – Son – Grand Son in a family or CEO – Vice President – General Manager – Manager in a company. Consider an hierarchical structure followed in a typical college shown in Fig. 12.1. These kind of hierarchical structures can best be represented by data structure called **Tree**. Let us understand more about these structures. Look at the picture, in case you want to know the details of student number 10 of Section A of CSE branch, you need to approach Principal – Dean academics – Head CSE – In Charge Students – Section A. In the process you have not bothered to visit Dean admin, thus saving access time. It is this feature which makes Trees a most useful and widely used data structure in Computer Science in the areas of data storage, parsing, evaluation of expressions, and compiler design.

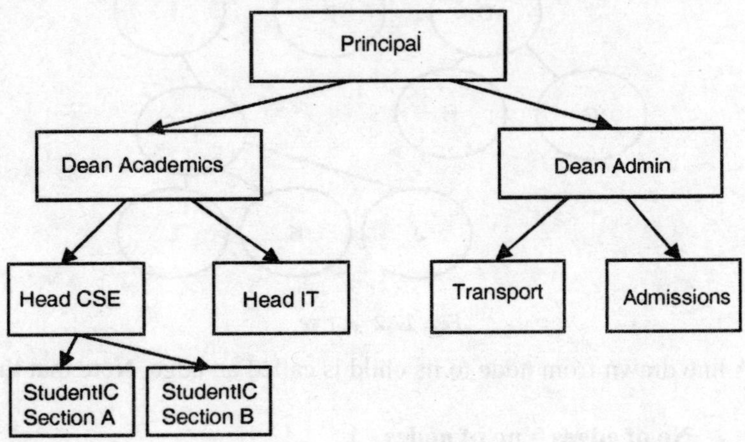

Fig. 12.1 A tree organization

■■■ 12.2 TERMINOLOGY AND DEFINITIONS OF TREE

Root is at the top of the hierarchy. Principal is the root. Parent Node : Each node except root has a parent. Head CSE node is parent node for in charge Admin and in charge Students. Principal, being root, does not have parent.

Levels: Note that we have also indicated levels starting at the root as level 0. Number of nodes at a level m is given by 2 ^ m.

Child Nodes or Siblings: Observe that a node has 2 or 1 or Nil child nodes directly under it. Nodes with same parent are called siblings.Dean Computing has two siblings Head IT and Head CSE. Observe that Section A, Section B and In Charge Admin have no child nodes.

Note that Principal, Deans, HODs, and In charges are all called Nodes. Nodes with siblings are called the internal nodes. Inter connecting lines are called Edges.

Leaf Nodes: Nodes with no Child nodes are called leaf nodes or terminal nodes or external nodes. . For example section A and Section B, In charge admin are all leaf nodes.

Trees: Collection of nodes and Edges. One of the nodes is a root, and remaining nodes are partioned as collection of sub trees, each of which is a tree by itself.

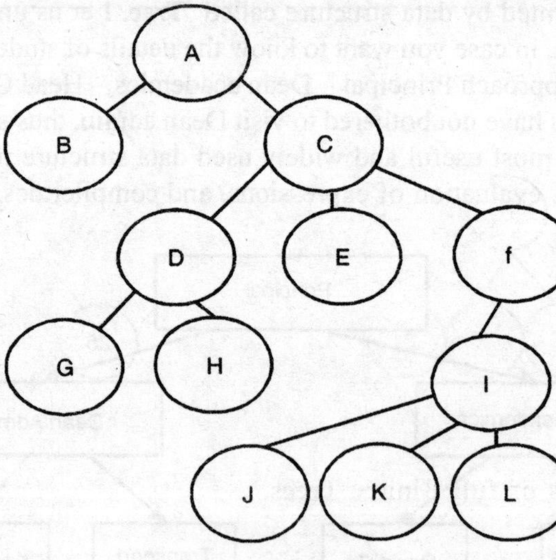

Fig. 12.2 A tree

Edge or Branch: A line drawn from node to its child is called an edge. Note that there are 12 Nodes. But edges are 12.

No of edges = no of nodes - 1

Path : It is a list of vertices from root node to leaf node connected by edges. For example A-C-F-I-J is a path. Note that there is only one path between nodes.
Path Length : No of edges in a path. The path **A-C-F-I-J** has a path length of 4.

Depth of node : It is the path length from the root. Node J is at depth 4 and node D has a depth of 2

Degree of a Node : The number of edges incident on a node is called degree of a node. Node C is of degree 4 and node D has a degree of 3.

■■■ 12.3 BINARY TREES

A binary tree is an empty or comprises a root node and two disjoint sub trees left sub tree(LST) and right sub tree(RST). LST and RST are themselves binary trees. Look at the fig 12.3 depicting a full binary tree.

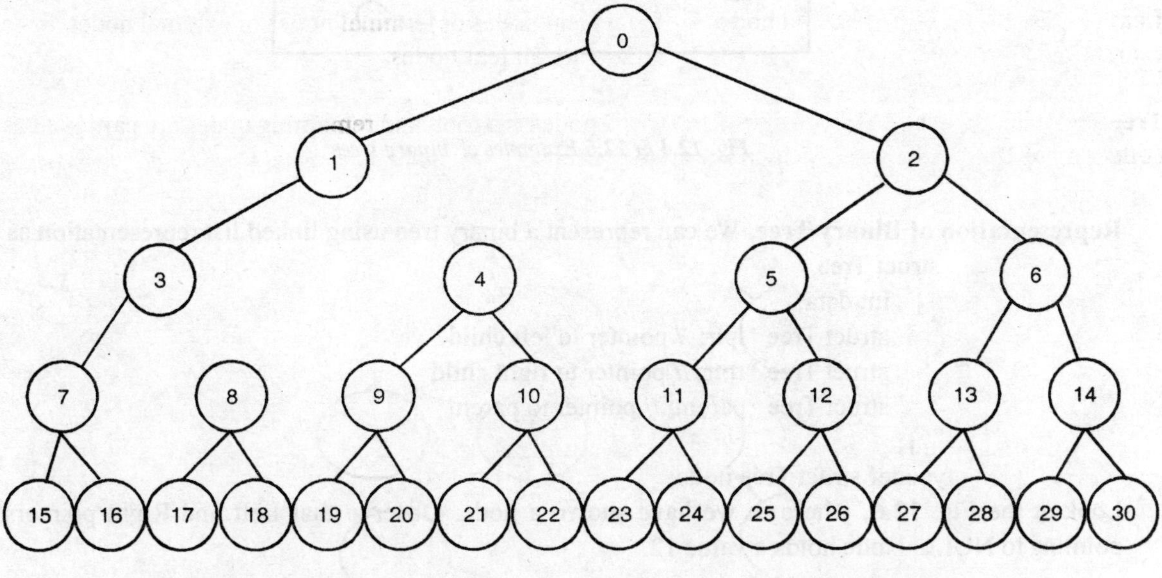

Fig. 12.3 A full binary tree with nodes = 31, levels = 5 (level 0 to level 4)

Some interesting properties of full Binary Trees.

Number of levels L = 5 (level 0 to level 4)
Number of nodes N = 2 ^ L – 1 = 32 -1 = 31 (numbered 0 to 30)
Number of nodes in a level m = 2 ^ m ;
Number of nodes at level 3 = 2 ^3 = 8

Number of internal nodes = Sum of nodes at (L0+L1+L2+L3) levels = 1+2+4+8=15
Number of external nodes (leaf nodes) = No of Internal nodes + 1 = 15 +1 = 16.
Height /Depth of Binary Tree with x internal node = $\log_2 (x+1) = \log_2 (15+1) = 4$

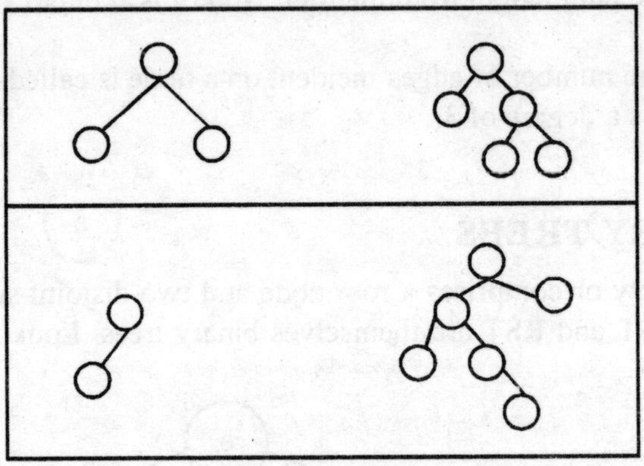

Fig. 12.4 & 12.5 Examples of binary trees

Representation of Binary Tree. We can represent a binary tree using linked list representation as

```
struct Tree
{ int data;
  struct Tree *lptr; // pointer to left child
  struct Tree *rptr; // pointer to right child
  struct Tree *parent; // pointer to parent
};
typedef struct Tree node;
```

Look at the Fig. 12.6, where in we have shown a node. Observe that Left and Right pointers are pointing to NULL. Node holds a value 12.

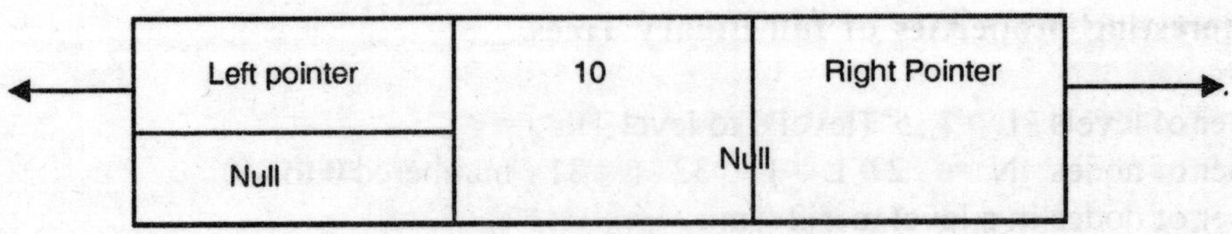

Fig. 12.6 Representation of a node

■■■ 12.4 BINARY SEARCH TREE

Binary Search Tree (BST) is an ordered Binary Tree in that it is an empty tree or value of root node is greater than all the values in Left Sub Tree(LST) and less than all the values of Right Sub Tree (RST). Right and Left sub trees are again binary sub trees by themselves.(Fig. 12.7a and b)

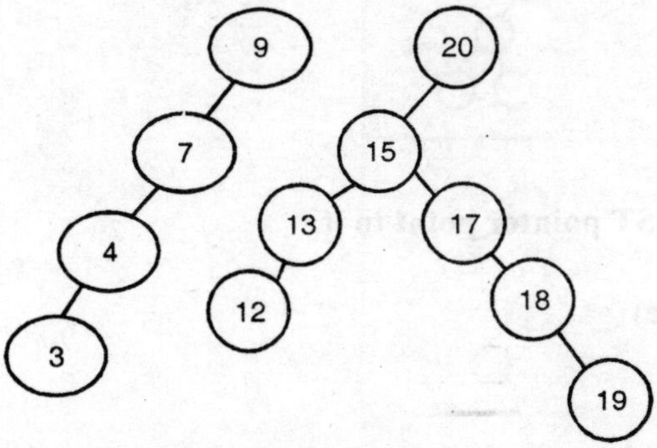

12.7 a .Example of BST

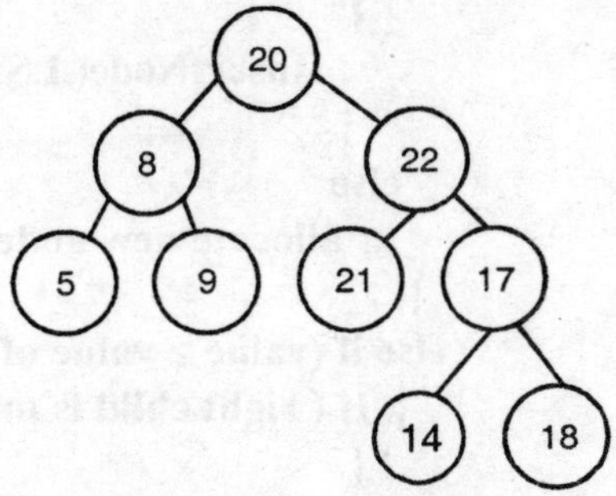

12.7 b Not a BST. Node 17 violates RST rule

We will be using BST structure to demonstrate features of Binary Trees. The operations possible on a binary tree are

a) Create a Binary Tree
b) Insert a node in a Binary tree
c) Delete a node in a Binary Tree
d) Search for a node in Binary search Tree
e) Traversals of a Binary Tree
   i) In Order traversal
   ii) Pre Order Traversal
   iii) Post Order Traversal

12.4.1 Creating Binary Tree

Algorithm

Step 1: Do step 2 to 3 till stopped by the user
Step 2 : Obtain a new node and assign value to the node
Step 3 : Insert on to a Binary Search tree
Step 4 : return

12.4.2 Insertion A Node in A Binary Search Tree (BST)

InsertNode (node, value)
{ Check if Tree is empty
If (empty)

```
        Enter the node as root

    // find the proper location for insertion
    Else
      If (value < value of current node)

        { If ( left child is present)
            {
                InsertNode( LST, Value);
            }
          else
              allocate new node and make LST pointer point to it
        }
      else if (value > value of current node)
        { If ( right child is present)
            {
                InsertNode( RST, Value);
            }
          else
              allocate new node and make RST pointer point to it
        }
  }
```

12.4.3 Deleting A Node from A Binary Search Tree. There are three distinct cases to be considered when deleting a node from a BST. They are

a) **Node to be deleted is a leaf node.** Make its parent to point to NULL and free the node. For example to delete node 4. Right pointer of 5 to point to NULL and free(node4).

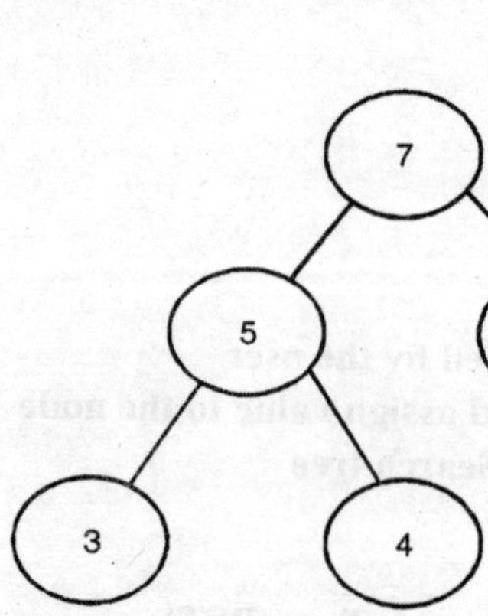

Fig. 12.8a Deleting a leaf node

b) **Delete a node with one child only, either left child or Right child.** For example we will delete node 9 that has only a right child. The right pointer of node 7 is made to point to node 12. The new tree after deletion is shown in 12.8 c.

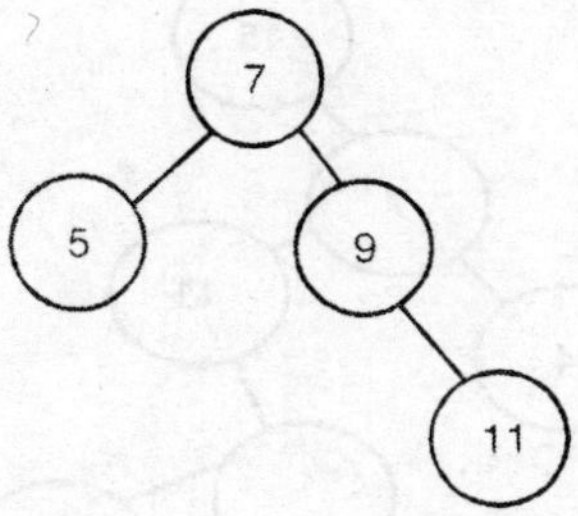

Fig. 12.8 b Deletion of node with only one child

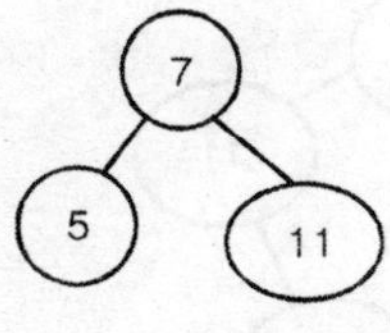

Fig. 12.8 c New tree after deletion

c) **Node to be deleted has two children.** The replace the value with smallest value in the right sub tree or largest value of left sub tree. We will replace it smallest value of Right sub tree. Node 9 that has two children,needs to be deleted from Fig. 12.9.

12.4.4 Searching A Binary Search Tree

```
SearchNode( int val, node * root)
{
 Step 1:  set root to pointer P
 Step 2 : Repeat step 3 – 4 till completion
 Step 3   if val = data of P
                Search is successful
          else
             { if val < data of P
                   Set P pointing to LPTR
                Else
                   Set  P pointing to RPTR
             }
 Step 4 : If ( P= = NULL)
                Value does not exist
 Step 5 : Return
```

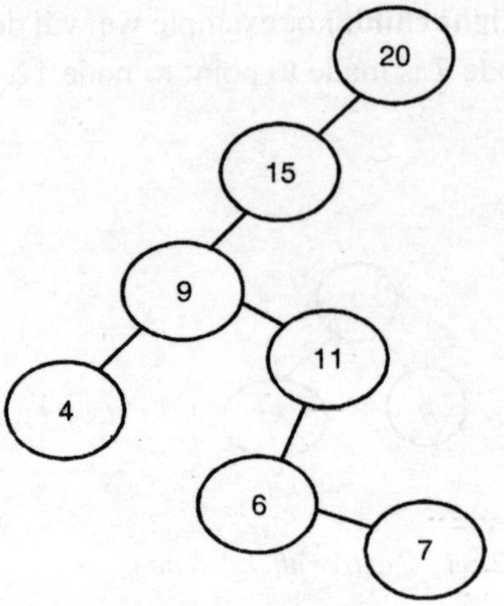

Fig. 12.9a Node 9 to be deleted

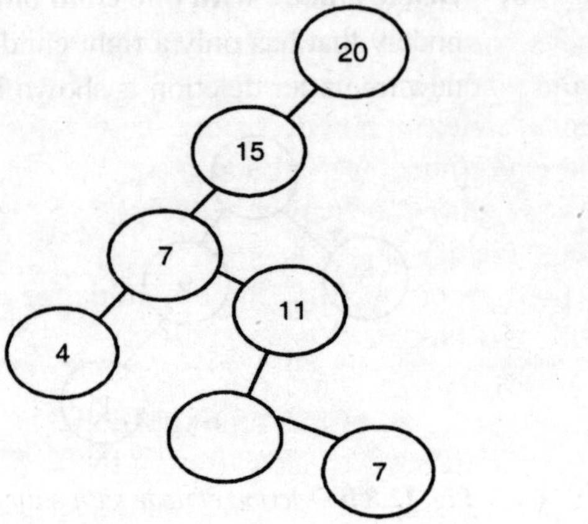

Fig. 12.9b Replace smallest of right sub tree i.e replace 9 with 6

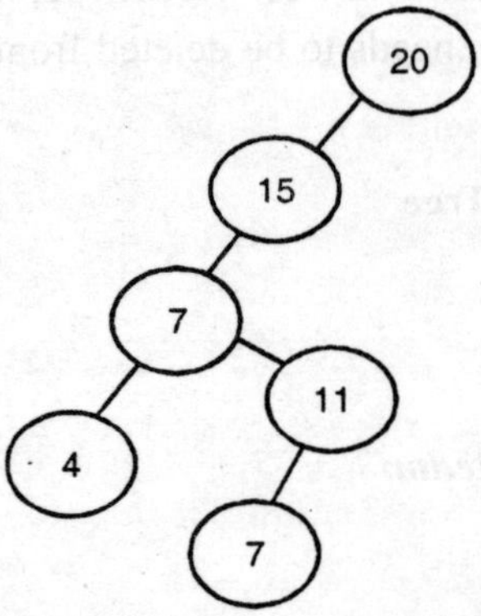

Fig. 12.9c Adjust the pointer of 11 to point to 7 and free empty node procedure at Fig. 12.8b

We now provide complete c program covering aspects of creation, insertion,deletion,and searching of a binary search tree.

```
//Example 12.1 : bintree.c
// a program for creation, deletion,insertion, and searching a binary search tree
#include<stdio.h>
#include<stdlib.h>
struct Tree
{  int data;
   struct Tree *lptr; // pointer to left child
        struct Tree *rptr; // pointer to right child
};                      // will be pointing to NULL in case of leaf nodes
typedef struct Tree node;
//Function prototypes
```

```
 node *createtree(node *root);
node *insert(int n,node *root);
void search(int n,node *root);
node *delet(int n,node *root);
int isLeft(node *parent,node *p);
int isRight(node *parent,node *p);
 void main()
{  node *root=NULL; //initially initialize root to null
  int n,n1,ch;
  while(1)
        {          printf("\n\n\t\tMENU");
     printf("\n\t1: CREATE\n\t2: INSERTION\n\t3: DELETION\n\t4:SEARCH");
                   printf("\n\t5: EXIT");
                   printf("\n\n\tEnter your choice\t");
                   scanf("%d",&ch);
                   switch(ch)
                   {
                             case 1:root=NULL;
                                        root=createtree(root);
                                        break;
                             case 2: printf("\n Enter Number");
                                            scanf("%d",&n);
                                           root=insert(n,root);
                                        break;

                             case 3:printf("\nEnter number to be deleted:");
                                    scanf("%d",&n1);
                               root=delet(n1,root);
                                    break;
                             case 4: printf("\nEnter no to be searched:");
                                        scanf("%d",&n);
                                         search(n,root);
        break;
                             case 5: exit(0);
                                            break;
                   default: printf("\n Invalid choice press between 1 and 8 only");

                   }//end  switch
        }//end while
}//end main

 node *createtree(node *root)
 {
```

```
 int n;
        do{ printf("\nEnter number<0 to stop>:");
                scanf("%d",&n);
                if(n!=0)
                        root= insert(n,root);
              }while(n!=0);
 return(root);
}

node *insert(int n,node *root)
{
 node *temp1=NULL;
 node *temp2=NULL;
 node *p=NULL;
 p=(node *)malloc (sizeof(node));//dynamic allocation of memory foe each element
p->data=n;   //initialize contents of the structure
p->lptr=NULL;
p->rptr=NULL;

  //A new node has been created now our task is to insert this node
        //in the appropriate place. If this is the first node to be created
        //then this is the root of the tree.
              if(root==NULL)
                     root=p;
              else
                     // We will use temp1 for traversing the tree.
                     // Temp2 will be traversing parent
                     // p is the new node we have created.

                     { temp1=root;
              while(temp1!=NULL)
                     { temp2=temp1; // store it as parent
                       // Traverse through left or right sub tree
                       if(p->data < temp1->data)
                  temp1 = temp1->lptr; // left subtree
                else
                        if(p->data > temp1->data)
                              temp1 = temp1->rptr; // right sub tree
                        else
                              {
                                    printf("\n\tDUPLICATE VALUE");
                                    free(p);
                                    break;
                              }//end else
                     } //end of while
```

```
                    // we have traversed to the end of tree
                    // node ready for insertion
                    if(temp1 == NULL)
                    { // attach either as left son or right son of parent temp2
                        if(p->data<temp2->data)
                            temp2->lptr=p; // attach as left son
                        else
                            temp2->rptr=p; // attach as right son
                    }
               printf("\n successful insertion\n");
              }//end of else
  return(root);
}//end of create tree

void search(int n,node *root)
{
  node *p;
  p=root; //initially assign p to root
  while(n!=p->data)
        {  if(n<p->data) //if n is less than curr node data
             p=p->lptr; //traverse the left sub tree
         else
               p=p->rptr; //else if n is greater than curr node data
            //travel right subtree
         if(p==NULL) //if temp1 points to null it implies no value  in the tree
        break;      //so exit loop
        }

        if(p==NULL)
         printf("value is not present in the tree\n");
        else
          printf("\n value found");
}

node *delet(int n,node *root)
{
        node *temp1=NULL; //
        node *temp2=NULL; // temp1 and temp2 are used for traversing the tree
        node *p=NULL; // p node indicates current node that has to be deleted
        int val;
        int ans;
   temp1=root;  //initialize temp1 to root
  while(n!= temp1->data)
```

```
{ temp2=temp1;  //store temp1 in temp2
        if(n<temp1->data) //if n is less than curr node data
 temp1=temp1->lptr; //traverse the left sub tree
else
  temp1=temp1->rptr; //else if n is greater than curr node data
        //travel right subtree
if(temp1==NULL)  //if temp1 points to null it implies value not present in the tree
 break;        //so exit loop
}
```

/*after the successful completion of the above loop temp1 will be pointing to the node having the data and temp2 will be pointing to the parent of this node, please note in case temp1 is pointing to root then temp2 will be pointing to NULL as root has no parent*/

```
if(temp1==NULL)
 printf("\n value not present in the tree");

else
{ // store in p, the node to be deleted
   p= temp1;
  //checking if node to be deleted is a leaf node
  if(p->lptr==NULL && p->rptr==NULL)
       { printf("\n Deleting leaf node with value: %d",p->data);
       //if the leaf node is root of the tree no need to check if it is left or
      //right son
       if(temp2==NULL)
           printf("\n Deleting root of the tree which is a leaf node");
        // check if leaf node is left son or right son of parent
         else
         {   ans=isLeft(temp2,p);
               if(ans==0) // p is the left son
                     temp2->lptr=NULL;
             ans=isRight(temp2,p);
                 if(ans==0) // p is the right son
                     temp2->rptr=NULL;
          }
 free(p);
 }//end of if deletion of leaf node

//checking if node to be deleted is a non leaf node with one child
else
  if(p->lptr==NULL || p->rptr==NULL)
    { printf("\n Deleting node with one child with value %d",p->data);
```

```
                if(p->lptr !=NULL)//implies left child is present
                {
                    if(temp2==0)
                     { printf("\n Deleting root with only left subtree");
                        root=p->lptr,
                      }//end of if
                  else
                   {
                     ans=isLeft(temp2,p);
                     if(ans==0)    // p is left son of parent
                       // assign left pointer of parent to left pointer of p
                      temp2->lptr=p->lptr;
                    ans=isRight(temp2,p);
                       if(ans==0)  // p is  right son of parent
                      // assign right pointer of parent to left pointer of p
                            temp2->rptr=p->lptr;
                   }//end of else
             }//end of if

        if(p->rptr !=NULL)//implies right child is present
        {  if(temp2==0)
            { printf("\n Deleting root with only right subtree");
                root=p->rptr;
             }//end of if
          else
            { ans=isLeft(temp2,p);
                if(ans==0) // p is left son of parent
                // assign left pointer of parent to right pointer of p
                   temp2->lptr=p->rptr;
                 ans=isRight(temp2,p);
                   if(ans==0) // p is right son of parent
                    // assign right pointer of parent to right pointer of p
                     temp2->rptr=p->rptr;
                }//end of else
      }//end of if
            free(p);
}//end of else if
 //checking if node to be deleted is non leaf node with two children
else if(p->lptr!=NULL && p->rptr!=NULL)
 { printf("\n Deleting node with two children with value=%d",p->data);
   //finding node with least value in the right tree of the node
   printf("\n Finding minimum value in right sub tree\n");
   temp1=p->rptr;
```

```
        while(temp1->lptr !=NULL)
        temp1=temp1->lptr;
            // temp now points to least value in right sub tree of node p
              printf("\n min value=%d",temp1->data);
              printf("\n Deleting and re-adjusting");
               val=temp1->data;
               delet(val,root); // recursive call
               p->data=val;
     }
    printf("\n successful deletion\n");
  }//end of else
  return(root);
}//end of delete

//This routine checks if a node is the left child of the parent
//arguments passed are the parent and current node pointers
//returns 0 if successful else returns 1
 int isLeft(node *parent,node *p)
 {  int ans;
    if(parent->lptr==p)
         ans=0;
    else
         ans=1;
      return ans;
 }
//This routine checks if a node is the right child of the parent
//arguments passed are the parent and current node pointers
//returns 0 if successful else returns 1
  int isRight(node *parent,node *p)
 {int ans;
   if(parent->rptr==p)
    ans=0;
   else
    ans=1;
    return ans;
 }
/*output
          MENU
      1  :  CREATE
      2  :  INSERTION
      3  :  DELETION
      4  :  SEARCH
      5  :  EXIT
```

```
    Enter your choice    1
Enter number<0 to stop>:10
Enter number<0 to stop>:20
Enter number<0 to stop>:30
Enter number<0 to stop>:40
Enter number<0 to stop>:50
Enter number<0 to stop>:60
Enter number<0 to stop>:0

Enter your choice    4
Enter no to be searched:50
value found

Enter your choice    3
Enter number to be deleted:50
Deleting node with one child with value 50
successful deletion

Enter your choice    4
Enter no to be searched:50
value is not present in the tree

Enter your choice    2
Enter Number50
Successful Insertion.

Enter your choice    4
Enter no to be searched:50
value found      */
```

■■■ 12.5 TREE TRAVERSALS

Tree being a non linear data structure, there is no fixed mode or sequence of traversal. There are three modes for traversal of a tree. All algorithms use recursive call feature. They are

In Order Traversal
Traverse Left sub Tree inorder
Visit the root
Traverse the Right sub tree inorder

Pre Order Traversal (Depth First Order – Stack data structure)
Visit the root
Traverse left sub Tree preorder.
Traverse the right sub tree preorder

Post Order Traversal (Breadth First Traversal – queue data structure)
Traverse left sub Tree postorder.
Traverse the right sub tree postorder
Visit the root

12.5.1 Tree Traversal Problems

1. Construct a tree for the expression given and give pre order and post order expression. ((a+ (b / c) ^ ((a + b) * C))

Step 1 Include brackets as per rule of algebra and precedence of operators and check correctness of parenthesis.

Step 2 ; Number the parenthesis as shown

((a+ (b / c)) ^ ((a + b) * C))
1 2 3 3 2 4 5 5 4 1

Step 3: Assign governing operator ^ of outer most bracket (no 1) to root. Assign expression to the left as LST and expression to the right of ^ as RST

^

((a+ (b / c))   **((a + b) * C))**
2 3 3 2   **4 5 5 4**

Inorder Traversal Traverse Left sub Tree inorder
Visit the root
Traverse the Right sub tree inorder

Identify the root : ^
Consider LST. Root now is +
Traverse LST again till you reach node A (LPTR of Node A points to NULL)
Visit the root +
Consider the RST. Root now is /
Traverse LST again till you reach node B (LPTR of Node B points to NULL)
Visit the root –
Continue till you visit all the nodes in the tree.

Step 4 Continue Step 3 for LST and RST to get the tree

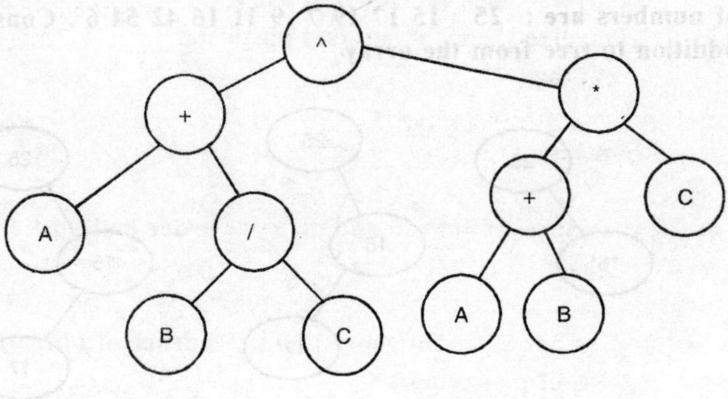

Inorder Traversal : (a+ (b / c) ^ ((a + b) * C). Note that this is nothing but infix notation, you have studied in chapter on stacks.

Preorder Traversal: Visit the root
Traverse left sub Tree preorder.
Traverse the right sub tree preorder

^
LST ROOT = +
LST preorder is A(A lptr points to null)
RST Root is /
LST preorder is B(B lptr points to null)
RST preorder is C(C lptr points to null)
Till now the expression is ^+A/BC

Continue till you visit all the nodes to realize pre order travel

Preorder Expression ^+A/BC*+ABC

Post order Traversal : Traverse left sub Tree postorder.
Traverse the right sub tree postorder
Visit the root

LST root is +
LST A
RST root /
LST is B
RST is C
Visit root is /
Expression till now is ABC/
Continue further to realize the full expression
ABC/+AB+C*^

12.5.2 Construction of Binary Search Tree Problems

1. The sequence of numbers are : 25 15 17 19 7 9 11 16 42 54 6 . Construct a BST. * represents latest addition to tree from the array

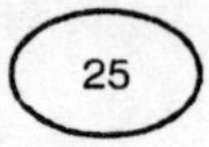

1

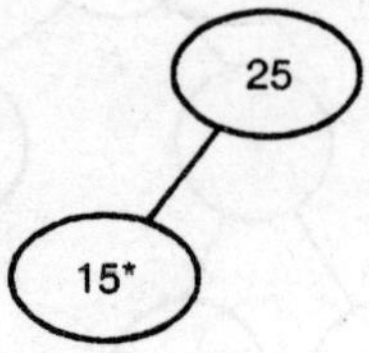

2

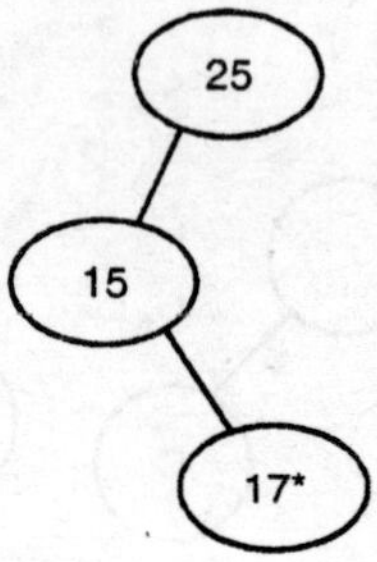

3

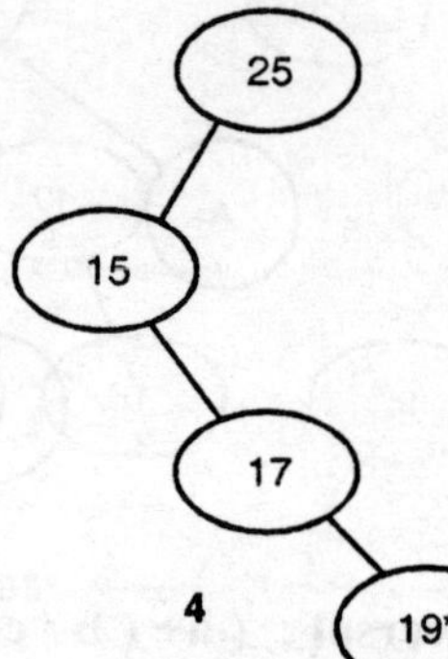

4

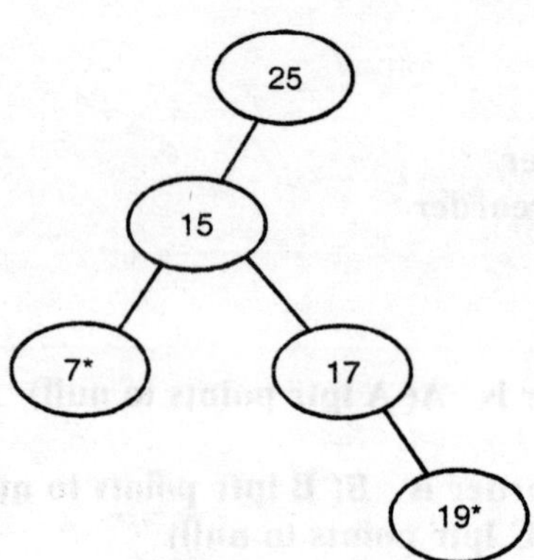

5&6

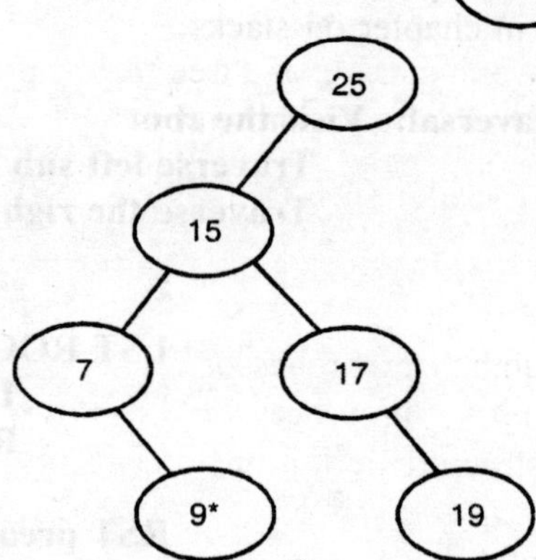

7

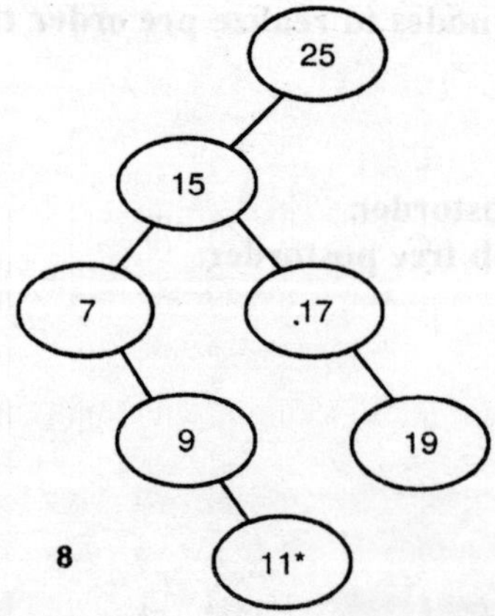

8

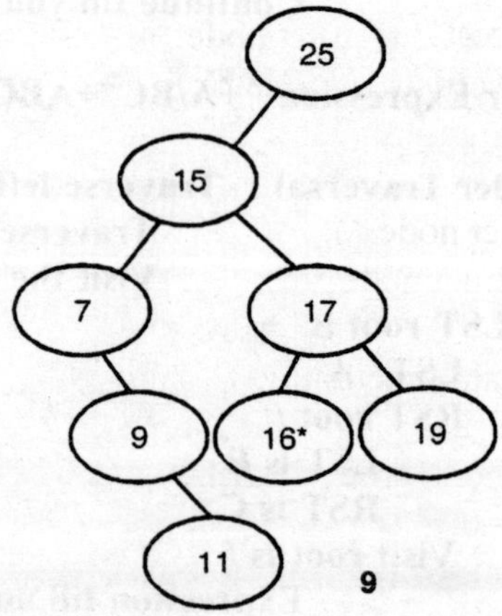

9

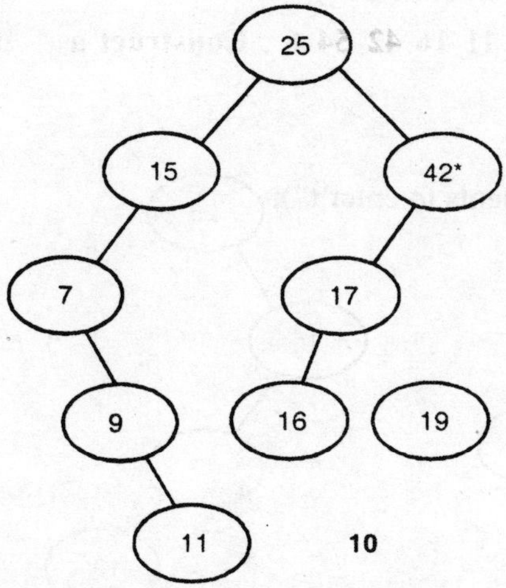

10

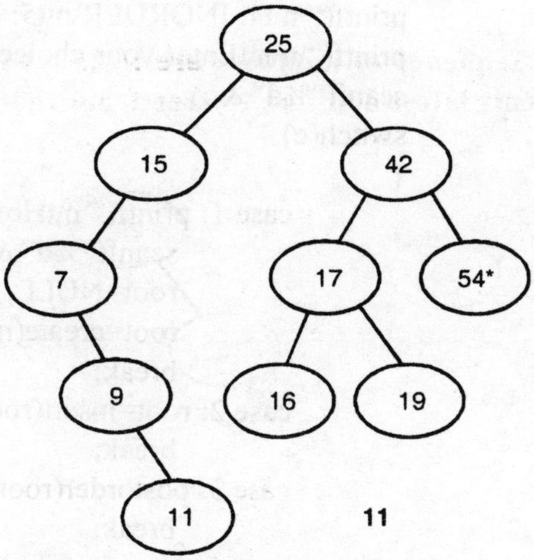

11

We have shown th making of a tree for the problem at 12.5 in the above diagrams. It may be noted that node entry in to the tree is shown by *

Example 12.2 : Tree traversals using recursion

```
//bstrecur.c
#include<stdio.h> //preprocessor
#include<stdlib.h>//preprocessor
struct node//structure definition
{
        int info;
        struct node *lptr,*rptr;
};
struct node *create(int,struct node *);
struct node *insert(struct node *);
//function declarations
int preorder(struct node *);
int inorder(struct node *);
int postorder(struct node *);

void main()//main function
{
        struct node *root=NULL;
        int n,c=0;
        while(c!=6)
        {
                printf("\n\n\t\tMENU");
                printf("\n\t1: CREATE\n\t2: INSERTION\n\t3: POSTORDER");
```

```
            printf("\n\t4: INORDER\n\t5: PREORDER\n\t6: EXIT");
            printf("\n\n\tEnter your choice\t");
            scanf("%d",&c);
            switch(c)
            {
                    case 1: printf("\n\tHow many elements to enter\t");
                            scanf("%d",&n);
                            root=NULL;
                            root=create(n,root);
                            break;
                    case 2: root=insert(root);
                            break;
                    case 3: postorder(root);
                            break;
                    case 5: preorder(root);
                            break;
                    case 4: inorder(root);
                            break;
            }//end switch
        }//end while
}//end main
struct node *create(int n,struct node *root)//create function
{
        struct node *p,*parent,*temp;
        int i;
        for(i=1;i<=n;i++)
        {
            p=(struct node *)malloc(sizeof(struct node));
            printf("Enter data\t");
            scanf("%d",&p->info);
            p->lptr=p->rptr=NULL;
            if(root==NULL)
                    root=p;
            else
            {
                    temp=root;
                    while(temp!=NULL)
                    {parent=temp;
                      if(p->info < temp->info)
                     temp=temp->lptr;
                     else
                                if(p->info > temp->info)
                                        temp=temp->rptr;
```

```
                        else
                        {
                                printf("\n\tDUPLICATE VALUE");
                                free(p);
                                break;
                        }//end else
                }//end while
                if(temp==NULL)
                {
                if(p->info < parent->info)
                        parent->lptr=p;
                else
                        parent->rptr=p;
                }//end if
        }//end else
    }//end for
    return(root);
}//end function
struct node *insert(struct node *root) //insert function
{
    struct node *p,*temp,*parent;
    p=(struct node *)malloc(sizeof(struct node));
    printf("\n\tEnter element\t");
    scanf("%d",&p->info);//scan elements
    p->lptr=p->rptr=NULL;
    if(root==NULL)
        root=p;
    else
    {
        temp=root;
        while(temp!=NULL)
        {
            parent=temp;
            if(p->info < temp->info)
                temp=temp->lptr;
            else
                if(p->info > temp->info)
                    temp=temp->rptr;
                else
                {
                    printf("\n\t DUPLICATE NODE\n");
                    free(p);
                    root=insert(root);
```

```
                        break;
                    }//end else
            }//end while
            if(temp==NULL)
            {
                if(p->info < parent->info)
                        parent->lptr=p;
                else
                        if(p->info > parent->info)
                            parent->rptr=p;
            }//end if
    }//end else
    return(root);
}//end function
int preorder(struct node *root)//preorder function
{
    if(root==NULL)
    {
            printf("\n\tEMPTY TREE");
            return 0;
    }//end if
    printf("%5d",root->info);
    if(root->lptr!=NULL)
            preorder(root->lptr);
    if(root->rptr!=NULL)
            preorder(root->rptr);
return 0;
}//end preorder
int inorder(struct node *root)//inorder function
{
    if(root==NULL)
    {
            printf("\n\tEMPTY TREE");
            return 1
                        ;
    }//end if
    if(root->lptr!=NULL)
            inorder(root->lptr);
    printf("%5d",root->info);
    if(root->rptr!=NULL)
            inorder(root->rptr);
return 0;
}//end inorder
```

```
int postorder(struct node *root)
{
        if(root==NULL)
        {
                printf("\n\tEMPTY TREE");
                return 0;
        }//end if
        if(root->lptr!=NULL)
                postorder(root->lptr);
        if(root->rptr!=NULL)
                postorder(root->rptr);
        printf("%5d",root->info);
return 0;
 }//end postorder
/*output

        MENU
    1  :  CREATE
    2  :  INSERTION
    3  :  POSTORDER
    4  :  INORDER
    5  :  PREORDER
    6  :  EXIT

    Enter your choice  .   1

    How many elements to enter      15
Enter data      14
Enter data      15
Enter data      4
Enter data      9
Enter data      7
Enter data      18
Enter data      3
Enter data      5
Enter data      16
Enter data      4
DUPLICATE VALUE
Enter data      20
Enter data      17
Enter data      9
DUPLICATE VALUE
Enter data      14
```

DUPLICATE VALUE
Enter data 5
DUPLICATE VALUE

Enter your choice 4
3 4 5 7 9 14 15 16 17 18 20
Enter your choice 5
14 4 3 9 7 5 15 18 16 17 20
Enter your choice 3
3 5 7 9 4 17 16 20 18 15 14
Enter your choice */

■■■ 12.6 NON RECURSIVE ALGORITHMS FOR BINARY SEARCH TREES

You have studied recursive algorithms for creation and tree traversals in section 12.5. In this section we will study non recursive implementation. We will use either Do ... While or While (1) control structure to achieve same functionality.

12.6.1 Inorder Traversal Traverse Left sub Tree inorder
Visit the root
Traverse the Right sub tree inorder

We will be using stack data structure to store the nodes for retrieval later.

```
Inordernr ( node * root)
{ //define a stack of type node to hold maximum of MAX and initialize the stack
   node *stack[MAX], *cur ; // current, we will use for traversal
   tos = -1; // tos is top of stack

Step 2; Repeat steps 3 to 12 till loop breaks
Step 3 : do steps 4 to 6 while cur !=NULL
Step 4: Check if stack is full. if full exit
Step 5 : Else push it on to stack stack [++tos] = cur;
Step 6 : cur =cur->lptr
Step 7 : check if tos is empty. If empty break the loop.
Step 8 : Un stack the node from the top of stack.
Step 9 : cur=stack[tos—];
Step 10: print the node for output
Step 11: // now traverse the right sub tree in order
Step 12 : cur=cur->rptr
}
```

12.6.2 Pre Order Traversal (Depth First Order)
Visit the root
Traverse left sub Tree preorder.

Traverse the right sub tree preorder

```
preordernr ( node * root)
  { //define a stack of type node to hold maximum of MAX and initialize the stack
    node *stack[MAX], *cur ; // current, we will use for traversal
    tos = -1; // tos is top of stack
    Step 1 : repeat step 2 to 11 till cur !=NULL
    Step 2: repeat Step 3 to 6 till cur!=NULL
    Step 3: print the node for output
    Step 4: push cur on to stack
          stack[++tos]=cur
    Step 5: // now traverse the left sub tree in order
    Step 6: cur=cur->lptr
    Step 7 : repeat steps 7  to 10  till cur !=NULL
    Step 8 : // pop the node from top of stack
    Step 9 : cur=stack[tos—];
    Step 10:// now traverse the right sub tree.
    Step 11 : cur=cur->rptr;
    // We will loop back to perform preorder traversal with cur
  }
```

12.6.3 Post Order Traversal (Breadth First Order)

Traverse left sub Tree postorder.
Traverse the right sub tree postorder
Visit the root

```
postordernr ( node * root)
  { //define a stack of type node to hold maximum of MAX and initialize the stack
    node *stack[MAX], *cur ; // current, we will use for traversal
    tos = -1; // tos is top of stack

    Step 1 : repeat step 2 to11 till cur !=NULL
    Step 2: repeat Step 3 to5 till cur!=NULL
        // now traverse the left sub tree post order
    Step 3:  Check if stack is full. if full exit
    Step 4 : Else push it on to stack stack [++tos] = cur;
    Step 5 : cur =cur->lptr
        // now traverse the right sub tree post order
    Step 7 : cur=cur->rptr
    Step 8 : check if tos is empty. If empty break the loop.
    Step 9: Un stack the node from the top of stack.
    Step 10: cur=stack[tos—];
    Step 11: print the node for output
```

```
}
```

Example 12.3. itertraves.c We present a program for Inorder and preorder traversals using iterative (non recursive) program. Post order traversal, we leave it to reader for completion.

// itertraves.c.A Program to demonstrate tree traversal using iteration

```
#include<stdio.h>
#include<stdlib.h>

struct Tree
{
  int data;
  Tree *lptr;
  Tree *rptr;
};
typedef struct Tree node;

node *stk[30];
int tos=-1;
 //Routines associated with tree
node *createtree(node *root);
node *insert(int n,node *root);
void preorder(node * root);
void inorder(node * root);

void main()
{ int ch;

   node *root=NULL;
   node *p=NULL;
         printf("Enter values to create tree\n");
   root=createtree(root);
         while(1)
         { printf("\n1: Inorder\n2: Preorder\n3: Exit");
      printf("\nEnter Choice:");
                        scanf("%d",&ch);

                              switch(ch)
                              {
                              case 1: printf("\ninorder sequence");
                                          inorder(root);
            break;
                        case 2:printf("\npreorder sequence\n");
```

```
                    preorder(root);
                         break;
          case 3: exit(0);
     break;
  default : printf("\nenter choice between 1 and 3 only");
               }
     }//end of while
}//end of main
void preorder(node *root)
{  int flag=0;
     node *p;
     p=root;
     while(1)
     {
          while(p!=NULL)
          { printf("\t%d",p->data);
       tos++;
           stk[tos]=p;    //push element onto stack
           if(p->lptr==NULL && p->rptr==NULL)
             flag=1;   //if left child is present for current node set flag to 1
             p=p->lptr;
          }
          if(flag==1)  //leaf node has been inserted into stack it so pop it out
          { p=stk[tos];
           tos—;
           flag=0;
          }
          if(tos==-1)
           break;
          p=stk[tos];  //get parent node from stack
          tos—;
   p=p->rptr;  //now traverse to the right of parent
     }
}
void inorder(node * root)
{      tos=-1;
       node *p;
  p=root;
  while(1)
     {  while(p!=NULL)
        { tos++;
         stk[tos]=p;
          p=p->lptr;
```

```
            }
        if(tos==-1)
         break;
                p=stk[tos];
                tos—;
                printf("\t%d",p->data);
                p=p->rptr;
        }
}
node *createtree(node *root)
 { int n;
        do{ printf("\nEnter number<0 to stop>:");
            scanf("%d",&n);
                if(n!=0)
                    root= insert(n,root);
                }while(n!=0);
  return(root);
 }
node *insert(int n,node *root)
{
  node *temp1=NULL;
  node *temp2=NULL;
  node *p=NULL;

                p=(node *)malloc (sizeof(node));//dynamic allocation of memory foe each element
                p->data=n;    //initialize contents of the structure
                p->lptr=NULL;
                p->rptr=NULL;

   //A new node has been created now our task is to insert this node
        //in the appropriate place.If this is the first node to be created
        //then this is the root of the tree.
                if(root==NULL)
                    root=p;
                 else
                    // We will use temp1 for traversing the tree.
                    // Temp2 will be traversing parent
                    // p is the new node we have created.
                    { temp1=root;
                 while(temp1!=NULL)
                      { temp2=temp1; // store it as parent
                       // Traverse through left or right sub tree
                       if(p->data < temp1->data)
```

```
                temp1 = temp1->lptr;  // left subtree
              else
                    if(p->data > temp1->data)
                         temp1 = temp1->rptr; // right sub tree
        else
                      {
                           printf("\n\tDUPLICATE VALUE");
                           free(p);
                           break;
                      }//end else
                  } //end of while
                // we have trvered to the enode of tree
                // anode ready for insetion
                if(temp1 == NULL)
                { // attach either as left son or right son of parent temp2
                     if(p->data<temp2->data)
               temp2->lptr=p; // attach as left son
      else
               temp2->rptr=p; // attach as right son
                }
              }//end of else
      return(root);
}//end of create tree
/*Output:
Enter values to create tree
Enter number<0 to stop>:45
Enter number<0 to stop>:23
Enter number<0 to stop>:56
Enter number<0 to stop>:67
Enter number<0 to stop>:78
Enter number<0 to stop>:12
Enter number<0 to stop>:25
Enter number<0 to stop>:47
Enter number<0 to stop>:0
1: Inorder
2: Preorder
3: Exit
Enter Choice:1
inorder sequence
   12   23   25   45   47   56   67   78
1: Inorder
2: Preorder
3: Exit
Enter Choice:2
preorder sequence
```

45 23 12 25 56 47 67 78 */

OBJECTIVE QUESTIONS

1. A binary tree can have empty left sub tree and empty right sub tree TRUE/FALSE)
2. Formula for number of nodes in a complete binary tree, given no of levels L is........
3. Number of nodes in a 5 level binary tree is ....
4. Degree of a node in a binary tree is ....
5. Given that a full binary tree has n nodes, number of edges are............................
6. Nodes with no siblings are called .... Nodes
7. Depth of a node is defined as a length of the node from ....
8. Number of nodes in a depth d full binary tree is given by ....
9 Binary Search tree is an .... binary tree.

REVIEW QUESTIONS

1. Construct a binary tree for the following preorder and inorder traversals. Explain with a neat diagram:

   (a)Preorder: ABDIEHJCFKLGM
   Inorder: DIBHJEAFLKCGM

   (b)Preoeder:ABDEFCGHJLK
   Inorder:DBFEAGCLJHK

2. Write an algorithm for each of the following
   (a) In order traversal (b) preorder and
   (c) post order traversal
3. Write a C program to implement binary tree traversals
4. Write an algorithm to count the no of leaf nodes in a binary tree. What is its computing time?
5. Write an algorithm, given the address of an input binary tree, prints the equivalent infix expression with minimum number of parenthesis.
6. Give a brief note about different representations of binary tree.
7. Prove that the total no of edges in a complete binary tree with n terminal nodes is 2(n-1)
8. Formulate non –recursive and recursive algorithm for postorder traversal of binary tree.
9. Write an algorithm for determining whether two binary trees a and b are similar based on the traversal method
10. Write in detail binary tree

11. Distinguish Binary tree and Binary Search trees.
12. Write non recursion algorithm and code for
    a) insert in to a binary search tree
    b) Search for a key node in a binary search tree
13. Write non recursive and recursive algorithms and C Code for following traversals
    a) Preorder
    b) Post order
    c) In order
14. Write algorithm/code for traversing a binary tree level by level.[Hint: start at the root and use array[queue] structure to determine next node.
15. Write an algorithm/code for finding height of a tree.
16. Write a C function to determine number of internal and external(leaf) nodes
17. Write a C function to test if two given trees are identical.[Hint: in order traversal]
18. Write a C function to find a mirror image of a given tree. Right child and left child of parent have to be interchanged to obtain the mirror image.

SOLVED PROBLEMS

1. Write a program to find the height of full binary tree.

```
//nodedepth.c
#include<stdio.h>
#include<stdlib.h>

struct Tree
{ int data;
  struct Tree *lptr;
  struct Tree *rptr;
};
typedef struct Tree node;

node *createtree(node *root);
node *insert(int n,node *root);
void finddepth(int n,node *root);

void main()
{
  int n;
        node *root=NULL;
        root=createtree(root);
  printf("Enter node:");
```

```
        scanf("%d",&n);
        finddepth(n,root);
}
node *createtree(node *root)
{  int n;
   do{ printf("\nEnter number<0 to stop>:");
      scanf("%d",&n);
      if(n!=0)
      root= insert(n,root);
            }while(n!=0);
   return(root);
 }
node *insert(int n,node *root)
{
  node *temp1=NULL;
  node *temp2=NULL;
  node *p=NULL;

                 p=(node *)malloc (sizeof(node));//dynamic allocation of memory foe each element
                 p->data=n;   //initialize contents of the structure
                 p->lptr=NULL;
                 p->rptr=NULL;

   //A new node has been created now our task is to insert this node
          //in the appropriate place.If this is the first node to be created
          //then this is the root of the tree.
                 if(root==NULL)
                        root=p;
                 else
                        // We will use temp1 for traversing the tree.
                        // Temp2 will be traversing parent
                        // p is the new node we have created.
                        {  temp1=root;
                  while(temp1!=NULL)
                           { temp2=temp1; // store it as parent
                            // Traverse through left or right sub tree
                            if(p->data < temp1->data)
                     temp1 = temp1->lptr; // left subtree
                   else
                            if(p->data > temp1->data)
                                      temp1 = temp1->rptr; // right sub tree
                 else
                                  {
```

```
                                        printf("\n\tDUPLICATE VALUE");
                                        free(p);
                                        break;
                                }//enode else
                        } //end of while
                        // we have trvered to the end of tree
                        // node ready for insetion
                        if(temp1 == NULL)
                        { // attach either as left son or right son of parent temp2
                                if(p->data<temp2->data)
                    temp2->lptr=p; // attach as left son
        else
                    temp2->rptr=p; // attach as right son
                        }
                     }//end of else
    return(root);
 }//end of insert tree

void finddepth(int n,node *root)
{
  node *p=root;
  int i=0;
  while(p->data!=n)
  { if(p->data>n)
        p=p->lptr;
        else
        p=p->rptr;
        i++;
   if(p==NULL)
        {printf("node does not exist in the tree");
        exit(1);
        }
        }
 printf("Depth=%d",i);
}
/*Output:
Enter number<0 to stop>:45
Enter number<0 to stop>:23
Enter number<0 to stop>:56
Enter number<0 to stop>:67
Enter number<0 to stop>:12
Enter number<0 to stop>:78
Enter number<0 to stop>:0
```

```
Enter node:78
Depth=3 */
```

2. Write a program to find the height of the full binary tree.

```
//treeheight.c.Program to compute height of a full binary tree
#include<stdio.h>
#include<stdlib.h>
#include<math.h>

struct Tree
{ int data;
  struct Tree *lptr;
  struct Tree *rptr;
};
typedef struct Tree node;

node *createtree(node *root);
node *insert(int n,node *root);
int inorder(node *root);
void findheight(node *root);

void main()
{  node *root=NULL;
  printf("Create a full Binary Tree\n");
   root=createtree(root);
   findheight(root);
}
node *createtree(node *root)
 {
   int n;
             do{ printf("\nEnter number<0 to stop>:");
                      scanf("%d",&n);
                      if(n!=0)
                             root= insert(n,root);
                  }while(n!=0);
    return(root);
 }
node *insert(int n,node *root)
{
  node *temp1=NULL;
  node *temp2=NULL;
  node *p=NULL;
```

```
p=(node *)malloc (sizeof(node));//dynamic allocation of memory foe each element
p->data=n;    //initialize contents of the structure
p->lptr=NULL;
p->rptr=NULL;

//A new node has been created now our task is to insert this node
//in the appropriate place.If this is the first node to be created
//then this is the root of the tree.
    if(root==NULL)
        root=p;
    else
        // We will use temp1 for traversing the tree.
        // Temp2 will be traversing parent
        // p is the new node we have created.
        {  temp1=root;
    while(temp1!=NULL)
        { temp2=temp1; // store it as parent
          // Traverse through left or right sub tree
          if(p->data < temp1->data)
        temp1 = temp1->lptr;  // left subtree
      else
          if(p->data > temp1->data)
                temp1 = temp1->rptr; // right sub tree
    else
                {
                    printf("\n\tDUPLICATE VALUE");
                    free(p);
                    break;
                }//enode else
        } //end of while
        // we have trvered to the end of tree
        // node ready for insetion
        if(temp1 == NULL)
        { // attach either as left son or right son of parent temp2
                if(p->data<temp2->data)
        temp2->lptr=p; // attach as left son
    else
            temp2->rptr=p; // attach as right son
            }
        }//end of else
    return(root);
}//end of insert tree
//For a full binary tree height=level-1,where level=log2(no of nodes+1);
```

```
//log2(x) can be rewritten as log10(x)/log2(x)
void findheight(node *root)
{ int i,height;
  i=inorder(root);
  height=(log10(i+1)/log10(2))-1;
  printf("\nheight of tree =%d",height);
}
//inorder traversal is used to calculate the total number of nodes
int inorder(node *root)//inorder function
{ static int i=0; //This is a recursive program if we use just int then it will increment only once
        if(root==NULL)
        {printf("\nEMPTY TREE");
         return 0;
        }//end if
        if(root->lptr!=NULL)
                inorder(root->lptr);
        i++;
        if(root->rptr!=NULL)
                inorder(root->rptr);
return i;
}//end inorder
/*Output:
Create a full Binary Tree
Enter number<0 to stop>:45
Enter number<0 to stop>:23
Enter number<0 to stop>:56
Enter number<0 to stop>:12
Enter number<0 to stop>:25
Enter number<0 to stop>:50
Enter number<0 to stop>:67
Enter number<0 to stop>:0

height of tree =2*/
```

3. Write a program to sort the given array of numbers using BST properties

//treesort.c

```
//Program to sort numbers using Trees
#include<stdio.h>
#include<stdlib.h>

struct Tree
{ int data;
  struct Tree *lptr;
```

```
  struct Tree *rptr;
};
typedef struct Tree node;

node *createtree(node *root);
node *insert(int n,node *root);
void sort(node *root);//this is same as inorder traversal of a tree

void main()
{
  node *root=NULL;
  root=createtree(root);
  printf("Sorted List.......\n");
  sort(root);
}
node *createtree(node *root)
 {
   int n;
          do{ printf("\nEnter number<0 to stop>:");
                    scanf("%d",&n);
                    if(n!=0)
                          root= insert(n,root);
                  }while(n!=0);
   return(root);
 }
node *insert(int n,node *root)
{
  node *temp1=NULL;
  node *temp2=NULL;
  node *p=NULL;

                p=(node *)malloc (sizeof(node));//dynamic allocation of memory foe each element
                p->data=n;   //initialize contents of the structure
                p->lptr=NULL;
                p->rptr=NULL;

   //A new node has been created now our task is to insert this node
        //in the appropriate place.If this is the first node to be created
        //then this is the root of the tree.
                if(root==NULL)
                         root=p;
                else
                         // We will use temp1 for traversing the tree.
```

```
// Temp2 will be traversing parent
// p is the new node we have created.
{ temp1=root;
while(temp1!=NULL)
  { temp2=temp1; // store it as parent
    // Traverse through left or right sub tree
    if(p->data < temp1->data)
  temp1 = temp1->lptr; // left subtree
  else
      if(p->data > temp1->data)
          temp1 = temp1->rptr; // right sub tree
else
          {
              printf("\n\tDUPLICATE VALUE");
              free(p);
              break;
          }//enode else
  } //end of while
  // we have trvered to the end of tree
  // node ready for insetion
  if(temp1 == NULL)
  { // attach either as left son or right son of parent temp2
      if(p->data<temp2->data)
  temp2->lptr=p; // attach as left son
else
  temp2->rptr=p; // attach as right son
  }
  }//end of else
return(root);
}//end of create tree
void sort(node *root)
{
 if(root==NULL)
 {printf("\nTree is empty");
  exit(1);
 }

 if(root->lptr!=NULL)
      sort(root->lptr);
 printf("%5d",root->data);
      if(root->rptr!=NULL)
      sort(root->rptr);
```

```
/*Output:
Enter number<0 to stop>:45
Enter number<0 to stop>:23
Enter number<0 to stop>:12
Enter number<0 to stop>:67
Enter number<0 to stop>:56
Enter number<0 to stop>:89
Enter number<0 to stop>:0
Sorted List.......
12  23  45  56  67  89 */
```

4. Write a program to swap left sub tree and a right sub tree.

```
//swaptree.c.Program to swap left and right binary subtrees
#include<stdio.h>
#include<stdlib.h>

struct Tree
{  int data;
   struct Tree *lptr;
   struct Tree *rptr;
};
typedef struct Tree node;

node *stk[30];
int tos=-1;   //stack data structure

node *createtree(node *root);
node *insert(int n,node *root);
void inorder(node *root);
void swap(node *root);

void main()
{
         node *root=NULL;
   root=createtree(root);
         printf("inorder traversal before swapping: ");
   inorder(root);
   swap(root);
   printf("\ninorder traversal after swapping: ");
         inorder(root);
}
void swap(node *root)
```

```
{
node *temp,*p;
int flag=0,flag1=0;
p=root;
tos++;
stk[tos]=p; //initially push root into the stack

while(tos !=-1)//while stack is not empty
{
  while(flag==0 && p->lptr!=NULL)
        { p=p->lptr;
          tos++;
          stk[tos]=p;
          flag1=1;
        }
 //while traversing the last leaf node is also pushed on the stack,so we use
        //flag1 to indicate if traversal has occured if flag1=1 it means that traversal
        //has occured and the node on the top of the stack is not a parent node but a
        //leaf node which has to be removed
        if(flag1==1)
        { p=stk[tos]; //so remove it from the stack
          tos—;
          flag1=0; //reset flag1
        }
  p=stk[tos]; //retrive the last parent from the stack
        tos—;
 //swap the left and right children
  temp=p->lptr;
        p->lptr=p->rptr;
        p->rptr=temp;
 //after swapping if the left child exists then its children also have to be swapped
        //so push left child onto stack
  if(p->lptr !=NULL)
        {p=p->lptr;
         tos++;
         stk[tos]=p;
         flag=0;
        }
 //if left child does not exist then set flag=1 this disables traversing the tree again
        //and simply retrives the last parent from the stack and processes it
        else
  flag=1;
}
```

```
}
node *createtree(node *root)
 {
   int n;
          do{ printf("\nEnter number<0 to stop>:");
                    scanf("%d",&n);
                    if(n!=0)
                          root= insert(n,root);
                  }while(n!=0);
   return(root);
 }
node *insert(int n,node *root)
{
  node *temp1=NULL;
  node *temp2=NULL;
  node *p=NULL;

                  p=(node *)malloc (sizeof(node));//dynamic allocation of memory foe each element
                  p->data=n;   //initialize contents of the structure
                  p->lptr=NULL;
                  p->rptr=NULL;

   //A new node has been created now our task is to insert this node
        //in the appropriate place.If this is the first node to be created
        //then this is the root of the tree.
                  if(root==NULL)
                          root=p;
                   else
                          // We will use temp1 for traversing the tree.
                          // Temp2 will be traversing parent
                          // p is the new node we have created.

                          { temp1=root;
                   while(temp1!=NULL)
                            { temp2=temp1; // store it as parent
                             // Traverse through left or right sub tree
                             if(p->data < temp1->data)
                      temp1 = temp1->lptr; // left subtree
                      else
                              if(p->data > temp1->data)
```

```
                                        temp1 = temp1->rptr; // right sub tree
                else
                                        {
                                                printf("\n\tDUPLICATE VALUE");
                                                free(p);
                                                break;
                                        }//enode else
                                } //enode of while
                                // we have trvered to the enode of tree
                                // anode ready for insetion
                                 if(temp1 == NULL)
                                 { // attach either as left son or right son of parent temp2
                                        if(p->data<temp2->data)
                        temp2->lptr=p; // attach as left son
        else
                        temp2->rptr=p; // attach as right son
                                        }
                                }//enode of else

    return(root);
 }//end of create tree
void inorder(node *root)//inorder function
{
        if(root==NULL)
        {printf("\n\tEMPTY TREE");
          exit(1);
        }
        if(root->lptr!=NULL)
                inorder(root->lptr);
        printf("%5d",root->data);
        if(root->rptr!=NULL)
                inorder(root->rptr);
}//end inorder

/*Output:
Enter number<0 to stop>:45
Enter number<0 to stop>:23
Enter number<0 to stop>:56
```

```
Enter number<0 to stop>:67
Enter number<0 to stop>:47
Enter number<0 to stop>:25
Enter number<0 to stop>:12
Enter number<0 to stop>:10
Enter number<0 to stop>:0
inorder traversal before swapping:   10  12  23  25  45  47  56  67
inorder traversal after swapping:   67  56  47  45  25  23  12  10 */
```

Solutions to Objective Questions

1) TRUE	2) 2^L -1	3) 31	4) no of incident edges	
5)	6) n+1	7) leaf	8) root	9) 2^(d+1) -1

CHAPTER 13
GRAPHS

■■■ 13.1 INTRODUCTION

Graph is an important mathematical representation of a physical problem, for example finding optimum shortest path from a city to another city for a traveling sales man, so as to minimize the cost. Unlike trees, which you have learnt, graphs can have loops or cycles. A graph can have unconnected node. Further there can be more than one path between two nodes.

We can write a graph G, a collection of Edges (E) and Vertices (V) as **G = (V, E)**

V (G) = {A, B, C, D, E, F}
E(G) = { (C,A), (A,B), (B,E), (B,D), (C,E), (C,A), (E,A)}

Each edge is specified by two nodes it interconnects. Two nodes are called adjacent nodes if they are connected by an edge. In fig 13.1 vertices A and C are adjacent. Also note that edges can be directed or bidirectional. We have shown directed edges in Fig. 13.1. A directed graph is also known as ***digraph.***

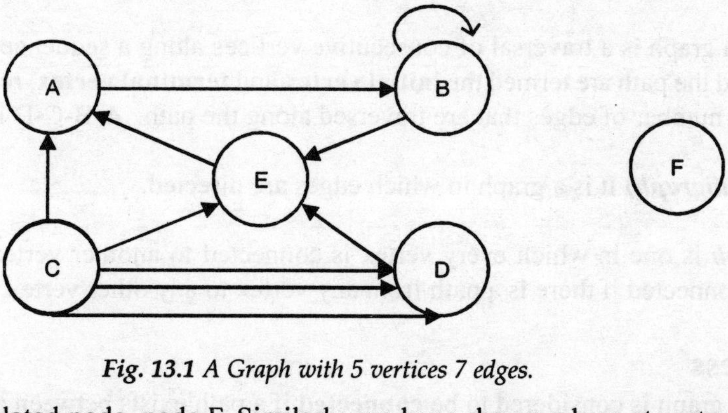

Fig. 13.1 A Graph with 5 vertices 7 edges.

A graph can have an isolated node, node F. Similarly, we have shown a loop at vertex B. A graph can have more than one edge between vertices. Then we call such graphs as multiple graphs. For example between C and D, there are 3 directed edges shown.

Degree of a node is number of edges incident on a node. Degree of node E = 3. Further in degree is number of incoming edges and out degree is number of edges leaving a node. For example in degree of node E is 3 and out degree of node E is 1.

A ***weighted graph*** is a graph whose edges have weights. These weights can be thought as cost involved in traversing the path along the edge. Fig. 13.2 shows a weighted graph.

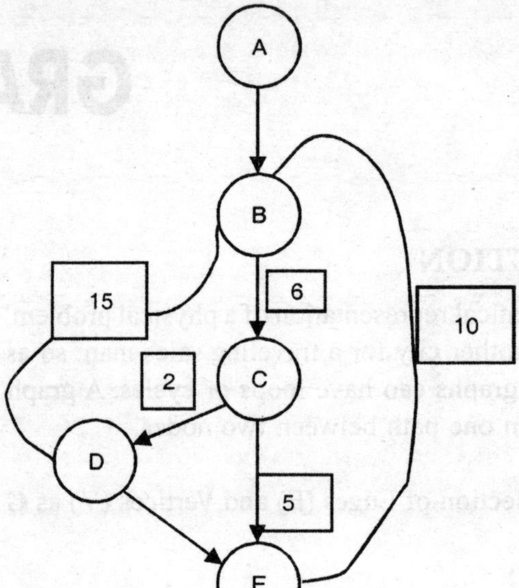

Fig. 13.2 A weighted graph

Adjacent Vertex *A* vertex V_2 is said to be adjacent to vertex V_1 if there is an edge connecting these two vertices. In Fig. 13.2 B&C, D&E are adjacent vertices.

A **path** through a graph is a traversal of consecutive vertices along a sequence of edges The vertices that begin and end the path are termed the **initial vertex** and **terminal vertex**, respectively. The **length** of the path is the number of edges that are traversed along the path. A-B-C-D is path.

Directed Graph(digraph) It is a graph in which edges are directed.

Connected Graph is one in which every vertex is connected to another vertex. Further a digraph is called strongly connected if there is a path from any vertex to any other vertex.

Connectedness

An undirected graph is considered to be **connected** if a path exists between all pairs of vertices thus making each of the vertices in a pair reachable from the other. An unconnected graph may be subdivided into what are termed connected subgraphs or connected components of the graph.

The **connectedness** of a simple directed graph becomes more complex because direction must be considered. For instance, if vertex a is reachable from vertex b, vertex a may not be reachable from vertex b. For the road map example when the map is considered to be a directed graph, it can not be considered a connected graph, because while Calgary is reachable from Saskatoon, Saskatoon is not reachable from Calgary.

Cycle: A graph is said to be cyclic if starting vertex and ending vertex in a path of the graph is the same. B-C-E-B is a cycle. A **cycle** is a path in which the initial vertex of the path is also the terminal vertex of the path. When a simple directed graph does not contain any cycles is termed **acyclic.**

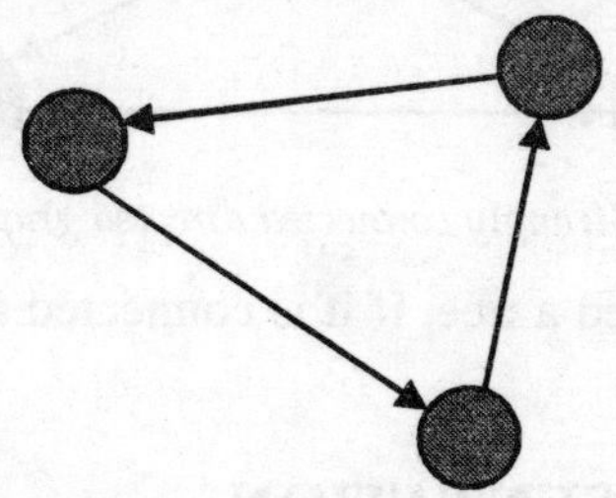

Directed graph cycle

Cycle for undirected Graph :A simple cycle for an undirected graph must contain at least three different edges and no repeated vertices, with the exception of the initial and terminal vertex.

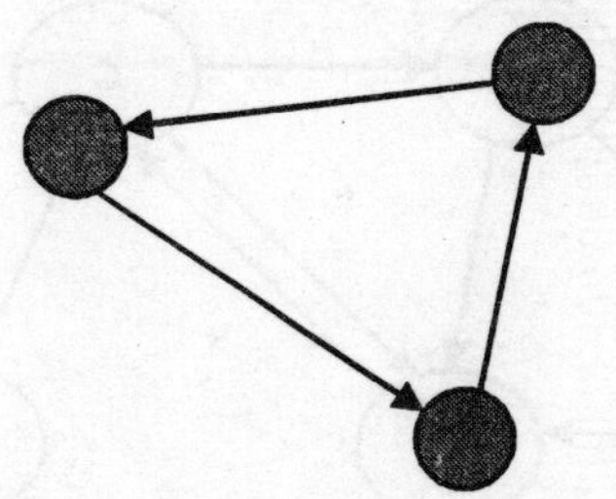

Directed graph cycle

Simple directed graphs can be classified as **weakly connected** and **strongly connected. A weakly connected graph** is where the direction of the graph is ignored and the connectedness is defined as if the graph was undirected. For example in the figure shown below we can not reach **a** from **c.**

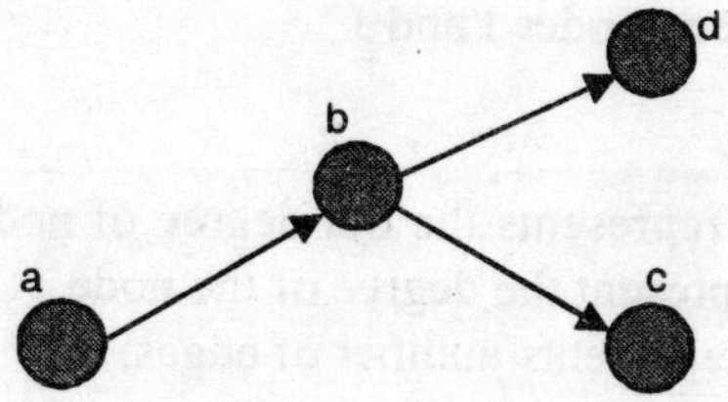

Weakly connected directed graph

A strongly connected graph is one in which for all pairs of vertices, both vertices are reachable from the other. A strongly connected graph is a directed graph that has a path from each vertex to every other vertex. In other words formally a strongly connected graph can be defined as a directed graph D=(V, E) such that for all pairs of vertices u, v " V, there is a path from u to v and from v to u.

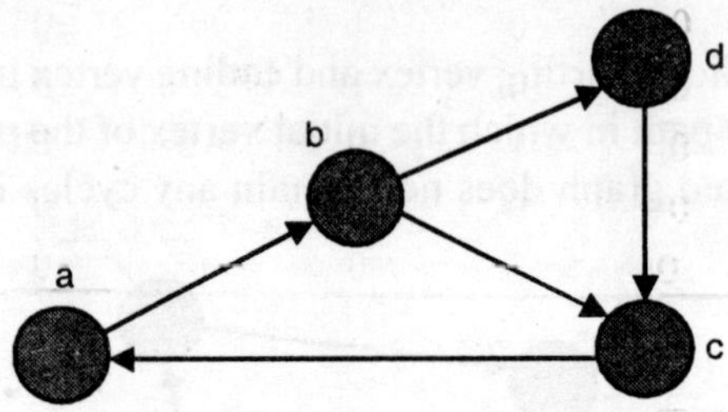

Strongly connected directed graph

Tree vs. Graph: A graph can be called a tree, if it is connected and there are no cycles.

13.2 GRAPH REPRESENTATION

A graph is a mathematical structure and it is required to be represented as a suitable data structure so that very many applications can be solved using digital computer. These data structures are adjacency Matrix Representation and Adjacency List Representations. We will consider graph at Fig. 13.3 to illustrate these two representations.

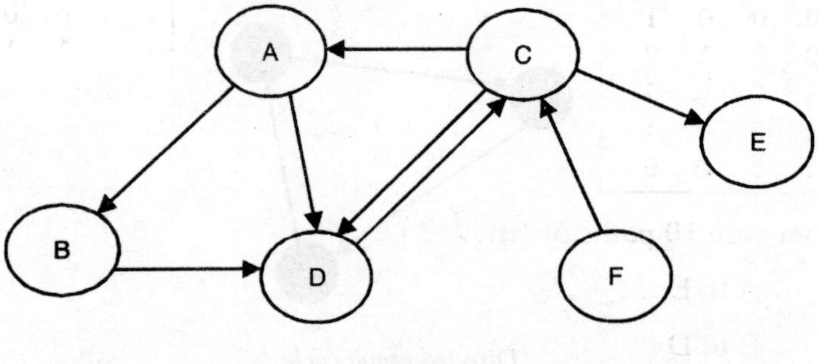

Fig. 13.3 A graph with 6 vertices and 8 edges

13.2.1 Adjacency Matrix Representation: A graph with N nodes can be represented as N x N Adjacency Matrix A such that an element A_{ij}

A_{ij} = 1 if there is an edge between nodes I and J
= 0 Otherwise

Note that number of 1 s in a row represents the out degree of node. Out degree of A is 2. In case of undirected graph number of 1 s represent the degree of the node.
Total number of 1 s in the matrix represents number of edges.

An interesting mathematical property is that an element of matrix A^m represents number of paths of length m between vertices V_i and V_j. Let us consider a 5X5 graph at Fig. 13.4

	A	B	C	D	E	F
A	0	1	0	1	0	0
B	0	0	0	1	0	0
C	1	0	0	1	1	0
D	0	0	1	0	0	0
E	0	0	0	0	0	0
F	0	0	1	0	0	0

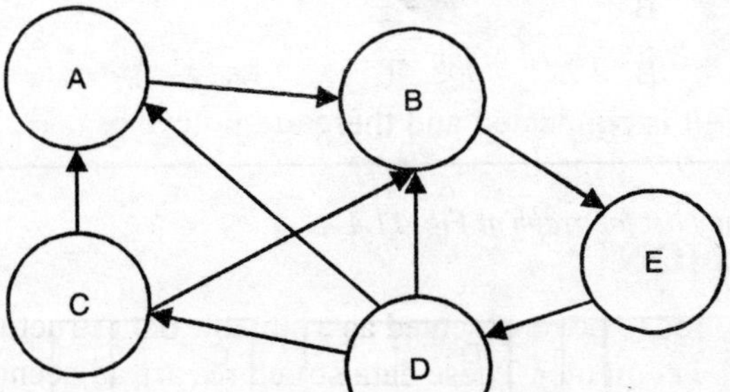

$$A = \begin{matrix} 0 & 1 & 0 & 0 & 0 \\ 0 & 0 & 0 & 0 & 1 \\ 1 & 1 & 0 & 0 & 0 \\ 1 & 1 & 1 & 0 & 0 \\ 0 & 0 & 0 & 1 & 0 \end{matrix}$$

$$A^2 = \begin{matrix} 0 & 0 & 0 & 0 & 1 \\ 0 & 0 & 0 & 1 & 0 \\ 0 & 1 & 0 & 0 & 1 \\ 1 & 2 & 0 & 0 & 1 \\ 1 & 1 & 1 & 0 & 0 \end{matrix} \qquad A^3 = \begin{matrix} 0 & 0 & 0 & 1 & 0 \\ 1 & 1 & 1 & 0 & 0 \\ 0 & 0 & 0 & 1 & 1 \\ 0 & 1 & 0 & 1 & 2 \\ 1 & 2 & 0 & 0 & 1 \end{matrix}$$

Note from A^2 that there are 10 paths of length 2 i.e.

First row : A to E

Second row : B to D

Third row : C to B , C to E

Fourth row : D to A , D to B (two paths) , D to E

Fifth row : E to A, E to B , E to C

Note from A^3 that there are 14 paths of length 3 i.e.

First row : A to D

Second row : B to A , B to B, B to C

Third row : C to D , C to E

Fourth row : D to B , D to D, D to E (two paths)

Fifth row : E to A, E to B (two paths), E to E

13.2.2 Adjacency List Representation

In Linked List representation, we store graph a linked List. Firstly, we have the full list of vertices, say A,B,C,D,E, and F. Then for each vertex, we would have linked list of its adjacent vertices. Consider the graph at Fig. 13.4

Adjacency List. Here we keep all the adjacency list for each node

Node	Adjacency	List	
A	B		
B	E		
C	A	B	
D	A	B	C
E	D		

Fig. 13.5 Adjacency list for graph at Fig. 11.4

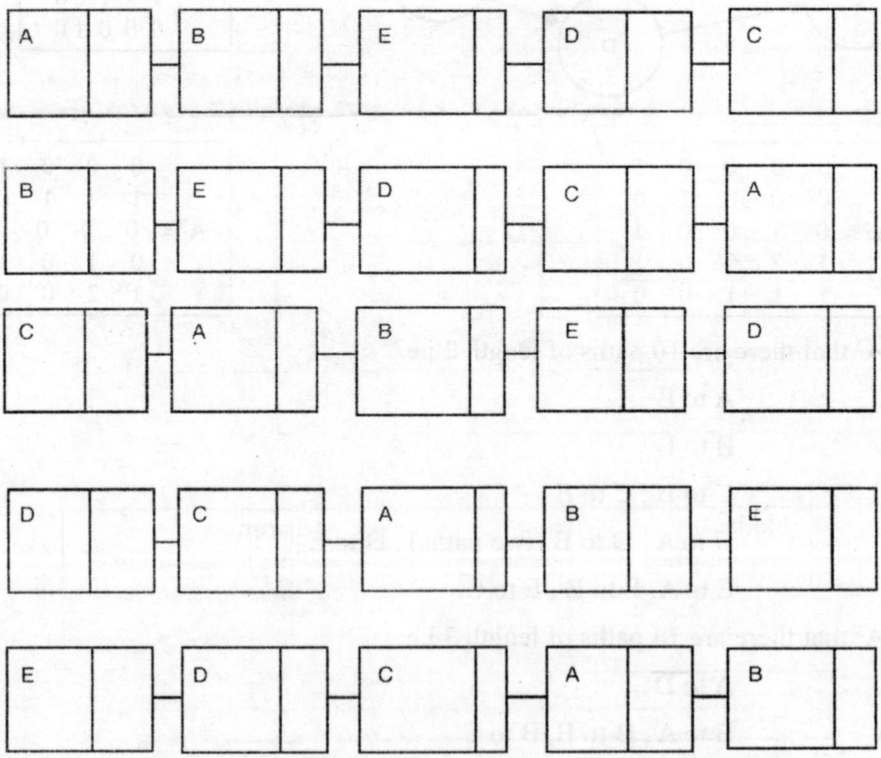

Fig. 13.6 Single linked list representation

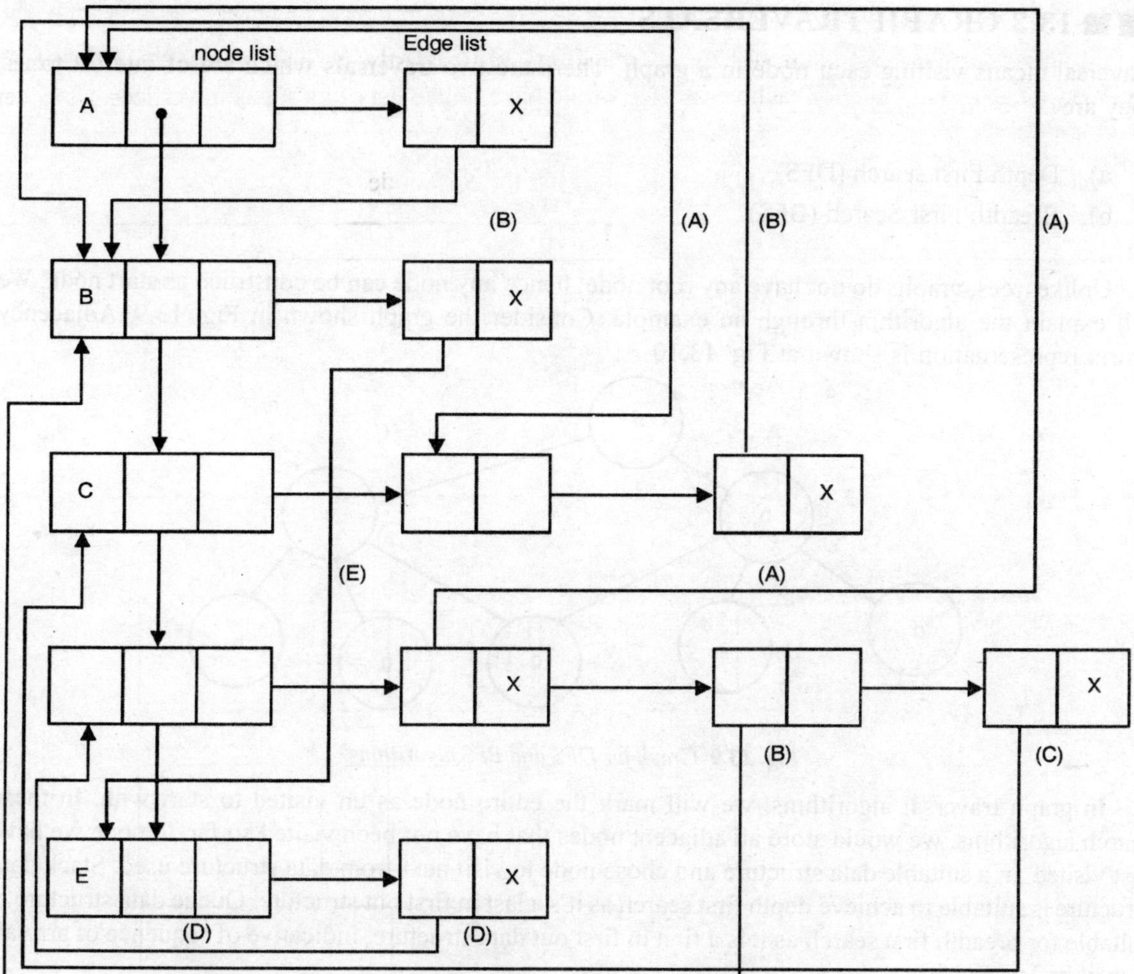

Fig. 13.7 Double linked list representation of a graph

Node In a graph	Next pointer To next Node in the Node List	Adjacent points to first node in the adjacency List

Fig. 13.8a A node list - fields

Pointer to Terminal node of the Edge in the graph	Pointer to Next node in the adj. List

Fig. 13.8b Edge list - fields

13.3 GRAPH TRAVERSALS

Traversal means visiting each node in a graph. There are two traversals which are of interest to us. They are

a) Depth First search (DFS)
b) Breadth First Search (BFS)

Unlike trees, graphs do not have any root node; hence any node can be construed as start node. We will explain the algorithm through an example. Consider the graph shown in Fig. 13.9. Adjacency matrix representation is shown at Fig. 13.10

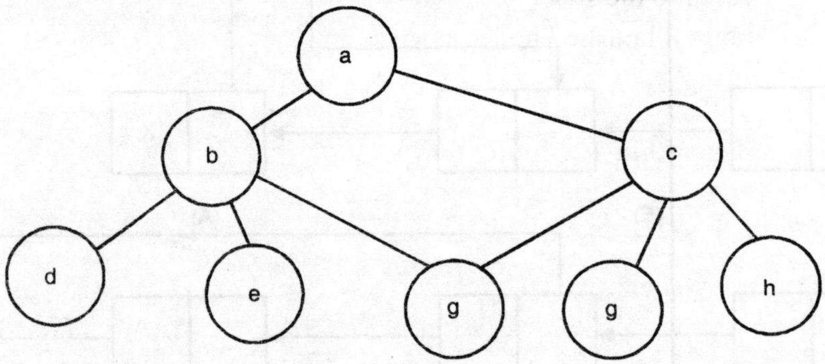

Fig. 13.9 Graph for DFS and BFS algorithms

In graph traversal algorithms, we will mark the entire node as un visited to start with. In these search algorithms, we would store all adjacent nodes that have not been visited so far, to node we have just visited in a suitable data structure and chose node to visit next from data structure used. Stack data structure is suitable to achieve depth first search as it's a last in first out structure. Queue data structure is suitable for breadth first search as it is a first in first out data structure, indicative of sequence of arrival. (Level by level visit)

Also note that we have to keep track of node which have been visited. In either case, we will continue the process; till all the nodes are visited i.e. stack or queue is empty. Following example will make your ideas clear.

	0 a	1 b	2 c	3 d	4 e	5 f	6 g	7 h
0a	0	1	1	0	0	0	0	0
1b	1	0	0	1	1	1	0	0
2c	1	0	0	0	0	1	1	1
3d	0	0	0	1	0	0	0	0
4e	0	0	1	0	0	0	0	0
5f	0	1	1	0	0	0	0	0
6g	0	0	1	0	0	0	0	0
7h	0	0	1	0	0	0	0	0

Fig. 13.10 Adjacency matrix representation

13.3.1 DFS Algorithm

Step 1: Initialization

a) Initialize Stack to empty

b) Mark all nodes as not visited

c) Push node 0 onto the stack and mark it as visited

Step 2: While (stack is not empty)

{

a) Pop value from stack

b) Push all nodes adjacent to popped node and which have not been visited as yet onto the stack

c) Mark all pushed nodes as visited

}

Depth First Search Algorithm-implementation

Step 1: Initialization

* Mark all nodes as not visited

Push 'a' onto the stack

and 'a' is visited

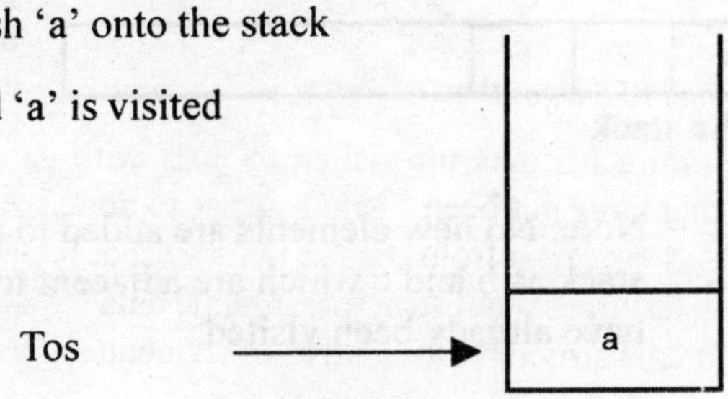

DFS Array

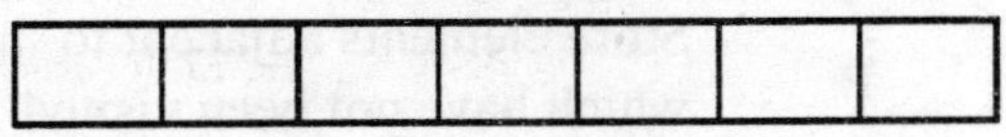

Empty

Step 2:

- Pop (Stack)
- Store in Array
- Push elements adjacent to a onto the stack
- Mark 'b' and 'c' as visited

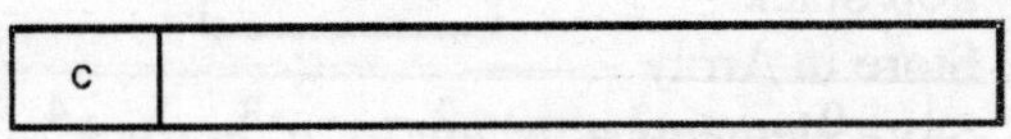

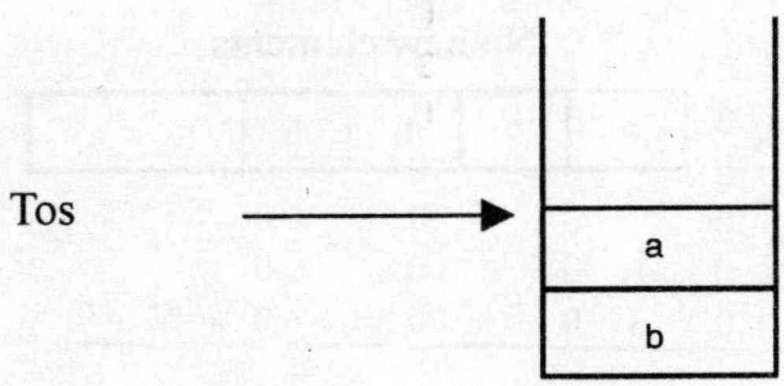

Step 3:

- Pop (Stack)
- Store in Array
- Push elements adjacent to c and which have not been visited on to the stack

a	c	

- Mark f, g, h as visited
-

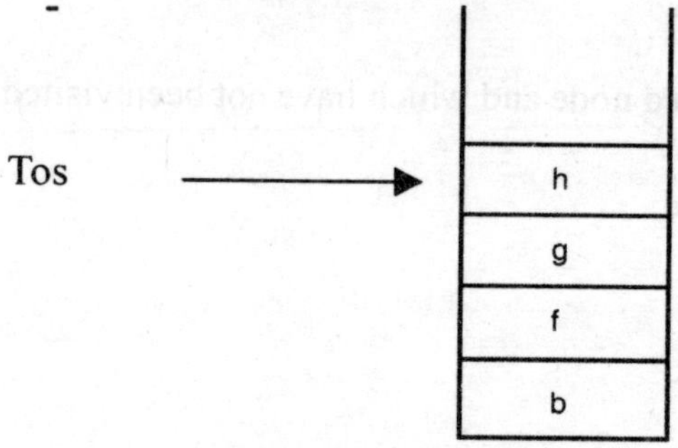

Step 4:

- Pop Stack
- Store in Array
- Store elements adjacent to 'h' which have not been visited on to the stack

a	c	h	

Note: No new elements are added to the stack as b and c which are adjacent to h have already been visited

Tos

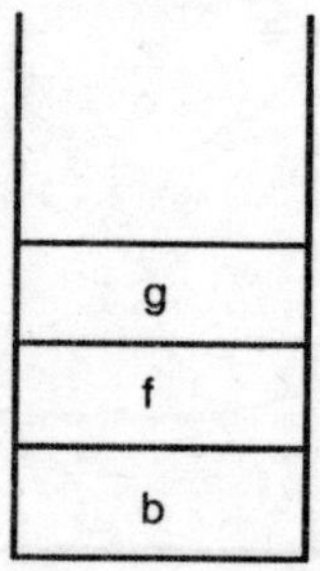

Step 5:

- Pop Stack
- Store in Array
- Store elements adjacent to 'g' in stack

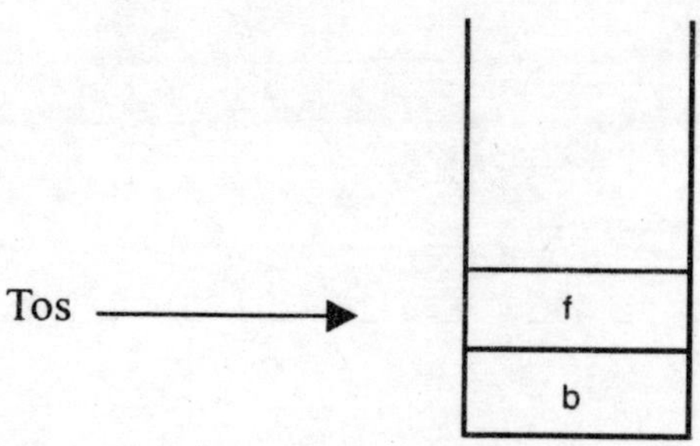

No new elements

a	c	h	h	

Step 6:

- Pop Stack
- Store popped value in array
- Store elements adjacent to 'f' in stack

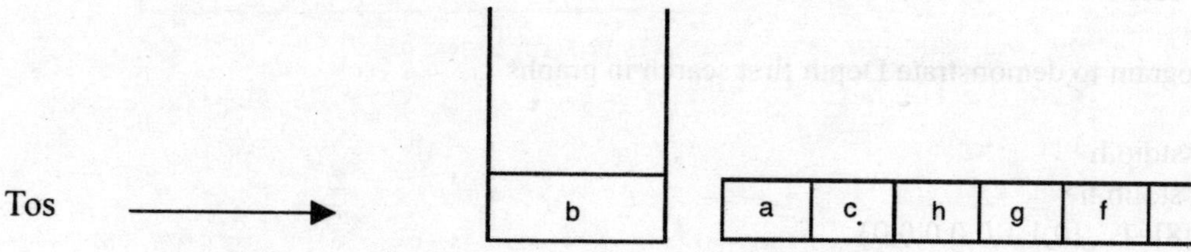

Step 7:

- Pop Stack
- Store elements in 'b' array
- Push elements adjacent to 'b' onto the stack

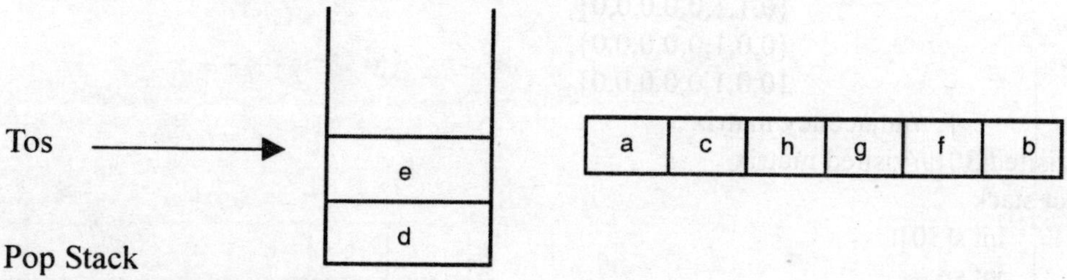

Step 8:

- Pop Stack
-Store elements in array
- Push elements adjacent to 'e' onto the stack

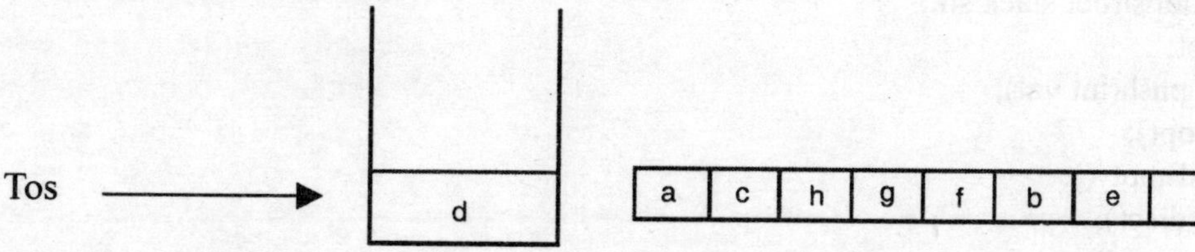

Step 9:

- Pop Stack
- Store elements in array
- Push elements adjacent to 'd' onto the stack

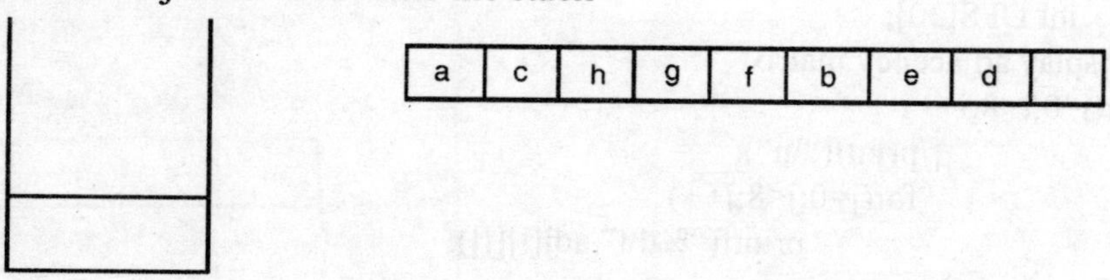

(Stack is empty)

DFS Traversal is : a c h g f b e d

Program to demonstrate Depth first search in graphs

Example 13.1

//**dfs.c** Program to demonstrate Depth first search in graphs

```
#include<stdio.h>
#include<stdlib.h>
int adj[8][8]={    {0,1,1,0,0,0,0,0},
                    {1,0,0,1,1,1,0,0},
                    {1,0,0,0,0,1,1,1},
                    {0,0,0,1,0,0,0,0},
                    {0,0,1,0,0,0,0,0},
                    {0,1,1,0,0,0,0,0},
                    {0,0,1,0,0,0,0,0},
                    {0,0,1,0,0,0,0,0}
            }; //adjacency matrix
int visited[30];//visited matrix
struct stack
{       int s[30];
        int sp;
};

 typedef struct stack stk;
  stk st;
 void push(int val);
 int pop();
 int isEmpty();
 void disp();
 void main()
 {       //initialize stack pointer
         st.sp=-1;
         int i,j,val;
         int DFS[30];
    //display adjacency matrix
    for(i=0;i<8;i++)
                { printf("\n");
                  for(j=0;j<8;j++)
                        printf("%d\t",adj[i][j]);
                }
   i=0;//reinitialize i
```

```
        push(i);//push first element onto the stack
    visited[i]=1;
        disp();

 while(isEmpty()==0)
        {  val=pop();
          DFS[i]=val;
          //now read the adjacency martrix and push
        //nodes onto stack which have not been visited
                for(j=0;j<8;j++)
                {          if(adj[val][j]==1)
                           {   if(visited[j]==0)
                                   {  push(j);
                                      visited[j]=1;
                                   }
                           }
                }//end of for
           //disp();
           i=i+1;
        }// end of while
     printf("\nDFS for the graph\n");
   for(i=0;i<8;i++)
                printf("%d\t",DFS[i]);
 }// end of main

 int isEmpty()
  {  if(st.sp==-1) //if top is equals to null
        {          //printf("Stack is Empty");
                   return 1;
        }
 else
    return 0;
}// end of isEmpty()


void push(int val)
{   st.sp++;//increment sp to next position
   st.s[st.sp]=val;//assigning val to st[sp]
} // end of int push ().

int pop()
{          int val, ans ; // ans hold the return value fro isEMpty(). 1 if it is
             // empty. Else it hold 0.
```

```
      ans = isEmpty();
    if (ans == 0) // The stack is not empty
     {       val=st.s[st.sp];
             st.sp—; //decrement stack[sp]
     }
    else
     printf( "\n Stack is Empty no items to pop");
     return(val);
}// end of int pop

void disp()//display function
{       int i ;
        printf("\n");
         if (isEmpty()== 0)
          {      printf("\n ****elements of stack****");
                 for(i=st.sp;i>=0;i—) //display stack items
                   printf("\n %d\t",st.s[i]);
     }
    else
     printf("\n stack is Empty.");
}//end disp()
/*

Enter no of nodes in the graph:8


0   1   1   0   0   0   0   0
1   0   0   1   1   1   0   0
1   0   0   0   0   1   1   1
0   0   0   1   0   0   0   0
0   0   1   0   0   0   0   0
0   1   1   0   0   0   0   0
0   0   1   0   0   0   0   0
0   0   1   0   0   0   0   0


DFS for the graph
0   2   7   6   5   1   4   3 */
```

13.3.2 BFS Algorithm

<u>Step 1:</u> Initialization

a) Initialize Queue to empty
d) Mark all nodes as not visited
e) Enque node 0 and mark it as visited

Step 2: While (queue is not empty)

{

Deque element from stack

d) Enque nodes adjacent to deque node and which have not been visited as yet onto the stack

e) Mark all enqued nodes as visited

}

Breadth First Search Algorithm

Step 1: Initialization

Mark all nodes as not visited

Enque 'a' mark it as visited

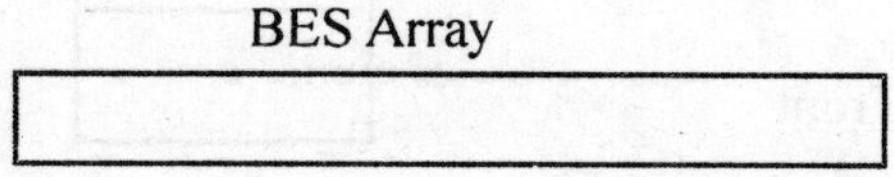

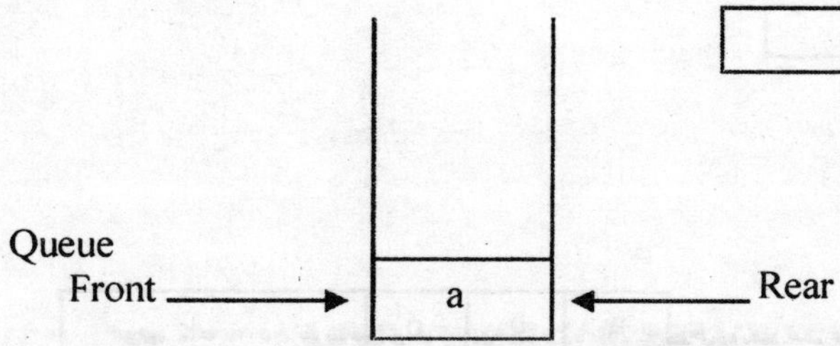

Step 2:

- Deque (Queue)
- Store in Array
- Enque nodes adjacent to 'a' into the queue
- Mark 'b' and 'c' as visited

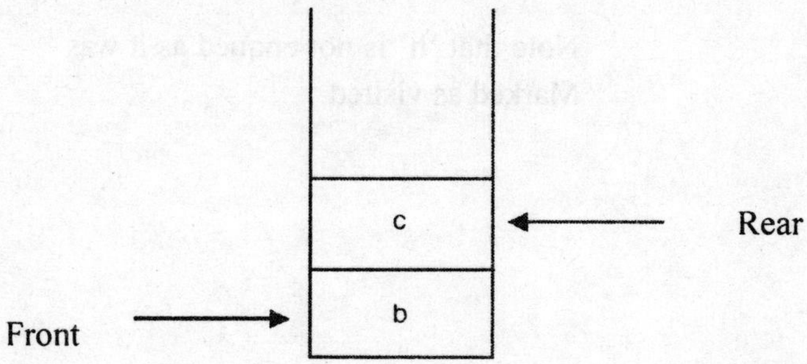

Step 3:

- Deque (Queue)
- Store in Array

- Enque nodes adjacent to 'b' into the stack
- Mark d,e,h as visited

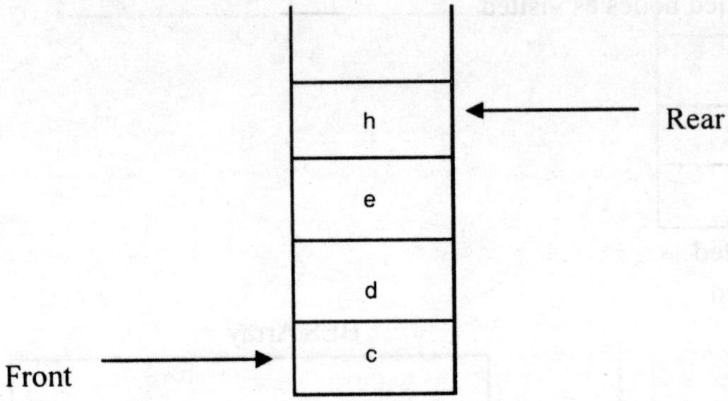

Step 4:

- Deque (queue)
- Store in Array
- Enque nodes adjacent to 'c' into the queue
- Mark 'f' and 'g' as visited

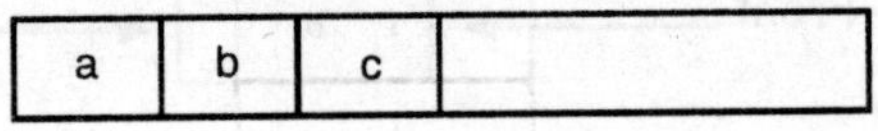

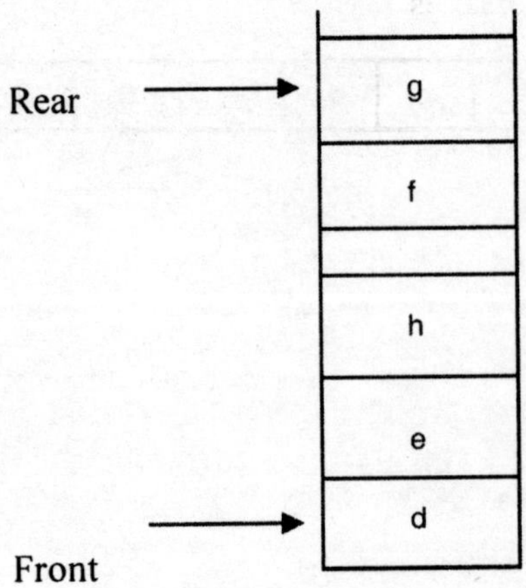

Note that 'h' is not enqued as it was Marked as visited

Step 5:

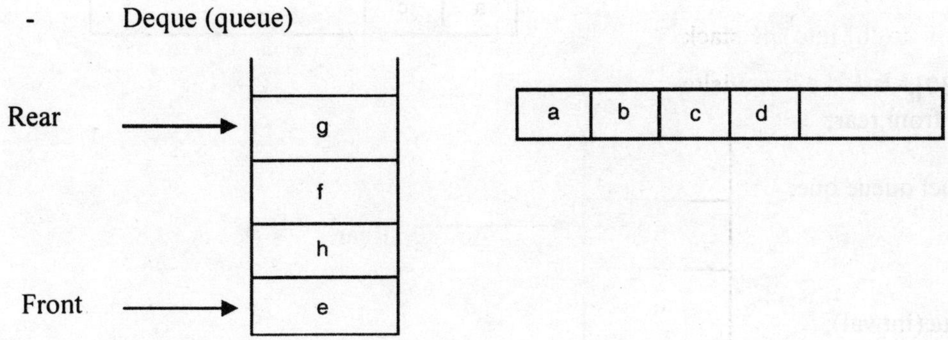

Step 6:

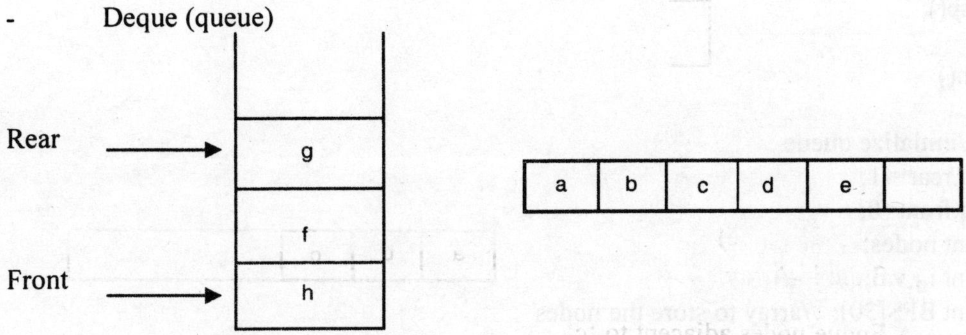

Step 7:

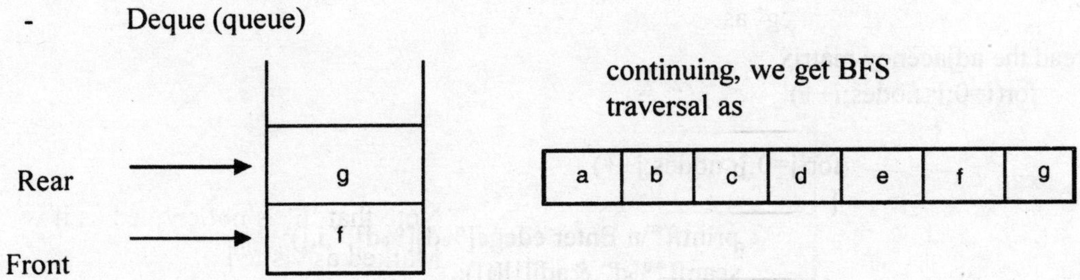

Example 13.2 bfs.c

```
//Program to demonstrate Breadth first search in graphs

#include<stdio.h>
#include<stdlib.h>

int adj[30][30]; //adjacency matrix
int visited[30];//visited matrix
```

```
struct queue
  {
    int data[30];
        int front,rear;
  };
  typedef struct queue que;
  que q;


  void enqueue(int val);
  int dequeue();
  int isEmpty();
  void disp();

void main()
{
        //initialize queue
        q.rear=-1;
        q.front=0;
        int nodes;
        int i,j,val;
        int BFS[30];  //array to store the nodes
     printf("\nEnter no of nodes in the graph:");
                        scanf("%d",&nodes);

    //read the adjacency matrix
        for(i=0;i<nodes;i++)
            {
                    for(j=0;j<nodes;j++)
                    {
                            printf("\n Enter edege[%d][%d]:",i,j);
                            scanf("%d",&adj[i][j]);
                    }
            }

    //display adjacency matrix
    for(i=0;i<nodes;i++)
            {
                    printf("\n");
                for(j=0;j<nodes;j++)
                        printf("%d\t",adj[i][j]);
            }
```

```
  i=0;//reinitialize i
        enqueue(i);//push first element onto the queue
   visited[i]=1;
        disp();
  while(isEmpty()==0)
        {
                  val=dequeue();
     BFS[i]=val;

                  //now read the adjacency martrix and push nodes onto stack which have not been visited
                  for(j=0;j<nodes;j++)
                  {
                         if(adj[val][j]==1)
                         {
                                if(visited[j]==0)
                                {
                                       enqueue(j);
                                       visited[j]=1;
                                }

                         }
                  }//end of for
          disp();
     i=i+1;
        }

 printf("\nBFS for the graph\n");
 for(i=0;i<nodes;i++)
                  printf("%d\t",BFS[i]);
}

void enqueue(int val)
{   q.rear++;//increment rear to point to next empty slot
    q.data[q.rear]=val;
}
int dequeue()
{   int k,ans;
  k=isEmpty();
       if(k==0)//queue is not empty
              { ans=q.data[q.front];
                 q.front++;
              }
     else
```

```
    {                   printf("Queue is empty\n");
                   ans=-1;
    }
    return(ans);
}

int isEmpty()
{ int ans;
 if(q.rear<q.front)
   ans=1;
          else
                   ans=0;
   return(ans);
}
void disp()
{   int ans,i;
   printf("****data elements in queue****\n");
    ans=isEmpty();
    if(ans ==0)
           { for(i=q.front;i<=q.rear;i++)
            printf("%d\n",q.data[i]);
    }
    else
           printf("queue is empty\n");
 }
```

13.4 MINIMAL SPANNING TREES(MST)

Dictionary meaning of spanning is to extend across from the present state. Minimal spanning tree means get connected to all other nodes so that cost of such connection is minimal. It means Minimal spanning tree is a fully connected graph. Solution of minimal spanning tree is very attractive for network designers, say for example a cable laying company with head quarters at Hyderabad and get connected to all district head quarters. How do they plan laying the cables and connect all district head quarters, keeping the total cost minimum. Therefore the constraints are:

- The set of edges to be included should be a minimal set.
- No cycle in MST

13.4.1 MST Problem

Kruskals algorithm builds a minimum spanning tree by adding at each step the smallest weighted edge that hasn't already been added, provided it does not create a cycle. The algorithm stops when all edges are connected (it is a spanning tree).

An algorithm that makes an optimal choice at each stage is called a *greedy algorithm*.

13.4.2 Example Spanning Tree Problem:

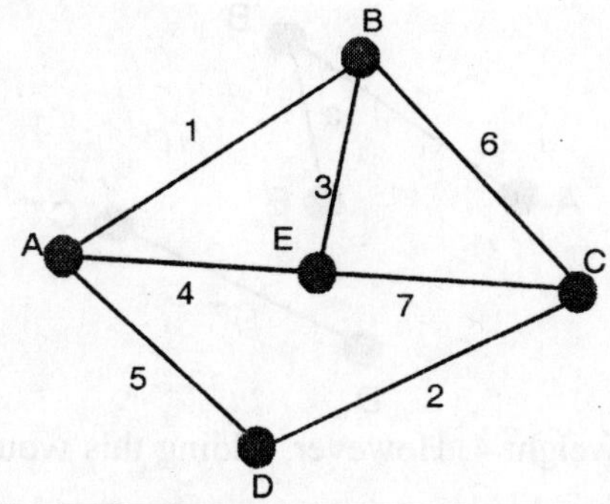

	0 a	1 b	2 c	3 d	4 e
0a	0	1	0	5	4
1b	1	0	6	0	3
2c	0	6	0	2	7
3d	5	0	2	0	0
4e	4	3	7	0	0

Fig. 13.11 Graph for minimal spanning tree & adjacency matrix

Following Kruskal's algorithm:

1. The smallest weight edge is of weight 1. Adding this doesn't create a cycle, so we add it

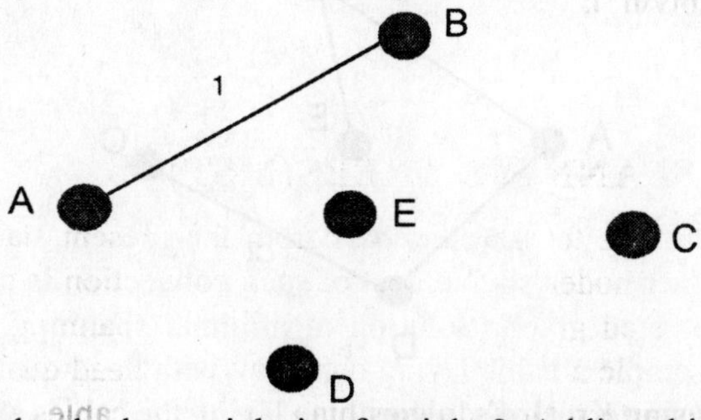

2. The next smallest weighted edge weight is of weight 2. Adding this doesn't create a cycle, so we add it.

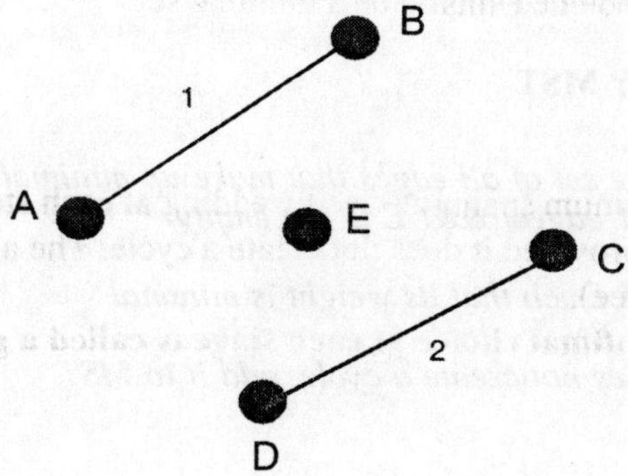

3. The next smallest weighted edge is of weight 3. Adding this doesn't create a cycle, so we add it.

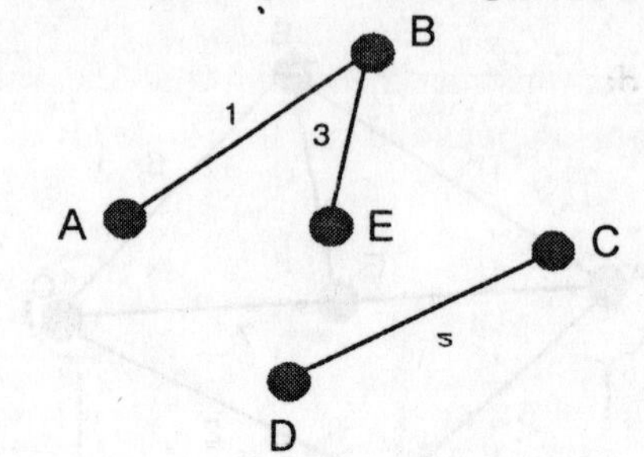

4. The next smallest edge is of weight 4. However, adding this would create a cycle (see below), so we don't add it.

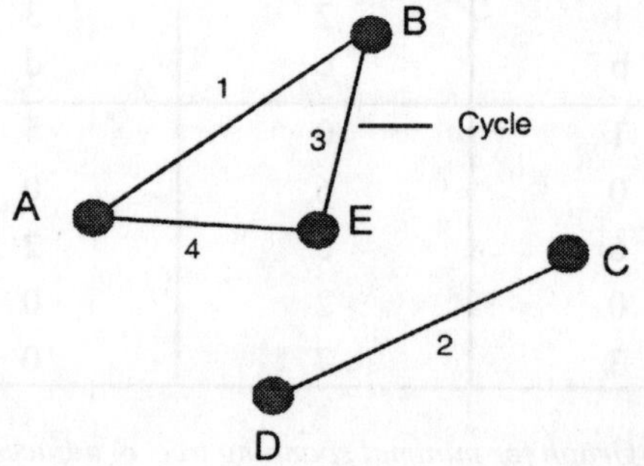

5. The next smallest edge is of weight 5. Adding this doesn't create a cycle, so we add it.

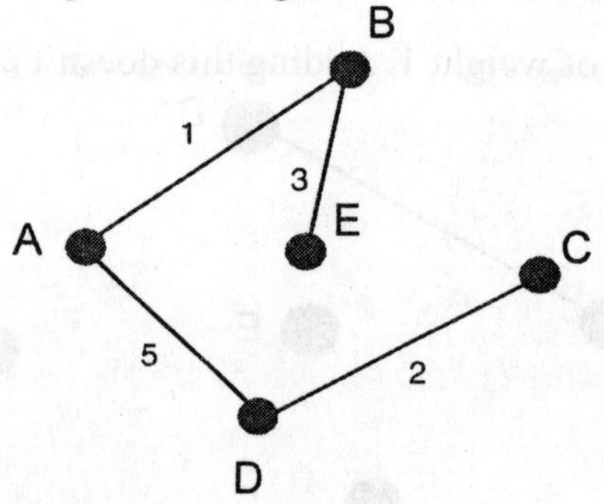

1. The above is MST using Kruskal's algorithm.
2. The edges selected are (A,B) (D,C) , (B,E) ,(A,D)
3. Cost of MST = 1+2+3+5=11 Units

13.4.3 Kruskals Algorithm for MST

```
Let G = { V, E} be a graph
    MST = { } // MST is the set of all edges that make up minimal spanning tree
    While ( MST has < n-1 edges) &&( E is not empty)
    {
        select ( u,v) fron E Duch that its weight is minimal
        delete ( u, v) from E
        if adding (u,,v) does not create a cycle, add it to MST
    }
```

Example 13.3 gkruskal.c

The graph we would consider for demonstrate the working of kruskal algorithm is shown below. The corresponding Adjacency matrix is also appended

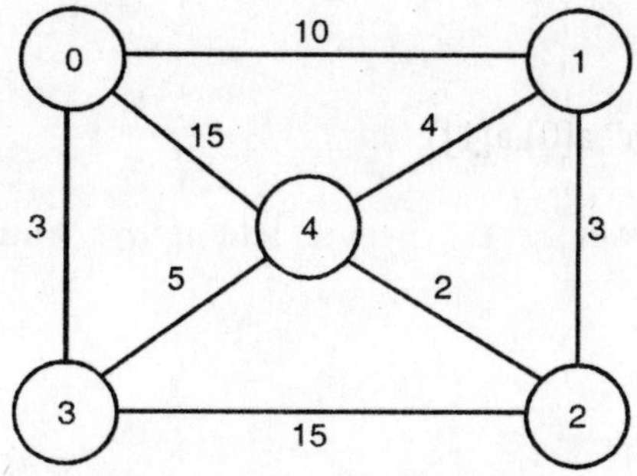

Fig. 13.12 Graph for solving Kruskals algorithm

```
adj[max][max]={ {HIGH,10,HIGH,3,15},
                {10,HIGH,3,HIGH,4},
                {HIGH,3,HIGH,15,2},
                {3,HIGH,15,HIGH,5},
                {15,4,2,5,HIGH}
              } ; //adjacency matrix
```

Note: adj[0][1]=10 and also adj[1][0]=10 so when we delete a edge we have to delete both adj[I][j] and adj[j][I]

```
// gkruskal.c. A program to demonstrate kruskals algorithm
#include<stdio.h>
#define max 5
#define HIGH 65535

int adj[max][max]={
                    {HIGH,10,HIGH,3,15},
                    {10,HIGH,3,HIGH,4},
                    {HIGH,3,HIGH,15,2},
                    {3,HIGH,15,HIGH,5},
                    {15,4,2,5,HIGH}
                    }; //adjacency matrix

void findminedge(int a[]); //finds the the edge with minimum cost
void delminedge(int a[]); //deletes the edge with minimum cost from graph
```

```
int  iscycle(int a[],int mst[][2],int edge);//checks if addition of edge to MST produces a cycle
                                            //returns 1 if yes else 0
void main()
{  int i=0,cycle,edge=0;
   int a[2]={0,0};//array to store the current minimum edge
   int mst[max-1][2];//array to store the mst
        while(edge<max-1)
        { findminedge(a);
   printf("min edge i=%d,j=%d\n",a[0],a[1]);
   delminedge(a);
   cycle=iscycle(a,mst,edge);
   if(cycle==0)
         {mst[i][0]=a[0];
          mst[i][1]=a[1];
          edge++;
          printf("mst=%d %d \n",mst[i][0],mst[i][1]);
          i++;
         }
        }//end of while
  printf("edges included in MST........\n");
        for(i=0;i<edge;i++)
    printf("%d %d\n",mst[i][0],mst[i][1]);
}
void findminedge(int a[])
{ int i,j;
 int min=HIGH;
 for(i=0;i<max;i++)
  {
   for(j=0;j<max;j++)
        {
        if(adj[i][j]<min)
        {min=adj[i][j];
         a[0]=i;
         a[1]=j;
        }//end of if
        }//end of for:j loop
  }//end of for:i loop
}//end of findminedge()

void delminedge(int a[])
{
  int i,j;
  i=a[0];
```

```
  j=a[1];
  adj[i][j]=HIGH;
  adj[j][i]=HIGH;
}//end of delminedge function
```

/*cycle checking
suppose edges1: 2 4 and edges2: 1 2 are already present in the MST,now suppose the new min is minedge: 1 4 to check if the current edge will form a cycle we will have to first check if i of newmin(1 in this case) and j of newmin(4 in this case), are already present in some i and j of the MST(in this case 1 is present in i of edge of 2 and 4 is present in j of edge1),once we have established that both are present we have to check if the second vertex of i and the first vertex of j are equal, if they are equal we can conclude that addition of this edge forms a cycle and hence should not be included in the MST(you can see that 2 is common to both edges1 and 2).*/

```
int iscycle(int a[],int mst[][2],int edge)
{ int i=0,j=0;
  int flag1=0,flag2=0;

  //the two for loops below find out if i and j of current min are already present in the MST
  //if yes it sets the flags to 1
  for(i=0;i<edge;i++)
       { if(mst[i][0]==a[0])
              { flag1=1;
                break;
              }//end of if
       }//end of for
  for(j=0;j<edge;j++)
  { if(mst[j][1]==a[1])
              { flag2=1;
                break;
              }//end of if
  }//end of for
  if(flag1==1 && flag2==1 && mst[i][1]==mst[j][0])
  { printf("cycle formed:not included in mst\n");
       return(1);
  }//end of if
  else
  return(0);
}//end of iscycle()
/*Output:
min edge i=2,j=4
mst=2 4
min edge i=0,j=3
```

mst=0 3
min edge i=1,j=2
mst=1 2
min edge i=1,j=4
cycle formed:not included in mst
min edge i=3,j=4
mst=3 4
edges included in MST........
2 4
0 3
1 2
3 4 */

13.4.4 Prims Algorithm for MST

Kruskal's algorithm has two main drawbacks. A second algorithm is required to sort the edges in ascending order of weight before we can select to be part of MST It is further necessary to check at each stage that a cycle isn't formed.

Prims algorithm solves these problems. It works by always choosing the closest unconnected vertex, from any connected vertex (not just the last connected vertex).

For the example network:

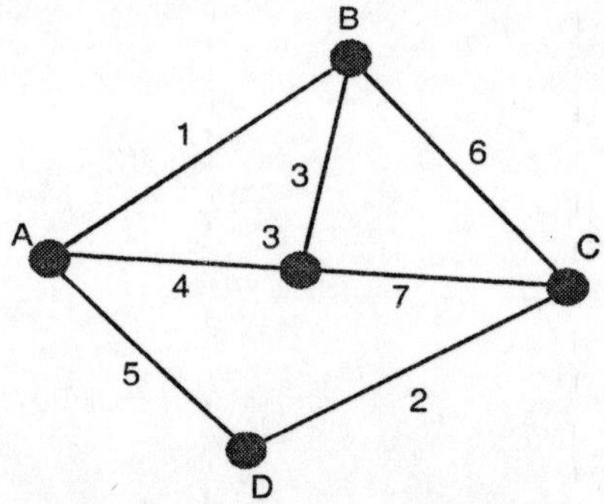

1. Choose a starting vertex. We'll choose A. Now add the closest , i.e. least cost from the vertex A. This is B, so B is added.

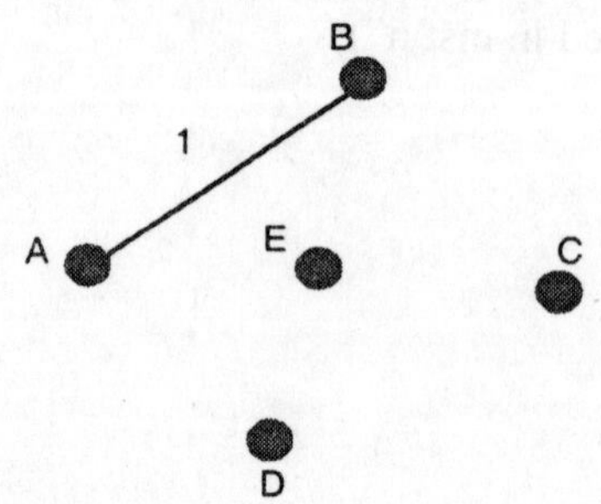

2. Now connect the vertex that is closest to any of the connected vertices (A and B). B connects to

E with a weight of only 3, so this is added

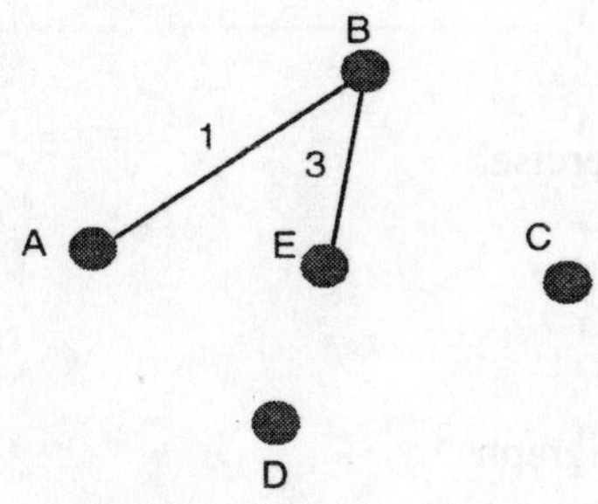

3. The closest to A,B or E is the connection from A to D, with weighting 5, so this is added.

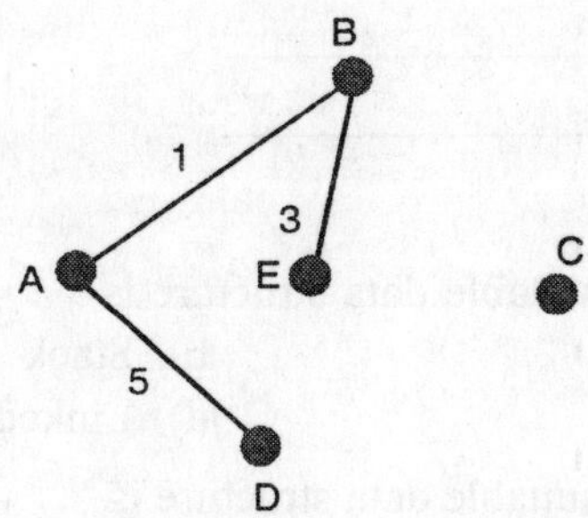

4. The closest connection to the only remaining vertex,C, is from D to C, so this is added.

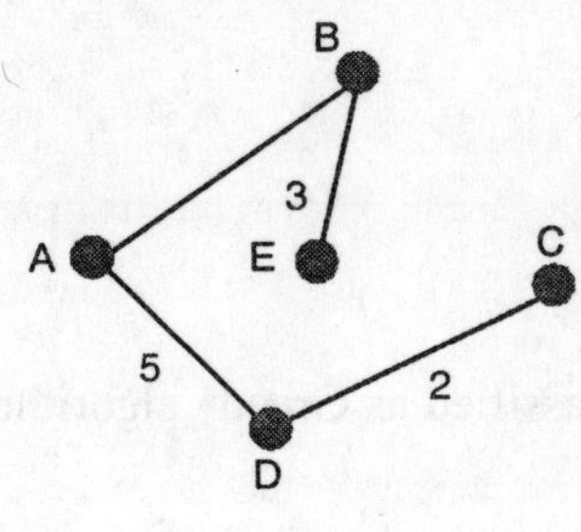

Prims Algorithm for MST

Let G = { V, E} be a graph
MST = { } // MST is the set of all edges that make up minimal spanning tree

Select the starting node
While (MST has < n-1 edges) &&(E is not empty)
{

select a node,v from adjacent nodes to the node selected such that its weight is minimal. if adding edge denoted by (u,,v) does not create a cycle, add it to MST delete edge (u, v) from E select the node closest to any of the previously selected nodes such that its weight is minimal.

}

We leave the coding as an exercise.

OBJECTIVE QUESTIONS

1. A directed graph is called digraph True/False
2. A degree of node is number of edges ____________ on it.
3. A tree is a graph with cycle True/False
4. A graph can be represented as

   ____

   ____

5. Graph has a root node. True/False
6. For Depth First Traversal, suitable data structure is
   a) Queue b) Stack
   c) Circular queue d) Linked List
7. For Bredth First Traversal, suitable data structure is
   a) Queue b) Stack
   c) Circular queue d) Linked List
8. In Minimal Spanning Tree edges are shortest paths. True/False
9. In MST which is NOT True.
   a) MST has no cycle
   b) Set of edges are minimal
   c) Total cost is minimum.
   d) none of the above
10. Kruskals algorithm can be classified as Greedy algorithm True/False

REVIEW QUESTIONS

1. *Write in detail about the following;*
   a. *Weekly connected graphs*
   b. *Strongly connected graphs*
2. *A digraph is strongly connected if it contains a directed path from j to I for every pair of distinct vertices I and j. Show that for every n, n>=2,there exists a strongly connected digraph that contains exactly n edges*

Show that every n vertex strongly connected digraph contains at least n edges where n>=2

3. *Explain about the following graph traversal methods with suitable*
   a) *Depth first search*
   b) *Breadth first search*
4. *Define a graph. Explain the properties of a graphs*

Solutions to Objective Questions

1. True 2) Incident 3) False
4) Adjacency matrix representation & adjacency list representation
5) False 6) b 7) a 8) False 9) d 10) True

CHAPTER 14

SEARCHING AND SORTING

14.1 INTRODUCTION

We are interested in evaluating a program or algorithm and compare the performance analysis of the programs. Generally, two of the most important factors we would like to consider are ***speed*** of execution and ***storage requirements***. Time is not actual time taken by the algorithm, not time units but it measures change in time consumed by the algorithm for change in input i.e.. increase in input. An algorithm has some key operations that would decide the time consumption, for example, in case of sorting algorithms, we would like to compare two records using some key. Number of key comparisons is one of the criteria for comparison of sorting algorithms.

We can carry out analysis of a program and decide the best case and worst case performance and arrive at a formula for program execution. Suppose that **n** is the input size, and as per analysis carried out average time (or number of critical operations) is given by formula

$$\mathbf{f(n) = 0.05 * n^2 +* n} \quad \ldots\ldots 14.1$$

The variation of **a, b,** and **f(n)** with varying input size is shown in Table 14.1 and Fig. 14.1. Observe that for n >= 100, the value of **a** increases much faster than value of **b.**

Table 14.1 Variation of a , b , and f(n) with input size - n

n	a=.05n*n	b=5n	f(n) =a+b
10	5	50	55
60	180	300	480
80	320	400	720
100	500	500	1000
200	2000	1000	3000
300	4500	1500	6000
400	8000	2000	10000
500	12500	2500	15000

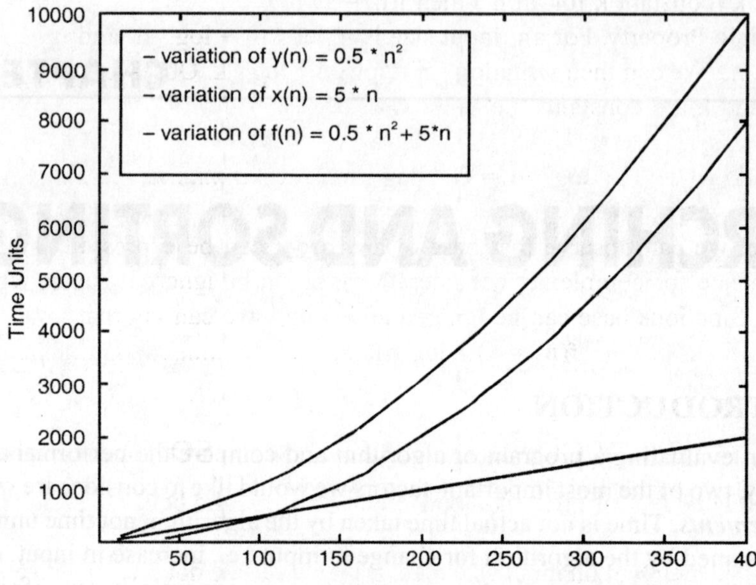

Fig. 14.1 Variation of a , b , and f(n) with input size - n

14.2 BIG OH-O NOTATION

To describe the behavior of f(n) as n varies, we can use Big O notation, where in we would say ***f(n) is on the order of y(n)*** and write

f(n) = O (y(n)) if there exists two numbers a and b such that
f(n) <= a*y(n) for all n>=b

For example if $f(n) = 0.05\, n^2 + 5\, n$, We have

5* n <= 0.05*n^2 for n>=100 ....14.3

add 0.05*n^2 on both sides to get

0.05*n^2 + 5* n <= 2 (0.05*n^2) 14.4

LHS is nothing but f(n), hence we have

f(n) <= 2 (y(n)) for n >= 100 where y(n) = 0.05*n^2 .....14.5

We can say that f(n) is bounded by y(n) from above i.e. f(n) is permanently smaller than y(n) for values of a = 2 and b = 100. Hence we can say that complexity is algorithm is of the order O(y(n)) i.e. O(0.05*n^2) = O(n^2)

A few important properties

a) Transitive Property : If f(n) O(y(n)) and y(n) = O (z(n)) then f(n) = O(z(n)

b) if f(n) = k (constant k for all n) then f(n) = O (1)

c) Logarithmic Property. For an input size is n, let $f(n) = \log_m n$ and $y(n) = \log_k n$. We can then write $\log_m n = \log_k n * \log_m k$. Observe that $\log_m k$ is a constant as both m and k are constants. i.e.

$$\log_m n = C * \log_k n \quad \text{.......... 14.2}$$

From above, we can observe that base of any order can be expressed as base of any other order and hence for complexity considerations, it can be ignored. Hence when dealing with logarithmic functions base can be ignored and simply we can say that

$$f(n) = O(\log n) \quad \text{.......... 14.3}$$

14.3 EFFICIENCY CONSIDERATIONS IN SORTING ALGORITHMS

If the algorithm is independent of problem size then O(1), this is the best situation that one can be in.

If the algorithm is dependent on input size n i.e. if the input size doubles, then if time consumed by algorithm also doubles, we can say complexity is O(n).

If the input size doubles and algorithm takes just one more step, then we can say that O(log n). If the input size is 8. $\text{Log}_2 8 = x$, where x is the number of steps an algorithm takes, we have x = 3. Now if input size doubles to 16 $\text{Log}_2 16 = x$, then x = 4 i.e. x increases only by 1.

If the input size doubles and algorithm takes more than twice that of n, the complexity is of the order of O(n log n)

Lastly, the worst case is when the algorithm takes n^2 steps for an input of n, we would say that complexity is $O(n^2)$.

14.4 SEARCHING

Searching is an important and most frequently performed in computer operations. The program usually searches for a record with an identification number. For example, if you are a bank manager you would search for a particular transaction involving a customer. Similarly, if you are a students you may search for your record containing marks. Note that, in real life files are usually very large files, for example Municipal corporation may hold millions of records. To search your record out of say ten million records must be fast. Here comes the need for an efficient algorithm.

There are several types of searches like linear search, binary Search, and hash search etc. However we would be concentrating on linear and binary search. usally we carryout search using a key. This key is an identifier for the record holding data. Examples of key are, customer id, student roll number etc. The output from a search algorithm is normally the position of the record or the contents of the record.

14.4.1 Linear Search

This is most frequently used search method. We simply traverse the list or array or records and check if the identification number matches with the id number of our interest.

Algorithm:

```
Begin:
        Found = false
    Count = 0
    Obtain the input array.
      Obtain number of terms, key
      Do
      {  If array[count]== key
            Found = true.
         Else
               Count ++
         } while ( count <=N) && found==false)
      if false declare the key is not present in the array
      Else declare the position and value of the element
End
```

We have done several of linear searches in the areas we have covered. for example all our array traversal are linear searches.

14.4.2 Analysis of Linear Search

The critical parameter of linear search is how many comparisons. we have to carry out to get the result. How many times we have to execute the do … while loop in our algorithm. Obviously the larger the data set, the larger will be time of execution. It also depends on the position of the record in the file.

For example if there are 10000 records and record of our interest is at 9999 the we have to traverse 9998 records to access 9999 record. Similary if we are lucky and our record is at position 2, then only one access and check would suffice. Therefore average number of comparisons **C** is given by

$$C = 1+2+3+4+ \ldots\ldots\ldots\ldots +N /N$$
$$C = (N * (N+1))/2*N$$
$$C = (N+1)/2$$

Sequential search os efficient for small number of records but very inefficient for large set of records. In the worst case, the sequential search has complexity of O(N) as N comparisons would be required.

14.4.1 Example 14.1. **linsrch.c** A program to perform linear search

Program:

```
//program to demonstrate linear serach
#include<stdio.h>
#include<stdlib.h>

int linsearch(int sort[],int val,int len);
void main()
{int len,i=0,val,key;
 int sort[30];
  printf("\n enter no<0 to stop>");
  scanf("%d",&sort[i]);
  while(sort[i]!=0)
        {i++;
   printf("\n enter no<0 to stop>");
        scanf("%d",&sort[i]);
        }
  len=i; //length is taken as i and not as i+1 as 0 is also stored in the array
   printf("\n **** Array **** \n");
        for(i=0;i<len;i++)
         printf("%d\t",sort[i]);
  printf("\n\nEnter value to be searched:");
        scanf("%d",&val);
       key=linsearch(sort,val,len); //call the function binsearch which will serach the element
    if(key==-1)
         printf("\n Value not present in the array");
        else
         printf("\n Value %d Found at location %d in the array\n",val,key);
}
int linsearch(int sort[],int val,int len)
{int i;
 for(i=0;i<len;i++)
        {if(sort[i]==val)
         return(i);
        }
 return(-1);
}
/*Output:
enter no<0 to stop>56
enter no<0 to stop>45
enter no<0 to stop>12
enter no<0 to stop>36
enter no<0 to stop>76
```

enter no<0 to stop>0
**** Array ****
56 45 12 36 76
Enter value to be searched:36
Value 36 Found at location 3 in the array*/

■■■ 14.5 BINARY SEARCH

While linear search is easy to implement for large data sets it is highly inefficient. Binary search on the other hand is very efficient and complexity is of the order of O(logN) only. In this method, in each iterartion we would partition the array exactly in to two halfs. Check out if the number required is exactly in the middle or to the left or to the right of the Middle number, shown in Fig. 14.2a Accordingly consider only left or right sub array.

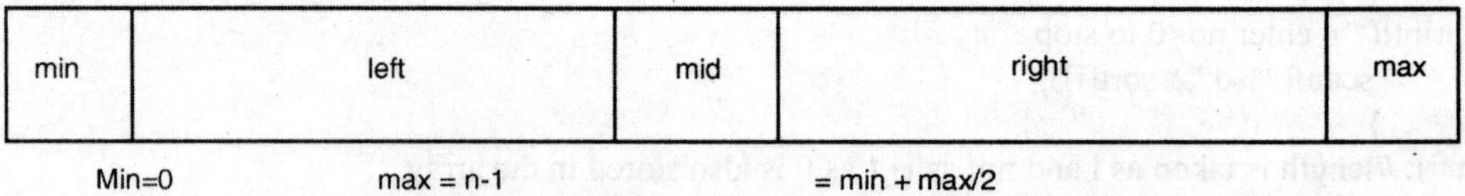

***Fig. 14.2a** Binary search technique. Original array*

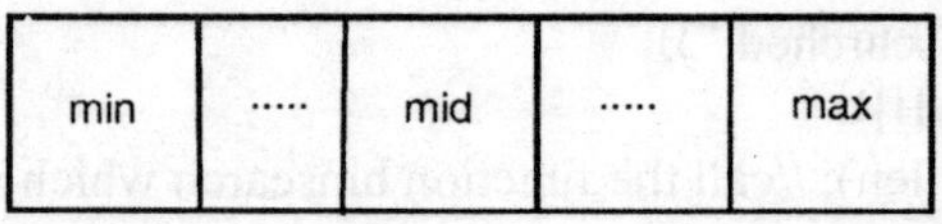

***14.2b. Left of the array :** Key is less than the mid value*

For example if the original array contained 32 elements i.e. 2^5. If the input size is 32. $\text{Log}_2\ 32 = x$, where x is the number of steps an algorithm takes, we have x = 5 Now if the input size is doubled to 64, $\text{Log}_2\ 64 = x$, where x is the number of steps an algorithm takes, we have x = 6. We can observe that as the input size is doubled the algorithm has taken only one step extra from 5 to 6. Hence we can conclude that binary search algorithm has complexity of the order of O(logN).

14.5.1 Binary Search Algorithm

```
begin :
        max=length-1
        min=0;
        success=false
      while ((!success) && max>=min)
        {
          mid=max+min/2
```

```
            if ( mid==key)
                  declare the result. Mid is the position. success=true;
            else
               if  key < array[mid]
                  // adjust max to left sub array
                  Max = Mid-1
               Else
                  Min=min+1
      end
```

Here comes the program on binary search

Example 14.2 binsrch.c A program to search an array on binary search using recusrion.

```
//program to demonstrate binary serach using recurssion
#include<stdio.h>
#include<stdlib.h>

int binsearch(int array[],int val,int lo,int hi);
void main()
{int len,i=0,val,key;
 int array[30];
   printf("Enter sorted input\n");
       printf("\n enter no<0 to stop>");
        scanf("%d",&array[i]);
       while(array[i]!=0)
       {i++;
   printf("\n enter no<0 to stop>");
        scanf("%d",&array[i]);
       }
       len=i; //length is taken as i and not as i+1 as 0 is also stored in the array
   printf("\n **** Array **** \n");
   for(i=0;i<len;i++)
        printf("%d\t",array[i]);
       printf("\n\nEnter value to be searched:");
         scanf("%d",&val);
       key=binsearch(sort,val,0,len-1); //call the function binsearch which will serach the element
   if(key==-1)
         printf("\n Value not present in the array");
       else
                 printf("\n Value %d Found at location %d in the array\n",val,key);
}
int binsearch(int array[],int val,int lo,int hi)
{ int mid,key;
   if(lo>hi)
```

```
            key=-1;
  else
            { mid=(lo+hi)/2;
       if(val==array[mid])
                              key=mid;
       else
                    if(val< array[mid])
                      {hi=mid-1;
                           key=binsearch(sort,val,lo,hi);
                      }
       else
                    if(val>array[mid])
                    { lo= mid+1;
                      key=binsearch(sort,val,lo,hi);
                    }
            }
  return(key);
}
/*Output:
Enter sorted input
enter no<0 to stop>56
enter no<0 to stop>67
enter no<0 to stop>78
enter no<0 to stop>100
enter no<0 to stop>120
enter no<0 to stop>0
**** Array ****
56      67      78      100     120
Enter value to be searched:78
Value 78 Found at location 2 in the array*/
```

Example 14.3 binsrchrec.c. A program to demonstrate binary search using iteration

```
#include<stdio.h>
#include<stdlib.h>
int binsearch(int array[],int val,int lo,int hi);
void main()
{int len,i=0,val,key;
 int array[30];
 printf("enter sorted array\n");
 printf("\n enter no<0 to stop>");
   scanf("%d",&array[i]);
 while(array[i]!=0)
         {i++;
```

```
    printf("\n enter no<0 to stop>");
        scanf("%d",&array[i]);
        }
        len=i; //length is taken as i and not as i+1 as 0 is also stored in the array
  printf("\n **** Array **** \n");
        for(i=0;i<len;i++)
                printf("%d\t",array[i]);
      printf("\n\nEnter value to be searched:");
        scanf("%d",&val);
      key=binsearch(array,val,0,len-1); //call the function binsearch which will serach the element
   if(key==-1)
              printf("\n Value not present in the array");
        else
         printf("\n Value %d Found at location %d in the array\n",val,key);
}
int binsearch(int array[],int val,int lo,int hi)
{int mid;
  while(lo<=hi)
  { mid=(lo+hi)/2;
       if(array[mid]==val)
        return(mid);
       else
   if(array[mid]<val)
              lo=mid+1;
       else
        if(array[mid]>val)
              hi=mid-1;
  }
  return(-1);
}
/*Output:
enter sorted array
enter no<0 to stop>34
enter no<0 to stop>45
enter no<0 to stop>56
enter no<0 to stop>67
enter no<0 to stop>78
enter no<0 to stop>89
enter no<0 to stop>0
 **** Array ****
34    45    56    67    78    89
Enter value to be searched:56
Value 56 Found at location 2 in the array*/
```

14.6 BUBBLE SORT

Bubble sort is the simplest of all the sort algorithms. Its name is derived from the fact that in each iteration the largest element bubbles to the end of the array, thus during the next iteration we need not consider this element as it has already been sorted.

14.6.1. Example :

Input Array :

22	34	10	55	14

Iteration 1 :

Before Comparison After Comparison

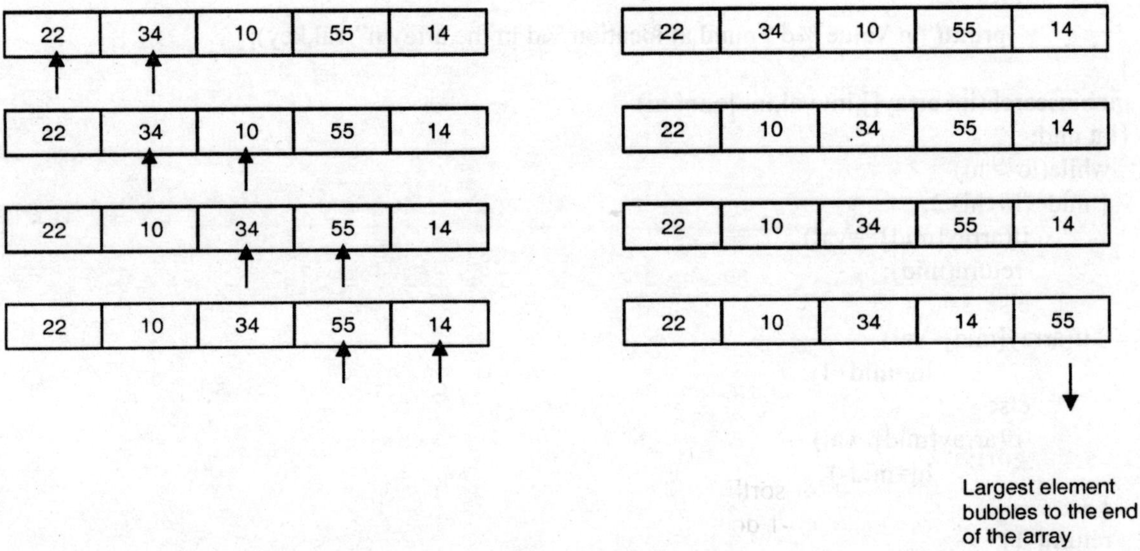

Now leave the sorted element 55 and consider the element 10 as sorting

Iteration 2 :

Before Comparison After Comparison

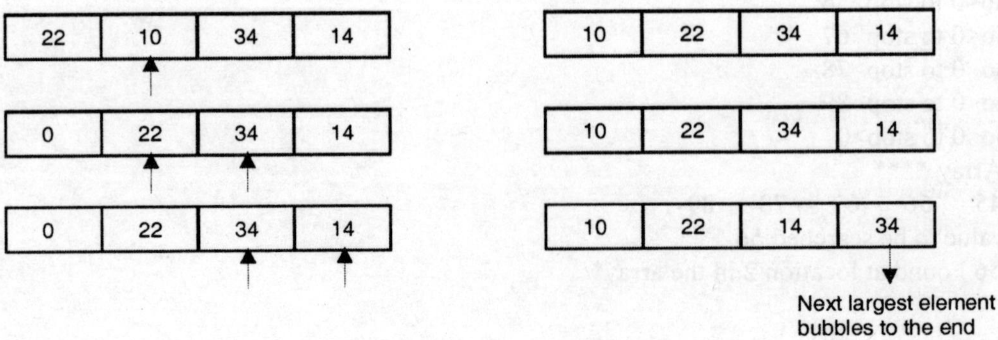

Iteration 3 : We need not consider 34 any more as it already sorted

Before Comparison

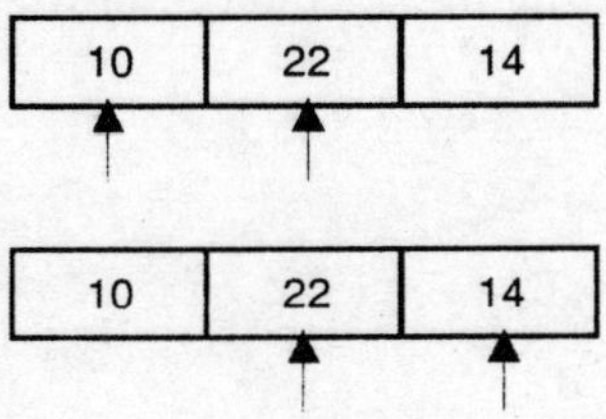

After Comparison

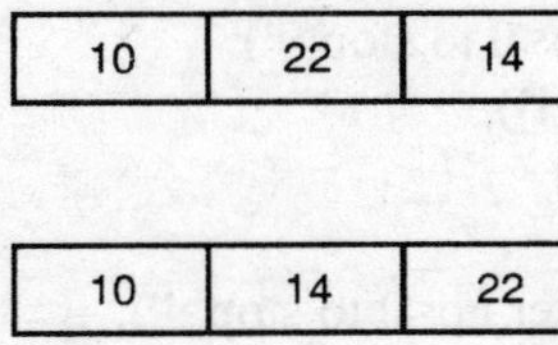

Iteration 4 :

Before Comparison

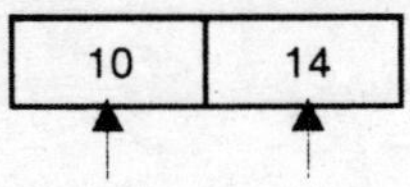

After Comparison

Complete Sorted List is

10	14	22	34	55

Note: Length of array n = 5
No. of outer loop iterations = 4 = (n-1)
No. of inner loop iterations = (n-i)

14.6.2 Algorithm

```
Procedure bubblesort(sort[],len)
        for i=1 to len-1 do
        begin
                for j=0 to len-i do
                begin
                        if [sort[j] > sort[j+1]
                                swap (sort[i],sort[j+1])
                        end
        end
return
```

14.6.3. Example bubble.c

```
#include<stdio.h>
#include<stdlib.h>

void bubblesort(int sort[],int len);
```

```
void main()
{
        int len,i=0;
   int sort[30];
    printf("\n enter no<0 to stop>");
   scanf("%d",&sort[i]);
     while(sort[i]!=0)
        {i++;
        printf("\n enter no<0 to stop>");
         scanf("%d",&sort[i]);
        }
        len=i; //length is taken as i and not as i+1 as 0 is also stored in the array
  bubblesort(sort,len); //call the function bubblesort which will sort the array
    printf("\n **** Sorted Array **** \n");
         for(i=0;i<len;i++)
                  printf("%d\t",sort[i]);
}
void bubblesort(int sort[],int len)
{int i,j,temp;
  for(i=1;i<len;i++)
        {for(j=0;j<len-i;j++)
          {if(sort[j]>sort[j+1])
            {temp=sort[j];
              sort[j]=sort[j+1];
               sort[j+1]=temp;
            }//end of if
        }//end of for(j)
     }//end of for(i)
}//end of bubblesort
/*Output:
enter no<0 to stop>34
enter no<0 to stop>12
enter no<0 to stop>45
enter no<0 to stop>32
enter no<0 to stop>16
enter no<0 to stop>0
 **** Sorted Array ****
12    16    32    34    45 */
```

14.6.4 Complexity of Bubble Sort

Let n be the input data size then we can see that during the first iteration the number of inner loop iteration (n-1) for the second iteration the number of inner loop iterations is (n-2), continuing

Iteration No.	No. of inner loop iterations
1	n-1
2	n-2
3	n-3
.	....
.	....
.	....
n-1	1

Total no. of iterations = (n-1)+(n-2)+(n-3)+.....1

= 1+2+3+........(n-1)

= n(n+1)/2

For sufficiently large value n the above value can be approximated to n^2 thus the complexity of bubble sort is $O(n^2)$

■■■ 14.7 SELECTION SORT

Compare 1st element with all other elements in each iteration set lowest as minimum(Min). At the end of iteration swap min and 1st element. Now continue with 2nd element same procedure. Continue with this procedure till entire array is exhausted.

14.7.1 Example :

Input 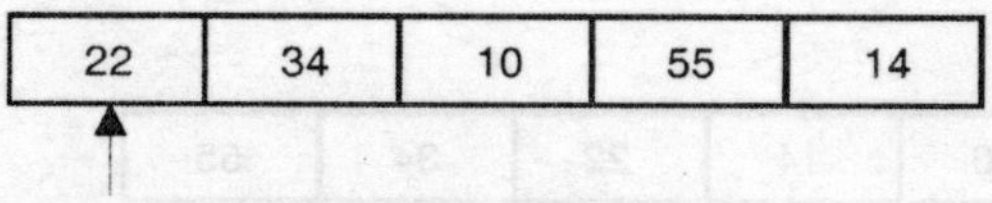

Array :

Initialization set Min = 22

Iteration 1 :

Comparison new Min

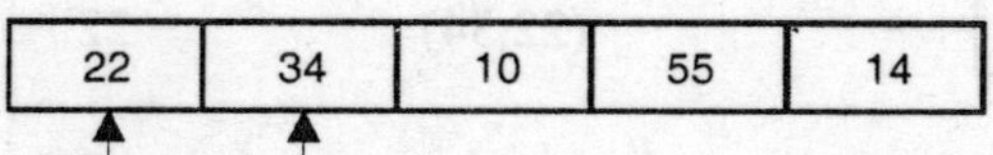

(22,34) 22

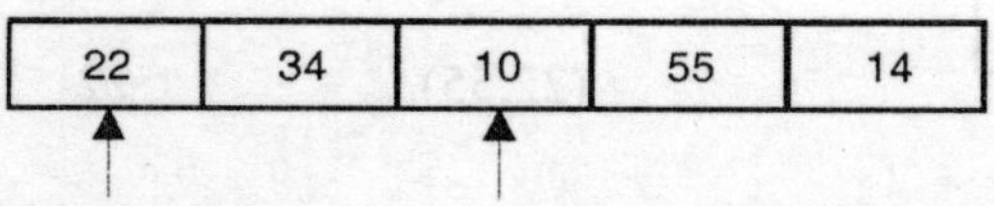

(22,10) 10

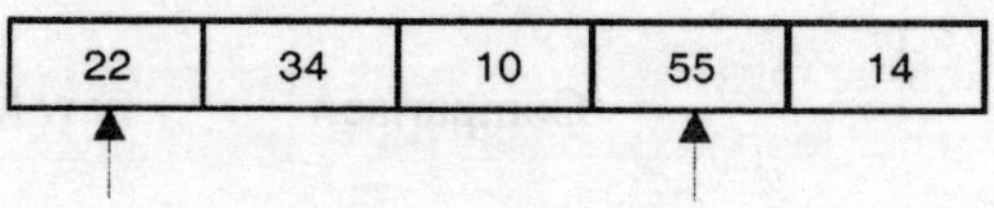

(10,55) 10

22	34	10	55	14	(10,14)	10

Swap (22,10)

10	34	22	55	14

Min value is put into place

Iteration 2 :

					Comparison	new Min
10	34	22	55	14	(34,22)	22
10	34	22	55	14	(22,55)	22
10	34	22	55	14	(22,14)	14

Swap (34,14)

10	14	22	34	55

Iteration 3 : (Min = 22)

					Comparison	new Min
10	14	22	34	55	(22,34)	22
10	14	22	34	55	(22,55)	22

Iteration 4 : (Min = 34)

Comparison new Min

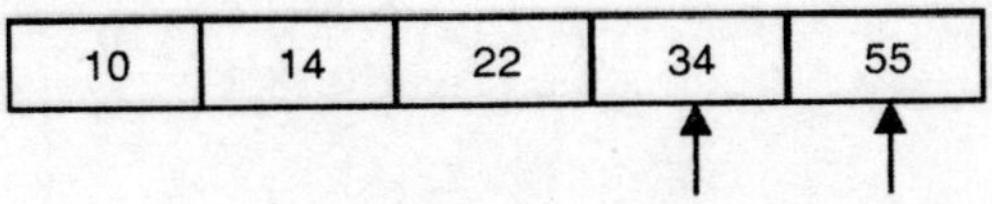

(34,55) 34

Sorted Array = | 10 | 14 | 22 | 34 | 55 |

Length of array = 5

Note: No. of iterations = 4 = (5-1) = (length – 1)

14.7.2 Algorithm :

```
Selectsort(sort[],len)
for i=0 to i<len-1 do
begin
        min=i
        for j=i+1    j<len do
        begin
                if[sort[j] < sort[min]
                        min=j
                end
        if(min != i)
                swap(sort[min],sort[i])
        end
```

14.7.3 Program:selection.c

```
//program to demonstrate selection sort
#include<stdio.h>
#include<stdlib.h>
void selectsort(int sort[],int len);

void main()
{int len,i=0;
 int sort[30];
 printf("\n enter no<0 to stop>");
  scanf("%d",&sort[i]);
  while(sort[i]!=0)
        {i++;
   printf("\n enter no<0 to stop>");
        scanf("%d",&sort[i]);
        }
        len=i; //length is taken as i and not as i+1 as 0 is also stored in the array
   selectsort(sort,len); //call the function selectsort which will sort the array
 printf("\n **** Sorted Array **** \n");
        for(i=0;i<len;i++)
                printf("%d\t",sort[i]);
```

```
}
void selectsort(int sort[],int len)
{int i,j,temp,min;
  for(i=0;i<len-1;i++)
        {min=i;
  for(j=i+1;j<len;j++)
       {if(sort[j]<sort[min])
               min=j;
       }
  if(min!=i)
       {temp=sort[min];
               sort[min]=sort[i];
               sort[i]=temp;
       }
      }//end of for(i)
}//end of select sort
```

Output:

```
enter no<0 to stop>45
enter no<0 to stop>12
enter no<0 to stop>34
enter no<0 to stop>65
enter no<0 to stop>10
enter no<0 to stop>0
**** Sorted Array ****
10    12    34    45    65
```

14.7.4 Selection Sort Complexity Analysis

For the first iteration the number of inner loop iterations is n-1 for the second iteration the no. of inner loop iterations is n-2 continuing we get total no. of iterations is

$$(n-1)+(n-2)+(n-3)+\ldots\ldots+1 = n(n-1)/2$$

Therefore, complexity of Selection sort is $O(n^2)$. The number of interchanges is always n-1. Hence selection sort is $O((n^2)$ for both best case and the worst case.

■■■ 14.8 INSERTION SORT

This is an interesting sort and very efficient for small amount of input data. To understand the concept, imagine how a class teacher sorts a column of students as per their heights. We have to insert elements in to correct slots. Two activities involved in insertion are

Finding correct position to insert.

Moving other element and make space for this new element to b inserted

14.8.1 Example

Consider an input array 'a' as shown

Insertion 1 :

Step 1: Assign a pointer 'i' to the second element of the array and place this element in temp.

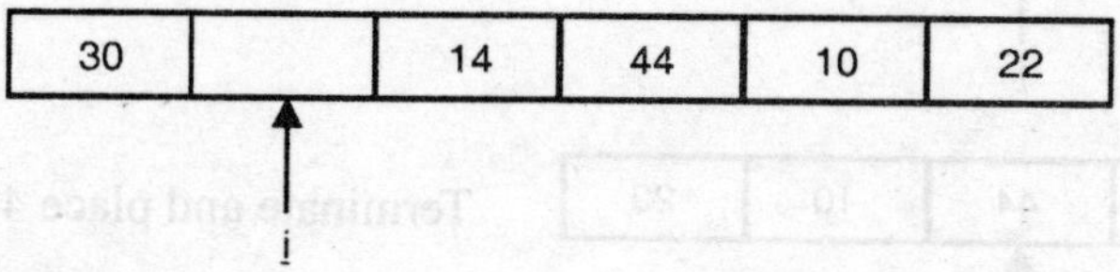

Temp

12

Step 2: Now shift elements which are to the left of i and which are greater than temp, by one position to the right. Continue this process till you find an element which is smaller than temp or you if you reach the beginning of the array.

As 30 is greater than 12 shift it to the right

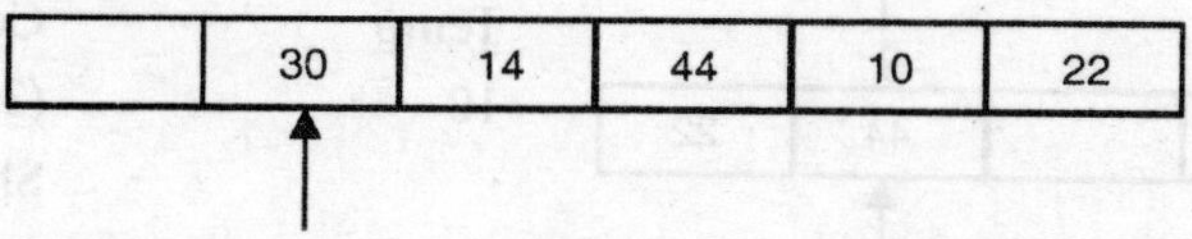

Temp

12

Step 3: Now place the temp value 12 in the slot that has been created

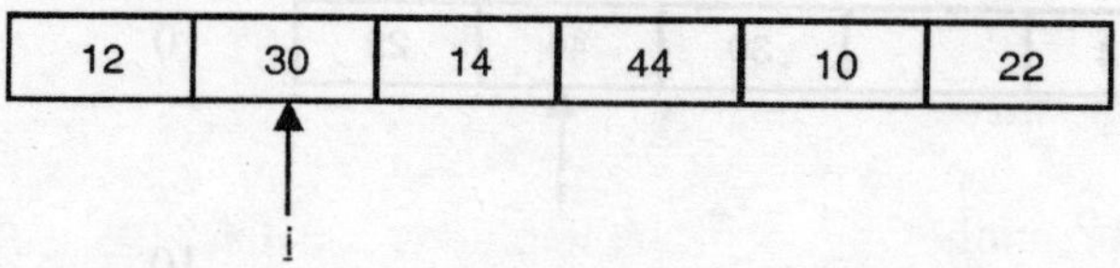

Step 4: Increment 'i' to point to 14 and repeat steps 1 to 4. Keep continuing this process till 'i' reaches the end of the array

Insertion 2:

Temp Compare

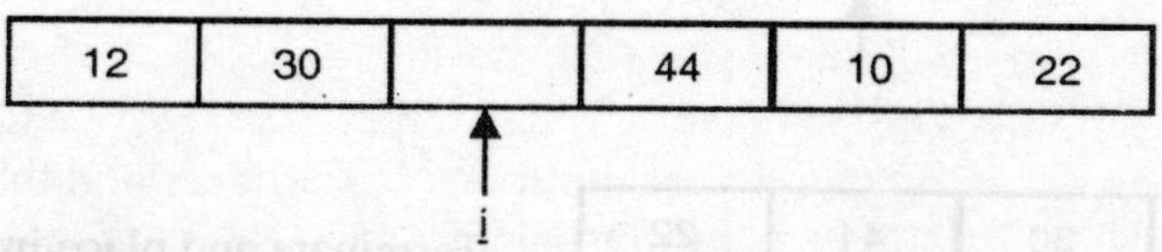

14 (30,14)

shift

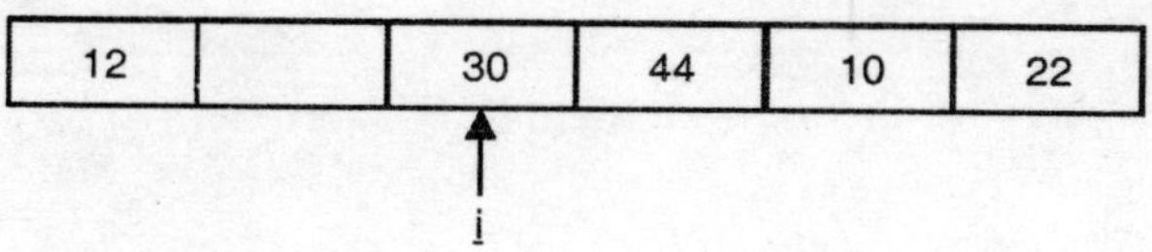

14 (12,14)

12	14	30	44	10	22	Terminate and place 14 in slot
		↑ i				

Insertion 3:

						Temp	Compare
12	14	30		10	22	44	(30,44)
			↑ i				

12	14	30	44	10	22	Terminate and place 44 in slot
			↑ i			

Insertion 4:

						Temp	Compare
12	14	30	44		22	10	(44,10) Shift
				↑ i			

						Temp	Compare
12	14	30		44	22	10	(30,10) Shift
				↑ i			

12	14		30	44	22	10	(14,10) Shift
				↑ i			

12		14	30	44	22	10	(12,10) Shift
				↑ i			

	12	14	30	44	22	10	Terminate
				↑ i			

10	12	14	30	44	22	Terminate and place in 10 in slot
				↑ i		

Insertion 5:

10	12	14	30	44		22	(44,22) Shift
10	12	14	30		44	22	(30,22) Shift
10	12	14		30	44	22	(14,22) Terminate
10	12	14	22	30	44		Terminate and place 22 in slot

14.8.2 Algorithm for Insertion Sort

```
for i=1 to i<len
begin
        temp = sort[i]
        for j=I to j=1
for j=i to j=1
begin
        if [sort[j-1] > temp]
                sort[j] = sort[j-1]        // shift one position to the right
        end
        sort[j] = temp
end
```

14.8.3 Program:insort.c

```
//program to demonstrate insertion sort
#include<stdio.h>
#include<stdlib.h>

void insort(int sort[],int len);

void main()
{int len,i=0;
 int sort[30];
  printf("\n enter no<0 to stop>");
  scanf("%d",&sort[i]);
  while(sort[i]!=0)
       {i++;
```

```
    printf("\n enter no<0 to stop>");
        scanf("%d",&sort[i]);
        }
        len=i; //length is taken as i and not as i+1 as 0 is also stored in the array
    insort(sort,len); //call the function qsort which will sort the array
   printf("\n **** Sorted  Array **** \n");
        for(i=0;i<len;i++)
         printf("%d\t",sort[i]);
}
void insort(int sort[],int len)
{int temp,i,j;
   for(i=1;i<len;i++)
        {temp=sort[i];
   for(j=i;j>0 && sort[j-1]>temp;j—)
                   sort[j]=sort[j-1];
     sort[j]=temp;
        }
}
/*Output:
 enter no<0 to stop>67
 enter no<0 to stop>34
 enter no<0 to stop>42
 enter no<0 to stop>35
 enter no<0 to stop>14
 enter no<0 to stop>0
 **** Sorted  Array ****
14    34    35    42    67 */
```

14.8.4 Insertion Sort Complexity Analysis :

For the first iteration the no. of inner loop iterations is 1 for the second iteration the no. of inner loop iterations is 2 continuing we get for the last iterations i.e. the (n-1)th iteration number of inner loop iterations is (n-1). Thus the total number of iterations is

$$1+2+3+\ldots\ldots\ldots(n-1) \quad = \quad n(n-1)/2$$

Therefore, complexity of Insertion Sort is $O(n^2)$

Consider the following input array

10	11	12	13	14	15

We can observe that for the first iteration the number of inner loop iterations is 1 for the second iteration the number of inner loop iterations is 1 and even for the (n-1)th iteration it is 1, thus the total number of iterations is

1+1+1+.......................1 = (n-1)

Therefore we can conclude that for an already sorted input the complexity for insertion sort O(n).

In many applications we will come across input arrays that are nearly sorted, in that case it is advisable to choose insertion sort over bubble or selection sort as for a nearly sorted array insertion sort will have a linear complexity[O(n)]. Whereas both Bubble and Selection Sorts will have a complexity of O(n)

14.9 QUICK SORT

In Quick sort we divide the array to be sorted into two sub arrays, and then recursively sort each of these sub arrays. Division into sub array involves choosing a pivot element, this pivot element could be the first element, last element, or any element of the array. Once the pivot element is chosen rearrange the array such that values smaller than the pivot element are placed to the left of it and values larger than the pivot element are placed to the right of it.

14.9.1 Example:

20	44	12	23	78	56	14	89	40
↑ i							↑ J	↑ Pivot

Step 1 : Choose 40 as Pivot element choose two pointers to point to the first element of the array and the element immediately preceding the Pivot element.

Step 2 : Keep incrementing 'i' till a[i] < a[Pivot]

20	44	12	23	78	56	14	89	40
	↑ i						↑ J	↑ Pivot

Step 3 : Keep decrementing 'j' till a[j] > a[Pivot]

20	44	12	23	78	56	14	89	40
	↑ i					↑ J		

Step 4 : Swap a[i] and a[j]

20	14	12	23	78	56	44	89	40
	↑ i					↑ J		

Step 5 : Repeat Step 2 i.e.. Keep incrementing 'i' till a[i] < a[Pivot]

20	14	12	23	78	56	44	89	40
				↑ i		↑ J		↑ Pivot

Step 6 : Repeat Step 3 i.e.. Keep decrementing 'j' as long as a[j] > a[Pivot]

20	14	12	23	78	56	44	89	40
			↑ J	↑				↑ Pivot

Step 7 : At this point 'i' has crossed 'j' and we can observe that all element from 'i' upto Pivot – 1 are largest than the Pivot element. And all elements from 'j' to the starting of the array are less than the Pivot elements.

Now swap a[i] and a[Pivot] i.e. swap [78,40]

20	14	12	23	40	56	44	89	78
			↑ J	↑ i				↑ Pivot

Now if you see 40 occupies correct place in the array as all elements to the right of it are larger and to the left of it are smaller to it

Step 8 : Partition the array into smaller arrays

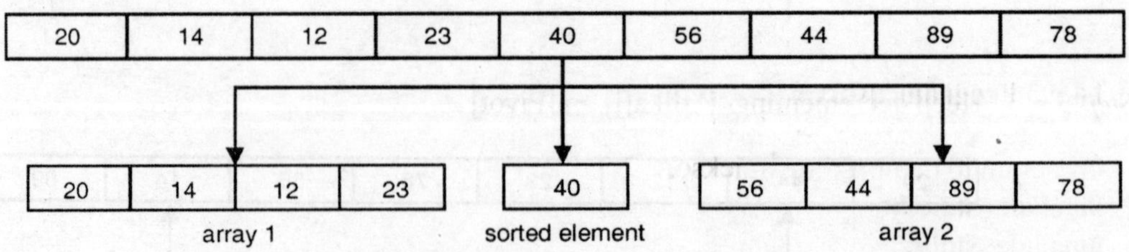

Step 9 : Now for each of the sub array proceed with steps 1-8 to obtain a fully sorted array

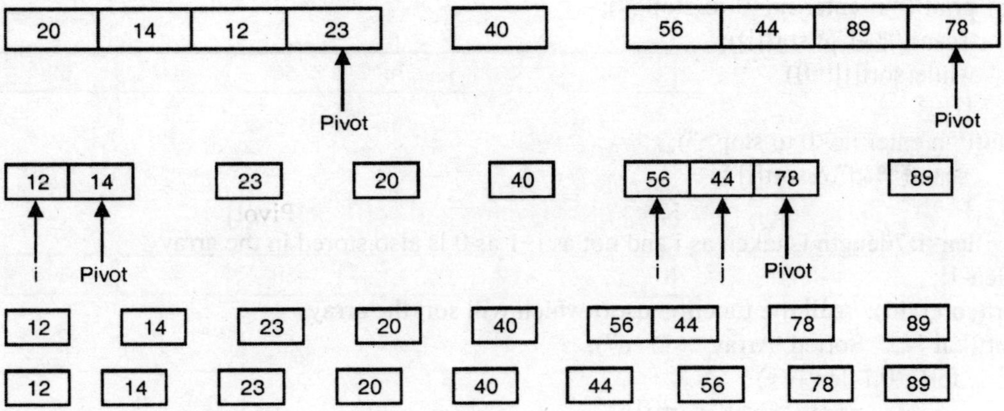

14.9.2 Algorithm for Quick Sort

Procedure QSort[int sort[], int lo, int hi]

Where sort[] is the input array which has to be sorted, 'lo' and 'hi' are indexes to the first and last elements of the sub array that has to be sorted.

```
If (lo >= hi)
        Return;
Initialize :
        i = lo-1
        j = hi
        pivot = sort[hi]     // set pivot element to print to last element of the array
while (i < j)
        {
                while (Sort[++i] < pivot);
                        while (j>=0 && sort[—j] > pivot);
                                if (i<j)
                                swap(sort[i],sort[j])
        }
```

14.9.3 Program:qsort.c

```
//program to demonstarte quicksort
#include<stdio.h>
#include<stdlib.h>

void qsort(int sort[],int lo,int hi);

void main()
{int len,i=0,hi;
 int sort[30];
```

```
        printf("\n enter no<0 to stop>");
         scanf("%d",&sort[i]);
        while(sort[i]!=0)
        {i++;
    printf("\n enter no<0 to stop>");
         scanf("%d",&sort[i]);
        }
        len=i; //length is taken as i and not as i+1 as 0 is also stored in the array
  hi=len-1;;
  qsort(sort,0,hi); //call the function qsort which will sort the array
  printf("\n **** Sorted Array **** \n");
        for(i=0;i<len;i++)
                printf("%d\t",sort[i]);
}
void qsort(int sort[],int lo,int hi)
{ if(lo>=hi)
   return;
  int temp;
  int j=hi;
  int i=lo-1;
  int num=sort[hi];  //it is the number we choose to divide the array
  while(i<j)
        {while(sort[++i]<num);
         while(j>=0 && sort[—j]>num);
          if(i<j)  //swap sort[i] and sort[j]
                {temp=sort[i];
        sort[i]=sort[j];
                 sort[j]=temp;
                }
        }
  temp=sort[i];
   sort[i]=sort[hi];
   sort[hi]=temp;;
   qsort(sort,lo,i-1);
   qsort(sort,i+1,hi);
}
/*Output:
 enter no<0 to stop>78
 enter no<0 to stop>12
 enter no<0 to stop>32
 enter no<0 to stop>45
 enter no<0 to stop>54
 enter no<0 to stop>10
 enter no<0 to stop>9
```

```
enter no<0 to stop>0
**** Sorted  Array ****
9      10      12      32      45      54      78*/
```

14.9.4 Complexity of Quick Sort

Best Case Analysis

In this case the pivot element divides the array into two sub arrays of equal length. To compute the complexity consider two arrays with input data size of 4(n) and 8(2n) respectively.

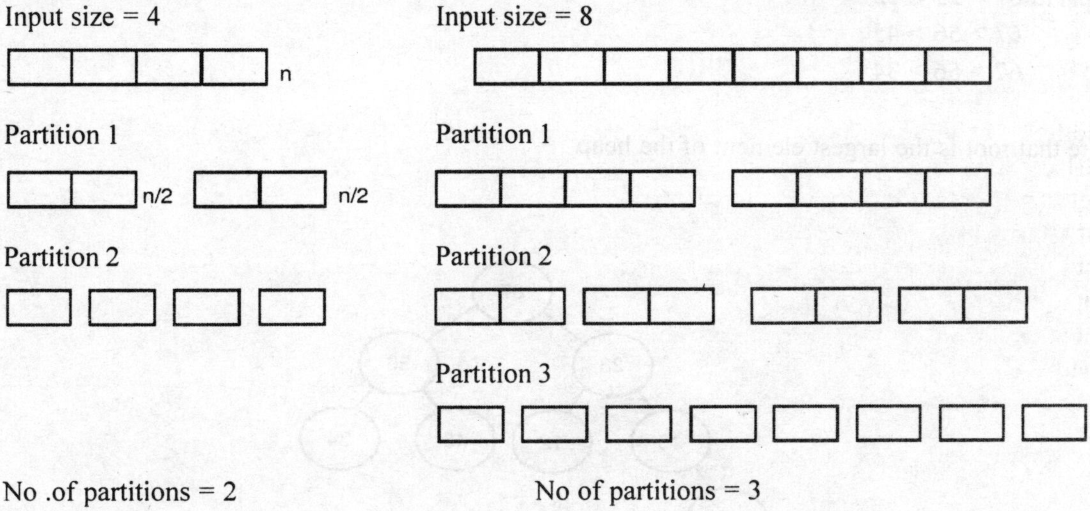

As seen from the figure the number of partitions required for an array with input data size 4 is 2 and for the array with input data size 8 is 3. As doubling the input data size from 8 to 4 resulted in only one extra partition. Thus we can conclude by definition that partitioning proceeds with log n complexity. During each partition the number of comparisons is n-1 which can be approximated to n for large n. Thus the complexity of Quick Sort is o(nlogn).

Worst Case Analysis

Suppose the input is an already sorted or almost sorted, and if we choose our pivot as either the first or the last element, then as seen from the figure the input array gets divided into two sub arrays of size (n-1) and 0, continuing the array further gets divided into (n-2) during the 2nd iteration, (n-3) during the 3rd iteration and so on. The number of comparisons for the 1st iteration would be (n-1), for the 2nd iteration it would be (n-2), continuing the total no. of iterations is

$$(n-1) + (n-2) + (n-3) + \dots\dots\dots\dots + 1$$

which can be approximated to n(n+1) /2 thus the worst case time complexity of Quick Sort is $O(n^2)$ if the input is almost or already sorted. One way to overcome this problem is to choose the pivot element randomly, rather than choosing the first or the last element.

■■■ 14.10 HEAP SORT

Heap is a complete binary tree, whose each path from the root to leaf is in ascending order i.e.. parent is always grater than or equal to its children

Fig. 14.3 represents a heap as all paths from root to leaf are in ascending order.

67 > 23 > 15 > 10
67 > 23 > 12
67 > 56 > 45
67 > 56 > 34

note that root is the largest element of the heap

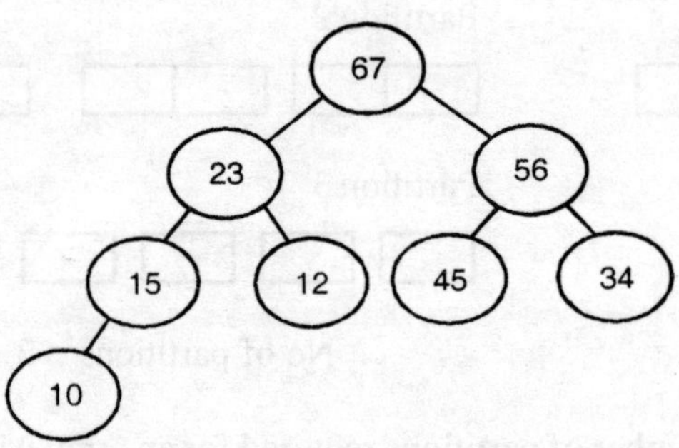

Fig 14.3 A heap tree

14.10.1 Mapping of Complete Binary Tree

A natural mapping exits by in which a complete binary tree can be mapped into an array. To map a complete binary tree into an array follow the steps shown below.

<u>Step 1:</u> Mark all nodes as shown in the fig. start by marking root as 0, and proceed level by level until all nodes have been marked.

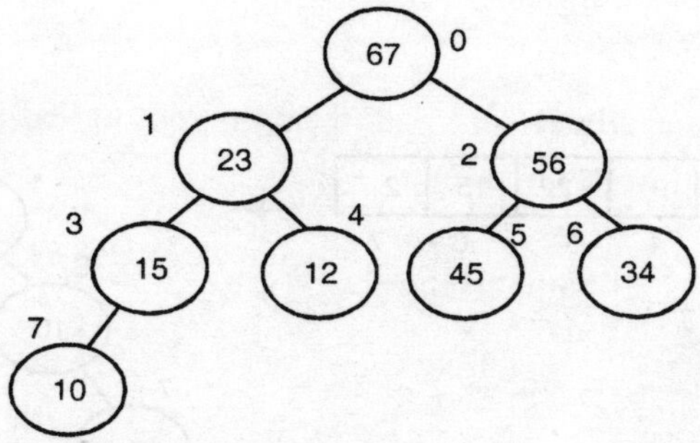

Step 2 : Map elements to their corresponding locations in the array i.e.. node 0 maps to location 0 in the array, node 1 maps to location 1 and so on.

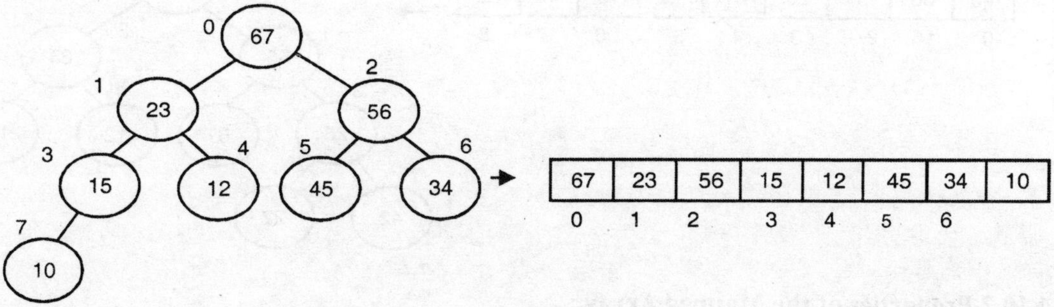

The mapping of a complete binary tree into an array is a two way mapping i.e.. an array can be mapped back into a complete binary tree, to map the array onto a complete binary tree map the elements at index 0 to node 0, element at index 1 to node 1 and so on.

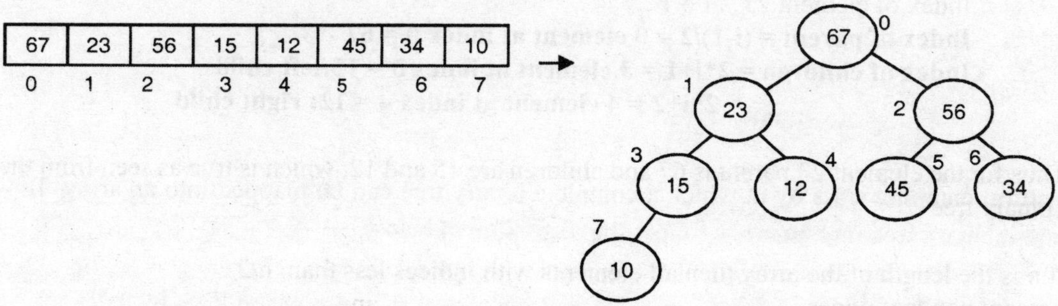

An array is said to have a heap property if the corresponding complete binary tree to which it is mapped has the heap property. Array 1 shown in the figure has the heap property where as array 2 does not have the heap property.

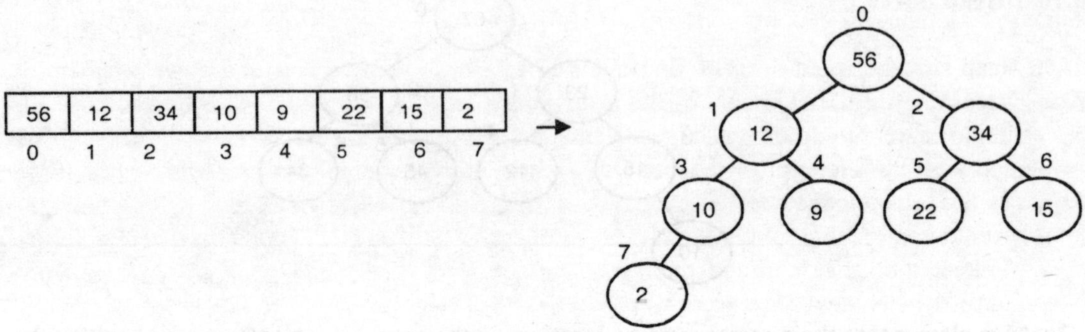

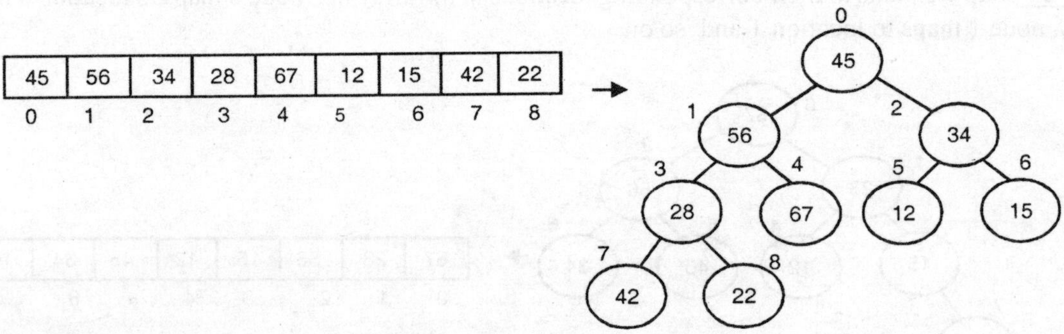

14.10.2 Properties of the Mapped Array :

For an element with index 'i' in the array, (i-1)/2 represents index of its parent and 2i+1 represent indices of its children

For eg: Consider element 23 in fig 14.3

Index of element 23 = i = 1

Index of parent = (i-1)/2 = 0 element at index 0 = 67

Index of children = 2*i+1 = 3 element at index 3 = 15:left child

2*i+2 = 4 element at index 4 = 12: right child

Thus for the element 23 parent is 67 and children are 15 and 12, which is true as seen from the complete binary tree

If n is the length of the array then all elements with indices less than n/2 represent non leaf nodes.

For eg : size of array n=8 n/2 = 3

Therefore elements with indices 0,1,2 and 3 which are 67,23,56 and 15 respectively represent non leaf nodes

14.10.3 Heap Sort

In Heap sort the input array is first made in to a heap. Converting the input array in to a heap involves rearranging the elements of the array so that it now possesses the heap property. Once the conversion to heap is complete the largest element now occupies the first position the array, this element is swapped with last element of the array so that the largest element occupies its correct place in the array, now the last element is left out and the remaining array is again converted to heap and once again the largest element of this remaining array occupies the first position, the largest element is swapped with last element so that it now occupies its correct position in the original array and the process is continued till all elements are sorted.

Example Heap create :

Iteration 1 :

Structure

45	23	56	67	12	15	78	34

Equivalent Graph

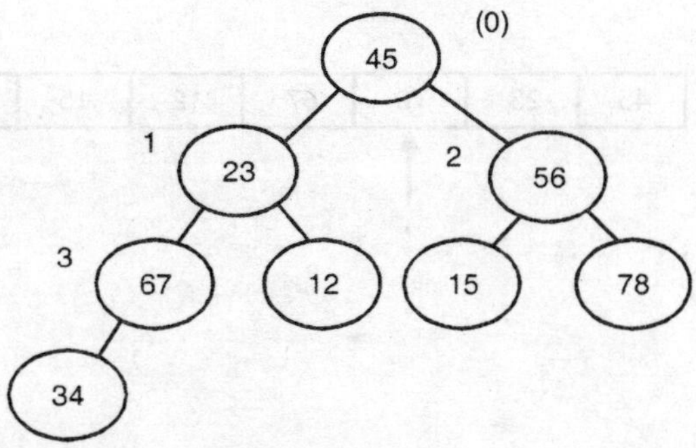

Step 1 : Set 'i ' so that i = len / 2 -1 i.e.. 'i' points to the last non leaf node

45	23	56	67	12	15	78	34
			↑ i				

Step 2 : Set pointer 'j' to the point to the larger of the two children of the current parent. In the present case only one child 34 is present so point 'j' to 34

45	23	56	67	12	15	78	34
			↑ i				↑ J

Step 3 : Compare Sort[i] and Sort[j] if Sort[i] < Sort[j] swap Sort[i] and Sort[j]. In this case as 67 > 34 no swapping is required.

45	23	56	67	12	15	78	34
			↑ i				↑ J

As 'j' is pointing to a leaf node it implies that processing of the current node(67) is complete. So we can begin to process the next leaf node which in this case is 56.

Iteration 2 :

Step 1 :

45	23	56	67	12	15	78	34
			i			J	

As seen 56 has two children 15 and 78. So set 'j' to point to the larger of the children, which in this case is 78

Step 2 : As Sort[i] < Sort[j] i.e. (56 < 78)

Swap Sort[i] and Sort[j]

45	23	78	67	12	15	56	34
		i				J	

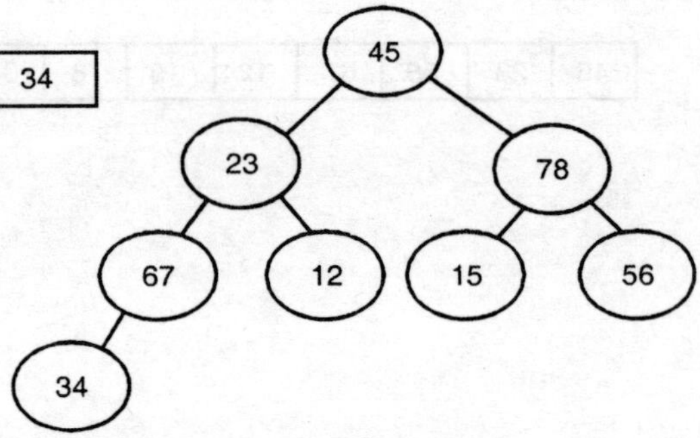

Step 3 : 'j' is pointing to a non leaf node so move on to process the next elements

Iteration 4 : Repeat steps 1 to 2 as shown in Iteration 3 to process the current node which is 45

45	67	78	34	12	15	56	23
i		J					

78	67	45	34	12	15	56	23
i		J					

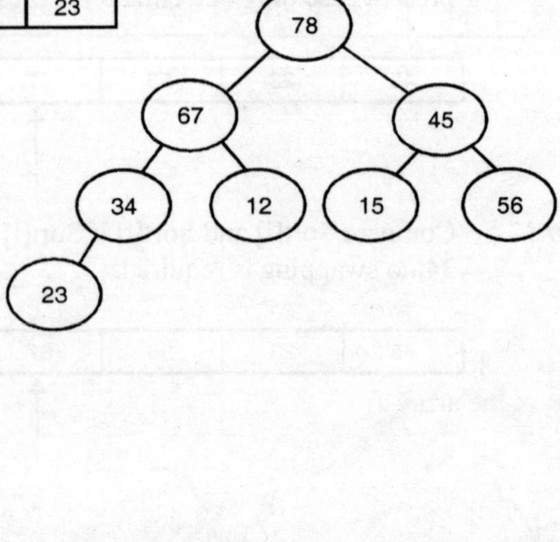

78	67	45	34	12	15	56	23

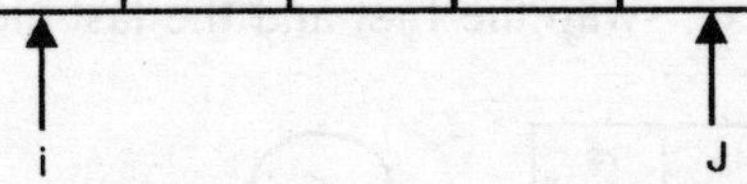

78	67	56	34	12	15	45	23

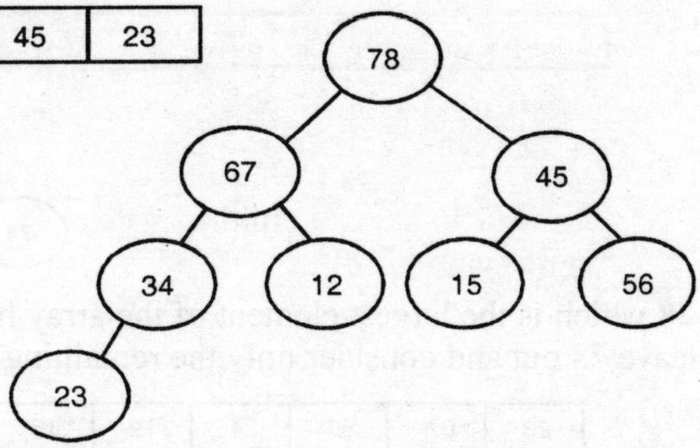

We can see that the array now has the heap property as

$$78 > 67 > 34 > 23$$

$$78 > 67 > 12$$

$$78 > 56 > 15$$

$$78 > 56 > 45$$

14.10.4 Example Heap Sort

Initialization : Given an input array, as a first step rearrange the array so that it has the heap property for doing this use heap create algorithm as discussed above

Let input array be

45	23	56	67	12	15	78	34

By rearranging using the heap create algorithm, we get

78	67	56	34	12	15	45	23

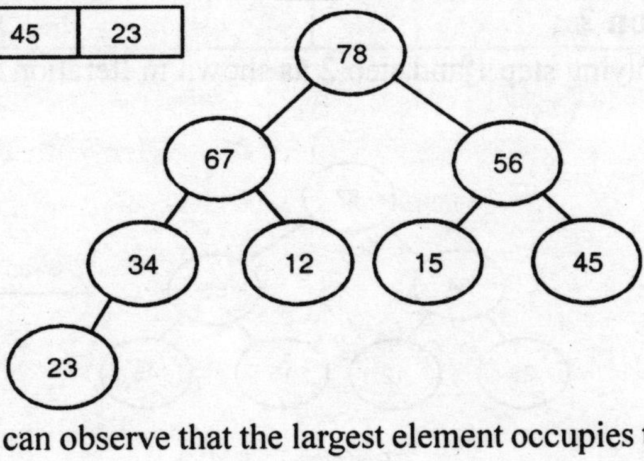

After performing the heap create operation we can observe that the largest element occupies the first position in the array.

Iteration 1 :

Step 1 : Swap (Sort[0] and Sort[len-1]) i.e.. swap the first and the last element

23	67	56	34	12	15	45	78

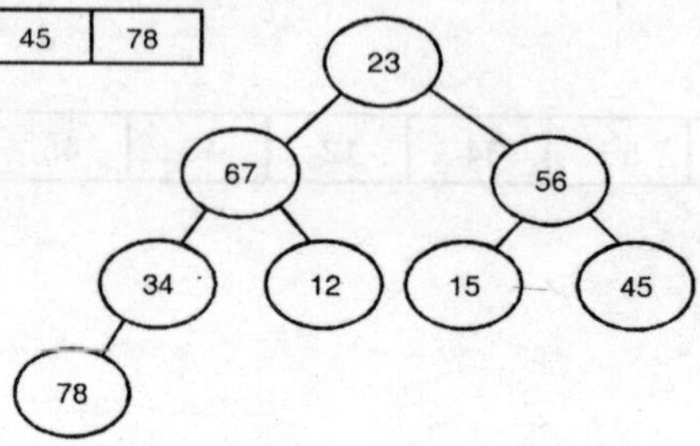

78 which is the largest element of the array has now been placed at its correct position so now we can leave 78 out and consider only the remaining elements

23	67	56	34	12	15	45		78

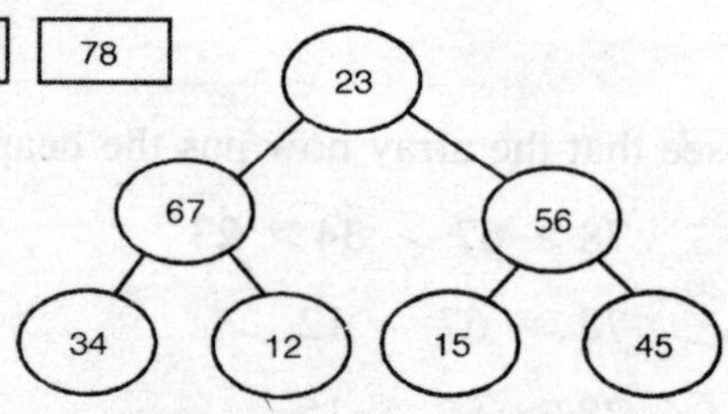

Step 2 : After swapping and removal operation the array has lost its heap property. So we once again apply the heap create algorithm to restore the heap property

23	67	56	34	12	15	45

Heap create →

67	34	56	23	12	15	45

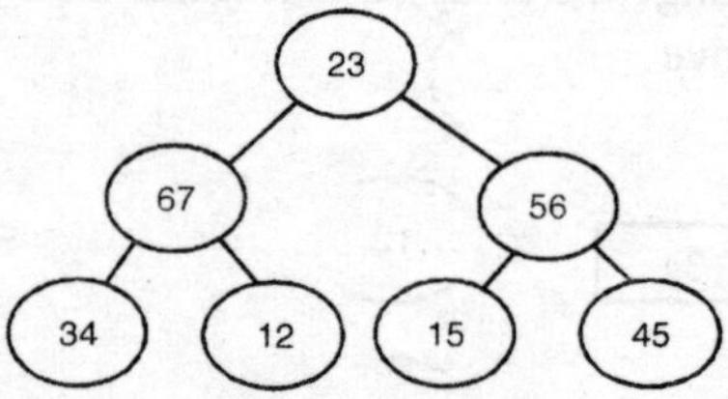

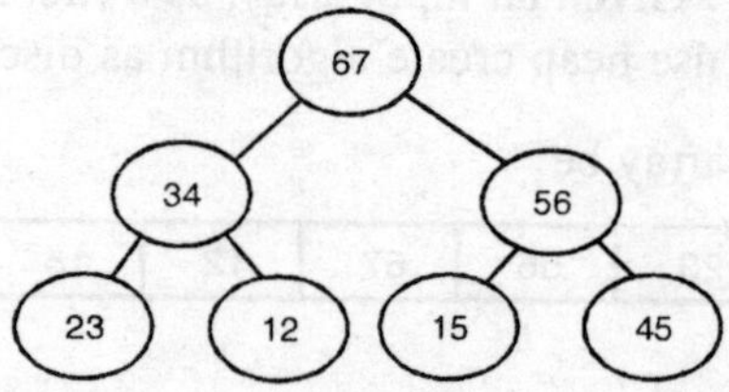

Iteration 2 :

Applying step 1 and step 2 as shown in Iteration 1 we get

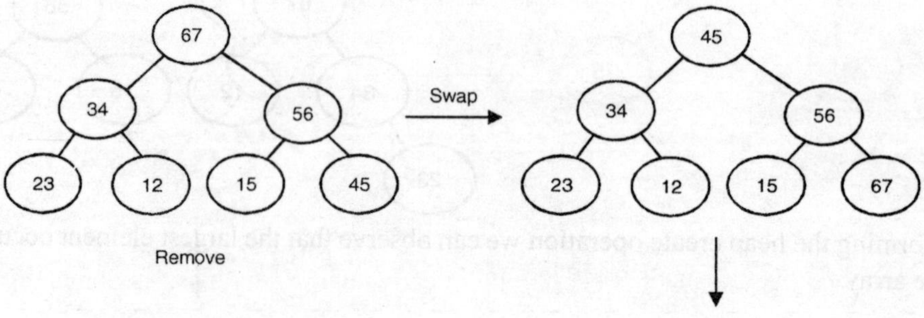

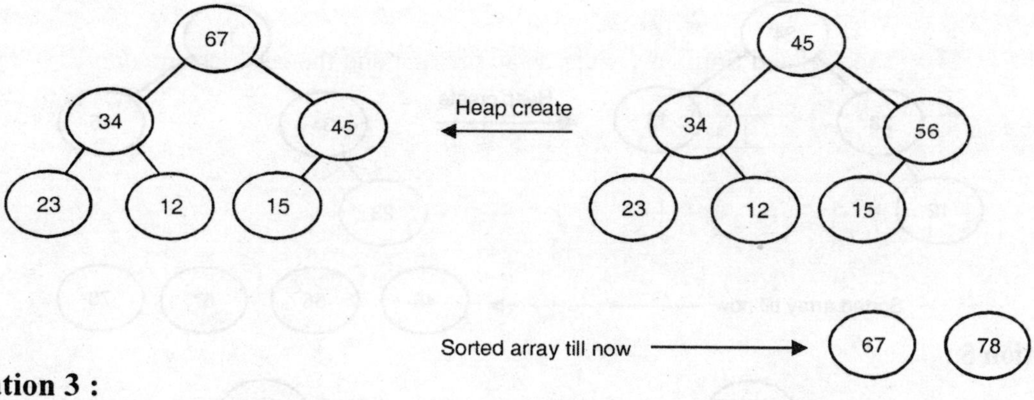

Iteration 3 :

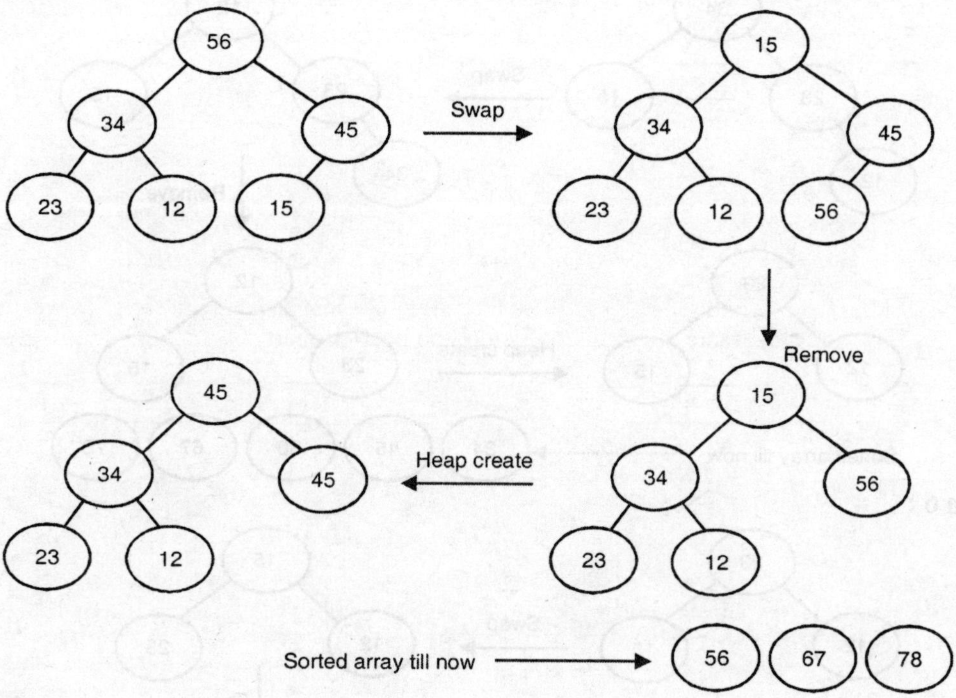

Iteration 4 :

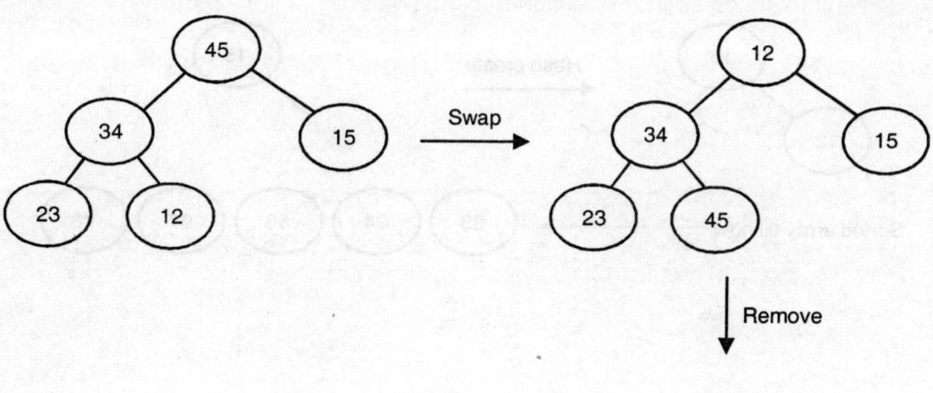

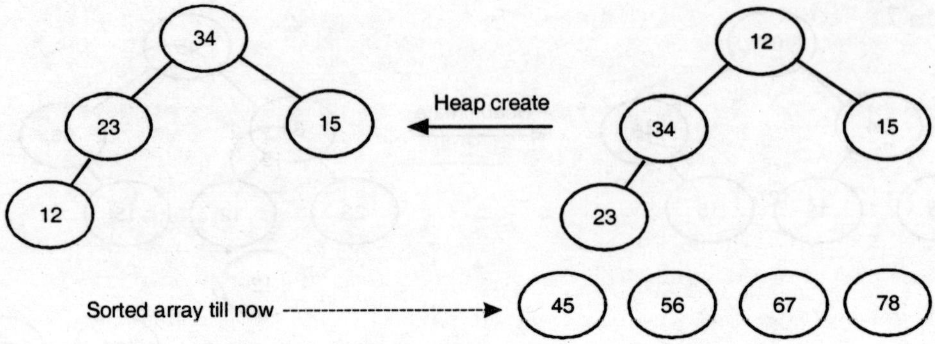

Iteration 5 :

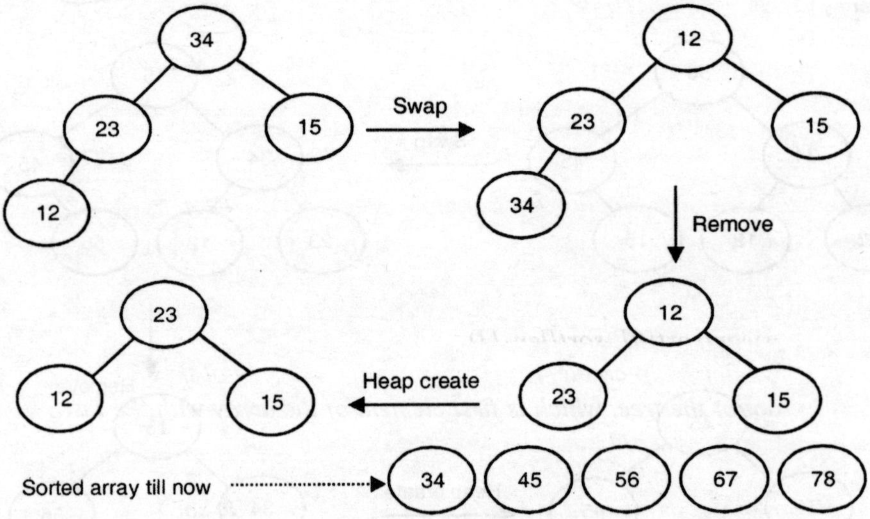

Iteration 6 :

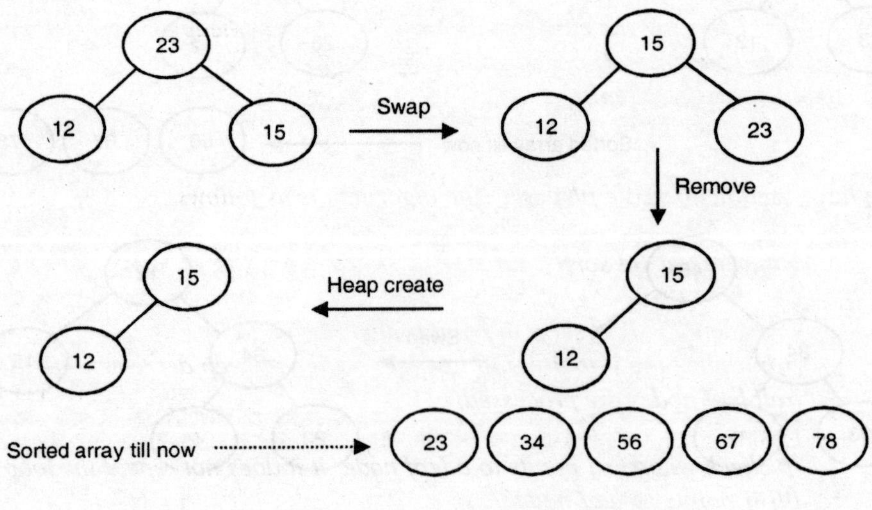

Iteration 7 :

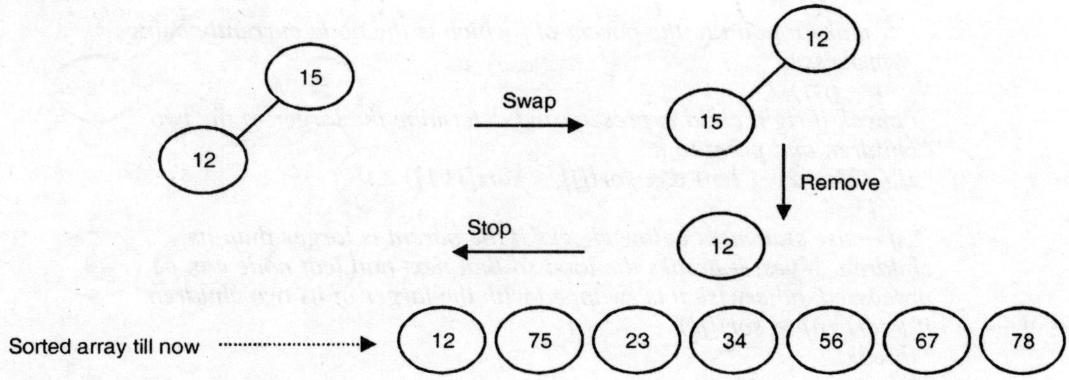

14.10.5 Algorithm for Heap Sort

Procedure heapSort (int sort[], int len)

```
Initialization
// call the heapcreate function so that input array has the heap property
Heapcreate(sort,len)
    While(len>0)
    {
       swap(sort[0], sort[len-1])
      /* after heap create, largest element is  the root of the tree. Swap
      root of the tree, which is first element of the array with the last
      element  so that largest element is sorted.*/

      len—;   // decrement the array to leave out already sorted element

      //By restoring the elements the array has lost the heap property. Hence
    // call heapcreate() once again.
   heapcreate (sort,len);
   } // end of while
```

We have used heapcreate function. The algorithm is as follows

```
    Heapcreate( int sort[], int len)
    {
       n=len/2 – 1; // set n to point to last leaf node.
    // Initialize the i  to point to last leaf node and keep decrementing till
    //all leaf nodes are processed.
    j=i;
    /* check whether j points to a leaf node, it it does not repeat the loop
    till it points to leaf node*/

    while( j*len/2 -1)
```

```
{  // set i to point to left child of  j, as left child is always present
    i =  2*j +1  ;
   // make n point to the parent of j which is the node currently being
  // processed
    n= (j-1)/2;
// check if right child is present and determine the larger of the two
//children and point to it.
 if ( (2*n+2) < len) && sort[j] < sort[j+1])
      j++
/* if – else statement below checks if the parent is larger than its
children. If yes, it breaks the loop so that next non leaf node can be
processed, otherwise it is swapped with the larger of its two children.
if ( sort [n] > sort[j])
   break;
else
 Swap ( sort[n], sort[j])
 }// end of while
}// end of Heapcreate function
```

PROGRAM:HEAP.C

```
//program to demonstarte heapsort
#include<stdio.h>
#include<stdlib.h>

void heapsort(int sort[],int len);
void heapcreate(int sort[],int len);

void main()
{int len,i=0;
 int sort[30];
  printf("\n enter no<0 to stop>");
   scanf("%d",&sort[i]);
  while(sort[i]!=0)
       {i++;
   printf("\n enter no<0 to stop>");
        scanf("%d",&sort[i]);
       }
       len=i; //length is taken as i and not as i+1 as 0 is also stored in the array
  heapsort(sort,len); //call the function heapsort which will sort the array
   printf("\n **** Sorted  Array **** \n");
        for(i=0;i<len;i++)
                printf("%d\t",sort[i]);
}
void heapsort(int sort[],int len)
{int temp,k;
  heapcreate(sort,len);
  k=len;
        while(len>0)
          {temp=sort[0];
```

```
    sort[0]=sort[len-1];
            sort[len-1]=temp;
  len---;
        heapcreate(sort,len);
        }
}
void heapcreate(int sort[],int len)
{int n,i,j,temp;
  n=(len/2)-1;
   for(i=n;i>=0;i--)
         { j=i;
     while(j<=len/2-1)
                 {j=2*j+1;
                       n=(j-1)/2;
                 if(2*n+2<len && sort[j]<sort[j+1])
                       j++;
       if(sort[n]>=sort[j])
                 break;
         else
                       {temp=sort[n];
                 sort[n]=sort[j];
                       sort[j]=temp;
                       }
         }
       }
}
/*Output:
 enter no<0 to stop>34
 enter no<0 to stop>45
 enter no<0 to stop>12
 enter no<0 to stop>56
 enter no<0 to stop>21
 enter no<0 to stop>0
 **** Sorted  Array ****
12     21     34     45     56*/
```

14.10.6 Complexity of Heap Sort

We know that a complete binary tree with N nodes has log (N+1) levels. For example if N = 31 then the number of levels is log(32) i.e. 5 levels

The insertion in create heap function is O(log N) as a complete binary tree with N nodes has log (N+1) levels and we have to access at leaf on node per level.

During the adjustment of heap while sorting, if one node per level is required to be accessed, the complexity is O(log N+1).

Therefore heap sort containing creation and adjustment is O(N Log N).

14.10.7 Which is better Heap or Quick sort

To recall quick sort has best case performance of N log N and a worst case performance of N^2.

Heap Sort is far superior to heap sort in the worst case. Heap sort is only NLogN whereas Quick Sort is N^2. Interestingly heap sort is O(NLogN) for both best and worst case. Then what is the catch?

Heap Sort is NOT efficient for small size data sets, as it requires considerable over heads for creation and adjustment of heaps. Computation of fathers and sons is also an overhead. Further Heap Sort require additional space to hold the record for swapping during heap adjust operation.

OBJECTIVE QUESTIONS

1. The two most important factors to consider in evaluating an algorithm are ________ and ________.
2. The big O notation is used to describe the variation of f(n) as n varies TRUE/FALSE
3. if f(n) = constant for all n then the complexity is of the order
   a) O(N) b) O(1)
   c) O(k) d) O(constant)
4. The worst case complexity of linear search is
   a) O(N) b) O(1)
   c) O(k) d) O(constant)
5. The best case for complexity of algorithm one can expect is is
   a) O(N) b) O(1)
   c) O(NlogN) d) $O(N^2)$
6. If the input size doubles, then if time consumed by algorithm also doubles, we can say complexity is.
   a) O(1) b) O(NlogN)
   c) $O(N^2)$ d) O(N)
7. when the algorithm takes N^2 steps for an input of N, we would say that complexity is
   a) O(1) b) O(NlogN)
   c) $O(N^2)$ d) O(N)
8. If the input size doubles and algorithm takes more than twice that of n, the complexity is of the order of
   a) O(1) b) O(NlogN)
   c) $O(N^2)$ d) O(N)
9. The worst case complexity of binary Search is for input of numbers is ________
10. The worst case complexity of bubble Sort is,for input of n numbers is________
11. The worst case complexity of bubble Sort is,for input of n numbers is
    a) O(1) b) O(NlogN)
    c) $O(N^2)$ d) O(N)

12. The worst case complexity of Insertion Sort input of n numbers is
    a) $O(N^2)$ b) O(1)
    c) O(NlogN) d) O(N)
13. The best case complexity of Insertion Sort input of n numbers is for an almost sorted input array
    a) $O(N^2)$ b) O(1)
    c) O(NlogN) d) O(N)
14. The best case complexity of Quick Sort input of n numbers is
    a) $O(N^2)$ b) O(1)
    c) O(NlogN) d) O(N)
15. The worst case complexity of Quick Sort input of n numbers is for an almost sorted input array
    a) $O(N^2)$ b) O(1)
    c) O(NlogN) d) O(N)
16. Average performance of Heap Sort is inferior to quick sort True/False.

REVIEW QUESTION

1. *Write and explain linear search procedure with a suitable example.*
2. *Discuss in detail about the following searching methods*
   a) sequential search
   b) Binary search using iteration technique
3. *Write in detail about the following*
   a) selection sort
   b) Heap sort
4. *Explain the Big O notation.*
5. *Discuss time and space requirements of a algorithm.*
6. *Explain why binary search is superior to linear search.*
7. *Write algorithm for insertion sort. Explain with an example.*
8. *Compare the algorithms for Quick Sort and Insertion sort. For an almost sorted array which is better and why?*
9. *Compare the algorithms for Heap sort and Quick sort.*

SOLVED PROBLEMS

1. Write a program to sort a list of names using heap sort

```
// charheapsort.c. Aprogram to sort the two dimensional
//array of strings using heap sort
#include<stdio.h>
#include<string.h>
```

```
void heapcreate(char name[][10],int len);
void heapsort(char name[][10],int len);

void main()
{char name[10][10];//10 names max size 10
 int len,i=0;
  printf("\nEnter name<stop to end>:");
  scanf("%s",name[i]);
   while(strcmp(name[i],"stop"))
         {i++;
    printf("\nEnter name<stop to end>:");
            scanf("%s",name[i]);
         }
  len=i;
         heapsort(name,len);
  printf("\n***sorted list***");
  for(i=0;i<len;i++)
   printf("\n%s",name[i]);
}

void heapsort(char name[][10],int len)
{
  char temp[10];
  heapcreate(name,len);
  while(len>0)
  {//swap first and last element
          strcpy(temp,name[len-1]);
          strcpy(name[len-1],name[0]);
          strcpy(name[0],temp);
          len—;
          heapcreate(name,len); //name array has lost heap property so retsote it
   }
}

void heapcreate(char name[][10],int len)
{
 int n,i,j;
 char temp[10];
 n=len/2-1; //point n to the last non leaf node
  for(i=n;i>=0;i—)
  { j=i;
   while(j<=len/2 -1)
   { j=2*j+1;
     n=(j-1)/2;
```

```
        if(2*n+2<len &&(strcmp(name[j],name[j+1])==-1))//check if right son exists and also find
           j++;                                    //greater of two children
      if(strcmp(name[n],name[j])==1||strcmp(name[n],name[j])==0)
              break;
            else
                  { strcpy(temp,name[j]);
        strcpy(name[j],name[n]);
                    strcpy(name[n],temp);
                  }
          }
        }
}

/*Output
Enter name<stop to end>:sachin
Enter name<stop to end>:arvind
Enter name<stop to end>:rohit
Enter name<stop to end>:srinivas
Enter name<stop to end>:anil
Enter name<stop to end>:stop
***sorted  list***
anil
arvind
rohit
sachin
srinivas*/
```

2 Write a program to search for a name given a two dimensional char array named List. Use binary search technique.

```
//charbinsearch.c
#include<stdio.h>
#include<string.h>

int binsearch(char name[],char list[][10],int lo,int hi);

void main()
{
  char list[10][10];
  char name[10];
  int len,i=0,key;
  int lo=0,hi;
  printf("\nenter sorted list only.....");
  printf("\nEnter name<stop to end>:");
```

```
 scanf("%s",list[i]);
  while(strcmp(list[i],"stop"))
        {i++;
  printf("\nEnter name<stop to end>:");
          scanf("%s",list[i]);
        }
 len=i;
        hi=len-1;
 printf("\nnames in list......\n");
        for(i=0;i<len;i++)
         printf("%s\t",list[i]);
  printf("\nenter name to search:");
         scanf("%s",name);

        key=binsearch(name,list,lo,hi);

 if(key==-1)
           printf("\nname does not exist in the list");
 else
                   printf("name found at index %d in the list\n",key);
}


int binsearch(char name[],char list[][10],int lo,int hi)
{
  int mid,key;
        if(lo>hi)
          key=-1;
        else
        {mid=(lo+hi)/2;
  if(strcmp(list[mid],name)==0)
             key=mid;
        else
   if(strcmp(list[mid],name)==-1)
          {lo=mid+1;
           key=binsearch(name,list,lo,hi);
          }
   else
          { hi=mid-1;
           key=binsearch(name,list,lo,hi);
          }
   }
         return(key);
 }
```

```
/*Output
enter sorted list only.....
Enter name<stop to end>:barath
Enter name<stop to end>:gurudutt
Enter name<stop to end>:raman
Enter name<stop to end>:ravi
Enter name<stop to end>:sumit
Enter name<stop to end>:stop

names in list......
barath gurudutt raman  ravi   sumit
enter name to search:raman
name found at index 2 in the list
*/
```

ASSIGNMENT QUESTIONS

1. Formulate recursive algorithm for binary search with its timing analysis
2. Write a, c, program that searches a value in a stored array using binary search (worst case and best case)
3. Explain the algorithm for selection sort and give a suitable example
4. Suppose that the list contains the integers 1,2, 8 in this order. Trace through the binary search to determine what comparisons of keys are done in searching.
   a) to locate 3
   b) to locate4,5
5. Write and explain non-recursive algorithm for binary search with suitable example and discuss the various complexities of binary search
6. Explain quick sort algorithm. Analyze the worst case performance of quick sort and compare with selection sort.
7. Write a program to sort the array of integers
8. Construct a tree for the expression given and give pre order and post order expression.

a) A * B + C **b) (A^B) * C** **c) A + (B^C) * D ^(E + F)**

Solutions to Objective Questions

1) speed , space	2) True	3) b	4) a	5) b	6) d
7) c	8) b	9) log n	10) n^2	11) c	12) a
13) d	14) c	15) a	16) True		

JNTU QUESTION PAPERS Fully Solved

Code No: RR10203 **Set No.2**

Apr/May 2006

1(a). What are different types of integer constants? What are long integer constants? How do these constants differ from ordinary integer constants? How can they be written and identified?

a) **Integer Constants :** An integer constant refers to a sequence of digits. There are three types of integer namely, decimal, octal and hexadecimal.They can be sub divided into

Decimal integer constants : 0 10 -745 999

Unsigned integer constant an be specified by appending letter U at the end. Ex : 55556U or 55556u

Long integer constant can be specified and identified by appending the letter l s at the end . For example 789654234L or 7896s

Octal integer constants :only digits between 0 to 7 are allowed. All Octal numbers must start with 0 digit to identify as octal number

Allowed octal constants	:	0777 , 001 , 0197 , 07565L (octal long)
Illegal octal constants are	:	089 - 8 is illegal , 777 - does not start with 0
	:	-0675.76 - . is illegal

Hexa decimal constants : A hexa decimal number must start with 0x or 0X followed by digits 0 to 9 or alphabets a to f, both upper case or lower case allowed. Allowed hexa decimal constants are : 0xffff , 0xa11f , 01 , 0x65000UL
Illegal hexa decimal constants are : 0x14.55 , illegal character "."

1(b). Describe two different ways that floating – point constants can be written in C. What special rules apply in this case?

Ans: Integer numbers are inadequate to represent quantities that continuously, such as distance, heights, temperatures, prices, and so on. These quantities are represented by numbers containing fractional parts like 17.548. Such numbers are called real or floating point constants. They are base – 10 number that can be represented either in ***exponent form*** or ***decimal point representation.*** Examples of real constants shown in decimal notation, having a whole number followed by a decimal point and the fractional part are:

0.0083 -0.75 435.36 +247.0

It is possible to omit digits before decimal point or digits after the decimal point

215. .95 -.71 +.5

A real number may also be expressed in exponential (or scientific) notation. For example, the value 215.65 may be written as 2.1565e2 in exponential notation. E2 means multiply by 10^2. The general form is **Mantissa e exponent**

The mantissa is either a real number expressed in decimal notation or an integer. The exponent is an integer number with an optional plus or minus sign.

Valid floating point constants are : 0.01 , 789.89765 , 5E-5 , 1.768E+9
Invalid floating point declarations are:

6 invalid . must contain exponent or float point.

5E+12.5 Invalid as exponent can not be float.

6,789.00 Invalid character ","

1(c). What is a character constant? How do character constants differ from numeric type of constants?

Ans: **Character constants.** Character constants can be declared based on the character set followed in a computer. ANSI have standardized these values as shown below.

A	65	a	097	NULL	000
B	66	b	098	LF(line feed)	010
Z	90	z	122	CR(carriage return)	013

A character constant contains a single character enclosed within a pair of single quote marks. Examples of character constants are:

'5' 'X' ';' ' '

Note that the character constant '5' is not the same as the number 5. the last constant is a blank space. Character constants have integer values known as ASCII values. For example, the statement

printf("%d",'a');

would print number 97, the ASCII value of letter a. Since each character constant represent an integer value it is also possible to perform arithmetic operations on character constants.

Special Characters that can not be printed normally , double quote(") ,apostrophe('), question mark(?) and backslash(\) etc can be represented by using *escape sequences. An escape sequence always starts with \ followed by special character stated ove .*

2.(a) Write a program to sort set of strings in an alphabetical order ?

Ans: To sort the given set of strings we can use any sorting algorithm here we use Bubble sort, to compare two strings we use function

strcmp(const char *s1,const char *s2)

which returns an integer <0 if s1 is less than s2

=0 if s1 is equal to s2

>0 if s1 is greater than s2

```
//stgsort.c
#include <stdio.h>
#include <string.h>
main()
{   int i,j,n;
    char a[10][20],t[20];
    printf("Enter the number of strings :");
    scanf("%d",&n);
    for(i=0;i<n;i++)
        scanf("%s",a[i]);// read the strings
    for(i=0;i<n-1;i++) //bubble sort
    for(j=0;j<n-1-i;j++)
if(strcmp(a[j],a[j+1])>0)
{       strcpy(t,a[j]);
        strcpy(a[j],a[j+1]);
            strcpy(a[j+1],t);
    }
    printf("The strings after sorting are : \n");
    for(i=0;i<n;i++)
    {
printf(" %s",a[i]);// print the strings
printf("\n");
    }
}
```

3(a). Differentiate between a structure and union with respective allocation of memory by the compiler. Give an example of each.

Structure:

A *structure* is a collection of variables referenced under one name, providing a convenient means of keeping related information together. A structure declaration forms a template that can be used to create structure objects (that is, instances of a structure). The variables that make up the structure are called *members*. (Structure members also commonly referred to as elements or fields)

The keyword struct tells the compiler that a structure is being declared.

```
Struct addr
    {
        char name[30];
        char street[40];
```

```
        char  city[20];
        char  state[3];
        unsigned long int zip;
    };
```

To declare a variable of type addr, we write

```
        Struct addr  addr_info;
```

This declares variable of type addr called addr_info. Thus, addr describes the form of a structure(its type),and addr_info is an instance of the structure.

When a structure variable (such as addr_info)is declared, the compiler automatically allocates sufficient memory to accommodate all of its members.

Name	30 bytes
Street	40 bytes
City	20 bytes
State	3 bytes
Zip	4 bytes

The above diag ram shows addr_info structure in memory.

Union:

Unions are useful when memory conservation is the criteria. Union , like structure holds data types like *int , char , float etc.* However , the major difference is that union holds only one data object at a time. Union calculates which of its declarations require maximum storage requirements and allocates memory space accordingly. It means that all the variables declared in a Union share the same memory location.

Compiler handles different memory requirements of various data types automatically but it is users responsibility to keep track of which data type is stored at a particular instant of time. Otherwise garbage result. The general syntax of Union is

```
Storage class union  nametag
{ data member 1;
   data member 2;
} var1 , var2 , var3;
```

Let us declare a union called details to make the working clear.

```
        union details
        {  char country[12];
```

```
        float networth;
    }indian, nri;
```

We have declared two variables resident and nri. They are of type details. Each of the variable resident and nri can represent either country or networth at any one particular instant of time. The country[25] requires more storage slot 25 bytes than a float value. Therefore union allocates a block memory space to each of the variable declared in the union. The union can be declared with in a structure. Note that programmer has to keep track of the data variable that is active in the memory.

Methods of accessing union members are same as that of structure. As a matter of fact every thing we discussed about structures hold good for unions as well.

3(b). Write a program to read n records of students and find out how many of them passed. The fields are student's roll no, name, mark and result. Evaluate the result as follows

If marks > 35 then
Result="pass" else "Fail"

Ans: To program for this type of problems it is very hard to hold different values of one particular student hence we use structure's which gives the flexibility of housing various data types under one name and this name can be given to student since there are no. of students for whom details are to be checked so we use structure arrays the program is as shown below,

Program:

```
#include <stdio.h>
#include <string.h>
struct student {
        int roll_no;//roll number
        char name[20];//name of student
        int mark;//marks obtained by student
        char result[10];//result
        };

main()
{
struct student s[10];
int i,n,a=0;
printf("Enter the number of records : \n");
scanf("%d",&n);//n is no. of students
for(i=0;i<n;i++)
{
    printf("Enter roll_no , name , marks of student: \n");
    scanf("%d %s %d",&s[i].roll_no,s[i].name,&s[i].mark);//reading
}
```

```
for(i=0;i<n;i++)
if (s[i].mark > 35)
        {strcpy(s[i].result,"pass");a++;}//a has value of no.of passed
else
        strcpy(s[i].result,"fail");
printf("The results of students are : \n");
for(i=0;i<n;i++)
printf("%d%d%s%d%s\n",i,s[i].roll_no,s[i].name,s[i].mark,s[i].result);
printf("Out of %d students %d students passed",n,a);
}
```

The above program uses structure to take the details of all students since practically it is very hard to bind together the details of a particular student which we can do with the help of structures. After accepting the details the marks of students are checked and the variable result in structure is set appropriately to pass or fail.

4(a). Write a 'C' program to compute the sum of all elements stored in an array using pointers.

Ans: The usage of pointers in arrays gives us the advantage of Dynamic memory Management where the size of the array is decided by the program and memory can also be deallocated. Here is a program to calculate the sum of numbers in an array using pointers.

```
#include<stdio.h>
#include<malloc.h>
main()
{ int *a,i,n,result=0;
  printf("Enter the no. of elements to be stored in array :");
  scanf("%d",&n);
  a=(int *)malloc(n*sizeof(int));//allocating space
  printf("Enter the elements :");
  for(i=0;i<n;i++)
  scanf("%d",a+i);
  for(i=0;i<n;i++)
  result+=*(a+i);
  printf("The sum of elements in array is :%d",result);
  free(a);//deallocating space
}
```

As shown in the above program the locations address being provided by a+i whereas when we add elements we access the value stored in a+i location by *(a+i) . The space of array is not fixed but the requirement is given by theuser at run time using malloc. Also this allocated memory can be deallocated by using free which increases the reusability of space.

4(b). Write a 'C' program to using pointers to determine the length of a character string

Ans: String variable names are pointers to strings this is the reason we commonly do not use symbol '&' in scanf while accepting strings .Array names are pointers to the arrays . In the program shown below we use a function rs() which returns a string pointer having the string hence this pointer can be used wherever we require the string

```
//stglen.c
#include<stdio.h>
//function prototype declarations
int length(char x[]);
void main()
{  int ans;
   char x[20];  // dimension of string array x
        printf("enter a string:");
        scanf("%s",x);              /*input string from the user*/
        ans =length(x);              /*function call*/
   printf("length=%d\n",ans);
        getch();
}/*end of main*/
int length(char a[])          /*function definition*/
{           int i=0;
        while(a[i]!='\0')      /*when the character is not null*/
            i++;
        return i;
}/*end of function length*/
/*
enter a string:hello
length=5 */
```

5. Show how to implement a queue of integers in C by using an array int q[QUEUESIZE],where q[0] is used to indicate the front of the queue, q[1] is used to indicate its rear and where q[2] through q[QUEUESIZE -1] contain elements on the queue. Show how to initialize such an array to represent the empty queue and write routines remove, insert and empty for such an implementation.

Queues:

A queue is a linear list of information that is accessed in first-in, first-out order, known as FIFO. That is, the first item placed on the queue is the first item retrieved, and so on. This is the only means of storage and retrieval in a queue; random access of any specific item is not allowed.

The above diagram represents a queue first element is indicated by front and the rear points to ending of the queue. This is normal representation of queue.

According to the problem a queue of size QUEUESIZE is required which holds the information regarding front of the queue in q[0] and information regarding rear of queue in q[1] and the queue consists of elements from q[2] through q[QUEUESIZE-1]

This can be diagrammatically represented as follows:

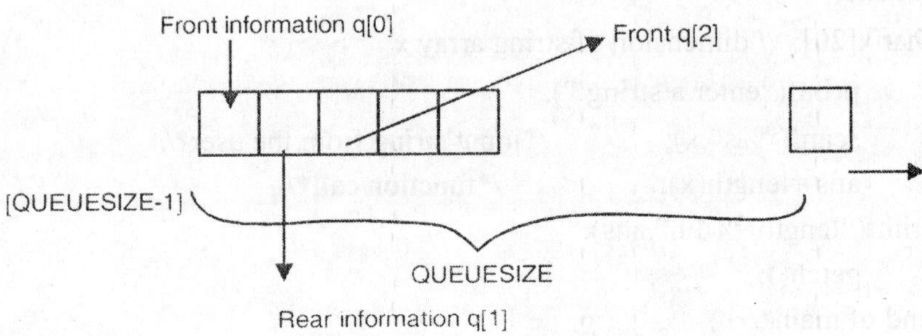

Initializing

First we take the queue as an array say q [QUEUESIZE] we initialize the first element that is q [0] with q [2] that is 2 which says that the first element is at location 2 of the array or the front of the queue is at location 2 of the array q []. Initially when the queue is empty the front and rear both mean the same location hence q [1] which has the information about rear of queue also has value 2 which says that queue is empty .

The initializing of such a queue is given as follows:

```
# define QUEUESIZE 10
struct queue
{
int q [QUEUESIZE];
}

INIT_queue (struct queue *A)
```

```
        {
            A -> q [0] = 2;
            A -> q [1] = 2;
        }
```

Now the queue is initialized and initially represents an empty queue which can be tested by the following function

```
int IsEmpty (struct queue *A)
{  return ( (A -> q [0] = = 2) && ( A-> q[1]==2) ? 1 : 0 );
}
```

The above function returns a value 1 if the queue is empty and 0. The function checks whether q [0] which signifies the front and q [1] which is the rear of a queue are same since they were initialized to same value that is 2. IsEmpty() returns 1 if the queue becomes empty.

Inserting

To insert a value into this type of queue we need to increment rear by using q[1]++ and inserting the value in position q [q[1]] this implementation is shown in the function below

```
Insert (struct queue *A, int x)
{
    if (A->q [1] = = (QUEUESIZE-1))
    {
        printf("Queue full");
        return(0);
    }
    else A->q[1]++;
    A->q [ A->q[1] ] = x;
}
```

The above function takes a structure queue and a value to be inserted in queue as arguments initially checks if queue is full if the queue is not full then the value of q [1] which is rear of queue is incremented and that value is used to place the value x in particular location of queue otherwise if queue is full q [1] is incremented to a value equal to QUEUESIZE hence the queue does not accept any more elements once a value is inserted the rear of queue increases by one more location showing a new element that has been added to the queue.

Removing

To remove an element from queue we use the function Remove which checks if currently the queue is empty if it is empty then no elements could be removed. Otherwise the function increments the value of front to show that a particular element which served as a front has been removed and its next element is the present front thus serving in a FIFO fashion.

```
int Remove (struct  queue *A)
```

```
{ int temp;
  if (Is_empty (A))
      {   printf("queue is empty");
          exit(1);
      }
  if(A->q [0] = = QUEUESIZE-1)
      printf("all elements removed")
  else
      {  temp= A->q [0];
         A->q[0]++ ; // increment the front value in the queue
      return ( A-> q [ temp] ); // return the deleted element
      }
}
```

Using the above function an element can be removed from the queue as q[0] is incremented the new value of q[0] becomes the new front of the queue and the element that is removed from the queue is returned by the function.

6 (a). Write routines a) to insert element at nth position b) to delete element at n th position in a doubly linked List.

In double linked list an additional pointer to previous node is provided so that traversal can be in any direction to the left of current node or to the right of current node.

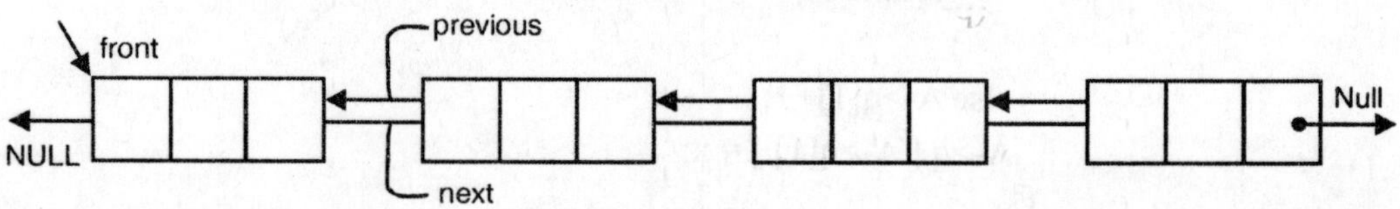


```
struct doublellist
{ int data;
  struct doublellist *left;
  struct doublellist *right;
};
typedef struct doublellist node;



node *insert(int n,int val,node *list)
{ node *p,*temp;
  temp=list;
```

```
p=(node *)malloc(sizeof(node));
p->data=val;
if(n==0)
{p->right=NULL;
 p->left=list;
 list->right=p;
 list=p;
}
else
{ while(temp->data!=n && temp->left!=NULL)
  temp=temp->left;  //find location oh n in the list

  if(temp->data!=n)
        {printf("node does not exist in list\n");
            exit(1);
        }
  else
        { p->left=temp->left;
            temp->left=p;
          p->right=temp;
          if(p->left!=NULL) //check if the node is to be added in the end
            (p->left)->right=p;
        }
}
return(list);
}
```

```
// deleting the node from a doubly linked list

node *delet(int n,node *list)
{ node *temp=list;
 while(temp->data!=n && temp->left!=NULL)
  temp=temp->left;  //find location oh n in the list
 if(temp->data!=n)
 {printf("node does not exist in list\n");
  exit(1);
 }
 else
 { //case 1:deletion of starting node
```

```
            if(temp->right==NULL)//check if it is the staring node
            {list=temp->left;
            list->right=NULL;
             free(temp);
            }
          //case 2:node is general node with left and right nodes
           else
            {(temp->right)->left=temp->left;
             if(temp->left!=NULL) //check if node is last node
        (temp->left)->right=temp->right;
             free(temp);
            }
      }
      return(list);
    }
```

7. **Write in detail about the following**
   a) Weakly Connected Graph
   b) Strongly Connected graph

We can write a graph G, a collection of Edges (E) and Vertices (V) as **G = (V, E)**

V (G) = {A, B, C, D, E, F}
E(G) = { (C,A), (A,B), (B,E), (B,D), (C,E), (C,A), (E,A)}

Each edge is specified by two nodes it interconnects. Two nodes are called adjacent nodes if they are connected by an edge . In Fig 13.5 vertices A and C are adjacent. Also note that edges can be directed or bidirectional. We have shown directed edges in Fig 13.5. A directed graph is also known as ***digraph***

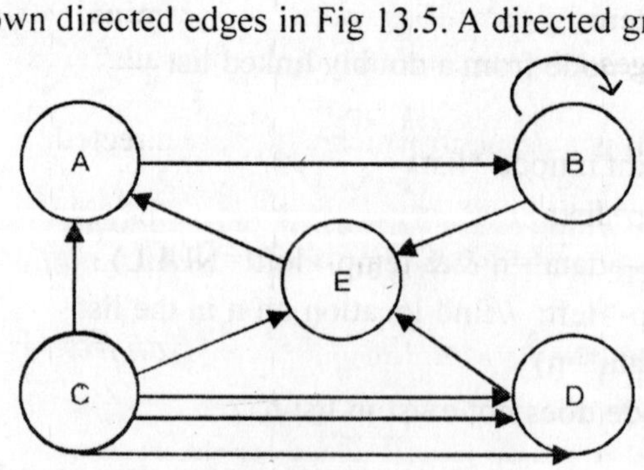

A Graph with 5 vertices 7 edges.

A graph can have an isolated node, node F. Similarly, we have shown a loop at vertex B. A graph can have more than one edge between vertices. Then we call such graphs as multiple graphs. For example between C and D, there are 3 directed edges shown.

Degree of a node is number of edges incident on a node. Degree of node E = 3. Further in degree is number of incoming edges and out degree is number of edges leaving a node. For example in degree of node E is 3 and out degree of node E is 1.

A ***weighted graph*** is a graph whose edges have weights. These weights can be thought as cost involved in traversing the path along the edge. Fig 13.6 shows a weighted graph

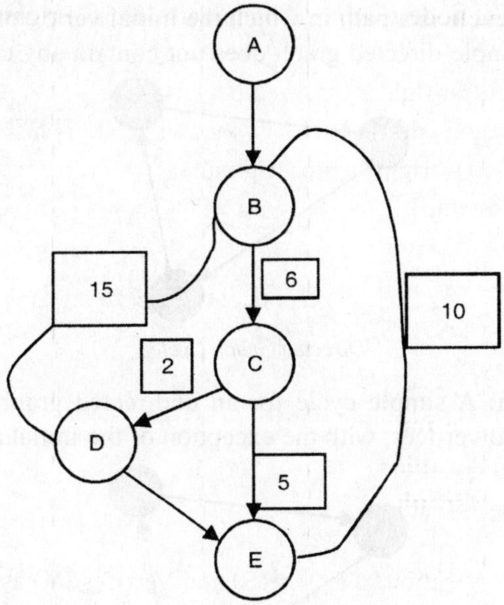

A weighted Graph

Adjacent Vertex A vertex V_2 is said to be adjacent to vertex V_1 if there is an edge connecting these two vertices. In Fig 13.6 B&C, D&E are adjacent vertices.

A **path** through a graph is a traversal of consecutive vertices along a sequence of edges The vertices that begin and end the path are termed the **initial vertex** and **terminal vertex,** respectively. The **length** of the path is the number of edges that are traversed along the path. A-B-C-D is path.

Directed Graph(digraph) It is a graph in which edges are directed.

Connected Graph is one in which every vertex is connected to another vertex. Further a digraph is called strongly connected if there is a path from any vertex to any other vertex.

A digraph is strongly connected if it contains a directed path from j to i for every pair of distinct vertices i and j.

Connectedness

An undirected graph is considered to be **connected** if a path exists between all pairs of vertices thus making each of the vertices in a pair reachable from the other. An unconnected graph may be subdivided into what are termed connected subgraphs or connected components of the graph.

The **connectedness** of a simple directed graph becomes more complex because direction must be considered. For instance, if vertex a is reachable from vertex b, vertex a may not be reachable from vertex b. For the road map example when the map is considered to be a directed graph, it can not be considered a connected graph. because while Calgary is reachable from Saskatoon, Saskatoon is not reachable from Calgary.

Cycle: A graph is said to be cyclic if starting vertex and ending vertex in a path of the graph is the same. B-C-E-B is a cycle. A **cycle** is a path in which the initial vertex of the path is also the terminal vertex of the path. When a simple directed graph does not contain any cycles is termed **acyclic**.

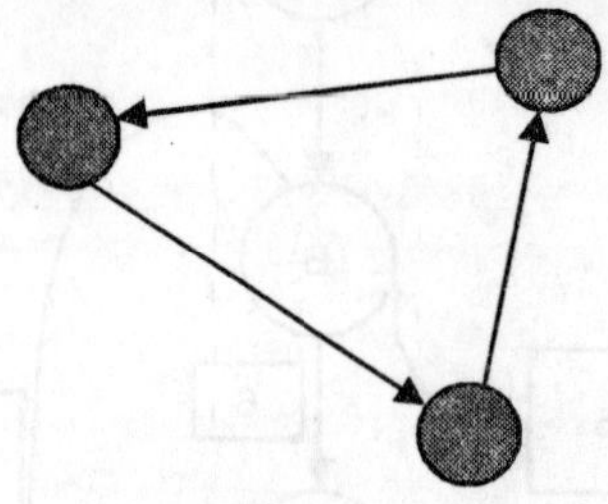

Directed Graph Cycle

Cycle for undirected Graph: A simple cycle for an undirected graph must contain at least three different edges and no repeated vertices, with the exception of the initial and terminal vertex.

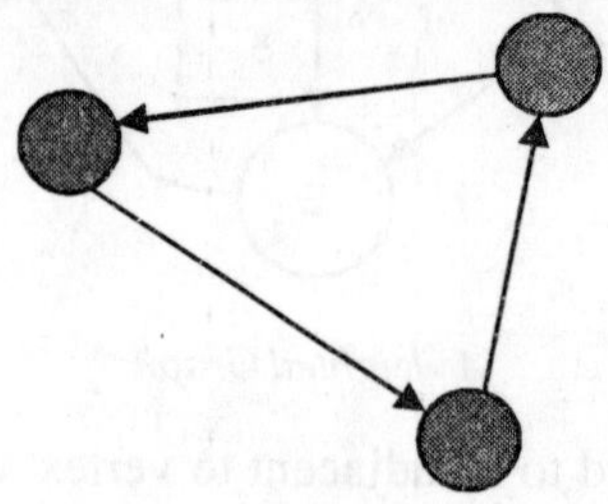

Directed Graph Cycle

Simple directed graphs can be classified as **weakly connected** and **strongly connected**. **A weakly connected graph** is where the direction of the graph is ignored and the connectedness is defined as if the graph was undirected. For example in the figure shown below we can not reach **a** from **c.**

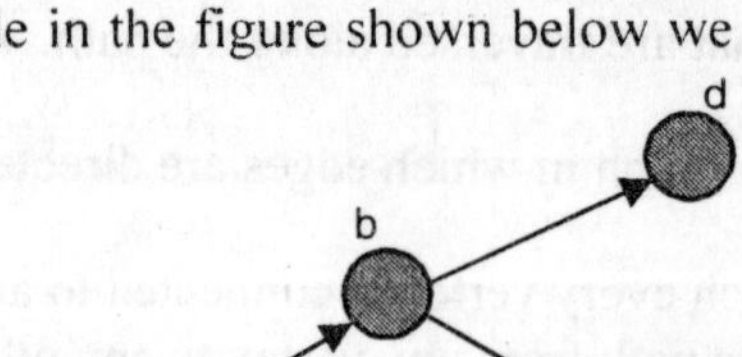

Weakly Connected Directed Graph

A strongly connected graph is one in which for all pairs of vertices, both vertices are reachable from the other. A strongly connected graph is a directed graph that has a path from each vertex to every other vertex. In other words formally a strongly connected graph can be defined as a directed graph D=(V, E) such that for all pairs of vertices u, v " V, there is a path from u to v and from v to u.

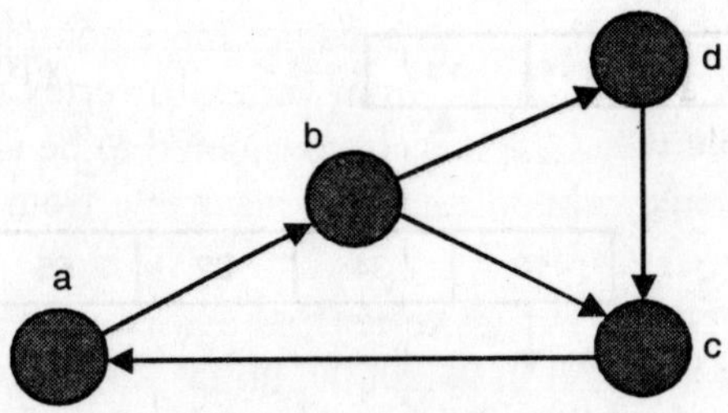

Strongly Connected Directed Graph

From the figure shown for strongly connected digraphs , we can conclude following theorems

a) *for every n, n>=2,there exists a strongly connected digraph that contains exactly n edges. Strongly connected digraph shown has 6 edges for n=6.*

b) *for every n vertex strongly connected digraph contains at least n edges where n>=2. In the figure , 4 vertex strongly connected digraph contains 5 edges.*

8(a). Write a 'C' program to sort the elements of an array using selection sort technique with a suitable example.

Selection Sort : Compare 1st element with all other elements in each iteration set lowest as minimum(Min). At the end of iteration swap min and 1st element. Now continue with 2nd element same procedure. Continue with this procedure till entire array is exhausted.

EXAMPLE :

Input

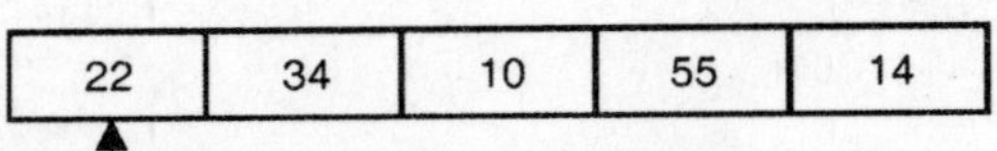

Array :

Initialization set Min = 22

Iteration 1 :

Comparison new Min

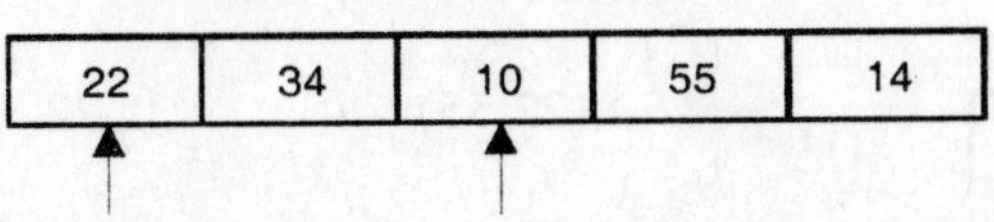

(22,34) 22

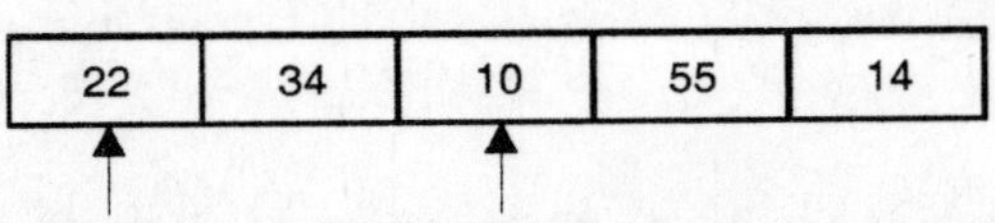

(22,10) 10

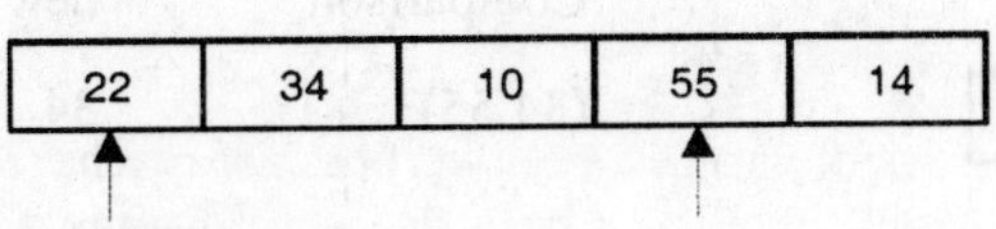

(10,55) 10

Array	Comparison	new Min
22 | 34 | 10 | 55 | 14	(10,14)	10

Swap (22,10)

10	34	22	55	14

Min value is put into place

Iteration 2 :

Array	Comparison	new Min
10 | 34 | 22 | 55 | 14	(34,22)	22
10 | 34 | 22 | 55 | 14	(22,55)	22
10 | 34 | 22 | 55 | 14	(22,14)	14

Swap (34,14)

10	14	22	34	55

Iteration 3 : (Min = 22)

Array	Comparison	new Min
10 | 14 | 22 | 34 | 55	(22,34)	22
10 | 14 | 22 | 34 | 55	(22,55)	22

Iteration 4 : (Min = 34)

Array	Comparison	new Min
10 | 14 | 22 | 34 | 55	(34,55)	34

Sorted Array	=	10	14	22	34	55

Length of array = 5

Note: No. of iterations = 4 = (5-1) = (length – 1)

Algorithm :

```
Selectsort(sort[],len)
for i=0 to i<len-1 do
begin
        min=i
        for j=i+1     j<len do
        begin
                if[sort[j] < sort[min]
                        min=j
                end
        if(min != i)
                swap(sort[min],sort[i])
        end
```

Program:selection.c

```
//program to demonstrate selection sort
#include<stdio.h>
#include<stdlib.h>
void selectsort(int sort[],int len);

void main()
{int len,i=0;
 int sort[30];
 printf("\n enter no<0 to stop>");
  scanf("%d",&sort[i]);
  while(sort[i]!=0)
        {i++;
   printf("\n enter no<0 to stop>");
        scanf("%d",&sort[i]);
        }
        len=i; //length is taken as i and not as i+1 as 0 is also stored in the array
   selectsort(sort,len); //call the function selectsort which will sort the array
  printf("\n **** Sorted  Array **** \n");
        for(i=0;i<len;i++)
```

```
            printf("%d\t",sort[i]);
}
void selectsort(int sort[],int len)
{int i,j,temp,min;
  for(i=0;i<len-1;i++)
        {min=i;
    for(j=i+1;j<len;j++)
          {if(sort[j]<sort[min])
                min=j;
          }
    if(min!=i)
          {temp=sort[min];
                sort[min]=sort[i];
                sort[i]=temp;
          }
        }//end of for(i)
}//end of select sort
```

8(b). What is the worst case and best case time complexities of selection sort?

For the first iteration the number of inner loop iterations is n-1 for the second iteration the no. of inner loop iterations is n-2 continuing we get total no. of iterations is

$$(n-1)+(n-2)+(n-3)+\dots\dots\dots+1 = n(n-1)/2$$

Therefore, complexity of Selection sort is $O(n^2)$. The number of interchanges is always n-1. Hence selection sort is $O((n^2)$ for both best case and the worst case.

Code No: RR10203 **Set No.3**

January 2005

1 (a). What is the difference between break and continue statement? Explain with examples.

THE break STATEMENT

The break statement is used to terminate loops or to exit from a switch. It can be used within a for, while, do-while, or switch statement. The break statement is simply written as **break** , without any embedded expressions or statements.

The break statement causes a transfer of control out of the entire switch statement, to the first statement following the switch statement.

EXAMPLE : Use of break in a switch statement:

```
switch (choice=toupper ( getchar() ))
      {
            case 'R':
                        printf("RED");
                        break;
            case 'W':
                        printf("WHITE");
                        break;
      }
```

EXAMPLE: Use of break in a for loop

```
      for ( ;;)   // for ever for loop
      {     if(count == 5)
            { printf("\n reached upper limit of 5: breaking the for loop");
              break;
            }
            else
            {
              printf("\n Enter value of %d number :", count);
              scanf("%d",&num);
              sum+=num;
              count++;
            }
      } // end of for
} // end of main
```

If a break statement is included in a while,do-while or for loop,then control will immediately be transferred out of the loop when the break statement is encountered. This provides a convenient way to terminate the loop if an error or other irregular condition is detected.

THE continue STATEMENT

The continue statement is used to bypass the remainder of the current pass through a loop. The loop does not terminate when a continue statement is encountered. Rather, the remaining loop statements are skipped and the computation proceeds directly to the next pass through the loop. The continue statement can be included within a while, a do-while or a for statement. It is written simply as

continue;

EXAMPLE OF CONTINUE IN DO ... WHILE STATEMENT

First, consider a do-while loop.

```
do
{       scanf ("%f",&x);
        if(x<0)
        {       printf("ERROR-NEGATIVE VALUE FOR X");
                continue;
        }
}while(x<=100);
```

EXAMPLE OF USAGE OF CONTINUE IN IF STATEMENT:

```
void main()
        {  int count=0;
           int sum;
           int avg;
           for ( ;;)    // for ever for loop  <---------------------------+
             { if( (count %2)== 0) // the number is even. % operator gives remainder
                 { printf("\n even number: breaking the for loop:%d " count);   |
                   continue; ------------> //control goes to here ------------+
                 }
               else
                 { count+=10; // means count = count + 10
                   printf("\n odd number : added 10%d",count);
                 }
             } // end of for
        } // end of main
```

1 (b). What is the purpose of go to statement? How is the associated target statement identified?

goto STATEMENT

The goto statement is used to alter the normal sequence of program execution by transferring control to some other part of the program. In its general form, the goto statement is written as

goto label;

where label is an identifier that is used to label the target statement to which control will be transferred. Control may be transferred to any other statement within the program. The target statement must be labeled, and the label must be followed by a colon. Thus, the target statement will appear as

label: statement

Each labeled statement within the program must have a unique label; i.e., no two statements can have the same label.

1(c). Write a C program to evaluate the power series
E^x=1+x+(x*x)+(x*x*x)+.....x^n, 0<x<1

```
        //sumseries.c
/*Program to evaluate the power series*/
#include<stdio.h>
#include<math.h>
#define n 2
void main()
{ float x,sum=0;
  int i;

  /* reading the value of x */
  printf("enter x value:\n");
  scanf("%f",&x);
  /* computing the value of the series */
  for(i=0;i<n;i++)
  {
              sum=sum+pow(x,i);
  /* pow is the function available in math.h */
  }
  /* displaying the value of sum of the series */
  printf("sum of the series is %f",sum);
  getch();
  }
```

2(a). In what way array is different from ordinary variables.

Arrays are defined in much the same manner as ordinary variables , except that each array name must be accompanied by a size specification(i.e., the number of elements). An array is a group of related data items of same data type that share a common name and are stored in contiguous memory locations.

For example:

int a[10];———————— array
int a; ———————————— variable

2(b). What conditions must be satisfied by the entire elements of any given array?

Ans:

1) All the data items of an array share a common name .

Eg:

salary[10]——————— array name is salary

2) All the elements should be same data type.

Eg:

int a[20]; ————— contains all its elements as integers only.

2(c). What are subscripts? How are they written? What restrictions apply to the values that can be assigned to subscripts?

Each array element (i.e., each individual data item) is referred to by specifying the array name followed by one or more subscripts, with is subscript enclosed in square brackets.

For example consider the following example

char **text[]** = "New Delhi"; // The string contains 9 characters . It will be stored in an array as shown below. Note that we have left blank for size of the array.

We could also declare specifying the size , but size to be correctly specified , taking care of null character as char text[9] = "New Delhi"

name of the array : text :	**N**	**e**	**w**		**D**	**e**	**l**	**h**	**i**	**\0**
Subscript value :	**0**	**1**	**2**	**3**	**4**	**5**	**6**	**7**	**8**	**9**

text[0] contains character N
text[9] contains null character (\0)

Each subscript must be expressed as a non negative integer. The value of each subscript can be expressed as an integer constant, an integer variable or a more complex integer expression .The number of subscripts determine the dimensionality of the array.

2(d). What advantage is there in defining an array size in terms of symbolic constant rather than fixed integer quantity?

Symbolic constants are defined in C language as shown below

```
#define MAX 20
```

It is convenient and also advantageous to define an array size in terms of symbolic constant rather than a fixed integer quantity.

```
int  array1{MAX];
```

This makes easier to modify a program that utilizes an array, since all references to the maximum array size (Eg., with in for loops as well as in array definitions) can be altered simply by changing the value of the symbolic constant.

2(e). Write a program to find the largest element in an array.

```
// maxarray.c Program to find maximum in an array using pointers
#include<stdio.h>
#include<conio.h>
#include<stdlib.h>
// Function prototypes
int FindMax( int *a , int n);
void SortArray( int *a , int n);

void main()
 {  int i, n, max; // n= no of values in an array
   int *x;  // x is a pointer to an array

   printf("how many elements in your array?<n>\n");
   scanf("%d",&n);

   // allocate dynamic memory space using malloc()
   x=(int*)malloc(n*sizeof(int));
   // read in the array
   for (i=0;i<n;i++)
     { printf("\n value for %d element=",i+1);
        scanf("%d",x+i); // scanf needs address. we have
     }                        // given address when we write x+i
   printf("\n The entered array is....\n");
   for (i=0;i<n;i++)
     printf("%d   ",*(x+i)); // same as writing x[i]
```

```
  // call Findmax function
  max=FindMax(x,n);//x is a pointer to array
  printf("\n maximum value of given array = %d ",max);
 }//end of main

// Fn definitions
int FindMax(int *x, int n)
{ int max,i;

  max=*x; // *x is the value of 1 element
  for(i=1;i<n;i++)
  { if (max<*(x+i))
        max=*(x+i);
  }
  return max;
} // end of FindMax
```

3(a). What is the use of struct keyword? Explain the use of dot operator? Give an example for each.

Ans:

"struct" is a required keyword for declaring the structures. C supports a constructed data type known as structure, which is a method of packing data of different types. A structure is a convenient tool for handling a group of logically related data items.

In general terms the composition of a structure may be defined as:

```
            struct tag
            {
                        member1;
                        member2;
                        …………
                        membern;
            };
```

Example:

```
            struct account
            {
                        int acct_no;
                        char acct_type;
                        char name[80];
                        float balance;
```

```
};
```

dot operator(.) :

The members of a structure are usually processed individually, as separate entities, Therefore, we must be able to access the individual structure members. A structure member can be accessed by writing

variable.member

where variable refers to the name of a structure-type variable, and member refers to the name of a member within structure. The period(.) that separates the variable name from the member name . This period is an operator; it is a member of the highest precedence group, and its associatively is left to right. From the above example, customer is a structure variable of type account. If we wanted to access the customer's account number, we would write

customer.acct_no

3(b). Write a C program to accept records of the different states using array of structures. The structure should contain cha state, population, literacy rate, and income. Display the state whose literacy rate is highest and whose income is highest.

```
//literat.c
#include<stdio.h>
#include<conio.h>
struct state
{
 char name[20];          /* structure to represent each state */
 int population;
 int literacy_rate;
 int income;
};
void main()
{
 struct state a[25]; /* array of type struct state */
                    /* i.e each element of the array is a structure of type state */
 int n,i;
 int highlit_rate,highincome;
 clrscr();

 printf("enter number of states\n");
 scanf("%d",&n);
 for(i=0;i<n;i++)
 {
        /* reading details of each state */
```

```
    printf("enter name,population(in millions),literacy rate and income(in crores) of state
   %d:\n",i+1);
    scanf("%s",a[i].name);
    scanf("%d",&a[i].population);
    scanf("%d",&a[i].literacy_rate);
    scanf("%d",&a[i].income);
  }
    /* code to compute the state with highest percentage of literacy */
  highlit_rate=0;
  for(i=1;i<n;i++)
  {
   if(a[i].literacy_rate > a[highlit_rate].literacy_rate)
    highlit_rate=i;
  }
  printf("the state with highest percent of literacy is %s\n",a[highlit_rate].name);

   /* code to compute the state with highest income */
  highincome=0;
  for(i=1;i<n;i++)
  {
   if(a[i].income > a[highincome].income)
   highincome=i;
  }
  printf("the state with highest income is %s\n",a[highincome].name);
  getch();
 }
```

4(a). How to use pointers as arguments in a function? Explain through an example.

Ans:

We can pass the address of a variable as an argument to a function. When we pass addresses to a function, the dummy parameters receiving these pointers which are pointers , should be pointers. The process of calling a function using pointers to pass the addresses of variables is known as **call by reference**.. Function once receives a data item by reference , it acts on data item and the changes made to the data item also reflects on the calling function.

Consider the following code:

```
        void change(int * val); // function prototypei
    void main()
        {
            int x;
```

```
        x=20;
        change(&x);
        printf("%d\n",x);
    }
void change(int * p)
{   int *p;
    *p= *p + 10;
}
```

When the function change() is called, **the address of the variable x i.e. & x , not its value i.e. x** , is passed into the function change(). Inside change(), the variable p is declared as a pointer and therefore p is the address of the variable x. The statement

*p=*p + 10;

means 'add 10 to the value stored at the address p'. Since p represents the address of x, the value of x is changed from 20 to 30. Therefore, the output of the program will be 30, not 20.

Thus, call by reference provides a mechanism by which the function can change the stored values in the calling function.

4(b). Write a C function using pointers to exchange the values in two locations in the memory.

The function for exchanging the values in two locations in the memory is as follows:

```
//ptrswap.c
#include <stdio.h>
#include <stdlib.h>
// declaration of function prototypes
void Swap( int a , int b); // call by value
void PtrSwap ( int *a , int * b); // Call by Ref. a & b are pointers by def.

void main()
{   int x = 5;
    int y=10;
    // call by value
    Swap( x,y);
    printf("\nafter call by value : x= %d  : y = %d " , x,y);
    // call by reference. Note that we have to send pointers i.e. addresses
    //of x & y . Hence we will pass &x , and & y.
    PtrSwap( &x, &y);
    printf("\nafter call by ref : x= %d  : y = %d " , x,y);
}//end of main
// Function definitions
void Swap ( int a, int b)
```

```
{   int temp ; // two local variables
    temp=a;
    a=b;
    b=temp;
    printf("\ninside  Swap  : a= %d   : b = %d " , a,b);
}
void PtrSwap ( int *a, int  *b)
 { // a & b are pointers . Hence we need a pointer called temp
    int *temp ;
    *temp=*a;
     *a =*b;
    *b= *temp;
    printf("\ninside  Swap  : a= %d   : b = %d " , a,b);
}
/*OUTPUT:
inside  Swap  : a= 10   : b = 5
after call by value : x= 5  : y = 10*/
```

5 (a). Write in detail about the following:

a) Recursion

b) Applications of Stacks and Queues

Ans:

a) Recursion

Recursion is a process by which a function calls itself repeatedly, until some specified condition has been satisfied. The process is used for repetitive computations in which action is stated in terms of a previous result. Many iterative problems can be written in this form:

In order to solve a problem recursively, two conditions must be satisfied. First the problem must be written in recursive form, and second, the problem statement must include stopping statement.

Eg: The following is the factorial of a number program:

```
#include<stdio.h>
long int factorial(int n);
main()
{
        int n;
        long int factorial(int n);
        printf(" n = ");
```

```
        scanf(" %d" , &n);
        printf(" n! = %ld \n" , factorial(n));
}

long int factorial(int n)
{
        if (n = =1)
                return (1);
        else
                return(n*factorial(n-1));
}
```

in the function module , it can be observed that finding factorial depends on the factorial of previous result i.e. factorial of (n-1). We are aware that 1! Is equal to 0. This is infact termination condition for a recursive call.

If a recursive function contains local variables, a different set of local variables will be created during each call. The names of the local variables will be the same as declared within the function. However variables will represent a different set of values each time the function is executed. Each set of variables will be stored in the stack. so that they will be available as and when recursive algorithm calls the previous values. The stack data structure is used for the recursive call mechanism.

b) Applications of stacks and queues

A queue is very similar to the way we queue up for any purpose. A Queue is a linear, sequential list of items that are accessed in the order First In First Out (FIFO). That is the first item inserted in a queue is also the first item to be accessed, the second item inserted will be the second item to be accessed and so on. We cannot store/ access the items in a queue arbitrarily or in any random fashion.

When we create a queue the two simple functions that are to be used are: write and read. The write function adds a new item to the queue, whereas the read function reads one item from the queue.

A queue can be used to store a list of interrupts in the operating system, which would get processed in the order in which they were generated. A queue can also be used to represent the records in a database in memory.

A Stack is exactly opposite to the queue. Items in the queue exit in the same way they had entered the queue. Therefore queue is called as a FIFO structure. A stack is called as Last In First Out (LIFO) structure, because the item that entered the stack last is the first item to get out. Similarly first item is the last item to go out from the stack.

Stacks are extensively used in computer applications. Their most notable use is in system software (such as compilers, operating systems etc).

Stack uses the following two functions: Push and Pop. To write a value to the stack we have to use the push operation, whereas to read a value from the stack we have to use the pop operation. The pop operation is destructive. That is, once an item is popped from the stack the value will no longer retain in the stack.

6. What is a single linked list? Explain various operations on single linked list with algorithms

Ans:

We know that a list refers to a set of items organized sequentially. An array is an example of a list. A completely different way to represent a list is to make each item in the list part of a structure that also contains a "link" to the structure containing the next item, as shown in the figure below.

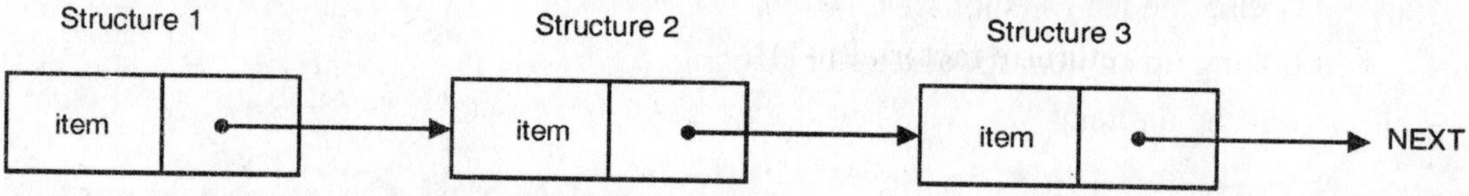

This type of list is called a linked list because it is a list whose order is given by links from one item to the next. Each structure of the list is called a node and consists of two fields, one containing the item and other containing the address of the next item (a pointer to the next item) in the list. A linked list is therefore a collection of structures ordered not by their physical placement in memory (like a carry) but by logical links that are stored as part of the data in the structure itself. The link is in the form of a pointer to another structure of the same type. Such a structure is represented as follows:

```
struct node
{
    int item;
    struct node *next;
};
```

The first member is an integer item and the second a pointer to the next node in the list as shown below. The item referred here can be any complex data type.

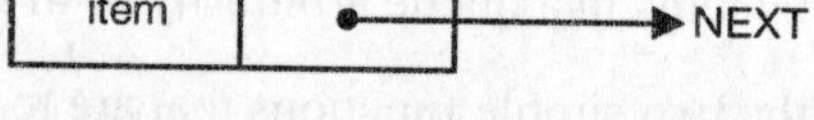

Such structures which contain a member field that point to the same structure type is called ***self referential structures.*** A node may be represented in general form as follows:

```
struct tag-name
{
    type member1;
    typemember2;
    ........
    ........
    struct tag-name *next;
};
```

The structure may contain more than one item with different data types. And in these, one of the items must be a pointer of the type tag-name.

BASIC LIST OPERATIONS:

We can treat a linked list as an abstract data type and perform the following basic operations:

1. Creating a list
2. Traversing the list
3. Counting the items in the list
4. Printing the list (or sublist)
5. Looking up an item for editing or printing
6. Inserting an item
7. Deleting an item
8. Concatenating two lists

INSERTING AN ITEM:

Inserting a new item, say X, into the list has three situations:

1. Insertion at the front of the list.
2. Insertion in the middle of the list.
3. Insertion at the end of the list.

The process of insertion precedes a search for the place of insertion. The search involves in locating a node after which the new item is to be inserted. A general algorithm for insertion is as follows:

```
Begin
        if the list is empty or
                the new node comes before the head node then,
                insert the new node as the head node,
        else
                If the new node comes after the last node, then,
                   Inset the new node as the end node,
            else
                Insert the new node in the body of the list.
End
```

Algorithm for placing the new item at the beginning of a linked list:

1. Obtain space for new node.
2. Assign data to the item field of new node.
3. Set the next field of the new node to point to the start of the list.
4. Change the head pointer to point to the new node.

Algorithm for placing the new node 'X' between two existing nodes: 'N1' and 'N2':

1. Set space for new node 'X'.
2. Assign value to the item field of 'X'.
3. Set the next field of 'X' to point to node 'N2'.
4. Set next field of 'N1' to point to 'X'.

Algorithm for placing the new item at the end of a linked list:

The algorithm is similar to the one for inserting in the middle except the next field of new node is set to 'NULL'.

1. Set space for new node 'X'.
2. Assign value to the item field of 'X'.
3. Set the next field of 'X' to point to NULL.
4. Set next field of 'N1' to point to 'X'.

Algorithm for deleting an element : we will delete node from linked list given a position.

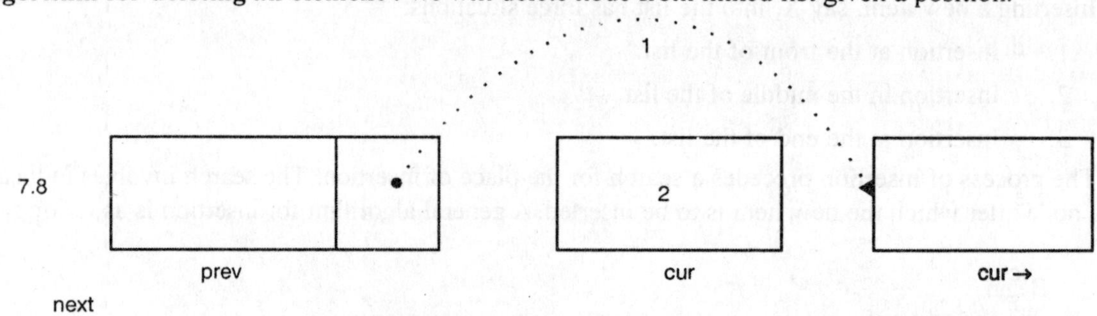

Linked List showing prev,cur,cur->next nodes

04. Locate the position to be deleted by traversing the List. Traversal can be based on finding position or finding a value of a node to be deleted. Cur is the node to be deleted.
05. Point prev → next to current → next.
06. Delete current node. We have to check if the node we are deleting is the first node. If yes we have to readjust the front pointer.

7(a). Write a C program to implement binary tree traversals

Tree being a non linear data structure , there is no fixed mode or sequence of traversal. There are three modes for traversal of a tree. All algorithms use recursive call feature. They are

In Order Traversal

Traverse Left sub Tree inorder

Visit the root

Traverse the Right sub tree inorder

Pre Order Traversal (Depth First Order – Stack data structure)

Visit the root

Traverse left sub Tree preorder.

Traverse the right sub tree preorder

Post Order Traversal (Breadth First Traversal – queue data structure)

Traverse left sub Tree postorder.

Traverse the right sub tree postorder

Visit the root

Tree traversals using recursion. recurtraves.c

```
/* binary tree operations and tree traversals */
// recurtraves.c
#include<stdio.h> //preprocessor
#include<stdlib.h>//preprocessor
struct Tree//structure definition
{ int data;
  struct Tree *lptr;
  struct Tree *rptr;
};
typedef struct Tree node;
//function declarations
node *createtree(node *root);
node *insert(int n,node *root);
void preorder(node *root);
void inorder(node *root);
void postorder(node *root);

void main()//main function
{
      node *root=NULL;
      int c=0;
      while(1)
      {
            printf("\n\n\t\tMENU");
            printf("\n\t1: CREATE\n\t2: POSTORDER");
            printf("\n\t3: INORDER\n\t4: PREORDER\n\t5: EXIT");
```

```
            printf("\n\n\tEnter your choice:");
            scanf("%d",&c);
            switch(c)
            {
                  case 1:root=createtree(root);
                        break;
                  case 2: postorder(root);
                        break;
                  case 3: inorder(root);
                        break;
                  case 4: preorder(root);
                        break;
                  case 5: exit(0);
                        break;
      default: printf("\nEnter values between 1 and 5 only");

            }//end switch
      }//end while
}//end main
void preorder(node *root)//preorder function
{
      if(root==NULL)
      { printf("\n\tEMPTY TREE");
        exit(1);
      }//end if
      printf("%5d",root->data);
      if(root->lptr!=NULL)
            preorder(root->lptr);
      if(root->rptr!=NULL)
            preorder(root->rptr);
}//end preorder
void inorder(node *root)//inorder function
{
      if(root==NULL)
      { printf("\n\tEMPTY TREE");
        exit(1);
      }//end if
      if(root->lptr!=NULL)
            inorder(root->lptr);
```

```
        printf("%5d",root->data);
        if(root->rptr!=NULL)
                inorder(root->rptr);
}//end inorder
void postorder(node *root)
{
        if(root==NULL)
        { printf("\n\tEMPTY TREE");
                exit(1);
        }//end if
        if(root->lptr!=NULL)
                postorder(root->lptr);
        if(root->rptr!=NULL)
                postorder(root->rptr);
        printf("%5d",root->data);
}//end postorder
node *createtree(node *root)
 { int n;
        do{ printf("\nEnter number<0 to stop>:");
            scanf("%d",&n);
                if(n!=0)
                        root= insert(n,root);
                }while(n!=0);
   return(root);
 }
node *insert(int n,node *root)
{
  node *temp1=NULL;
  node *temp2=NULL;
  node *p=NULL;

                p=(node *)malloc (sizeof(node));//dynamic allocation of memory foe each element
                p->data=n;    //initialize contents of the structure
                p->lptr=NULL;
                p->rptr=NULL;

   //A new node has been created now our task is to insert this node
        //in the appropriate place.If this is the first node to be created
        //then this is the root of the tree.
```

```
        if(root==NULL)
                root=p;
        else
                // We will use temp1 for traversing the tree.
                // Temp2 will be traversing parent
                // p is the new node we have created.
                {  temp1=root;
        while(temp1!=NULL)
                  { temp2=temp1; // store it as parent
                    // Traverse through left or right sub tree
                    if(p->data < temp1->data)
               temp1 = temp1->lptr;  // left subtree
             else
                     if(p->data > temp1->data)
                             temp1 = temp1->rptr; // right sub tree
        else
                             {
                                     printf("\n\tDUPLICATE VALUE");
                                     free(p);
                                     break;
                             }//end else
                  } //end of while
                // we have trvered to the enode of tree
                // anode ready for insetion
                 if(temp1 == NULL)
                 { // attach either as left son or right son of parent temp2
                         if(p->data<temp2->data)
               temp2->lptr=p; // attach as left son
    else
                temp2->rptr=p; // attach as right son
                 }
                }//end of else
    return(root);
}
```

8. Explain the algorithm for selection sort and give a suitable example.

Selection Sort : Compare 1st element with all other elements in each iteration set lowest as minimum(Min). At the end of iteration swap min and 1st element. Now continue with 2nd element same procedure. Continue with this procedure till entire array is exhausted.

EXAMPLE :

Input Array :

22	34	10	55	14

Array :

Initialization set Min = 22

Iteration 1 :

Array	Comparison	new Min
22, 34, 10, 55, 14	(22,34)	22
22, 34, 10, 55, 14	(22,10)	10
22, 34, 10, 55, 14	(10,55)	10
22, 34, 10, 55, 14	(10,14)	10

Swap (22,10)

10	34	22	55	14

Min value is put into place

Iteration 2 :

Array	Comparison	new Min
10, 34, 22, 55, 14	(34,22)	22
10, 34, 22, 55, 14	(22,55)	22
10, 34, 22, 55, 14	(22,14)	14

Swap (34,14)

10	14	22	34	55

Iteration 3 : (Min = 22)

Comparison new Min

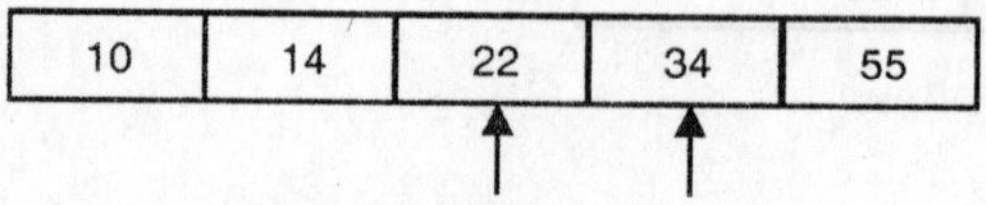

(22,34) 22

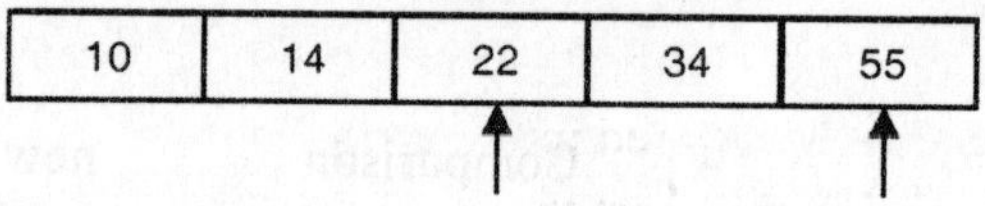

(22,55) 22

Iteration 4 : (Min = 34)

Comparison new Min

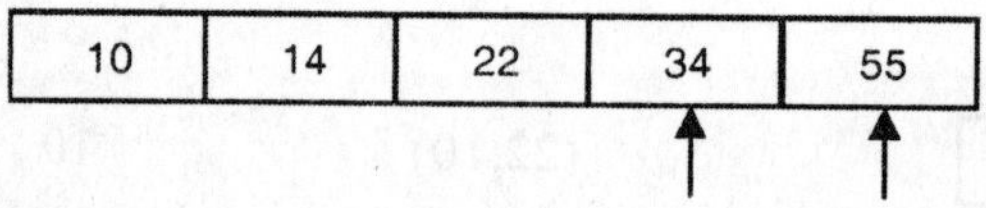

(34,55) 34

Sorted Array =

10	14	22	34	55

Length of array = 5

Note: No. of iterations = 4 = (5-1) = (length – 1)

Algorithm :

```
Selectsort(sort[],len)
for i=0 to i<len-1 do
begin
        min=i
        for j=i+1     j<len do
        begin
                if[sort[j] < sort[min]
                        min=j
                end
        if(min != i)
                swap(sort[min],sort[i])
        end
```

Program:selection.c

```
//program to demonstrate selection sort
#include<stdio.h>
#include<stdlib.h>
void selectsort(int sort[],int len);

void main()
{int len,i=0;
```

```
 int sort[30];
 printf("\n enter no<0 to stop>");
  scanf("%d",&sort[i]);
  while(sort[i]!=0)
        {i++;
   printf("\n enter no<0 to stop>");
         scanf("%d",&sort[i]);
        }
        len=i; //length is taken as i and not as i+1 as 0 is also stored in the array
   selectsort(sort,len); //call the function selectsort which will sort the array
  printf("\n **** Sorted Array **** \n");
         for(i=0;i<len;i++)
                   printf("%d\t",sort[i]);
}
void selectsort(int sort[],int len)
{int i,j,temp,min;
  for(i=0;i<len-1;i++)
        {min=i;
   for(j=i+1;j<len;j++)
          {if(sort[j]<sort[min])
                 min=j;
          }
   if(min!=i)
          {temp=sort[min];
                 sort[min]=sort[i];
                 sort[i]=temp;
          }
         }//end of for(i)
}//end of select sort
```

For the first iteration the number of inner loop iterations is n-1 for the second iteration the no. of inner loop iterations is n-2 continuing we get total no. of iterations is

$$(n-1)+(n-2)+(n-3)+\dots\dots\dots+1 = n(n-1)/2$$

Therefore, complexity of Selection sort is $O(n^2)$. The number of interchanges is always n-1. Hence selection sort is $O((n^2)$ for both best case and the worst case.

Code No: RR10203 Set No.1

Apr/May 2006

1(a). Write the various steps involved in executing a C program and illustrate it with a help of flowchart.

Executing a program written in C involves a series of steps. These are:

1. Creating the program.
2. Compiling the program.
3. Linking the program with functions that are needed from the C library.
4. Executing the program.

The following figure illustrates the process of creating, compiling and executing a C program.

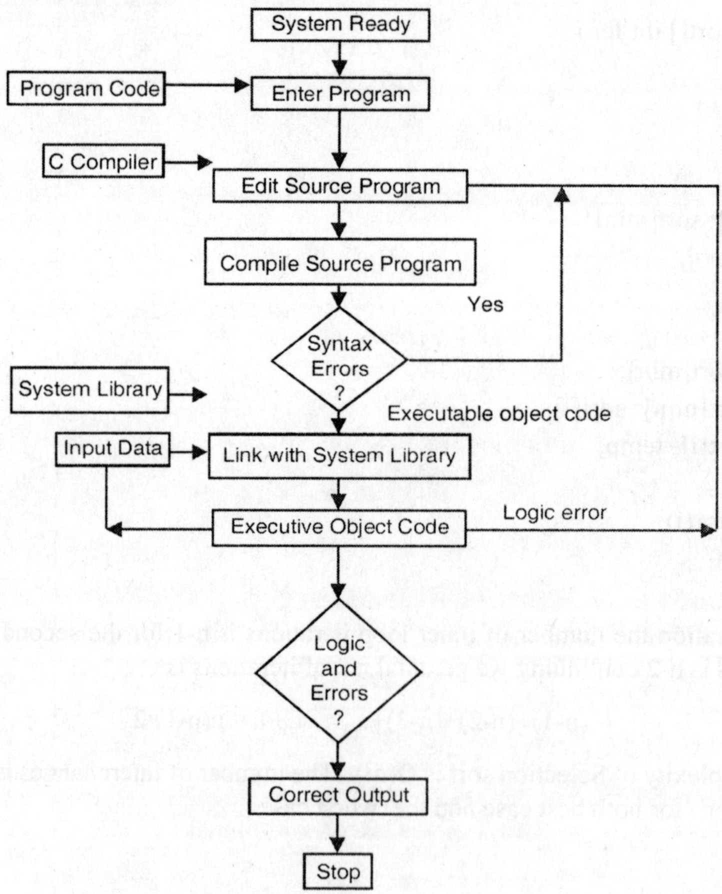

Creating the program:

Once we load the Operating system into the memory, the computer is ready to receive the program. The program must be entered into a file. Examples of valid filenames are hello.c, program1.c, etc. When the editing is over, the file is saved on the disk. The program that is entered into the file is known as the Source program, since it represents the original form of the program.

Compiling and linking:

When the compilation command for a file is given (varies for different versions) the source program instructions are translated into a form that is suitable for execution by the computer. The translation is done after examining each instruction for its correctness. If everything is alright, the compilation proceeds silently and the translated program is stored on another file with a different file name having .o or .obj extension called Object Code.

Linking is the process of putting together other program files and functions that are required by the program. If mistakes in the syntax and semantics of the language are discovered, they are listed out and the compilation process ends right there. The errors should be corrected in the source program with the help of the editor and the compilation is done again.

The compiled and linked program is called the Executable object code.

Executing the program:

Execution is a simple task. When the command for the execution is given, it will load the executable object code into the computer memory and execute the instructions. During execution the program may request for some data to be entered through the keyboard. If the program doesn't produce correct results, it means that there is a logic or data error in the program. Then it would be necessary to correct the source program or the data. In case the source program is modified, the entire process of compiling, linking and executing the program should be repeated.

Creation compilation and running your program

Use any text editor like notepad, vi editor etc and enter your code and save it as ball1.c.

Compile it using #gcc ball.c   Output using # a.out for Linux based system

Run —— Compile —— Execute for Turbo C

Compile and Run your program. Now we are ready for dabbling our foot ball using arrays!

Programming and executing in Linux environment:

1. Switch on the computer.
2. Select the Red hat Linux environment.
3. Right click on the desk top. Select 'New Terminal'.
4. After getting the $ symbol, type ***'vi filename.c'*** and press Enter.
5. ***Press Esc+I*** to enter into Insert mode and then type your program there.

   The other modes are Append and Command modes.

6. After completion of entering program, press ***(Esc + Shift + :)***.

   This is to save your program in the editor.

7. Then the cursor moves to the end of the page.

   Type 'wq' and press Enter.

   (wq=write and quit)

8. On $ prompt type, cc ***filename.c*** and press Enter.

9. If there are any errors, go back to your program and correct them.

   Save and Compile the program again after corrections.

10. If there are no errors, run the program by typing

    ./a.out and press Enter.

11. To come out of the terminal, at the dollar prompt, ***type 'exit'*** and press Enter.

1(b). Candidates have to score 90 or above in the IQ test to be considered eligible for taking further tests. All candidates who do not clear the IQ test are sent reject letters and others are sent call letters for further tests. Represent the logic for automating this task.

Ans:

From the data given call letters should be sent only to the students who scored 90 or above in the IQ test and others are sent reject letters.

Algorithm:

Step 1: Start.

Step 2: Read the name of the student.

Step 3: Read the value of marks scored.

Step 4: Continue the steps 2,3 until all students' marks are entered.

Step 5: Print the name of the student and send him the call letter if he scored 90 or above otherwise send them reject letters.

Step 6: Repeat the above step until all students are verified.

Step 7: Stop.

Program:

```
#include<stdio.h>
struct student
{
  char name[10];
  int marks;
};
main()
{
```

```
        struct student stud[20];
        int i,n;
        printf("Enter the number of students\n");
        scanf("%d",&n);
        for(i=0;i<n;i++)
        {
          printf("Enter the name of the student and his corresponding marks\n");
          scanf("%s %d",&stud[i].name,&stud[i].marks);
        }
        for(i=0;i<n;i++)
        {
          if(stud[i].marks>=90)
            printf("%s is selected \n",stud[i].name);
          else
            printf("%s is not selected \n",stud[i].name);
        }
      }
```

2. **The annual examination is conducted for 50 students for three subjects. Write a program to read the data and determine the following**

   (a) Total marks obtained by each student

   (b) The highest marks in each subject and roll number of the student who secured it.

   (c) The student who obtained the highest total marks.

```
    //stdmarks.c
#include<stdio.h>
struct student
{       int num,subject1,subject2,subject3;
        int total;
} st[20];
int max(int m,int n); // function prototype

void main()
{       int i,j,n;
        printf("enter the number of students\n");
        scanf("%d",&n);
        for(i=0;i<n;i++)
        {       printf("enter the number\n");
                scanf("%d",&st[i].num);
                printf("enter the marks of the three subjects\n");
                scanf("%d%d%d",&st[i].subject1,&st[i].subject2,&st[i].subject3);
```

```
        }
        for(i=0;i<n;i++)
        {           st[i].total=st[i].subject1+st[i].subject2+st[i].subject3;
                    printf("the marks secured by %d are %d\n",st[i].num,st[i].total);
        }
        j=max(1,n);
printf("maximum marks obtained in subject1 are %d by roll no %d\n",st[j].subject1,st[j].num);
        j=max(2,n);
        printf("maximum marks obtained in subject2 are %d by roll
        no%d\n",st[j].subject2,st[j].num);
        j=max(3,n);
        printf("maximum marks obtained in subject3 are %d by roll
        no%d\n",st[j].subject3,st[j].num);
        j=max(0,n);
        printf("maximum total marks obtained are %d by roll no%d\n",st[j].total,st[j].num);
}
//function definitions
int max(int m,int n)
{       int t=-1,i,j;
        for(i=0;i<n;i++)
        {   switch(m)
                {  case 1:
                        if(st[i].subject1>t)
                        {t=st[i].subject1; j=i;
                        }
                    break;
                  case 2:
                        if(st[i].subject2>t)
                        {t=st[i].subject2;j=i;
                        }
                    break;
                  case 3:
                        if(st[i].subject3>t)
                        {t=st[i].subject3;j=i;
                        }
                    break;
                default:
                        if(st[i].total>t)
                        { t=st[i].total;
                          j=i;
```

```
            }
        }//end of switch
    }// end of max
    return j;
}
```

3(a). How are structure elements accessed using pointer? Which operator is used? Give an example.

(b). Write a program to use structure within union. Display the contents of structure elements.

Ans:

(a) Structure is a collection of data items of different data types. A structure is a convenient tool for handling a group of logically related data items. They help us to organize complex data in a more meaningful way. The general format of a structure definition is as follows

```
struct  tag_name
{
    data_type  member1;
    data_type  member2;
    ....       ....
    ....       ....
};
```

Pointers and structures:

We know that the name of an array stands for the address of its zeroth element. The same thing is true of the names of arrays of structure variables. Suppose 'product' is an array variable of struct type. The name product represents the address of its zeroth element. Consider the following declaration

```
struct inventory
{
        char name[30];
        int number;
    float price;
        } product[2].*ptr;
```

This statement declares product as n array of two elements, each of the type struct inventory and ptr as a pointer to data objects of the type struct inventory.

The assignment ptr = product; would assign the address of the zeroth element of product to ptr. That is, the pointer ptr will now point to product[0]. Its members can be accessed using the following notation.

ptr->name
ptr->number
ptr->price

The symbol -> is called the arrow operator and is made up of a minus sign and a greater than sign. Note that ptr-> is simply another way of writing product [0]. When ptr is incremented by one, it is made to point to the next record, i.e., product[1].

We could also use notation (*ptr).number to access the member number.

EXAMPLE:

```
//structptr.c
#include<stdio.h>
#include<stdlib.h>
// struct declaration
struct date
{
 int dd;
 int mm;
 int yy;
};
struct Account
{
 int accNo;
 char accType;
 char name[20];
 float bal;
 struct date pdate;
};
typedef struct Account acct;
acct cust,*ptr; // ptr is a pointer to structure
// fn decl
void ReadInput(acct *cust); // cust is a pointer to structure
void Update(acct *cust);
void WriteOutput(acct *cust);

void main()
{
acct cust; // create an instance of structure acct
 // read data into structure by passing a pointer to structure
//to ReadInput().
```

```
  ReadInput(&cust); //&cust would imply address of cust i.e pointer
 // Update status of account
  Update(&cust); // we are again passing pointer
 //write output
  WriteOutput(&cust);
 }// end of main
// fn defenitions
void ReadInput(acct *cust)
{  float bal;
  printf("\n enter data for  account holder");
  printf("\nEnter <name>:");scanf("%s",cust->name);
  printf("\nEnter <accNo>:");scanf("%d",&cust->accNo);
  printf("\nEnter <accType>:");cust->accType=getche();
  printf("\nEnter <balance>:");scanf("%f",&bal);cust->bal=bal;
  printf("\nEnter pdate<dd mm yy>:");
  scanf("%d%d%d",&cust->pdate.dd,&cust->pdate.mm,&cust->pdate.yy);
  printf("\n------------------------------------------");

}
 void WriteOutput(acct *cust)
{  printf("\n------------------------------------------");
  printf("\nname:");printf("%s",cust->name);
  printf("\naccNo:");printf("%d",cust->accNo);
  printf("\naccType:");printf("%c",cust->accType);
  printf("\nbalance:");printf("%g",cust->bal);
  printf("\npdate<ddmmyy>:");
  printf("%d-%d-%d",cust->pdate.dd,cust->pdate.mm,cust->pdate.yy);
}

void Update(acct *cust)
{
 //if the balance is more than 1000.00 set accType as current(c)
 // and add 10% of balance to balance amount as Interst. Else
 //classify the account as inactive(I)
 if(cust->bal>=1000.00)
  {
   cust->bal+=cust->bal*0.1;
   cust->accType='C';
  }
```

```
else
  cust->accType='I';

}
```

b) A program to use a structure with in a union

```
/* program to use structure with in union */

//union1.c
#include<stdio.h>
#include<ctype.h>
// union declaration
struct Account
{char name[20];
};
union details
{ int accNo;
 char accType;
 struct Account acc;
};
typedef union details acct;
// fn decl
acct ReadInput(acct cust);
void WriteOutput1(acct cust);
void WriteOutput2(acct cust);
acct Update(acct cust);
acct Update2(acct cust);
void WriteOutput3(acct cust);
void main()
{  acct cust; // create an instance of union acct
 /* read data into union by union to ReadInput()
  that returns union filled with data*/
   cust=ReadInput(cust);
 // after ReadInput cust.accNo is active
   WriteOutput1(cust);
 // Update status of account
   cust=Update(cust);
   WriteOutput2(cust);
```

```
 cust=Update2(cust); Update2 modifies the name
//After Update2() function only cust.acct.name is active.
 WriteOutput3(cust);
}// end of main
// fn defenitions

acct ReadInput(acct cust)
{ printf("\n enter data for  account holder");
 printf("\nEnter <name>:");scanf("%s",cust.acc.name);
   printf("\nEnter <accNo>:");scanf("%d",&cust.accNo);
   printf("\n________________________________________");
  return cust;
}
void WriteOutput1(acct cust)
{ printf("\noutput after calling ReadInput()");
  printf("\n\nNow cust.accNo is active.....");
  printf("\naccNo:");printf("%d",cust.accNo);
}
acct Update(acct cust)
{ if(cust.accType=='C')
    cust.accType='D';
  else
     cust.accType='C';
  return cust;
}
void WriteOutput2(acct cust)
{ printf("\n\noutput after calling Update()");
  printf("\n\nNow cust.accType is active.....");
  printf("\naccType:");printf("%c",cust.accType);
}
acct Update2(acct cust)
{ printf("\nEnter Ammended <name>:");
  scanf("%s",cust.acc.name);
   return cust;
}
void WriteOutput3(acct cust)
{ printf("\n\noutput after calling Update2()");
  printf("\n\nNow cust.acc.name is active.....");
  printf("\nname:");printf("%s",cust.acc.name);
```

}

4.(a) Distinguish between the following functions
i. printf and fprintf
ii. eof and ferror

(b) Write a program to copy the contents of one file into another.

(a)

i) printf: It is a predefined (means that it is a function that has already been written and compiled, and linked together with our program at the time of linking) standard C function for printing output. The printf causes everything between the starting and the ending quotation marks to be printed out.

E.g. printf("this is demonstration");

In the above example the output will be

this is demonstration

The printf can take multiple arguments also including any values of the variables to be output.

The format for printf statement is : printf(format, arg1,arg2..)

Consider the following example

E.g. printf("%d\n",number);

The above example the first argument "%d" tells the compiler that the value of the second argument number should be printed as a decimal integer. The new line character \n causes the next output to appear on a new line. It prints out the data given to it on to the screen.

Other Control formats available for printf are:

%c	Character
%d	Decimal integer
%h	Short integer
%i	Decimal , octal(prefix by 0) , Hexadecimal(prefix by 0x)
%o	Octal integer
%u	Unsigned decimal integer
%x	Hexadecimal
%f	Float
%e	Float , double precision
%g	Float
%s	String followed by null character (\0 will be added automatically)

fprintf:

The function fprintf perform I/O operations that is identical to printf, except of course that they work on files. The first argument of this function is a file pointer which specifies the file to be used. The general form of fprintf is

fprintf(fp,"control string",list);

Where fp is a file pointer associated with a file that has been opened for writing. The control string contains output specifications for the items in the list. The list may include variables, constants and strings.

EXAMPLE :

```
fprintf(f1,%s %d %f",name,age,7.5);
```

```
/*a program demonstrating the usage of printf and fprintf */
  #include<stdio.h>
  main()
  {
    FILE *fp;
    char text[30];
    fp = fopen("text .txt","w");
    printf("enter text here\n");
    gets(text);
    fprintf(fp,"%s",text);
    fclose(fp);
  }
```

ii) EOF:

It specifies the end of file that is the end of a data in a file is indicated by entering an EOF character, which is control-Z in reference system. When any function encounters the ending of file it returns an EOF character.

ferror:

It is possible that an error may occur during I/O operations on a file. They include device overflow, trying to use unopened file, opening a file with an invalid filename, trying to read beyond the end-of-file mark, attempting to write a write protected file etc. they may result in abnormal termination of the program. To avoid such results ferror help us to detect I/O errors in the files.

The ferror function report the status of the file indicated. It also takes a FILE pointer as its argument and returns a nonzero integer if an error has been detected upto that point, during processing. It returns zero otherwise. The statement

```
if(ferror(fp)!=0)
        printf("an error has occurred\n");
```

would print the error message, if the reading is not successful.

```
/*a program to demonstrate the usage of EOF and ferror( ) */

        #include<stdio.h>
```

```
#include<process.h>
#include<conio.h>

void main()
{
  FILE *f;
  char c;
  f = fopen("test.c"."w");
  if(f == NULL)
  {
    printf("\n cannot open");
    exit(0);
  }
  while((c=fgetc(f))!= EOF)
  {
    if(ferror(f))
    {
      printf("\n can't read file");
      fclose(f);
      exit(1);
    }
    printf("%c",c);
    getch();
  }
  fclose(f);
}
```

(b) Write a program to copy a file on to another file

```
/*Write a program to copy a file from source to destinations*/
//fcopy.c
#include<stdio.h>
#include<stdlib.h>
void main()
{       char c;
        char file1[10],file2[10];
        FILE *fp1,*fp2;
        printf("Enter a input file name: ");
        scanf("%s",file1);
        printf("Enter output file name: ");
```

```
scanf("%s",file2);
fp1 = fopen(file1, "r");
if (fp1 == NULL)
{ printf("Error opening file \n");
   exit(1);
}
else
{        fp2=fopen(file2,"w");
         if (fp2 == NULL)
         { printf("Error opening file\n");
            exit(1);
         }
        else
            while( ( c=getc(fp1))!=EOF)
                putc(c,fp2);
          printf("successful copy operation\n");
}
} // end of main
```

5. Write in detail about the following
a) Circular queue b) Dequeue

(a) Circular queue-array representation

Linear queue suffers from one major drawback . When the first element is serviced , the front is moved to next element. However , the position vacated is not available for further use. Thus , we may encounter a situation , wherein program shows that queue is full , while all the whose elements have been deleted are available but unusable , though empty. The situation is shown in fig 1 As a solution , we would consider a superior data structure called circular queue . Look at the fig 2.showing an empty circular queue. Observe that both front and rear are initialized to the same position MAX-1 i.e. position9. For programmer only positions available are from 0 to 8. W have sacrificed one position , shown as * in the diagram , in order that we could identify the conditions empty and full for circular queue. Consider following two statements

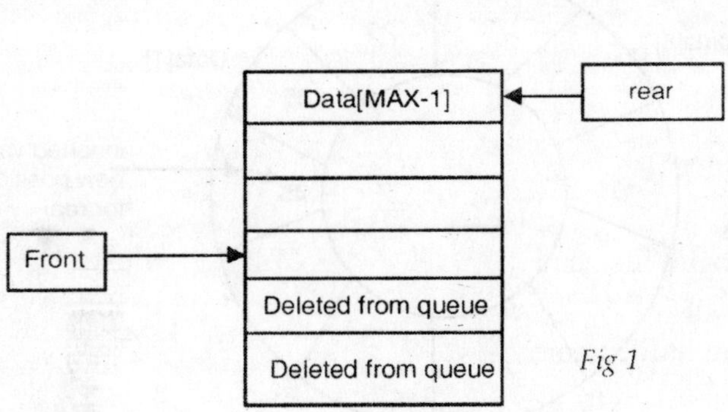

Fig 1

Circular queue is empty if q.rear = = q.front

For checking Full condition , we will increment q.rear and then check

if q.rear= = q.front

In a circular queue , there is no fixed positions for front and rear .

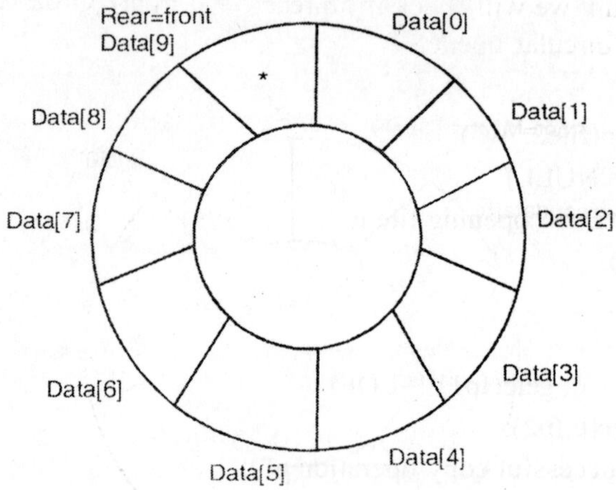

Fig. 2 An Empty circular queue capacity max = 12.

Front always points to beginning of the queue but it does not point to first element. It is always point to one less than first element of the queue.

On Insert operation , rear is incremented by 1.

On delete front pointer is decremented by 1 and front now points to next element in the queue.

In Fig. 3 , insertion of new element is simple operation as queue is NOT full i.e. rear != front. As we are dealing with circular queue , there is a need to wrap around rear if it exceeds Max -1 value. For this activity , we will use %(modulus operator) that give us remainder directly.

Rear = (Rear +1)%(Max)

Rear = (1+1)%10 = 2. Therefore insert element 45 at rear =2

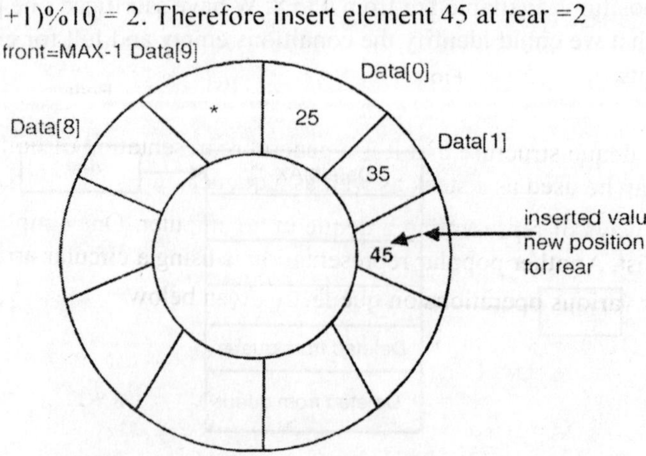

Fig. 3 Insertion in a circular queue that is not full

For checking overflow condition, shown in fig. 4 we will first increment q.rear and check if q.rear = = q.front. If condition is true, it implies that queue is full. Then we will decrement q.rear by one, which we have incremented prior to checking and return to calling function. For example, we want to add element 105 to the queue . as a first step, increment q.rear. Now, we find q.rear is equal to q.front.(9). It means that queue is full Hence we will restore q.rear to original position by decrementing by one. To check if circular queue is full, we will check if (q.rear = = q.front). Observe that condition is same as that of checking for empty circular queue.

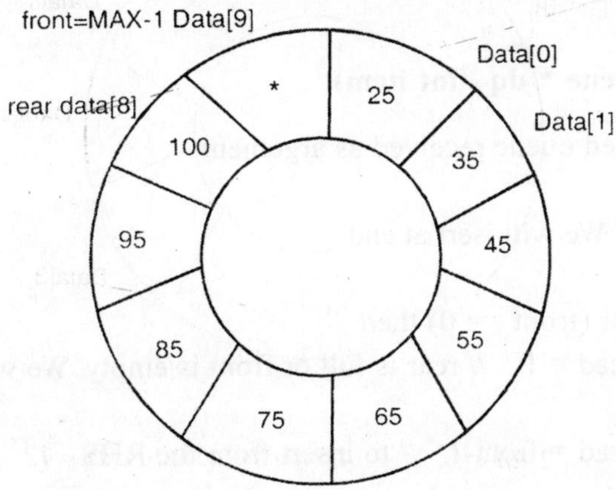

Fig. 4 : Insertion in a circular queue that is full

b) Dequeue

The term dequeue originated from Double Ended Queue. Unlike queue, in dequeue, both insertion and deletion operations can be made at either end of the structure. It can be as shown below.

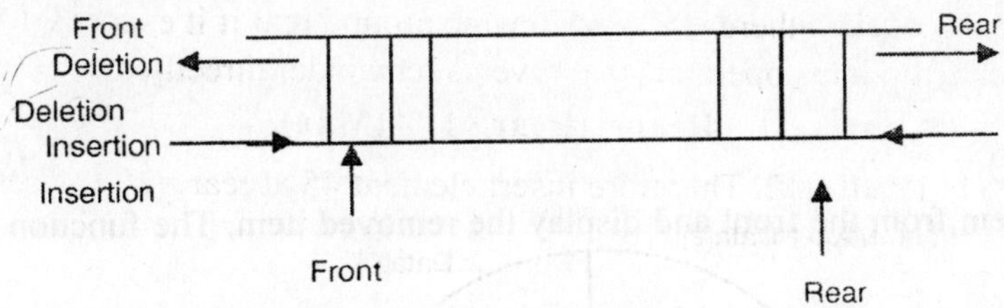

It is clear from the deque structure that it is a general representation of both stack and queue, or in other words, a deque can be used as a stack as well as a queue.

There are various ways of representing a deque in a computer. One simpler way to represent it is using a double linked list. Another popular representation is using a circular array.

The algorithms for various operations on queue are given below.

1. PushFront(item) : To insert ITEM at the front.
2. popfront() : To remove the front ITEM from dequeue
3. pushRear(item) : To insert ITEM at the REAR end of dequeue
4. poprear( ) : To remove the REAR ITEM from dequeue

These operations are described for a deque based on a circular array of size Length len.

The data structure most suited would be circular queue. The prototype function for pushfront() is as follows

dequeue * pushfront(dequeue * dq , int item);

```
    // dq = double ended queue received as argument
    if (front = 1) then
        ahead = len   // We will isert at end
    else
        if(front = len) or (front == 0) then
                    ahead = 1   // rear is full or front is empty. We will insert at LHS
        else
                    ahead = front-1  // to insert from the RHS
        end if
    if (ahead = rear) then
        print "deque is full"
        exit
    else
        front = ahead    // move Front as per insertion side LHS or RHS
        dq[FRONT]=ITEM// insert an item
    return dq;
    stop
```

Algorithm popfront()

To remove an item from the front and display the removed item. The function prototype is shown below.

int popfront(deque * dq)

```
    if (front= = 0) then
        print "queue is empty"
        exit
    else
        Item = dq(front)
        if (front ==REAR) then
```

```
                front = 0
                rear =0
        else
                front= (front % len)+1
        end if
    end if
    stop
```

Algorithm for pushing an element from the rear

```
dequeue * pushfront(dequeue * dq , int item);

        if(front==0) then
        front = 1;
        rear= 1
        dq[front] = item
    else
        nextt = (rear % len)+1
        if(next' != front) then
                rear = next
                dq[rear] = item
        else
                        print "queue is full"
        end if
    end if
    stop
```

Algorithm to pop an element from the rear

int poprear(deque * dq)

```
    if(front == 0) then
        print "deque is emplty"
        exit
    else
        if(front == rear) then
                        item = dq[rear]
                        front = rear = 0
        else
                if(rear == 1) then
                        item = dq[rear]
```

```
                    rear = len
            else
                    if(rear= len) then
                            item = dq[rear]
                            rear = 1
                    else
                            item= dq[rear]
                            rear = rear -1
                    end if
            end if
    end if
    stop
```

6. **Write a C program to implement addition of two polynomials**

Ans:

```
//addpoly.c
#include<stdio.h>
#include<malloc.h>

struct NODE
{
    int p;
    int coeff;
    struct NODE *next;
};

typedef struct NODE NODE;
NODE* CREATEPOLY(int c[],int ord);        /*creates a polynomial*/
void ADD(NODE *A,NODE *B)
{   int y;
    while(A||B)
    {       y = A->coeff+B->coeff;
            if(A->p>B->p)
            {       printf("%dx^%d+",A->coeff,A->p);
                    A = A->next;
            }
            else if(A->p<B->p)
            {       printf("%dx^%d+",B->coeff,B->p);
                    B = B->next;
```

```
                }
                else
                {       printf("%dx^%d+",y,A->p);
                        A = A->next;
                        B = B->next;

                }
        }
        printf("\b");
}
void main()
{       int *c,*d,x,y;
        struct NODE *A,*B,*P,*Q;
        int n,i,m;
        printf("enter the degrees of first and second polynomials\n");
        scanf("%d%d",&n,&m);
        c = (int*)malloc((n+1)*sizeof(int));
        d = (int*)malloc((m+1)*sizeof(int));

        printf("enter the coefficients of the first polynomial:\n");
        for(i=0;i<=n;i++)
                scanf("%d",&c[i]);

        printf("enter the coefficients of the second polynomial\n");
        for(i=0;i<=m;i++)
                scanf("%d",&d[i]);

        A = CREATEPOLY(c,n);
        B = CREATEPOLY(d,m);
        printf("\n the addition result is \n");
        ADD(A,B);
}
NODE* CREATEPOLY(int c[],int ord)       /*creates a polynomial*/
{       int i;
        NODE *H=0,*A;
        for(i=0;i<=ord;i++)
        {       A = (NODE*)malloc(sizeof(NODE));
                A->coeff = c[i];
                A->p = i;
                A->next = H;
```

```
            H=A;
        }
        return (H);
    }
```

7. Write in detail about the following
(a) AVL tree
(b) Binary search tree

(a) AVL tree:

Adilson Velski Landis tree is a height balanced binary search tree in which the balance factor of each node is 0,1,-1. balance factor of each node is defined as the height of left sub tree – the height of right sub tree.

Basic Operations:

1. Construction
2. Search and traversing as a binary search tree.
3. Insert a new item in the AVL tree in such a way that the height balance property is maintained.
4. Delete an item from an AVL tree in such a way that the height balance property is maintained.

Rotation of AVL tree:

A rotation rebalances the part of an AVL tree by rearranging the nods by preserving the relation ship, left<parent<right that must be maintained, for a tree to remain a binary search tree. After a rotation, the balance factors at the nodes in the rotated sub tree should have balance factors –1,0,1(any of them). The different types of rotations are

1. Left rotation
2. Right rotation
3. Left right rotation
4. right left rotation

Left rotation:

It is performed when unbalance occurred due to a new element is inserted into the left of left sub tree of tree T. The rotation steps are

i. Let the root be T and let left is the left child of root. To perform left rotations set the left pointer of T as a right child of left.

ii. Set the right pointer of left to T.

iii. Now left refers to the T.

Right rotation:

It is performed when unbalance occurred due to a new element is inserted into the right of right sub tree of tree T. steps include

i. Set the right pointer of T to the left child of the right.

ii. Set the left pointer of right to T.

Left right rotation:

It is performed when unbalance occurred due to a new element is inserted into the right sub tree of left sub tree of tree T. Let left be the left child of T and grandchild is right child of left. Steps include

i. We set the right pointer of left, to the left child of grandchild.

ii. Next set the left pointer of grand child to the left.

iii. Set the left pointer of T to the right pointer of grand child and right pointer of grand child to T. Finally T refers to the left.

Right left rotation:

It is performed when unbalance occurred due to insertion at the left sub tree of right child of the pivot node.

i. Right sub tree(Br) of the left child(B) of the right child(A) of the pivot node(P) becomes the left sub tree of A.

ii. Right child(A) of the pivot node(p) becomes the right child of B.

iii. Left sub tree(Bl) of the right child (B) of the right child(A) of he pivot node(p) becomes the right subtree of p.

iv. P becomes the left child of B.

Binary Search Tree : Binary search Tree (BST) is an ordered Binary Tree in that it is an empty tree or value of root node is greater than all the values in Left Sub Tree(LST) and less than all the values of Right Sub Tree (RST). Right and Left sub trees are again binary sub trees by themselves.

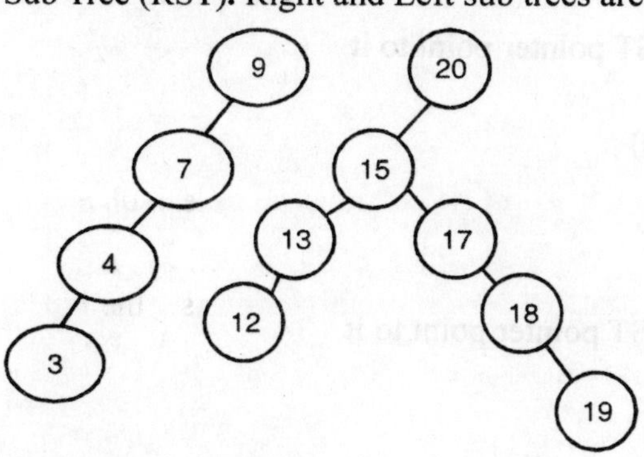

Example of BST

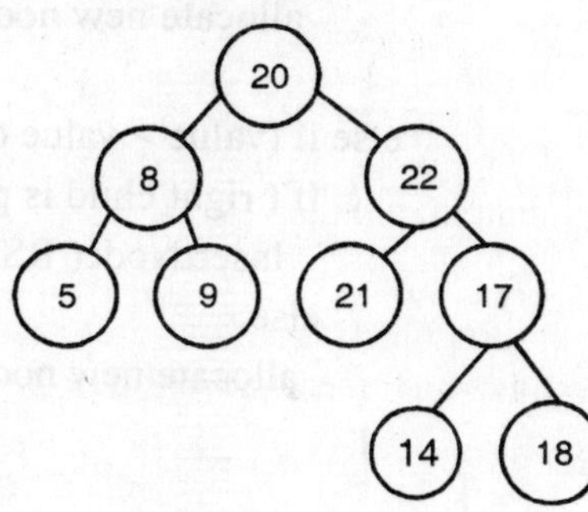

Not a BST. Node 17 violates RST rule

We will be using BST structure to demonstrate features of Binary Trees. The operations possible on a binary tree are

a) Create a Binary Tree
b) Insert a node in a Binary tree
c) Delete a node in a Binary Tree
d) Search for a node in Binary search Tree
e) Traversals of a Binary Tree
   i) In Order traversal
   ii) Pre Order Traversal
   ii) Post Order Traversal

Creating Binary Tree: Algorithm

Step 1: Do step 2 to 3 till stopped by the user
Step 2 : Obtain a new node and assign value to the node
Step 3 : Insert on to a Binary Search tree
Step 4 : return

Insertion a node in a binary search tree (BST)

```
InsertNode ( node , value)
    {   Check if Tree is empty
        If (empty )
          Enter the node as root
        / / find the proper location for insertion
        Else
          If (value < value of current node)
            { If ( left child is present)
                InsertNode( LST , Value);
              else
                allocate new node and make LST pointer point to it
            }
          else if (value > value of current node)
            { If ( right child is present)
                InsertNode( RST , Value);
              else
                allocate new node and make RST pointer point to it
            }
    }
```

Deleting a node from a binary search tree. There are three distinct cases to be considered when deleting a node from a BST. They are

a) Node to be deleted is a leaf node. Make its parent to point to NULL and free the node. For example to delete node 4 . Right pointer of 5 to point to NULL and free (node4).

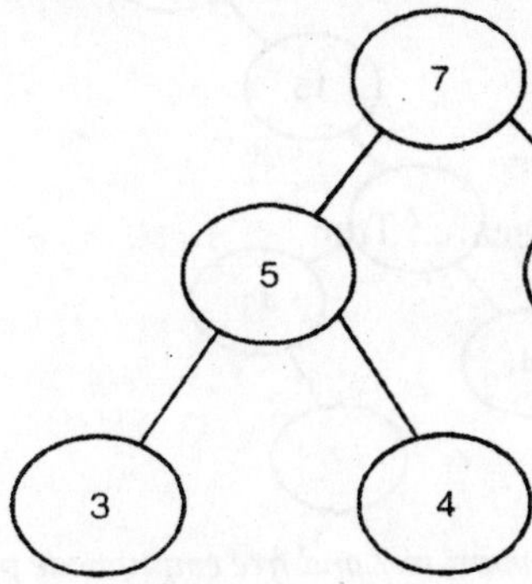

Fig. Deleting a leaf node

b) Delete a node with one child only, either left child or right child. For example we will delete node 9 that has only a right child. The right pointer of node 7 is made to point to node 12. The new tree after deletion is shown in figure given below.

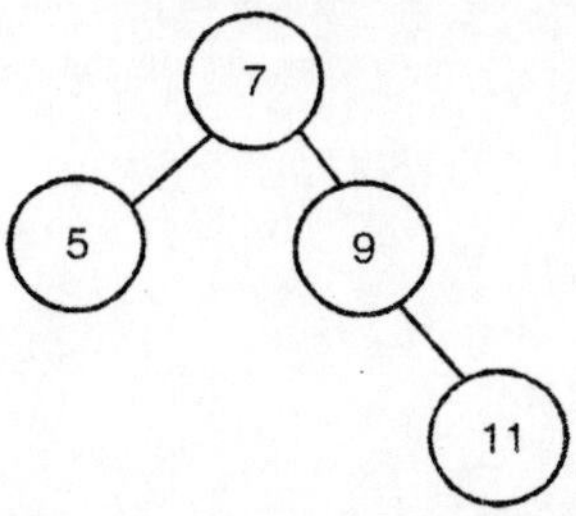

Fig. Deletion of node with only one child

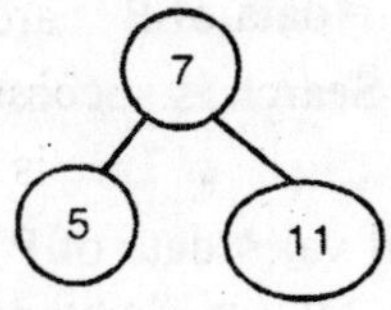

Fig. New tree after deletion

c) Node to be deleted has two children. The replace the value with smallest value in the right sub tree or largest value of left sub tree. We will replace it smallest value of right sub tree. Node 9 that has two children, needs to be deleted from figures.

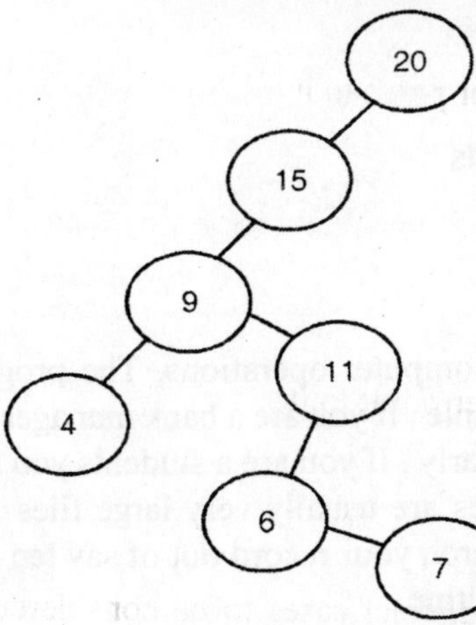

Fig. A node 9 to be deleted

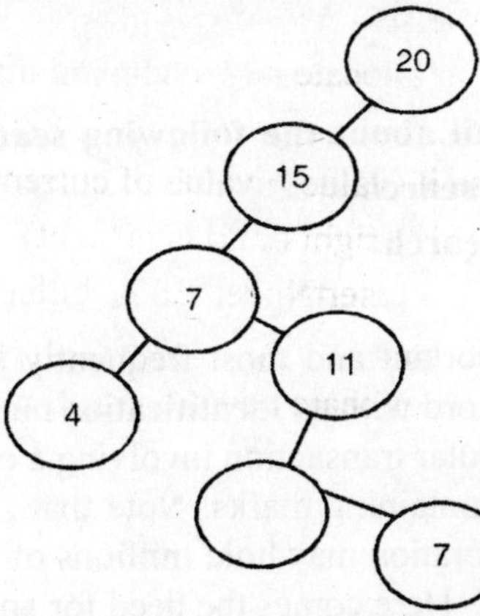

Fig. Replace smallest of right sub tree i.e replace 9 with 6

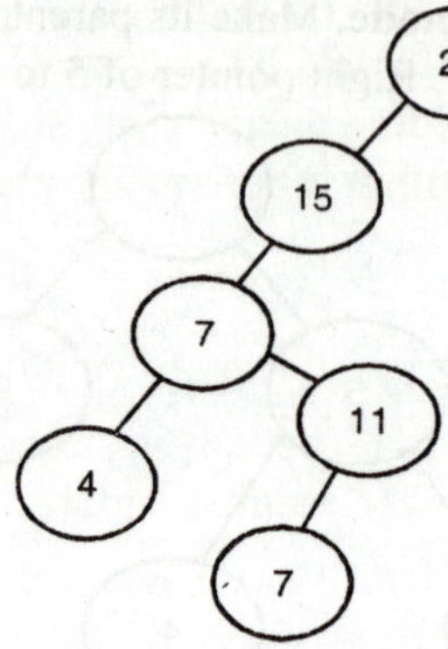

Fig. Adjust the pointer of 11 to point to 7 and free empty node procedure at fig 12.8 b

Searching a binary search tree

SearchNode(int val , node * root)
{
Step 1: set root to pointer P
Step 2 : Repeat step 3 – 4 till completion
Step 3 : if val = data of P
Search is successful
else
{ if val < data of P
Set P pointing to LPTR
Else
Set P pointing to RPTR
}
Step 4 : If (P= = NULL)
Value does not exist
Step 5 : Return

8. Discuss in detail about the following searching methods
(a) Sequential search
(b) Fibonacci search

Searching:

Searching is an important and most frequently performed in computer operations. The program usually searches for a record with an identification number. For example , if you are a bank manager you would search for a particular transaction involving a customer. Similarly , if you are a students you may search for your record containing marks. Note that , in real life files are usually very large files , for example Municipal corporation may hold millions of records. To search your record out of say ten million records must be fast. Here comes the need for an efficient algorithm.

There are several types of searches like linear search , binary Search , and hash search etc . However we would be concentrating on linear and binary search. usally we carryout search using a key. This key is an identifier for the record holding data. Examples of key are , customer id , student roll number etc. The output from a search algorithm is normally the position of the record or the contents of the record.

Linear Search

This is most frequently used search method. We simply traverse the list or array or records and check if the identification number matches with the id number of our interest.

Algorithm:

```
Begin:
        Found = false
    Count = 0
    Obtain the input array.
      Obtain number of terms , key
      Do
    {   If array[count]== key
          Found = true.
      Else
            Count ++
    } while ( count <=N) && found==false)
    if false declare the key is not present in the array
   Else declare the position and value of the element
End
```

We have done several of linear searches in the areas we have covered . for example all our array traversal are linear searches.

Analysis of Linear Search.

The critical parameter of linear search is how many comparisons . we have to carry out to get the result. How many times we have to execute the do ... while loop in our algorithm. Obviously the larger the data set , the larger will be time of execution. It also depends on the position of the record in the file.

For example if there are 10000 records and record of our interest is at 9999 the we have to traverse 9998 records to access 9999 record. Similary if we are lucky and our record is at position 2 , then only one access and check would suffice. Therefore average number of comparisons **C** is given by

$$C = 1+2+3+4+ \ldots\ldots\ldots\ldots +N/N$$

$$C = (N * (N+1))/2*N$$

$$C = (N+1)/2$$

Sequential search os efficient for small number of records but very inefficient for large set of records. In the worst case , the sequential search has complexity of O(N) as N comparisons would be required.

(c) Fibonacci Search:

The following search algorithm on a sorted array is known as the Fibonacci search because of its use of Fibonacci numbers. In this algorithm mid value is not simply an average of Beg and End but based on Fibonacci number. The code is shown below

```
/*code representing the Fibonacci search*/
        for(j=1;fib(j)<n;j++) ;
        mid = n-fib(j-2)+1;
        fi = fib(j-2);
        f2 = fib(j-3);
        while(key!=k[mid])           /*k is an array of elements on which the search has to be carried
        out*/
          if(mid<0 key>k[mid])        /* key is the element that has to be searched*/
          { if(f1==1)  return(-1);
            mid+=f2;
            f1-=f2;
            f2-=f1;
          }
        else
          {  if (f2==0)  return(-1);
             mid -=f2;
             t=f1-f2;
             f1=f2;
             f2=t;
        }
        return (mid);
```

In the above code fib(n) gives the nth fibonacci number. The code for it is

```
        int fib(int n)
          {  int x,y;
             if(n<=1)  return(n);
             x=fib(n-1);
             y=fib(n-2);
             return(x+y);
          }
```